1968
IN AMERICA

Music, Politics, Chaos, Counterculture, and the Shaping of a Generation

30th Anniversary Edition

CHARLES KAISER

Grove Press
New York

Due to limitations of space, permissions and acknowledgments appear on page 290.

THIRTIETH ANNIVERSARY EDITION

Published simultaneously in Canada
Printed in the United States of America

First Grove Atlantic hardcover edition: October 1988
This Grove Atlantic paperback edition: April 2018

Library of Congress Cataloging-in-Publication data available for this title.

ISBN 978-0-8021-2803-4
eISBN 978-0-8021-9324-7

Grove Press
an imprint of Grove Atlantic
154 West 14th Street
New York, NY 10011

Distributed by Publishers Group West

groveatlantic.com

18 19 20 21   10 9 8 7 6 5 4 3 2 1

For Joe,
for Jerry,
and for my parents

CONTENTS

INTRODUCTION TO THE
THIRTIETH ANNIVERSARY EDITION

A Crack in Time

WHERE were you in the nineteen-sixties? And what were you? A toddler, a grade schooler, a teenager? A young adult? Were you already old enough to form your own memories? Or were you old enough but in the "if you can remember the sixties you really weren't there" category?

Of course, if you're like most people, you were nowhere. You hadn't been born yet. You didn't exist. But wherever and whatever you were or weren't, it's a safe bet that you've *heard* about The Sixties—quite enough, maybe. Maybe *ad nauseam*.

Or maybe not. The fact that you're holding this book suggests that you're open to hearing (or rehearing) more. So welcome. Mix a drink, light a joint, make yourself comfortable.

Technically, the sixties began on January 1, 1960, and ended on December 31, 1969. But The Sixties are another story. The Sixties are too protean to be hemmed in by calendrical niceties. The sixties may be just another decade, but The Sixties are something more—a mood, a state of mind, a way of life, a congeries of sounds and images. The Sixties contain multitudes.

There is a continuing theological controversy among sixtiesologists concerning when The Sixties can properly be said to have begun and ended. Tuesday, November 8, 1960—the day Senator John F. Kennedy was elected president of the United States—has a pretty good claim to the beginning. Kennedy's campaign slogan, which appeared on every campaign poster, had been LEADERSHIP FOR THE 60's. Out with the dull, conformist, priggish, crewcut, Eisenhowerish Fifties! In with the dashing, exciting, daring, sexy, slightly longer-haired, Kennedyesque Sixties!

On Tuesday, November 8, 1960, I was a seventeen-year-old high school kid, spending the fall semester as an American Field Service exchange student at a boys' lycée in Toulouse, France. The next day, my pals, *mes copains*, made me stand on a chair in the courtyard and cheered as I delivered a victory speech in my less than perfect French. As usual, I had a Kennedy button on my lapel and a Kennedy bumper sticker on my book satchel. These displays, by the way, amazed my schoolmates. They explained to me that no Frenchman would risk flaunting his political preferences unless surrounded by like-minded comrades. There was a war in Algeria and bitter clashes over it in the streets, with tear gas and club-wielding *flics*. There was terrorism and actual Communists and armed neo-Pétainist extremists. French politics was *serious*. Not like the amiable American variety—which, of course, would soon enough get the smile wiped off its face.

A darker view—the view I take—sets the clock of The Sixties ticking three years later. The assassination of President Kennedy was a crack in time. Like Sunday, December 7, 1941, and like Tuesday, September 11, 2001, Friday, November 22, 1963, was "a date that will live in infamy." And, like them, it was a day that is remembered in vivid detail by those who experienced it. Just about every American whose age was in double digits on any of those three days can picture exactly where they were the moment they heard the awful news. I, for example, was taking a noontime shower in my Harvard dorm room, having been as usual up till dawn getting out the college daily, the *Crimson*. I heard a faint, muffled radio news bulletin coming through the wall from the neighboring room. I gathered that someone important had been shot, but I somehow heard the name as Francisco Franco, the Spanish dictator. Good, I thought. But then, as I dried off, I turned on my own radio. I can still see the edge of the shower stall and the little bathroom window next to it. On the grass below, a girl was standing under a tree, weeping. The *Crimson* put out an extra that afternoon, but without my help. It felt too much like a schoolboy stunt. Rightly or wrongly, I didn't want to play newspaperman. I didn't want to be distracted from the communal grief all around me.

As it happens, my class, the class of 1965, had taken it for granted that the commencement speaker at our graduation would be John F. Kennedy '40, as the *Crimson* always styled him. The former president would doubtless be in Cambridge anyway, attending his twenty-fifth reunion. And by 1990, the year of *our* twenty-fifth (and his fiftieth), Mr. Kennedy would be a vigorous, venerated, still uncannily youthful seventy-three-year-old. And the world would now be a better place.

So The Sixties, in this conceit, began either in 1960 or, like Philip Larkin's sexual intercourse, in 1963. And the ending? That too has long been a subject of debate. There are plenty of nominees, two of which may be considered the front-runners. Like the beginnings, one is light and one is dark. The light one: Friday, August 9, 1974, the day Richard Nixon resigned the presidency, freeing the nation from a quarter century of having had him to kick around. The dark one: Altamont. Sunday, December 6, 1969. Google it. Or see the movie.

Whenever The Sixties started and ended, it is universally recognized that 1968 was the peak year—the climactic year, a singular year, a year of events and sensations that cascaded with an intensity that was sometimes unbearable, sometimes ecstatic. In a modest way, 1968 was the kind of year that pushes history in some unforeseen, astonishing direction—a gentler little brother to 1492, 1776, 1848, 1914, 1945, and 2001. If you were there, you're about to go there again. If you weren't, you soon will be. Either way, with Charles Kaiser as your guide you're sure to have a good trip.

Kaiser's now-canonical account of the time is detailed and passionate, always insightful and often delightful, fully as much as it was when the first edition was published thirty years ago. He brings to it the scrupulousness of a scholar, the thoroughness of an archivist, the enthusiasm of a fan, the story-telling instincts of a novelist, and the curiosity and skepticism of a reporter whose byline has graced the trifecta of American journalism: the *New York Times*, the *Washington Post*, and the *Wall Street Journal*. He chooses to build his narrative around two currents of the year's events, currents that melded and crisscrossed and fed off each other, to startling effect: the music, mostly a kaleidoscopic, wildly imaginative explosion of rock and roll; and the politics, mostly a politics of protest—protest against the Vietnam War, against racial injustice, and, more broadly, against what was experienced as the joyless, stultifying blandness of mainstream American life.

Those two currents, the music and the protests, washed over me as they did over millions of others. In 1966, a year out of college and a newly minted cub reporter for *Newsweek*, I was lucky enough to land in San Francisco. Something was happening there, and I found myself in a position to absorb it.

Soon after I arrived the Beatles came to town and gave a concert in Candlestick Park, the Giants' baseball stadium. It was a disaster. Relegated to a rickety platform built over second base, far away from the audience and protected by a force of two hundred cops, real and rented, the fab four were tiny figures in the distance, and the primitive sound system was too feeble to overcome the unending screaming of the younger concertgoers. The boys left as quickly as they decently could. Other than the suprise set they played in 1969 from the rooftop of their London headquarters, they would never again perform in public. But over the next few years they would return to San Francisco many times, individually or in pairs, always without fanfare, simply to soak up the scene. And the scene, cultural and political, was quite something.

A new kind of music—rooted in blues, rock and electronica, and super-charged by psychedelia—was drawing motley-dressed weekend crowds to a couple of repurposed old dance halls, the Fillmore Auditorium and the Avalon Ballroom. For $2.50 you could spend hours listening and dancing to bands that were still unknown back east or down south in L.A.—bands still without record contracts but with wonderful names: Jefferson Airplane, the Grateful Dead, Big Brother and the Holding Company, Quicksilver Messenger Service—often paired with iconic bluesmen like Muddy Waters and James Cotton. The walls were mesmerizingly alive with rhythmically pulsating, ever-changing liquid projections. It was, in the patois of the moment, mind-blowing. For the gentle dreamers that Herb Caen, the *San Francisco Chronicle*'s gossip columnist, had dubbed hippies, the Fillmore and the Avalon were Carnegie Hall and the Philharmonic.

If San Francisco was the cultural capital of a new youth common-wealth, Berkeley was the political capital. The campus of the University of California was the staging area for demonstration after demonstration. Further left, would-be revolutionaries flirted with violence. The anger that in 1968 would explode in the streets of Chicago was growing apace. So was the reaction. A onetime movie star, Ronald Reagan, ran for gover-nor and won, largely on a promise to bring all those spoiled, unpatriotic campus brats to heel.

The last event I covered before I had to leave San Francisco took place in Golden Gate Park on January 14, 1967, and was called, in full, A Gath-ering of the Tribes for a Human Be-In. Organized by the elders of the Haight-Ashbury district, many of whom were Beat Generation artists and mystics in their thirties, the Be-In was envisioned as, among other things, a meeting of the minds and bodies of the hard-edged radicals of Berkeley and the soulful flower children of the Haight. The Grateful Dead played. The speakers and chanters ranged from Jerry Rubin, the brash political provo-cateur, to Allen Ginsberg, the poet and sage. Refreshments of a kind were provided by Owsley Stanley, security by the Hells Angels. The peaceful, happy, friendly crowd numbered thirty thousand. The Be-In was, among other things, the prototype for a profusion of mass gatherings, up to and including the Woodstock Music and Art Fair two and a half years later.

Like every young man of my generation, I had to reckon with the draft. I was against the war, of course, but I didn't think I had the stomach to go to jail over it. I had zero desire to go to any more schools, graduate or otherwise. I was unmarried and childless. Canada was not my country, my country was the United States of America. I wasn't physically or mentally ill and was too proud to fake it. And I wasn't a conscientious objector. On the other hand, I didn't want to get killed either. My solution was the US Navy.

A couple of weeks after the Be-In, I got a haircut and reported to the naval base at Newport, Rhode Island, for three months of officer training. From there I asked to be sent to Vietnam, but it wasn't like it sounds. Unless you were a flier (like John McCain, the future senator), a Seal (like Bob Kerrey, also a future senator) or a member of the Riverine Force (like John Kerry, a future senator, presidential nominee, and secretary of state), being a naval officer in Vietnam, especially a "public affairs" officer like me, posed very little physical risk. Instead, however, the Navy, in its wisdom, assigned me to a desk job in lower Manhattan.

The job, consisting mainly of sending out canned press releases and writing the occasional anodyne speech for an about-to-retire admiral who hated public speaking and tried to avoid it whenever possible, was undemanding to say the least. I stole away from the office whenever I could, leaving a message that I was doing a bit of library research, and devoted the time to salving my conscience—doing my bit, piddling though it was, to end the war. I pitched in at the ramshackle headquarters of the War Resisters League, doing editorial chores for its feisty little magazine, *Win*. (The name was an acronym of Workshop In Nonviolence.) In March, after Robert Kennedy entered the presidential race, I took to hanging around his Manhattan headquarters, doing layouts and writing headlines for the *Kennedy Current*, the campaign's weekly tabloid.

As the year rushed on, the pace of events grew ever more frenzied: the bloody shock of the Tet Offensive; the electoral abdication of President Lyndon Johnson; the assassination of Martin Luther King, Jr. and the riots that followed; the murder of Robert Kennedy; the chaotic, riotous Democratic Convention in Chicago; Nixon's hairsbreadth victory over Hubert Humphrey in November. And me? Well, at Christmastime I got the orders to Vietnam (as a "recreation officer" at the US base in Da Nang) I'd hoped for two years earlier. Only this time I didn't want to go. My antiwar sentiments had hardened to the point that I decided I preferred jail to further military service, and I announced my intention to refuse the orders. But before I could achieve fame as a martyr for peace an unexpected medical difficulty developed, and the Navy quickly and quietly mustered me out. I guess I managed to have it both ways: veteran (kind of) and resister (in a way).

The sixties were almost over, but The Sixties never fully went away. For me, and no doubt for many others of my vintage, it's hard to believe that half a century now separates us from the momentous, tumultuous year of this book's title, and that 1968 is now as distant in time as 1918—the year of the end of World War I, the consolidation of Bolshevik power in Russia, and the flu pandemic that killed fifty million people—was in 1968. Thank you, Charles Kaiser, for making it all as fresh as tomorrow's tweets.

—Hendrik Hertzberg
New York City, October 2017

PREFACE

WHEN Theodore H. White published *The Making of the President, 1960,* the book that revolutionized the way Americans write about politics, every member of my family fell in love with it. It was 1961, and I was ten years old. A few months earlier, on January 20, I had shoveled the snow out of our driveway in Bethesda, Maryland, so that my mother could drive me downtown to watch the inaugural parade. As John F. Kennedy passed by hatless in an open car, I shouted out, "Good luck, Jack!" When the new president turned to look in my direction, a young friend who sat shivering next to me in the reviewing stand was sure our hero had heard me.

That was the closest I ever got to Kennedy. But Teddy White was a good friend of my parents, and I met him for the first time a couple of years later. No one has ever been kinder to kids who hoped to emulate him than Teddy. Unlike so many famous people, he never demanded reverence. He did not expect it, probably because he knew the arrogance of youth would not permit it. He loved young people and he loved politics, and he especially loved young people who loved politics, even when they argued with him, as I often did from the other side of the generation gap.

Teddy gave me every encouragement to become a writer, including the crucial one of his own example. He inscribed my family's copy of *The Making of the President, 1968:* "For *Charles,* and Hannah and Phil, and all the Kaisers whom I love, but mostly for *Charles,* who thinks politics may be worth *reading* and *writing* about." Through the generosity of his widow, Beatrice, and his children, Heyden and David, I was the first person to be given access to his massive archive after his death, in 1986. Without Teddy's documents it would have been impossible to produce this volume.

I WROTE this book to try to understand the impact of a single year when so many grew up so quickly. For a surprisingly large number of Americans, I think 1968 marked the end of hope. Twenty years later, it may now be possible to start unraveling the mystery of how its traumas and its culture changed us. If we can appreciate the triumphs, perhaps we can finally get over the tragedies.

This account is primarily about the people of all ages who believed that fundamental change was possible and necessary in America in 1968, and about the culture that shaped that conviction. It is a book about the power of idealism, the power of music, the power of the bullet, and the power of the press. It is also the story of what it felt like to grow up in a time when every established norm seemed to be under siege. Drugs such as marijuana, once confined to the ghetto (and the jazz musicians who discovered them there), were suddenly available on almost every college corridor. Broadway theatergoers accustomed to fully clothed actors were getting their first dose of full-frontal nudity in a "tribal-love-rock-musical" called *Hair.* Off-Broadway, straight and not-so-straight audiences were absorbed by an explicit (though still utterly self-loathing) depiction of gay life in *The Boys in the Band.* A computer named Hal in a movie called *2001: A Space Odyssey* replicated every human personality trait, and some viewers even speculated about Hal's sexuality.

The *New York Times* replaced its stolid movie critic with Renata Adler, a cerebral thirty-year-old whose reviews exploded off the paper's grey pages like torpedoes. *The Green Berets*, for example, was "so unspeakable, so stupid, so rotten and false in every detail" that it became an invitation to grieve "for what has happened to the fantasy-making apparatus in this country." (Strom Thurmond denounced her from the senate floor for that one.) Gore Vidal published *Myra Breckinridge*, the first mainstream American novel with a transsexual hero. *Newsweek* ran a cover story asking whether men should wear jewelry, as women's skirts inched higher above the knee than either man or woman had imagined possible. On daytime television, Tommy Hughes was toking up in *As the World Turns* and Tom Horton was impotent on *Days of Our Lives.* At the beginning of the year, you could pick up the phone in New York City and "Dial-a-Poem"; by June you could also "Dial-a-Demonstration."[1] That fall, for the first time ever, Columbia men gained the right to entertain women in their dormitory rooms twenty-four hours a day.

Blacks were beautiful—and growing Afros and raising their fists in a defiant Black Power salute at the Olympics to prove it. Violence was everywhere, especially during February in Vietnam, where the Tet offensive drenched that country in blood, and in American streets two months later, when 65,000 troops were needed to quell riots in 130 cities after Martin Luther King, Jr.'s killing. "Go home and get a gun" was Stokely Carmichael's advice. After the year's second major political assassination, the Advertising Council sponsored a campaign for gun control that urged Americans to "Write your senator—while you still have a senator." In August, thousands in Chicago fought pitched battles with Mayor Richard Daley's police and hundreds of undercover agents from the FBI, the CIA, and Army Intelligence, who alternated between photographing demonstrators and provoking them. In one instance of the media overload typical of the times, an Army Intelligence officer masquerading as a television-news camera operator in Chicago was inadvertently captured practicing his craft by the cinematographer who filmed *Medium Cool,* the fictional feature that used these riots for its *cinéma-vérité* background.[2]

I have tried to make reading the book as much as possible like living through the year. But one of the qualities that made 1968 so exhilarating—the virtue we made of nonconformity—also makes it especially treacherous to generalize about. There were so many separate movements for change, so many musical styles, and so many methods of mind alteration that it was unusually easy, even for two people the same age growing up in the same small town, to have opposite interests—and fierce disagreements about what it was that *really mattered.* The passage of time has done little to diminish the intensity of these controversies.

So I cannot tell the "truth" about the Beatles, Bob Dylan, Walter Cronkite, Gene McCarthy, Bobby Kennedy, or Martin Luther King. The same problem would arise in dissecting the social and political movements of any year; in this case it is particularly acute. The most I can do is to write what *I think* is important about some of the things we all experienced, because we all experienced them so differently. I only hope that even those who are infuriated by my very personal judgments will concede that the vehemence with which they are expressed is in keeping with the spirit of the era I love.

"Would you believe in a love at first sight?"
"Yes, I'm certain that it happens all the time."
—John Lennon and Paul McCartney

INTRODUCTION

Bringing It All Back Home

T HIS is the story of what happened to America in 1968, the most turbulent twelve months of the postwar period and one of the most disturbing intervals we have lived through since the Civil War. In the twentieth century only the Depression, Pearl Harbor, and the Holocaust punctured the national psyche as deeply as the dramas of this single year. Nineteen sixty-eight was the pivotal year of the sixties: the moment when all of a nation's impulses toward violence, idealism, diversity, and disorder peaked to produce the greatest possible hope—and the worst imaginable despair. For many of us who came of age in that remarkable era, it has been fifty years since we have lived with such intensity. That is one of the main reasons why the sixties retain their extraordinary power over everyone old enough to remember them.

Until the election of Donald Trump as president, the sixties and the thirties were the only modern decades in which large numbers of Americans wondered out loud whether their country might disintegrate. From this distance the massive unemployment of the Depression looks like a bigger threat than the upheavals of the more recent period. But unlike the still puzzling moods of the sixties, the nature of American despair in the thirties was never mysterious: people were miserable because they were hungry, fearful because they weren't sure anyone would ever figure out how to put them back to work again.

Nothing was quite so straightforward in the years leading up to 1968.

The role of affluence was the first imponderable. Particularly within the white middle class, Americans had assumed that their phenomenal postwar prosperity would be purely liberating. To those in college during the six-ties, it *was* liberating in one respect. Years of relatively low inflation had produced a cheap cost of living (a first-class letter cost 6¢, gas 37¢ a gal-lon, a custom-made shirt $7.50, marijuana $20 an ounce), so we felt little urgency to decide who we would become when we grew up. We were free to experiment and anything seemed possible: Everything could be changed. Paradoxically this same abundance was both deadening and radicalizing. Deadening because we couldn't emulate our parents' achievements even if we wanted to, since we had no Depression to climb out of (or Nazi men-ace to conquer); radicalizing because the absence of an obvious economic challenge forced us to think about how we might reinvent ourselves. And for the opposite reason, equally radicalizing for poor blacks, constantly reminded by practically everything on television of the chasm between ghetto life and white suburban life.

Disdain for our parents' materialism was only one factor in the search for some sort of new spirituality. The failure of religion was also signifi-cant, especially for those whose parents were the children of immigrants. My father's parents were Russian Jews who came to this country in 1906; his early rejection of an Orthodox upbringing was one shortcut to becom-ing completely American. In our family, faithful secular celebrations of Christmas *and* Passover were the answer to the religion question. Whatever belief my parents grew up with had been eroded by the Holo-caust and perhaps subconsciously shattered by Hiroshima. Like many of their contemporaries, they were convinced that Freud and Einstein had answered nearly every consequential question of the age. Awed by these men and the Bomb, they were propelled toward the conclusion that God had become obsolete.

The kids I knew who did get formal religious training were hardly more likely to be believers than I was. Especially to young Catholics, the old-fashioned orthodoxies seemed utterly implausible in the nuclear age. In the sixties religion was treated with unprecedented irreverence by popular culture in America. It was Easter 1966 when *Time* magazine's cover asked "Is God Dead?"; Christmas 1967 when Dustin Hoffman used a crucifix to barricade the church doors in *The Graduate*.[1]

In the summer of 1967, the *New York Times* reported, "Most campus activists are *comparatively* intelligent, stable and unprejudiced [emphasis added]." The story revealed that "a disproportionately high number of activists are Jewish" and "very few are Roman Catholic." Eight separate studies indicated that activists "are slightly less alienated than nonactiv-ists, and no more in rebellion against parental ideas and authority than the rest of the student body."[2] In 1968 just 43 percent of all Americans went to church weekly, according to a Gallup poll.[3]

We were the first generation to be born into the world with the Bomb, and our early intimacy with the reality of Armageddon gave us a unique adolescence. Like many leitmotifs of the sixties, this one burst forth during John Kennedy's presidency. Everyone who went to school in the fifties knew of the possibility of nuclear war through CONELRAD and those eerie air-raid sirens, commanding us to dive under our desks or curl up on the floors of windowless hallways to evade the imaginary radioactivity. By the spring of 1960, 70 percent of the public favored the construction of air-raid shelters in every community; by the fall of 1961, 53 percent thought a world war was likely within five years.[4]

Yet the threat of the definitive horror became palpable only once, in 1962, when President Kennedy peered over the edge of the abyss during the Cuban Missile Crisis. Going from routine air-raid drills to knowing that the world really could end at any moment was like the difference between watching a murder at the movies and coming home to find your parents pinned down in your living room by a stranger with a shotgun. The seeds of a much wider generation gap were sown when every one of us, simultaneously, for seven days, came home every afternoon to watch all our parents looking down the barrel of the same enormous shotgun. We did awake physically unscathed from this nightmare. But it eliminated our confidence in our parents' ability to control the world or protect us from its wickedness. It's the kind of experience that works subliminal wonders for one's willingness to question the wisdom of one's elders.

Barely one year later, the memory of the missile crisis was displaced by John Kennedy's assassination, still the most petrifying instant in my lifetime. The panic we felt that Friday wasn't simply the result of the love affair much of the nation was having with this sexy man who had defeated an evil-looking rival and then injected every aspect of his presidency with emotion. More important was the fact that no president had been murdered since McKinley was shot in 1901. After that gap of six decades, only Americans over sixty-five could remember a presidential assassination. The possibility of such a catastrophe had evaporated from the national consciousness. When White House aide Ralph Dungan called Hubert Humphrey on November 22 to tell him, "The president has been shot," Humphrey asked, "What president?"[5]

If nothing was more shocking than Kennedy's murder, probably nothing he accomplished was more significant than the simple fact of his election to the presidency. Until John Kennedy broke a 171-year-old barrier of prejudice, only undivorced Protestant men had served as American chiefs of state. Neither Democratic liberals (who infuriated the Kennedys by getting Eugene McCarthy to nominate Adlai Stevenson in 1960) nor Democratic Southerners supported this Irish Catholic's nomination: The power base he used to force the party's embrace was created by his family, almost entirely by his father. None of the Kennedys lost an election from 1948 until 1968—a record that preserved their fabled aura of invincibility throughout that period. John Kennedy did lose the fight for the 1956 Democratic vice-presidential *nomination* to Estes Kefauver. But after Adlai Stevenson lost to Eisenhower in another landslide, professional politicians regarded Kennedy's loss as the most fortunate failure imaginable.

In 1960 Kennedy carried the popular vote for president by an infinitesimal one-tenth of one percentage point. But he was still the first person to prove conclusively that a non-WASP could achieve unlimited upward mobility in America. His success made the country seem more susceptible to outsiders than it had been at any other time in the twentieth century—an exciting circumstance for everyone who nurtured the hope for substantial change through the quiescent fifties, especially those committed to achieving real equality between blacks and whites. Kennedy's selection in 1960 was one of the first volleys in the decade's war against all kinds of intolerance, hypocrisy, and exclusivity. This many-sided assault produced one of the proudest and least appreciated legacies of the sixties.

Thus, as 1968 began, these were some of the sources of the malaise gnawing away at many of the six million draft-age students in college, the largest group of undergraduates in American history: an absence of religious conviction; an unwanted intimacy with the nuclear void; an unexpected familiarity with political assassination—Malcolm X's in 1965, as well as John Kennedy's in 1963—and a yearning for the idealism that was the most evocative part of Kennedy's presidency. Together these disparate elements fed two seemingly contradictory but actually complementary impulses: the desire to create our own culture, a world of our own where we could retreat from the world of our parents; and the need to embrace causes larger than ourselves, crusades that would give us the chance to define ourselves as moral people. Neither impulse could have been satisfied without our two most powerful inspirations: the war and the radio.

Everyone from Marshall McLuhan to Theodore White has made what is now a reflex observation about the preeminence of television within the modern American psyche. They were not wrong; but as far as the Vietnam generation is concerned, I think they were only half right.

It was true that for viewers of every age, including thirteen-year-olds like myself, nothing could equal the shock of watching Lee Harvey Oswald's murder, live, on Sunday-morning television*—or the electronic catharsis produced by John Kennedy's televised funeral the following day. Five years later television news was bruising everyone's nerve endings nightly. In 1968 it brought the War in Vietnam and the war in the ghetto into every dorm room and living room with a power no other medium could match. The pictures Americans saw made millions of them intensely uncomfortable with themselves: pictures of the South Vietnamese national police chief shooting a suspected Vietcong in the head during Tet, of Martin Luther King's casket, and of Bobby Kennedy's bleeding body on a hotel kitchen floor; pictures of the uprisings all over America after King's death and the worst fires in the city of Washington since the War of 1812. Ghetto insurrections were followed by campus revolts, most dramatically at Columbia University. For the first time since their invention, televised pictures made the possibility of anarchy in America feel real. These scenes fueled the campaigns of Gene McCarthy, Bobby Kennedy, George Wallace, and Richard Nixon. They also destroyed Lyndon Johnson and crippled Hubert Humphrey's effort to succeed him.

For Americans from the generation that fought in World War II, I doubt that anything equaled the emotional power of these pictures. A young man, then a sophomore at Harvard, remembers his parents in Tell City, a tiny Indiana town, watching the riots in the streets of Chicago during the Democratic National Convention in 1968: "The beating of protesters was a very big shock. Nothing like that had ever happened in their lives—in their entire lives."[6]

But for everyone their son's age—all the men eligible for the draft during Vietnam and all the women who were not, the two million who fought in the war and the twenty-five million who, like me, never did—everything on the tube tearing us apart was almost perfectly balanced by the remarkable unity we achieved through the music on the radio. It was the only place in the history of the United States where, for a fleeting moment, we created a world of seemingly genuine racial and sexual equality, embraced by everyone under thirty—and millions more who fell in love with the beat.

---

* The gory eight-millimeter Zapruder film of John Kennedy's mutilation wasn't shown on television until many years later. The most gruesome frames were even omitted from the sequence of nine color stills published in *Life* immediately after his death.

To us, George Harrison, John Lennon, Paul McCartney, Ringo Starr, Bob Dylan, Janis Joplin, the Supremes, the Rolling Stones, Stevie Wonder, Aretha Franklin, Chuck Berry, Elvis Presley, the Four Tops, the Doors, the Jefferson Airplane, the Who, the Grateful Dead, the Everly Brothers, James Brown, Sam Cooke, Eric Clapton, Country Joe and the Fish, Chubby Checker, Laura Nyro, Simon and Garfunkel, Gerry and the Pacemakers, Otis Redding, Buddy Holly, the Band, Blood, Sweat and Tears, B. B. King, Marvin Gaye and Tammi Terrell, Martha and the Vandellas, the Mamas and the Papas, the Kinks, the Kingsmen, Judy Collins, Pete Seeger, Peter, Paul and Mary, the Lovin' Spoonful, Santana, Traffic, Bob Johnson, the Bee Gees, the Temptations, Jethro Tull, Brian Epstein, Arlo Guthrie, Joan Baez, the Byrds, the Beach Boys, the Moody Blues, the Blues Project, Muddy Waters, Them, Joni Mitchell, Bill Graham, Holland-Dozier-Holland, Ashford and Simpson, Herman's Hermits, Smokey Robinson and the Miracles, Percy Sledge, George Martin, ? and the Mysterians, Wayne Fontana and the Mindbenders, Sonny and Cher, Buffalo Springfield, Del Shannon, Berry Gordy, the Animals, the Searchers, the Safaris, the Zombies, Led Zeppelin, Frank Zappa, Dionne Warwick, Mary Wells, the Hollies, the Youngbloods, the Yardbirds, the Young Rascals, Ten Years After, the Righteous Brothers, the Walker Brothers, Roy Orbison, Paul Butterfield, the Persuasions, Neil Young, Crosby, Stills & Nash, the Dave Clark Five, Richie Havens, Phil Spector, Van Morrison, the Velvet Underground, Carole King, Petula Clark, Jan and Dean, Jimi Hendrix, and the Jackson 5 were the ones who mattered most. These black and white men and women from Liverpool, London, Hibbing, Detroit, New York, San Francisco, and the rest of the artistic kingdom of America and Great Britain were the composers, performers, managers, and producers who filled the airwaves with the most eclectic-electric-wrathful-revolutionary-romantic-soulful-psychedelic music ever played, simultaneously, on every rock-and-roll radio station in the world. The songs they produced kept us alive, even a little hopeful, through the most terrifying year of the decade.

Almost by osmosis, John Kennedy's adventurous spirit penetrated the culture, probably even more deeply than his politics. In 1960 his hair was considered unusually long for a presidential candidate, despite a new haircut for the campaign. After he became president, his private life stole a march on the decade in ways we never imagined at the time. Mary Meyer, one of his many girlfriends, introduced him to marijuana—and joked about getting high in the White House while the president had his finger on the Button.[7] When he traveled to Vienna in 1961 for his first summit meeting with Nikita Khrushchev, the notorious speed doctor Max Jacobson was one of his companions.*

If aspects of Kennedy's lifestyle anticipated the youth culture of the sixties, in a peculiar way, his murder expedited the inauguration of its icons. No other death depressed us as completely. More than ever before, we needed an emotional lift: distraction, a place to put it all, to bury our anguish and rediscover our joy. Just four weeks after his funeral, four very young, very sexy, and (we thought) *very* long-haired Englishmen didn't just fill this emotional void: They took absolute control of our hearts and minds in a way that no one else ever would again.

It began in America with the release of two minutes and twenty-four seconds of music on December 26, 1963, which by February 1 had become the number-one-selling single in the country. The utterly sentimental lyrics just happened to be a perfect fit for the sensibilities of the largest generation of adolescents America had yet produced. But there was much more than sentimentality to this song. Driven by Ringo's relentless, underrated drumming, it also had a chorus—mistaken by grown-ups for a screech—that we recognized as a primal scream.†

Christina Orth, high school senior, Piedmont, California: "I remember going round and round in circles in a Volkswagen convertible with the top down and the radio way up, with Dede Mitchell and her boyfriend, Pat Gilligan, and just screaming at the top of our lungs, 'I want to hold your hand!' We were the first three people in the whole school to hear the song."[8]

Jane Berentson, high school sophomore, Barrington, Illinois: "A boyfriend of mine had brought their records back from Europe. They were presented to me, like, here are these amazing people called 'the Beatles.' And I agreed. The girls all decided right away which one they were in love with. And the boys all decided which one they looked like."[9]

Sal Matera, eighth grader, Brooklyn, New York: "If you told the tough guys they [the Beatles] were better than Elvis, they beat you up." Did you think they were better than Elvis? "Yes. But I didn't say. Only to the girls."[10]

---

* Jacobson injected his numerous celebrity patients, including Tennessee Williams and Cecil B. DeMille, with what he described as a vitamin mixture. Amphetamine was actually its active ingredient. He finally lost his license to practice medicine in 1975. [*New York Times*, 12/4/72 and 4/26/75.]

† RCA's release of Elvis Presley's "Heartbreak Hotel" in 1956 and his subsequent explosion on the national scene were probably more revolutionary cultural events—but in that instance, there was no synergy with the Eisenhower administration.

And there was also this witness from Minnesota: "We were driving through Colorado. We had the radio on, and eight of the Top Ten songs were Beatles songs. In Colorado! 'I Want to Hold Your Hand,' all those early ones. They were doing things nobody was doing. Their chords were outrageous, and their harmonies made it all valid. . . . But I kept it to myself that I really dug them. Everybody else thought they were for the teenyboppers, that they were gonna pass right away. But it was obvious to me that they had staying power. I knew they were pointing the direction where music had to go. . . . In my head, the Beatles were *it*. . . . It seemed to me a definite line was being drawn. This was something that never happened before."[11] The name of this witness was Bob Dylan.

Kennedy taught students of the sixties the power of the individual: how one man could change the way a whole country felt about itself, particularly if the man was young, charismatic, and followed an elderly general into the White House. The Beatles illuminated the power of collaboration, and *their* message was even more surprising. These Liverpudlians proved that four kids from a decaying British port, rock-and-roll musicians without money or connections, just good looks, a canny manager, and colossal talent, could change the way the whole world felt about itself, practically overnight.

By the time their masterpiece appeared in June 1967, the rarest thing in America was a teenager with his hair combed straight back with Vitalis— and the Beatles were the most famous people on the planet. Critic Langdon Winner explains: "The closest Western Civilization has come to unity since the Congress of Vienna in 1815 was the week the *Sgt. Pepper's* album was released. In every city in Europe and America the stereo systems and the radio played, 'What would you think if I sang out of tune. . . . Woke up, got out of bed . . . looked much older, and the bag across her shoulder . . . in the sky with diamonds, Lucy in the . . . ' and everyone listened. At the time I happened to be driving across country on Interstate 80. In each city where I stopped for gas or food—Laramie, Ogallala, Moline, South Bend—the melodies wafted in from some far-off transistor radio or portable hi-fi. It was the most amazing thing I've ever heard. For a brief while the irreparably fragmented consciousness of the West was unified, at least in the minds of the young."[12]

The release of *Sgt. Pepper's Lonely Hearts Club Band* in the summer of 1967 was even more important in one other respect. Our fiery embrace of this fabulous foursome wasn't merely the source of almost perfect happiness; it also represented our biggest bet ever against the supposedly better judgment of our elders. *(Newsweek* did make "Bugs About Beatles" its cover story in February 1964, but it dismissed them visually as "a nightmare" and musically as "a near disaster."[13]) With *Sgt. Pepper,* youth won its wager. Despite the explicit contribution of controlled substances to this album, it forced even the most skeptical adult critics to admit that rock and roll could be art. For the first time ever we had proved to the world, and to ourselves, that we really could be as perceptive as our parents.

To MANY, the Rolling Stones looked like the Beatles' archrivals, but the boys from Liverpool provided plenty of clues that they actually considered a slender fellow from Hibbing, Minnesota, to be their supreme competitor: the one who always wore his harmonica on his chest, the one George Harrison simply called "the man."[14]

Contrary to his own legend, Bob Dylan—born Robert Zimmerman—had actually been a model high school student. "His ratings by the teachers on personal appearance, social adaptability, courtesy, emotional stability, trustworthiness and honesty, dependability and self-reliance, industry and effort, civic responsibility, and cooperation were all very high," according to the Hibbing superintendent of public schools.[15] But his yearbook revealed that he planned "to join Little Richard."[16] He was distracted from that ambition when he read Woody Guthrie's autobiography, *Bound for Glory.*

From then on, "he wanted to have free rein," according to his father, Abe Zimmerman. "He wanted to be a folk singer, an entertainer. We couldn't see it, but we felt he was entitled to the chance. It's his life, after all, and we didn't want to stand in the way. So we made an agreement that he could have one year to do as he pleased, and if at the end of that year we were not satisfied with his progress, he'd go back to school."[17]

Dylan turned twenty-four in 1965. By then he had recorded four albums, *The New Yorker* had profiled him, the *New York Times* had canonized him ("the brilliant singing poet laureate of young America"), his father finally believed in him, and the former Bobby Zimmerman had abandoned the solo style that made him the most celebrated folk singer of modern times. He would never repeat himself.

From the beginning Dylan had an uncanny ability to anticipate trends and events. And like the Beatles, the chronology of his career was intertwined with John Kennedy's life and death. "The Times They Are A-Changin'," the only one of more than three hundred compositions he has ever described as "definitely a song with a purpose," was recorded four weeks to the day before Kennedy was killed. "I wanted to write a big song in a simple way," he told me in 1985. "I knew exactly what I wanted to say and for whom I wanted to say it." He was in Times Square when he learned Kennedy had died, and that night he sang the song in concert: "It sort of took over as the opening song and stayed that way for a long time."[18] More than anyone else it was Dylan who taught a generation to make quick and brutal judgments. His anger was our public badge; the saddest songs we ever learned became our secret link. *He* knew they were his secret weapon.

In June 1965 he released "Like a Rolling Stone," a rock-and-roll breakthrough. It was the first song big enough to explain his abandonment of simple acoustical accompaniment; it also came closest to being the anthem of the generation. It was revolutionary, and not only because of its six-minute length, which made it the longest cut ever played until then on rock radio. (There was a fitting subliminal message there: To make money off us on this one, at least they'll have to mangle their format.) With organ, piano, tambourine, drum, guitar, and harmonica accompaniment, this was the song that shouted out a generation's deepest anxieties and most glorious dreams:

> *How does it feel?*
> *How does it feel*
> *To be on your own*
> *With no direction home*
> *Like a complete unknown*
> *Like a rolling stone?*[19]

To me, its lyrics meant: Trust yourself. Be grateful that you will never find peace until you figure out a way to reinvent yourself. To everyone else, they meant *everything* else.

In the thirties Woody Guthrie was the preeminent musician in a great American tradition: the artist who discovered how to merge culture with politics. In the sixties Bob Dylan became the modern master of this art. His persuasive example attracted hundreds of professional imitators, and on every high school and college campus in America, millions of amateur followers. By the beginning of 1968, his songs were ubiquitous on the radio, performed by everyone from Peter, Paul and Mary and Joan Baez to Elvis Presley and the Byrds. For a generation in turmoil, he had become a thousand times as influential as his spiritual father. His purposefully ambiguous lyrics cemented his connection to the growing collective he identified in "The Chimes of Freedom" as "every hung-up person in the whole wide universe." Bob Dylan's fusion of culture and politics produced more than combustion. This was alchemy: a mysterious mechanism that produced the locomotive power of the sixties.

So it was not the draft alone that spawned the unrest that would change the way Americans behaved at home—and the United States behaved abroad—not just in 1968, but for many years afterward. It was the Beatles and the Rolling Stones and marijuana and LSD and a thousand other things besides our vulnerability to the war that gave us that fleeting sense of ourselves as a generation apart, a generation with a mission. Certainly our opposition to the war was rooted in self-interest—or, more precisely, self-preservation—but it was the best example of enlightened self-interest of our time.

And it was this very young mystic poet from Minnesota, more than any other artist, who fostered the mood that would help persuade another poet—also a mystic, also from Minnesota—to accept the challenge that every other elected official in Washington rejected. The challenge was to run for the presidency of the United States to bring an end to the War in Vietnam. The man who accepted the challenge was Senator Eugene McCarthy. In 1968 no other nonviolent act would change American politics or American foreign policy so permanently.

1968
IN AMERICA

1

Four Democrats,
Three Ghosts,
One War

"This nation will keep its commitments, from South Vietnam to West Berlin."

—President Lyndon B. Johnson in his first
speech to a joint session of Congress,
November 27, 1963[1]

"The younger generation came on the world scene [after 1960], not having lived through any of these other events and so they think of communism as being in some cases a terrible system and, in other parts of the world, nothing much worse than some of our allies. [Those in] the older generation think back on all of these events and say, 'How can you trust a Communist?' or 'How can you ever accept the idea that there should be a Communist?' When we talk in our country of the struggle between the young and the old, I think part of it at least is due to that."

—Robert Kennedy to David Frost, 1968[2]

EUGENE McCarthy would seek the Democratic nomination for president in 1968 because of the War in Vietnam; after a painful interval, Robert Kennedy would emulate him. Lyndon Johnson would retire from politics because of the war, and Hubert Humphrey would be emasculated by it.

All four Democrats had complex, interconnected histories that stretched back over two decades. Each of them had served in the Senate; Johnson and Humphrey had both served as vice-president. The other two—McCarthy and Kennedy—had wanted to become Johnson's vice-president in 1964. For the victor in 1968, the prize was the heart of the Democratic party and—if that could be won without destroying its soul—the possibility of four years in the White House. But these men were not only running against each other; they also had to grapple with three ghosts.

Because these spirits were invisible, their existence was not always acknowledged. However, they had great influence over all the candidates. These were the ghosts of John Kennedy, Joseph McCarthy, and a crucial summit meeting called "Munich." How each aspirant dealt with these spirits, whether he chose to embrace them or exorcise them, would determine his position on the war, the dominant issue in America in 1968.

FROM 1956, when John Kennedy lost his fight for the Democratic vice-presidential nomination, until 1980, when Jimmy Carter beat back Edward Kennedy's challenge in the presidential primaries, every Democratic politician (and many Republicans) who aspired to national office measured his success largely in terms of the Kennedys. No other family had so dominated the dialogue in a major American political party for so long. Their larger-than-life presence in the minds of the public produced absolute devotion and almost unbelievable hatred. Franklin D. Roosevelt inspired emotions of equal intensity, but even his unprecedented twelve-year presidency lasted only half as long as the political era in which one's position on Jack, Bobby, or Teddy was the threshold question for every active Democrat. When national political correspondent David Broder quit the *New York Times* in 1966 to join the *Washington Post,* among his complaints was the fact that "Kennedy stories of any variety" were one of the "few stimuli" to which editors of his former paper always reacted.[3] In 1986 Caroline Kennedy was the only presidential daughter whose wedding would still rate the page-one treatment the *Times* normally reserves for royalty—twenty-three years after her father's presidency.

All the leading major-party candidates for president in 1968 were very much a part, if not a prisoner, of this syndrome. Richard Nixon had run against John Kennedy (and his brother Bobby, who was JFK's campaign manager) for president in 1960. Nixon lost the popular election by just 112,881 votes, out of nearly sixty-nine million cast.[4] In 1968 he planned to avenge that humiliation, running as "the New Nixon" to distinguish himself from the pallid man with the five o'clock shadow who had been defeated by a dashing Bostonian eight years earlier.

Hubert Humphrey had been mentioned as a potential presidential candidate every four years since his 1948 speech on civil rights—and every time he ran for national office, he bumped into a Kennedy. When he sought the Democratic nomination for vice-president in 1956, he came in fifth—behind Estes Kefauver, John Kennedy, Albert Gore, and Robert Wagner. In 1960 the Minnesota senator ran an underfinanced campaign for president; eighteen weeks after he announced his candidacy, the Kennedy machine had demolished him. The end came in West Virginia, where Franklin Roosevelt, Jr., campaigning for Kennedy, made the false charge that Humphrey had been a draft dodger in World War II. (He had actually flunked his physical.) Later Humphrey confronted Roosevelt over the smear.

"Frank," he said, "you know goddamn well that what you said wasn't true."

"I know that," said Roosevelt, "but Bobby asked me to do it."[5]

After West Virginia, Humphrey had flirted with the idea of coming out for Kennedy before the first ballot at the Democratic National Convention, until McCarthy told him sardonically that it was the "right decision," adding that "all those stories about Bobby bringing FDR, Jr., into West Virginia and calling you a slacker—they're totally unfounded." A furious Humphrey immediately abandoned the idea of endorsing Kennedy.[6]

In 1964 Lyndon Johnson chose Humphrey to be his running mate, and the Minnesotan was finally elected to a national office—but only after Johnson felt strong enough to ignore the movement urging him to make Bobby Kennedy his vice-president.

Gene McCarthy was the other senator from Minnesota, and two disparate facts made his relations with the Kennedys particularly intricate. First, like them, he was a Catholic, but a very different kind of Catholic. Second, he was from the same state as Hubert Humphrey, a geographical coincidence that made him Humphrey's ally when he ran against John Kennedy in 1956 and 1960.

McCarthy entered the House of Representatives in 1949, two years after John Kennedy. Fred Marshall, another Minnesota Democrat elected to the House in 1948, remembered the young academic from Minnesota being briefly infatuated with the Irishman from Massachusetts. "A lot of things attracted them to each other," said Marshall. "I remember that Gene was more or less enamored of Jack Kennedy and his family at first."[7] McCarthy was even invited to Kennedy's wedding in 1953. But it was a doomed romance: Those early feelings of friendliness rapidly dissolved into rivalry and resentment.

Their common religion caused other complications. Many of McCarthy's friends thought part of his resentment of the Kennedys came from his conviction that *he* should have been the first Catholic president. McCarthy denied this. "Why be first anyway?" he asked. "That had nothing to do with it."[8]

The fact that Kennedy was not particularly religious actually made him the ideal Catholic to break the chain of prejudice that had confined the presidency to Protestants since 1789. From a political standpoint, it was also helpful that abortion was not legal—or even widely debated—in America in 1960. As a result, it was not yet an issue that would put a liberal Catholic into conflict with his church. (The landmark Supreme Court decision striking down restrictive abortion laws wasn't rendered until 1973.) The enlightenment of Pope John XXIII, who led the church from 1958 to 1963, was another blessing for the Kennedy campaign.

Anticipating criticism of his Catholicism, Kennedy told a national magazine in 1959, "Whatever one's religion in private life may be, for the office-holder nothing takes precedence over his oath to uphold the Constitution and all its parts—including the First Amendment." This was a pragmatic, political approach and—perhaps for that reason—offensive to McCarthy. The Minnesotan was more devout than Kennedy; he had even spent ten months in two monasteries before deciding he was not cut out for the life of a Benedictine monk. Writing in *America*, a Catholic weekly, he disputed Kennedy's more secular view: "Although in a formal sense church and state can and should be kept separate, it is absurd to hold that religion and politics can be kept wholly apart when they meet in the consciousness of one man." The implication, of course, was that they did *not* meet in Kennedy. McCarthy continued, "If a man is religious—and if he is in politics—one fact will relate to the other if he is indeed a whole man." When Kennedy saw the piece, he recognized it as an attack on himself.[9]

Everything about the way Kennedys—especially Jack Kennedy—lived suggested that they believed what happened here on earth was more consequential than whatever might occur in an uncertain hereafter. The same could not be said of McCarthy, whose slightly mystical bearing made many of his friends unsure of the ultimate importance he placed on earthly events. This resulted in very distinct campaign styles (and levels of commitment) when Jack, Gene, and Bobby ran for president.

McCarthy seemed to go out of his way to offend his fellow Catholic when Kennedy ran for the presidency in 1960. After Humphrey had quit the race, the Kennedys asked Walter Ridder, a Washington newspaperman, to act as their emissary to obtain the support of the senator from Minnesota. Ridder's approach was immediately rebuffed. McCarthy "didn't say why," but Ridder gathered that the Minnesotan "didn't think Kennedy had been a very good senator or a very good Catholic and that he just didn't like him personally. . . . From that point on, as far as I could see, Gene was dead with the Kennedys."[10] McCarthy compounded the offense when he agreed to nominate Adlai Stevenson at the Democratic Convention in 1960.

Even though Kennedy's nomination was never really in doubt in Los Angeles, McCarthy briefly managed to steal the Kennedys' thunder. "We're going to have a lot of fun with this," he confided after receiving the assignment to deliver the Stevenson nominating speech. On that Wednesday evening in July, McCarthy revealed one of his finely tuned and seldom displayed talents: the ability to milk a moment for maximum emotional effect. Gene had never been particularly close to Stevenson.[11] His target (the Kennedys) probably gave him more inspiration than his subject. Like Humphrey's peroration on civil rights twelve years earlier, it was that rare rhetorical event: a speech so powerful, it transforms its author into a national figure overnight. Destiny would offer McCarthy an even more dramatic opportunity for impromptu oratory eight years later; but never again would he speak so effectively as he did that evening for Adlai Stevenson.

"Do not reject this man who made us all proud to be called Democrats," McCarthy implored. "Do not turn away from this man. . . . Do not leave this prophet without honor in his own party." Stevenson's supporters staged a wild demonstration for twenty-five minutes; but this was really a wake masquerading as a celebration. When it was over, Kennedy had won the nomination with 806 votes on the first ballot. Johnson was second with 409 votes; Stevenson, a very distant third at 79½. A quarter-century later McCarthy said he didn't think Kennedy was ready to be president in 1960. "If I'd had my pick then, I would have picked Stevenson and Kennedy as a ticket," he said.[12]

After John Kennedy was killed, McCarthy always insisted in public that he had admired him. Despite his ambivalence toward the young president, McCarthy was shaken by his death. On the Senate floor in 1963, he delivered this elegant tribute: "A mind that sought the truth, a will ready for commitment, and a voice to challenge and to move are ended for this age and time of ours." Mary McGrory, a *Washington Star* reporter friendly with both McCarthy and the Kennedys, said, "Gene

really felt terrible about Jack Kennedy being killed. I think he was very
jealous of him and resentful of him, but I can remember him calling me
up and saying, 'Nothing's any fun any more.' He was minded at one time
[after JFK's assassination] to go and see Bobby, and I said, 'I think you
should.' And he said, 'Yeah, but he might misunderstand.' I said, 'I don't
think he would: He's heartbroken.'" McCarthy never made the visit.[13]
And although he later claimed to be "more intimate with Kennedy in the
presidency than with Johnson or anyone else," in 1963 the Minnesotan
spent a long session with an old friend describing how much more effective
Johnson was than Kennedy.[14]

LYNDON Johnson became president in 1963 because John Kennedy had
selected him to be his running mate in 1960. Kennedy had needed the South
in order to win the election, and Johnson helped the Democrats carry seven
Southern states, including the crucial one: Texas.[15]

In 1968 Johnson was in danger of *losing* the presidency, partly because a
substantial element of the Democratic party longed for a restoration of the
Kennedy dynasty. To these dissenters, John Kennedy had been the glam-
orous product of a new generation, a Harvard man with a Boston accent
and the perfect tailor. Lyndon Johnson, an unworthy usurper with an ugly
Southern drawl, the vulgar alumnus of Southwest Texas State Teachers
College, looked like a throwback to the generation of Kennedy's father,
even though he was only nine years older than his predecessor. The babies
in John Kennedy's White House were his own; in Johnson's, they were the
president's grandchildren. But what was most unforgivable was Johnson's
status as the one clear beneficiary of the Kennedy assassination. In Theodore
White's words, "When Lyndon Johnson became President, all the yester-
days were restored. . . . For Robert F. Kennedy the title papers of Lyndon
Johnson to the Presidency [would be] forever flawed—flawed by the bullet
and flawed by the generation of his age."[16]

No one doubted the hatred between Johnson and Bobby Kennedy: Both
men could be brutal, almost to the point of bloodthirstiness. President Johnson realized the Kennedy clique thought of him as an accidental pretender
to the throne. He responded to these muttered feelings with all the cruelty
he could muster. Johnson used Pierre Salinger as his messenger, knowing
that Kennedy's former press secretary would deliver his vicious parable to
the dead president's brother. After Bobby heard the story from Salinger,

he repeated it to Arthur Schlesinger. Kennedy called it "the worst thing" Johnson had said.

This was Bobby's recollection of the president's words to Salinger: "When I was young in Texas, I used to know a cross-eyed boy. His eyes were crossed, and so was his character. . . . That was God's retribution for people who were bad, and so you should be careful of cross-eyed people because God put his mark on them." Then Johnson suggested John Kennedy might have been another victim of one of God's "marks": "Sometimes," he said, "I think that when you remember the assassination of Trujillo and the assassination of Diem, what happened to Kennedy may have been divine retribution."[17]

The campaign to convince Johnson to choose Bobby as his running mate in 1964 enraged the new president. "A tidal wave of letters and memos about how great a vice-president Bobby would be swept over me," he told his biographer, Doris Kearns.[18] The president considered *himself* "the custodian" of John Kennedy's will, "but none of this seemed to register with Bobby Kennedy, who acted like *he* was the custodian of the Kennedy dream, some kind of rightful heir to the throne." (In the early days of John Kennedy's administration, Washington wags twitted these dynastic notions this way: "We've got Jack until '68, then Bobby until '76, and then Teddy—and then it doesn't matter anymore, because then it's 1984.")

"It just didn't seem fair," Johnson continued. "I'd waited for my turn. Bobby should've waited for his. But he and the Kennedy people wanted it now. . . . No matter what, I simply couldn't let it happen. With Bobby on the ticket I'd never know if I could be elected on my own."[19] He was just as blunt with historian Eric Goldman: "That upstart's come too far and too fast. He skipped the grades where you learn the rules of life. He never liked me, and that's nothing compared to what I think of him."[20]

Johnson recalled a visit to a poor family in Appalachia with special bitterness: "They had seven children, all skinny and sick. I promised the mother and father I would make things better for them. . . . They seemed real happy to talk with me, and I felt good about that. But then as I walked toward the door, I noticed two pictures on the shabby wall. One was Jesus Christ on the cross; the other was John Kennedy. I felt as if I'd been slapped in the face."[21]

Like the other competitors for national office, Bobby and Lyndon were both prisoners of John Kennedy's legacy. Each of them would always feel inadequate after 1963 because he was not the late president—but they probably tried to disguise that fact from themselves, as well as each other.

John Kennedy knew he was easy to love. Lyndon Johnson and Bobby Kennedy knew they were easy to hate.

It was probably worse for Bobby. Three weeks after John Kennedy's assassination, Mary McGrory persuaded the attorney general to make his first public appearance at a Christmas party for homeless children at a Washington restaurant. "I had told the children that Robert Kennedy would be coming, and told them to be nice and all that," said McGrory. She particularly remembers a beautiful little boy named Michael Doyle, "the kind of child who melts you." The writer Peter Maas was also present. "The moment [Kennedy] walked in the room," Maas recalled, "all these little children—screaming and playing—there was just suddenly silence." Then Michael Doyle ran up to the attorney general and blurted out, "I know your brother, he's President Kennedy, and he's dead."

The adults froze. Bobby flinched. Then Kennedy picked Michael up, held him very close for a moment, and said: "That's all right. I have another brother."[22]

Some amateur psychologists thought this was Bobby's "turnaround moment." McGrory doesn't think he ever had one.[23] Theodore White believed Robert Kennedy "loved his brother more than himself" and saw him "as more than a person—as the flag of a cause."[24] Arthur Schlesinger, also intimate with both siblings, offers these comparisons: "One was a man for whom everything seemed easy; the other a man for whom everything had been difficult. One was always graceful, the other often graceless. John Kennedy, one felt, was at bottom a happy man; Robert, a sad man. John Kennedy seemed invulnerable; Robert, desperately vulnerable. One felt liked by John Kennedy, needed by Robert Kennedy."[25]

THIS was part of the history that made the ghost of John Kennedy so potent in 1968. In life, he had been an unusually romantic figure for an American president: youthful, funny, glib, much more intellectual than the average politician; husband of a beautiful, elusive wife; father of two beguiling children. After his death, we turned him into a demigod, his administration into a magical mystery—"Camelot." Since this Camelot was a myth, you could neither confirm nor deny it with objective facts. When Lou Harris asked Americans what they missed most about Kennedy a year after his death, "his dramatic personality" was the most frequent answer. "Strength of leadership" was a distant fourth.[26]

It had actually been a promising but stillborn presidency. Camelot attracted some very gifted men and women to Washington, but their judgment was erratic. The Cuban Missile Crisis was remembered as Kennedy's greatest triumph, but if his bluff hadn't worked, it might have destroyed the world. Had it really been worth it? His tax cut and civil rights bills, which were his major domestic initiatives, languished until his successor got them through Congress. Perhaps Kennedy also would have got them passed; perhaps he wouldn't have. He still looked so young when he died. Who could say what he would have become? His assassination precluded any final judgment. You could not play it out. Or rather, *everyone* could play it out: Everyone was free to invent his own ending for the Kennedy administration—and everyone did.

The question no one could really answer was what Kennedy would have done about Vietnam. Like a nimble oracle, he had left enough clues behind to support several different conclusions. His race for the presidency included militant rhetoric about a "missile gap" with the Soviets, but once safe inside the White House, his aides admitted that the shortfall Kennedy had described never really existed. In his inaugural address the new president promised to "pay any price, bear any burden, meet any hardship, support any friend, [and] oppose any foe to assure the survival and the success of liberty." A few months later, diplomat George Ball warned him that the defense of liberty in Vietnam might eventually require three hundred thousand American troops. Kennedy laughed. "Well, George," he said, "you're supposed to be one of the smartest guys in town, but you're crazier than hell. That will never happen."[27] Yet, by the end of his first year in office, there were 3,200 American military personnel in Vietnam—and Kennedy had become the first president to violate the Geneva accords, which prohibited the introduction of bombers into Indochina. When the first American B-26s and SC-47s arrived at the end of 1961, they were rechristened "reconnaissance bombers" to disguise the violation. The International Control Commission charged the United States with violating the Geneva accords—and North Vietnam with subversion—on May 25, 1962.[28]

During this period, the president was depressed by the disastrous invasion of Cuba at the Bay of Pigs and unsettled by Khrushchev's bullying in Vienna. After the summit, Kennedy confided to *New York Times* columnist James Reston, "Now we have a problem in making our power credible—and Vietnam is the place" to make it credible.[29]

In 1962 the number of Americans in Vietnam more than tripled, to eleven thousand. Two and a half months before he died, Kennedy rejected French president Charles de Gaulle's proposal for a neutral, reunited Vietnam and ruled out the withdrawal of American troops before the Vietcong had been defeated. When the president was killed, there were 16,500 American military men in Vietnam.[30]

Kennedy's own top advisors—Secretary of State Dean Rusk, Secretary of Defense Robert McNamara, National Security Advisor McGeorge Bundy, and Bundy's successor, Walt Rostow—all played key roles in persuading Johnson to undertake his disastrous policy of escalation. But by 1967, Kennedy's brother Bobby and former Kennedy aides like Arthur Schlesinger were making some of the loudest protests *against* Johnson's war. One matter Bobby was reluctant to discuss, according to his friend George McGovern, was his role in formulating his brother's position on Vietnam—"other than to say that he was one of those involved in supporting the policy."[31]

BOBBY'S very recent past as his brother's chief lieutenant was one factor that made his transformation into one of the war's most vocal opponents particularly dramatic. Another was his history with the second ghost that played such a large role in the way politicians viewed the War in Vietnam in 1968: the ghost of Joe McCarthy.

First elected to the Senate from Wisconsin in 1946, Joe McCarthy was voted its worst member by the Senate press gallery in 1949, largely because of his visible preoccupation with drinking and gambling.[32] After Mao Tse-tung won his civil war against Chiang Kai-shek in 1949, the Republicans began charging that the Democrats had "lost" China to the Communists. The following year, McCarthy, searching for a catchy issue for his reelection campaign, launched the notorious crusade against alleged subversives that would make "McCarthyism" a permanent part of the political lexicon.

McCarthy began by pretending in February 1950 that he had a list of 205 Communists working in the State Department and known to the secretary of state. The charge was pure invention; there was no evidence whatsoever to support it. Three years later, he chose Roy Cohn, a young lawyer from New York who blended amorality with immense ambition, to be his chief counsel. With Cohn egging him on, McCarthy managed to destroy the careers of scores of government employees because of their ancient, imagined or (occasionally) real connections to the Communist party. As *New Yorker* writer Richard Rovere observed, no politician of this era had "surer, swifter access to the dark places of the American mind" than Joe McCarthy.[33]

In 1954 only Arkansas's J. William Fulbright had the courage to vote against a new appropriation for McCarthy's investigations. "The truth is," said Rovere, "that everyone in the Senate, or just about everyone, was scared stiff of him. Everyone then believed that McCarthy had the power to destroy those who opposed him, and evidence for this was not lacking"—all four of the Democratic senators McCarthy had campaigned against had been defeated.[34]

McCarthy was finally censured by the Senate at the end of 1954. Though he died in disgrace three years later, his relatively brief reign of terror left a durable, destructive legacy. Throughout the fifties and sixties, the ghost of this demagogue would exercise extraordinary power over American foreign policy. In 1968, eleven years after his death, most American politicians remained paranoid about the possibility of being perceived as "soft on communism." This was one of the principal reasons it took so many so long to express in public their private doubts about the course of the war.

Of the five leading major-party candidates running for president in 1968, Richard Nixon and Bobby Kennedy were most closely identified with McCarthyism in the public mind. Nixon had anticipated Joe McCarthy's methods and motives with his assault on Alger Hiss, a State Department official accused by Whittaker Chambers of having been a Communist. From then on, a virulent anticommunism had been the cornerstone of Nixon's political career.

Bobby Kennedy's name would always be tinged with McCarthy's shade because he had worked for him. It was Bobby's father, a friend and campaign contributor to McCarthy, who decided Bobby should go to work for the controversial legislator.

John Kennedy didn't like the idea of having his brother work for McCarthy because he knew many of his influential friends would be offended. "His reasons were political, not ideological," according to his scribe, Theodore Sorensen.[35] John Kennedy's own record on McCarthy always made liberals uncomfortable because Kennedy was in the hospital when the Senate censured McCarthy, and—unlike every other absent senator—Kennedy did not obtain a pair. As a result, his opposition to McCarthy was never recorded. James MacGregor Burns thought nothing caused Kennedy more trouble than this failure to vote on the final censure: "A sharp question from the audience on the McCarthy issue was the one thing that could ruffle his ordinarily immaculate composure."[36]

Within seven months of joining the committee's staff, Bobby Kennedy became disillusioned with McCarthy's methods, and he resigned in July 1953. Even so, four years later, he attended McCarthy's funeral. "It wasn't the easiest thing for him to go," John Kennedy remarked to Ben Bradlee.[37] And for the rest of his life, Bobby would never be completely free of McCarthy's stigma. A California voter who wrote Kennedy in 1968 to ask about his connection to Joe McCarthy received this standard reply: "When my complaints to the Senator about the reckless procedures employed in investigations were ignored, I submitted my resignation and, in fact, wrote the minority report which censured the Senator."[38] Accurate as far as it went, but the statement ignored the fact that McCarthy's recklessness was obvious to many three years before Kennedy had gone to work for him.

Many years later Peter Maas asked Kennedy how he ever could have had "anything to do with" Joe McCarthy. "I thought there was a serious internal security threat to the United States," Kennedy replied. "I felt at that time that Joe McCarthy seemed to be the only one who was doing anything about it. I was wrong."[39]

Hubert Humphrey was a vociferous liberal in the Senate in the early fifties, having first received national attention for his brilliant defense of civil rights before the Democratic National Convention in 1948. Even though he had played a key role in purging far-leftists from the Democratic Farmer-Labor party (Minnesota's version of the Democrats), as a liberal he was still a frequent victim of McCarthyites who accused him of being soft on Communists.

Like too many other progressives of the period, Humphrey tried to deflect Joe McCarthy's charges by emulating Harry Truman's technique. The Democratic president's strategy was to make himself appear to be even more violently anti-Communist than his Republican critics. In May 1946 President Truman reacted to the pre-McCarthy, post–World War II anti-Communist hysteria by establishing the Temporary Commission on Employee Loyalty. Every federal employee was ordered to take a new security test to determine whether he or she had "sympathetic association with" any group defined by the attorney general as "totalitarian." Many historians believe this was the real beginning of "official McCarthyism."[40] But rather than outflanking the anti-Communist extremists, Truman had inadvertently legitimized their dubious goals, if not their means.

Eight years later Humphrey still hadn't grasped what it was that made Truman's approach defective. Acting on a very bad suggestion from Max Kampelman—a lifelong supporter who would give him equally poor counsel in Chicago in 1968—Humphrey proposed something more drastic than anything McCarthy had advocated.[41] The Minnesotan offered an amendment to a Republican-sponsored bill that would outlaw the Communist party and provide criminal penalties for membership. The Communist

Control Act passed the Senate by a vote of 84 to 0, and Eisenhower signed the bill into law, but because of its doubtful constitutionality, it was never enforced.[42]

IN 1968 no one was more imprisoned by the ghost of Joe McCarthy than Lyndon Johnson. Few Americans perceived of Johnson as a McCarthyite when he was in the White House. Nevertheless, he bore a measure of responsibility for creating the atmosphere in which McCarthyism flourished throughout the postwar period.

Three years after Truman had instituted his new loyalty test, Johnson waged a classic McCarthyite campaign against Leland Olds, the man Truman had renominated to run the Federal Power Commission. Olds had saved consumers millions of dollars by keeping utility rates low; but Johnson saw the Olds nomination as the perfect opportunity to ally himself with the powerful Texas oil and gas interests he had denounced at the beginning of his political career.

Olds was a socialist in the twenties and he had shared a platform with a Communist leader in 1924. These meager facts became the basis for a vitriolic attack by the senator from Texas. Johnson told Truman his subcommittee was "shocked" by the views Olds had expressed twenty-five years earlier. The *Washington Evening Star* accused Johnson and his colleagues of staging an "inquisition" that was "reminiscent of the House Un-American Activities Committee." The Senate rejected Olds, 53 to 15.[43]

The irony of Johnson's actions as a young senator would not be evident until twenty years later. By participating in the anti-Communist witch-hunt of the late forties, Senator Johnson had fostered the climate that would push America into the very quagmire that would end his own presidency in 1968.

For five years beginning in 1945, the United States had spurned requests from the French for troopships to assist in their war against Ho Chi Minh's Communist-nationalist army in Vietnam. During this period, the Truman administration took the perfectly logical position that there was no reason for the United States to participate in one of France's colonial wars. But two months after Joe McCarthy began his hysterical campaign in 1950, Secretary of State Dean Acheson announced a new program of military aid for the French in Indochina.[44] In August, an American Military Assistance Advisory Group of thirty-five men arrived in Vietnam to teach troops receiving U.S. weapons how to use them.[45] During the next four years,

American support for the French campaign in Indochina topped $2.5 billion—more money than France had received through the Marshall Plan to rebuild its own economy after World War II.[46]

America's long march into military involvement in Vietnam had begun. Charles Yost, a careful diplomat, argued "that it was McCarthy's all-too-popular persecution of those he claimed 'lost' China that drove [Eisenhower's secretary of state] John Foster Dulles, John F Kennedy, and Lyndon Johnson into the morass of Vietnam." This fear of "losing" another country was "in large measure a posthumous exercise of power by Joe McCarthy."[47]

Of all the candidates for president in 1968, only Eugene McCarthy demonstrated real moral courage when Joseph McCarthy's influence was at its peak. Six months before Bobby Kennedy went to work for the erratic senator from Wisconsin, and two years before Humphrey's misguided amendment, Gene McCarthy became the first congressman to stand up to Joe McCarthy in a nationally televised debate.[48] While most of his colleagues in the Senate continued to cower before the bully from the Midwest, this second-term congressman quietly took Crazy Joe's arguments apart.

The two McCarthys appeared together on the *American Forum of the Air* on June 22, 1952. "We know we have lost an average of one hundred million people a year to communism since the shooting part of World War II ended," Joe McCarthy declared. "The total lost has been about seven hundred million people. Right, Gene?"

"Senator, I don't think you can say that we have lost them: We never had them," the thirty-six-year-old congressman replied. "Of course, it is not our policy to 'have' people," he added.[49]

The *Washington Evening Star* reported that Gene had exploded "the fallacy of Senator McCarthy's invincibility in debate." Gene McCarthy had emerged "unruffled and unscarred"—tantamount to "victory in this league." The fact that he shared his opponent's surname probably heightened the effect of the Minnesotan's success. For the rest of his career, Eugene would occasionally be mistaken for Joe—and some analysts have argued that as late as 1968 the less informed members of the electorate thought they were voting for the dead senator from Wisconsin rather than his living ideological opposite.

Gene's arguments in 1952 paralleled the anti-interventionist rhetoric he would use sixteen years later. More important, this was the first time he displayed a rare, and rarely used, capacity to recognize exactly when to ignore the conventional wisdom. It was partly this instinct, present in every brilliant politician, that would propel him into action fifteen years later, when every other potential peace candidate remained paralyzed with doubt.

"MUNICH" was the third ghost gnawing away at American politicians and foreign policy experts throughout the postwar period. British prime minister Neville Chamberlain flew to Munich on September 29, 1938. There he made the egregious mistake of trying to appease Hitler by giving him Czechoslovakia's Sudetenland. The Munich pact emboldened the German dictator, presented him with a huge strategic advantage, and made the bloodiest war of all time inevitable. Chamberlain hailed the moment as "peace for our time," while Winston Churchill correctly identified it as a "total and unmitigated defeat."

For the next thirty years, the respective judgments of Chamberlain and Churchill echoed away endlessly inside the heads of American foreign policymakers. (The mystery of the "man with the umbrella," who can be seen opening one in the Zapruder film as John Kennedy drove by in the fatal Dallas motorcade, was finally solved when its owner told congressional investigators he was using Chamberlain's trademark to make an oblique protest against Kennedy's supposed appeasement of Communists.) The memory of Munich was at the heart of the domino theory, the idea that the "loss" of Vietnam would jeopardize the independence of all of Southeast Asia. Lyndon Johnson was obsessed with it. On his first trip to Vietnam as Kennedy's vice-president, he hailed President Ngo Dinh Diem as the reincarnation of Churchill.[50] (Thirty months later, the Kennedy administration indirectly encouraged a coup that resulted in Diem's assassination.[51]) When Doris Kearns was helping Lyndon Johnson write his memoirs, he told her any suggestion that he might have chosen a different course in Vietnam was based on "complete ignorance. For if I had chosen otherwise, I would have been responsible for starting World War III. . . . It was the thought of World War III that kept me going every day. . . . As horrible as it was—and I hated it more than anyone—do you know what it's like to feel responsible for the deaths of men you love? Well, all that horror was acceptable if it prevented the far worse horror of World War III. For that would have meant the end of everything we know."[52]

To Johnson and his men, it was Munich that gave the War in Vietnam the overtones of a religious crusade. Francis Cardinal Spellman, vicar of the armed forces, called the conflict "Christ's war . . . a war for civilization."

Antiwar protesters responded to the cardinal's words at a high mass in New York City's St. Patrick's Cathedral by unfurling a banner with a picture of a wounded Vietnamese child and the words THOU SHALT NOT KILL.[53] But Johnson persisted in seeing the war as a moral necessity: We had to fight to prevent a repetition of the catastrophe at Munich, the most disastrous mistake of an earlier generation, the generation that sent its sons off to war in 1939. Until 1968 this misuse of the lessons of history made any compromise with the war's opponents impossible.

To the liberals who abandoned Johnson, Munich had far less to do with Vietnam. These men and women felt the failure to act quickly enough to restrain a savage tyrant who had revived a powerful industrial state in Central Europe had little or no relevance to a civil war in a small agricultural country eight thousand miles from the California coastline.

Those who by 1967 were questioning the war knew that it was no longer practical or reasonable to oppose communism everywhere, regardless of the cost in American lives and irrespective of the chances for success. Most of them (including Gene McCarthy) also believed that John Kennedy would have recoiled from the huge war Johnson had created, whereas those who continued to support the carnage cited the dead president's more militant rhetoric—and still quivered at the thought of "losing" another country to the Communists.[54]

The tension between these two groups was played out at social gatherings all over the capital. "You went out to dinner and you took your life in your hands," said Mary McGrory. "I can still remember the screaming—and the misery." Hubert Humphrey felt trapped among his old friends.

In the fifties, when Johnson was the Senate majority leader and Humphrey was trying to ingratiate himself with the Senate establishment, the Minnesotan often acted as Johnson's emissary to the liberal wing of the party. By the end of his third year as Johnson's vice-president, that role was becoming increasingly distasteful. Though he would sometimes express private doubts about the course of the war, in public he remained unconditionally loyal to his commander-in-chief. To many of his old comrades-in-arms, it was a repellent spectacle. Gene McCarthy thinks Humphrey behaved in a sycophantic way because he felt the Kennedys had ended his career in national politics in 1960. McCarthy believed that Humphrey had concluded about himself, "You're a loser, you can't win, you can only run in Minnesota." Then Johnson resurrected him by choosing him as his running mate in 1964. "He was back again," said McCarthy. "When the Chinese used to save a man from drowning, why, he was yours forever. He's your slave—and Hubert was always that way with Lyndon. He was *so* grateful."[55] To White House reporters visiting him on his Texas ranch, Johnson described Hubert's loyalty this way: "I've got his balls in my pocket."[56] But Humphrey's anguish boiled over at a dinner party Joseph Rauh held for the vice-president in the spring of 1967.

Joe Rauh was a grand old man among American liberals: He had been prominent in nearly every important progressive crusade in postwar America. He had worked for Humphrey's presidential campaign in 1960,[57] represented Lillian Hellman when she was called before the House Un-American Activities Committee in 1952, and served as one of the chief lobbyists for the landmark Civil Rights Act of 1964. On one April evening in 1967 his dinner guests were, among others, Hubert Humphrey, Arthur Schlesinger, Harvard professor (and former Kennedy ambassador to India) John Kenneth Galbraith, *New Republic* editor Gil Harrison, and two columnists, James Wechsler and Clayton Fritchey. The gathering for old friends remained pleasant as long as the subject of Vietnam could be avoided; then it dissolved into forty-five minutes of belligerence. In the tone of the conversation you can hear the onset of a liberal tendency that would become so prevalent in 1968: the instinct of these deeply committed men and women to attack one another with more venom than they would ever direct at their real enemies in the Republican party. This is one participant's recollection of the debate at Rauh's dinner table:

"It was when Humphrey referred to the Indonesian situation that the biggest explosion occurred. He said almost parenthetically that he thought our stand in Vietnam had been a key factor in the anti-Communist resistance in Indonesia." Schlesinger blew up and said, "Hubert, that's shit, and you know it." In his response, Humphrey never defended Rusk. The vice-president said he favored a bombing halt, adding, "The president's advisors obviously don't agree." Then "Schlesinger said with some feverishness that 'everybody in the State Department identified with Dean Rusk has to be thrown out' if there was to be a real new direction in policy. Humphrey, for one of the few times in the evening, raised his voice and responded angrily: 'Arthur, these were *your* guys. *You* were in the White House when they took over. Don't blame them on us.' Arthur did not answer back."[58]

To MANY political analysts, the tremendous prosperity most Americans were enjoying in 1967 was far more important to Lyndon Johnson's future than the growing dissension at Washington dinner parties over Vietnam.

The economy was booming: There were new fears about inflation, but prices were still rising by just 3.1 percent annually; unemployment averaged 3.8 percent, and the gross national product had reached a robust $789.7 billion a year. The interest rate on a typical home mortgage was only 6.5 percent.

These statistics convinced many Washington "pros" in 1967 that Lyndon Johnson remained invulnerable. For one thing, during this period the polls offered encouragement to hawks and doves alike. In the middle of 1967 George Gallup reported that 41 percent of his sample thought it had been a mistake to send U.S. troops to Vietnam—up from 24 percent just two years before—but a Harris survey revealed similar growth in the same period in the number of Americans favoring "total military victory": 45 percent in May 1967, compared with 31 percent at the end of 1966.[59]

In a typical example of widely accepted (but historically false) conventional wisdom, the experts declared no incumbent could be denied his party's nomination when he wanted it. Actually, five American presidents have been denied renomination, though never in the twentieth century. They were John Tyler, Millard Fillmore, Franklin Pierce, Chester Arthur, and, in 1868, Andrew Johnson. The pros' analysis also ignored another bit of history that was particularly relevant to the national condition in 1968: At the height of the Korean War in 1952, President Truman had taken himself out of the race—eighteen days after Estes Kefauver defeated him in the New Hampshire primary.

The herd instinct has always been particularly powerful within the Washington establishment. Once they had enshrined Johnson as the "master politician," these specialists—politicians and journalists alike—had a vested interest in his survival. Anyone willing to question this ignorance masquerading as insight quickly felt the consequences. Those who believed in the inevitability of Lyndon Johnson didn't tolerate dissent any better than the president himself did.

At the beginning of the Johnson administration, Walter Lippmann had briefly supported the president's bombing of North Vietnam. Now, in 1967, the columnist was almost alone among old-line, establishment Washington figures in his public rejection of the Munich parallel and in his brutal attacks on the disaster he saw unfolding in Southeast Asia. "Making this artificial and ramshackle debris of the old empires permanent and committing our lives and fortunes to its maintenance means unending war in Asia," he wrote in a typical article. The dean of Washington journalists called Lyndon Johnson "pathologically secretive," his conduct of foreign policy "willful, personal, arbitrary, self-opinionated."

Lippmann had never used such strong language against a president in his thirty-five years as a columnist. Gradually, his words made him such a pariah at the White House that Lyndon Johnson began to respond in kind, even attacking him in a toast at a state dinner. The writer who had spent a lifetime as the consummate Washington insider suddenly found himself on the outside. He was "snubbed and vilified" by old friends, according to his biographer, Ronald Steel, "and his sense of isolation increased." In the spring of 1967 he retreated from his home on Woodley Road, near the Washington Cathedral, to a Park Avenue duplex in Manhattan.* Lippmann denied he was leaving the capital because of Johnson. But few of his friends believed him. "I simply can't stand Washington," he said. "It's impossible to breathe or think in this town."[60]

Joe Rauh was another prisoner of this atmosphere. Although he was a strong opponent of the war, he resisted the earliest efforts to form a "Dump Johnson" movement, partly because he was afraid of splitting the party. Rauh was close to many of Johnson's more conservative allies in the labor movement as well as counsel to the Leadership Conference on Civil Rights. It had been liberal gospel for decades that the liberal-labor coalition was essential to victory at the polls. And Rauh knew the price Martin Luther King, Jr., had paid after his pointed criticism of the war in 1965. Many of King's white supporters (including the editorial page writers of the *New York Times*) reacted so negatively to his attack on the war that the civil rights leader backed away from the issue for eighteen months, until the conflict had grown huge and King identified it as the principal obstacle to domestic reform.[61]

Rauh worried that an unsuccessful assault on the presidency might even mask the full extent of peace sentiment within the party. In July 1967 he wrote down his arguments against participating in a "Dump Johnson" movement without a nationally known figure willing to oppose the president. Rauh thought the antiwar movement should focus on the adoption of a peace platform at the Democratic National Convention in 1968. Before mailing his memo out to three hundred liberal sympathizers, he took it to George McGovern. The South Dakotan was one of Bobby Kennedy's favorite senators as well as a prominent critic of the war in his own right. Rauh sat in front of McGovern for twenty minutes while the senator gave the fifteen-page document a careful reading. This is Rauh's recollection of the conversation:

---

* The new tenant of Lippmann's house in Washington happened to be another thoughtful opponent of the war: Eugene McCarthy.

"I'd like to throw it away if we had a candidate," said Rauh. "Are you a candidate?"

"No," McGovern replied.

"Are there any other circumstances that would bring you in?"

"No," the South Dakotan repeated.

"Is there any other senator who would be a candidate? Take all the peace people: Is there any who would run?"*

"No," McGovern answered again. "Neither Bobby nor anyone else is going to run. I am pretty sure of that."[62]

---

* By coincidence, nearly all of the senators opposed to the war—including McGovern, Joseph Clark of Pennsylvania, Wayne Morse of Oregon, Ernest Gruening of Alaska, J. William Fulbright of Arkansas, Gaylord Nelson of Wisconsin, and Frank Church of Idaho—were up for reelection themselves in 1968. And Rauh believed at this time that every Democratic governor, including Harold Hughes, was still a supporter of the war [Recorded interview with Joseph Rauh, 6/10/69, McCarthy Historical Project Archive, Georgetown University Library, Washington, D.C.].

2

Blowin' in the Wind

"A miasma of trouble hangs over everything. . . . It is unbearably hard to fight a limited war."
—Lady Bird Johnson, *A White House Diary,*
January 5, 1967[1]

A T THE beginning of 1967, very few Washingtonians anticipated the breadth of warfare that would break out all over America in 1968: in the streets, on the campuses, in the ghettos, and inside the Democratic party.

Outside the center of government, there was a different mood, an inkling among the more perceptive that a serious upheaval might be imminent in spite of, or because of, the capital's complacency. Johnson's war, the generation gap, Johnson's credibility gap, the spreading disorder in black ghettos (Detroit and Newark both exploded in the summer of 1967), the increase in black militancy, and the small but growing popularity of black separatism—these were all clues to the coming explosions. Working-class whites flocked to rallies celebrating the thinly veiled racism of Alabama governor George Wallace. Radicals argued that the war was the symptom of a decaying society. Normally pacifist liberals seriously discussed the possibility of guerrilla action inside the United States.[2] In April, Martin Luther King, Jr., called America the "greatest purveyor of violence in the world today."[3] One survey suggested that America had degenerated into an immense armed camp. Lou Harris reported that 55 percent of all whites and 32 percent of all blacks kept guns in their homes—and 51 percent of these gun owners said they would use them in a race riot.[4]

Elements of two generations of American students—some of whom had graduated from college in the fifties, others who were still attending college in the late sixties—were among the first to understand the opportunities implicit in this national uneasiness.

The civil rights crusaders of the fifties provided the original inspiration for many of these activists. The blacks who fought to end Southern segregation immediately after the landmark 1954 Supreme Court opinion in *Brown* v. *Board of Education* were important role models. The decision of the court reversed the fifty-eight-year-old doctrine of *Plessy* v. *Ferguson,* which permitted states to maintain separate but supposedly equal facilities. Apart from Jackie Robinson's integration of major league baseball in 1947, this was probably the greatest victory for American blacks since the Emancipation Proclamation. Segregation was finally illegal, although it would be years before the executive branch of the federal government would consistently enforce the new law of the land.

In this interim period, *Brown* v. *Board of Education* became a catalyst for courage. At a time when many white liberals were shell-shocked by McCarthyism, black men and women living below the Mason-Dixon Line reminded the rest of the nation of the power of the individual: the power to defy irrational injustice and, sometimes, to end it. Scores of future antiwar organizers worked within the civil rights movement; thousands of others, too young to participate in it, experienced it through newspapers and television.

Rosa Parks was a perfect example of an ordinary person almost casually assuming an extraordinary role. A forty-two-year-old tailor's assistant in Montgomery, Alabama, Mrs. Parks had been an active member of the NAACP (National Association for the Advancement of Colored People) since 1943. On December 1, 1955, with "no previous resolution until it happened," she refused to give up her seat on a city bus to spare a white man the indignity of sitting in the same row as a black woman. Her impulsive act of conscience sparked a black boycott of the bus system that lasted 382 days, until the city's resistance collapsed and a twenty-seven-year-old minister named Martin Luther King, Jr., became the first black passenger to sit in one of the first ten rows of a Montgomery bus.[5]

In "moderate" Little Rock—the state capital of Arkansas, where public transportation was already integrated by 1956—nine black high school students got such an ugly welcome in 1957 at a previously all-white public school that President Eisenhower was forced to send in paratroopers from the 101st Airborne Division to restore order. To ensure their safety *inside* Central High School, all the blacks were given individual military escorts to protect them while walking between the classrooms.

One of the Little Rock Nine would not make it through the school year, but the impact of her unprecedented protest may have been worth the punishment of expulsion. Disgusted with the constant badgering of a white boy in the cafeteria, Minniejean Brown suddenly emptied her chili bowl over his head. Her classmate Ernest Green recalled the scene: "There was just absolute silence. Then the help—all black—broke into applause. The white kids didn't know what to do. It was the first time, I'm sure, that white kids had ever seen someone black retaliate."[6]

And there were the four black students from North Carolina A & T College who started the sit-in movement on February 1, 1960, by taking seats at the whites-only Woolworth lunch counter in Greensboro, North Carolina; no one served them but they refused to leave.[7] Designed to desegregate public accommodations, this tactic quickly spread across the South. Fifteen days later Martin Luther King came to Durham, North Carolina, to address more than a thousand supporters of the sit-ins. "What is new in your fight," he declared, "is the fact that it was initiated, fed, and sustained by students. . . . When you have found by the help of God a correct course, a morally sound objective, you do not equivocate, you do not retreat—you struggle to win a victory." The struggle was for true personal freedom, for "freedom is necessary for one's selfhood, for one's intrinsic worth."[8]

Here were the roots of the moral certainty so many of us would discover through our opposition to the war, and the self-fulfillment we would achieve through those feelings of righteousness. As Thomas Powers observes in *The War at Home,* "The single most important influence on white students" in the early sixties was "the example of black students in the South."[9]

In DIFFERENT ways in different decades, the coastal states of New York and California have always welcomed the immigrant and the outcast—the avant-garde, the radical, the disadvantaged, the adventurer, the artist, the author, the beat, and the hip. In the sixties this lineage made San Francisco and New York City leading contenders in a flamboyant competition to become Counterculture Capital of the World. The weapons in this pacifist-dominated contest included long hair (Afros, Jewfros, ponytails, and Arthurs); Black Panthers; black politics; marijuana; guitars; folk-rock; acid rock; student politics; LSD; the Haight; the East Village; the Fillmore (the neighborhood); Greenwich Village; androgyny; speed; Andy Warhol; questioning authority; pop art; sexual politics; Bob Dylan; the Jefferson Airplane; Simon and Garfunkel; the Grateful Dead; Peter, Paul and Mary; Country Joe and the Fish; Bill Graham's Fillmores (East and West); radical politics; going back to nature; and putting your enemies up against the wall.

New York was arguably the first beacon for what would become the sixties: After all, Dylan moved to Manhattan to find Woody Guthrie the year the decade began, six years *before* Janis Joplin migrated from Texas to join Big Brother and the Holding Company in San Francisco in 1966.[10] Yet the West was still the home of many important firsts. Woodstock, in 1969, took place two years after San Francisco's Summer of Love, and students rose up in the name of free speech at Berkeley in 1964, four years before the explosion at Columbia University. The contest ended in a draw when the country between the coasts chose to emulate both of them.

The antiwar movement found two of its first safe-houses on these sea-boards: In the sixties, the politics of peace would be one of their most important exports. In March 1967 the left-liberal California Democratic Council announced it would run a slate of antiwar delegates in June 1968 unless steps were taken to bring peace to Vietnam within six months. On May 7, the Committee for Democratic Voters, the official arm of New York's reform movement, declared it would "work for the nomination . . . of a candidate other than Lyndon Johnson."[11] In the midst of these pronouncements, the Spring Mobilization to End the War in Vietnam held simultaneous marches on April 15 in New York and San Francisco, attracting about fifty thousand in the West and perhaps four times that number in Manhattan. In Central Park that day, more than a hundred young men fueled the rebellion by setting their draft cards on fire.[12]

IN 1967 there were two restless men who would exhaust themselves visiting hundreds of antiwar outposts on both coasts and in scores of cities, towns, and hamlets in between. These two men believed before almost anyone else did that Lyndon Johnson was not only hateful but vulnerable. The lives of these two men had repeatedly intersected with those of civil rights workers all over the South and other Americans throughout the country committed to change and social justice. It was their perpetual travels and ceaseless telephoning that would eventually knit together all of the war's opponents, convince them that they were not alone—that their goal was not preposterous—and prepare the way for Gene McCarthy's presidential campaign. These men were Curtis Gans and Allard Lowenstein.

Gans was born in Brooklyn in 1937, the son of a German merchant who had made and lost a fortune on the Berlin stock exchange before coming to New York in 1925. His father began life in America sweeping up coffee grounds on the floor of a business that eventually became his own.[13] Lowenstein was born in Newark, New Jersey, in 1929. His father had arrived here from Lithuania as a child, attended college, and become a scientist, only to abandon that career during the Depression to go into the restaurant business.

Lowenstein was much more political than his parents. Because he skipped a grade in elementary school, he was smaller than the other kids. "I wore glasses, and I was funny looking. I was picked on and left out a lot. Maybe because of that I always identified with ugly girls at dancing school, with blacks in the back of the bus, with anybody that was in some way hurt or excluded. My political involvement, I think, came from some emotional identification with people like that rather than from some ideology."[14]

These two sons of immigrants first met in 1957 at the University of North Carolina, where they began their acquaintance as political enemies. Gans was a UNC undergraduate and student-newspaper columnist; the peripatetic Lowenstein held the improbable post of graduate-student counselor for the athletics department. When Lowenstein concluded that the student-newspaper editor (elected by the student body) was making irresponsible attacks on the university's hospital, he started a recall campaign against him. Gans thought the attacks *might* be irresponsible, but after all, what did you expect from a student-newspaper editor? So he fought the recall, unsuccessfully. After that he decided he might as well recruit Lowenstein if he couldn't defeat him—so he asked him to manage the *Gans* campaign for newspaper editor.

Lowenstein had been an assistant to Eleanor Roosevelt and served as national chairman of Students for Stevenson in 1952. In 1958 he would work for Hubert Humphrey, and in 1964 write speeches for his vice-presidential campaign. When he accepted Gans's invitation, it marked the beginning of a long, uneasy alliance. "In that period he taught me an awful lot about politics," said Gans, "and I won the election." His earliest memory of Lowenstein is of a "liberal and a personalist. The most important cause of the moment was whatever Allard's cause was." Gans was always ambivalent about his confederate, partly because Lowenstein tended to take all the credit for what Gans believed they had achieved together.[15]

After graduating from UNC in 1959, Gans became a vice-president of the National Students Association. Since Lowenstein "was always operating on the fringe" of the NSA, which he had headed in 1951, their paths crossed quite frequently. When Lowenstein went to South-West Africa in 1959 to help smuggle out a student, Hans Beukes, Gans substituted for him at some speaking engagements back in the States and helped raise the $750 needed to fly Beukes to New York.[16]

Lowenstein had also been an undergraduate at UNC, graduating ten years before Gans. In 1950 he was elected president of the National Students Association. To Lowenstein, the value of the NSA "was that it reached a broad stream of American students. It was a mass movement, and at the conventions every year were fraternity jocks and Midwestern pom-pom girls, kids from little Catholic colleges and student-body presidents who were not particularly interested in partisan politics. . . . I think if you took a vote in the NSA congresses on the Eisenhower-Stevenson races in 1952 and 1956, Eisenhower would have won. Yet I think NSA contributed to liberalizing a wide range of student opinion."[17]

For thirty years, beginning with its founding in 1947, the NSA was a crucial meeting ground for young people committed to social change. As with the sit-in movement, the Mississippi Summer Project of 1964, the March on Montgomery, and other major episodes in the struggle for civil rights, the NSA was an incubator for organizers from all over the country. These men and women would eventually form the nucleus not only of the antiwar movement, but of all the other liberation movements of the sixties and seventies as well.

In the early sixties, Lowenstein worked with the Student Nonviolent Coordinating Committee in Mississippi and earned the enmity of radicals like Stokely Carmichael and Jim Foreman, who insisted, according to Lowenstein, "that the white middle-class way of life was itself sick, and they did not want to get poor black people into it."[18] Foreman charged that Lowenstein represented "a whole body of influential forces seeking to prevent SNCC from becoming too radical and to bring it under the control of what I have called the liberal-labor syndrome."[19]

Gans's connections to the civil rights movement included an active role in the sit-in movement, right from its inception in Greensboro. He saw himself as a "backstop" to the protests, "coming down to give tactical advice, bailing people out, raising money up North, finding new colleges for people who were expelled, doing everything possible to keep that movement alive." He was part of "a corps of backup people in the sit-in movement who were invisible, because the image we wanted to project was of well-dressed, well-groomed, well-spoken blacks against the unruly forces of white order." Gans was learning the value of appearances, knowledge that would become indispensable eight years later, when thousands of bearded and blue-jeaned young college students succumbed to the command to become "Clean for Gene" in McCarthy's presidential campaign.

By the time he was hired by Americans for Democratic Action in 1965, Gans had one of the most unlikely résumés in America: He had studied European intellectual history at graduate schools in California and North Carolina; helped the Student Nonviolent Coordinating Committee separate itself from the Southern Christian Leadership Conference; worked for six months as a recruiter for the Peace Corps; gone to dealer's school so that he could get a summer job at Harrah's Casino in Lake Tahoe; joined and left Students for a Democratic Society before its 1962 statement of principles at Port Huron, Michigan; enlisted in the Marine Corps reserves to dodge the draft and learned—"in the most rudimentary form"—how to be an air-traffic controller; driven a taxi for four months in Berkeley to earn enough money to go back East and look for a job in journalism; and worked for the *Miami News* during the Bay of Pigs. In 1963 he was a member of United Press International's bureau in Dallas, where, he complained to his friends, "nothing ever happens."

Curtis Gans was sleeping when his phone rang on the afternoon of November 22; he had been working the night shift.

"Curt," said the voice in the receiver. "Did you hear what happened?"

"No. What happened?"

"The president has been assassinated, and I want you to meet the casket at the airport."

"WHAAT???"

Gans did not believe his editor; he called a local radio station to make sure he was not the victim of a sadistic prank. Then he sped off to the airport.[20]

The next day, Gans was "hashing over" the assassination with a fellow UPI reporter, Terry McGarry. "We decided that if it was a conspiracy—and we made no judgment about it—but if it was a conspiracy, somebody who was as unstable as we began to know Oswald was could not be allowed to live. So based on that, we each took one of the police stations on Sunday morning that he was to be either transferred from or to." It was during that nationally televised transfer that Jack Ruby murdered Lee Harvey Oswald. "I got the wrong station," said Gans. Five years later his enemies in the McCarthy campaign would deride him as "the reporter who slept through the Kennedy assassination." Gans felt he had made up for his untimely slumber after becoming the wire service's Oswald expert. He thinks his biography of Lee Harvey Oswald holds the record for the longest story ever distributed on UPI's A-wire: It ran for one hour and forty-five minutes. Later on he wondered whether he had been transferred to Cheyenne, Wyoming, because he refused to give up on the Oswald story.[21]

GANS remembers becoming an opponent of the war the very next year, in 1964. When the bombing of North Vietnam began in 1965, he was "right at the hub" of the early opposition because he was working on foreign policy issues and editing the newspaper at Americans for Democratic Action, which came out strongly against the bombing in February of that year. In his spare time Gans made himself available as the "logistical coordinator" for any mass demonstration in Washington that would be "nonviolent, nonconfrontational, and persuasive." He worked with SANE (the Committee for a Sane Nuclear Policy) and SDS—and his list of contacts kept growing. "I didn't keep a good card file. But you can't imagine how much I kept in my head. I had networks in civil rights, networks in NSA, and networks in ADA." Only his addiction to Pepsi-Cola matched the intensity of his activism.

In the fall of 1966, Lyndon Johnson decided to cancel a previously scheduled campaign tour in the face of a probable Democratic disappointment, and forty-seven Democratic congressmen—as well as some great men like Paul Douglas, the Democratic senator from Illinois—were defeated in a Republican rout.[22] While the pros tended to look on these results as the normal corrective to Lyndon Johnson's landslide victory of 1964,* Gans saw the election as a devastating referendum on LBJ himself. He didn't think it proved the country was antiwar, just anti-Johnson. From that

---

* Lyndon Johnson won 61 percent of the vote. and the Democrats nearly doubled their majority in the House, from 82 to 155. After the 1966 election, the Democrats' majority shrank back to just 61.

point on he was convinced that "the Achilles' heel of the Vietnam War was the personality and leadership of Lyndon Johnson." The first time he saw Lowenstein after the November results, they greeted each other with the same sentiment: "Wasn't that a wonderful election?" They both thought that "Lyndon Johnson was vulnerable and beatable. This was not just a principled effort to try to do something; this could work."

Even though the trend seemed clear to Gans, Lowenstein was the only person he knew at this early stage who agreed that the president would be vulnerable in 1968. But they were hardly alone in their instinct: The day after the 1966 election, Adam Walinsky wrote a memo to his boss, Bobby Kennedy, explaining why he should challenge Johnson two years later. Gans found his personal poll most persuasive: "Not only could you stand on any street corner and turn to your left and turn to your right and talk to either person and find someone who hated LBJ, it was also the intensity of the feelings of hatred. The president was essentially quite devious and somewhat of a prevaricator and had a style that appealed to no one."[23]

One news story that broke in this period was especially helpful to two activists trying to encourage distrust of their president and his government. *Ramparts,* the radical magazine whose contributors ranged from black author Eldridge Cleaver to Cambodian prince Norodom Sihanouk, disclosed in 1967 that the CIA was the principal backer of the National Students Association. In rapid succession, Americans learned that the Congress of Cultural Freedom (which published the magazine *Encounter*), the National Council of Churches, the American Friends Service Committee in Philadelphia, several unions, and a number of educational institutions—even the YWCA[24]—had all received funds from the CIA. To liberals, the disclosures were shocking: disturbing proof of the government's willingness to engage in invisible manipulations of American society. To the Vietnam generation, it was just another illustration of the folly of putting your faith in the government.

Lowenstein insisted—and the agency officially confirmed—that he was the last president of NSA to be kept ignorant of the CIA connection. (A biography of the activist by Richard Cummings asserts that he not only knew of the relationship but actually worked for the agency on and off for many years. However, Cummings does not provide any credible evidence to support this allegation.[25])

Every NSA president after 1951 was informed of the CIA's involvement—and simultaneously forbidden to disclose it. Gene McCarthy complained that by requiring loyalty oaths from NSA presidents, the CIA had made these officers primarily responsible to the agency rather than to the members of their organizations, "who believed them to be free agents."[26]

Radicals were initially gleeful about the CIA revelations: Here at last was evidence that the government was just as duplicitous as they had suspected. But beneath the satisfied smiles there was an undercurrent of terror. Until these disclosures, radicals might boast about their telephones being tapped primarily to impress their friends. Now they had to worry that the imagined surveillance was real. This was more corroboration than they really wanted of one of the era's favorite epigrams: "Just because you're paranoid doesn't mean they're not after you."

Gans and Lowenstein began to do some more soundings. They were the quintessential Mr. Inside and Mr. Outside. Gans was always on the telephone, performing the behind-the-scenes organizing and the all-important name collecting. Lowenstein was the perfect public man, a spellbinding speaker whose myriad causes had already carried him from Spain to South Africa and back to Mississippi. To the slightly jaundiced eye of his less flamboyant collaborator, Lowenstein was also very good at "ingratiating himself with famous people he liked," from Eleanor Roosevelt to Bobby Kennedy.

Lowenstein abandoned the idea of a third-party effort headed by Martin Luther King, Jr., after the black leader made it clear in April that he did not want to run.[27] In New York, Gans and Lowenstein met with Norman Thomas, Andrew Young (an aide to King), and James Wechsler. Partly because Gans was working at Americans for Democratic Action and had helped get Lowenstein on its board in 1966, and partly because Wechsler was close to Joe Rauh, then the key figure in the ADA, the group agreed to work initially through that organization.[28]

On May 20, 1967, the ADA voted to support "that candidate of either party who offers a genuine hope for restraint in the conduct of the war in Vietnam and for its peaceful resolution on honorable terms."[29] At the same time, Rauh convinced his fellow board members they should make Lowenstein a vice-chairman of the ADA. "I figured if we didn't have student connections, we were missing what was probably the most important part of liberalism in America," said Rauh, "and I really had some feeling that Al was right when he talked about student participation in the campaign."[30]

Ironically, it was also at this point that Rauh became one of the principal impediments to what was already becoming known as the "Dump Johnson" movement.[31] Every time someone called Rauh to ask if he should contribute time or money to the Gans-Lowenstein effort, Rauh discouraged him. "In fairness to these people," Gans said of Rauh and his friends, "the Vietnam War was a very peculiar crisis for orthodox

American liberalism. Their base was still liberal anticommunism, and we were fighting communism in Vietnam." The liberal leaders of the oldest organized political party in the world had not yet confronted the limits of American power, or, as Gans put it, "how far you want to carry that fight."[32]

In August 1967, the NSA held its annual convention, and a young man named Sam Brown listened intently as Lowenstein spoke to a "screaming, shouting, foot-stomping, hurrah-hurrah kind of meeting" in the basement of the armory at the University of Maryland.[33] Lyndon Johnson's nemesis urged a grass-roots movement to get rid of the president, and Brown decided to participate in it. Two weeks later, Brown announced to 550 cheering student leaders the creation of an anti-Johnson group called Alternative Candidate Task Force (ACT '68).

Brown was the son of a small businessman, "sort of a pillar-of-the-church Republican, Rotarian type." As a youth growing up in the fifties in Council Bluffs, Iowa, Brown regarded Barry Goldwater and Richard Nixon as his heroes. He left home in 1961 to go to college in Redlands, California. Two weeks into his freshman year he was invited to a mountain retreat where he first met Lowenstein, who was just back from South Africa. Brown's conversion from libertarian to left-wing liberal began at that moment. When the college paper was closed down—partly because of an article Brown had written criticizing a rule banning Communist speakers on campus—he became the secret editor of an underground newspaper.

Later, after Brown had entered a master's program in "Christian ethics" at the Harvard Divinity School, he also met Gans. Brown was chairman of the Seminarians' National Emergency Committee, and Gans had helped him organize some antiwar picketing in front of the White House.

At Harvard, Brown spent a good deal of time researching regicide and tyrannicide, trying to determine whether it would be morally wrong to assassinate the president of the United States. He concluded that it "probably wouldn't be ethical" to kill President Johnson—even though he was waging a demonstrably unjust war in Vietnam—because Johnson's death was not likely to bring an immediate end to the conflict. Brown then considered the possibility of getting the job done by a "right-wing group," since that approach could produce a reaction against the right, which in turn might strengthen the antiwar movement. But even with that strategy Brown decided you "probably shouldn't" murder the president.[34] The student organization he founded after Lowenstein's August speech fizzled quickly for lack of funds, but the names of its leaders were immediately added to the Gans-Lowenstein Rolodex.

* * *

IN JUST three months in 1967, Gans had traveled to forty-two states, looking for people who might be able to carry out a campaign "once there was a campaign," for activists who could be "arms and legs" but not "leadership," and for all sizes and colors of student cadres. Usually Lowenstein would swoop in to speak to the groups Gans had located after he left, though sometimes Gans would do the follow-up himself. It remained a difficult relationship. "Allard really badly mistreated Curtis during that period of time," said Brown. "He sort of made a vassal out of him rather than any kind of partner in a process—which is not a very good way to get people to work."[35]

Lowenstein still hoped that he could persuade Bobby Kennedy to be a candidate. He had contributed ideas for some of Kennedy's speeches during his visit to South Africa in 1966, and they had remained friendly afterward. Kennedy's qualms about the course of the war grew steadily, even as his late brother's appointees—Rusk, the Bundy brothers, McNamara, and the Rostow brothers—had steadily enlarged it. Mary McGrory had a "very painful conversation" with Kennedy, urging him to run for president; he demurred on the ground that it would "split the party." When she reminded him he had never cared very much about the party before, Bobby responded "very dryly, 'My mother and my sisters all agree with you.' "[36]

On September 23, 1967, Kennedy met with Lowenstein and a few close friends to discuss his presidential prospects. "I would have a problem if I ran first against Johnson," Kennedy said. "People would say I was splitting the party out of ambition and envy. No one would believe that I was doing it because of how I felt about Vietnam and poor people. I think Al is doing the right thing, but I think that someone else will have to be the first to run. It can't be me because of my relationship to Johnson."[37]

Kennedy was right, though he must have known that staying out of the race would only result in a different sort of denunciation. The situation did not leave him with any desirable option. Most of his staff thought a race in 1972 would be wiser and easier; running now, they believed, would damage Bobby *and* the party, achieving nothing but a Republican victory in November. Only an occasional iconoclast like California assembly speaker Jesse Unruh or New York lawyer Justin Feldman suggested that, by then, someone else might have captured the imagination of America's activists. Feldman, a Kennedy friend and a savvy political operative, argued that the senator's hypothetical rival would run in 1972 on the slogan "Where was Bobby Kennedy in 1968?"[38]

To his enemies, this man of action's refusal to act was something much worse than a strategic error: It was proof of cowardice and calculation. To them it was obvious that Bobby was too preoccupied with the necessity of victory to devote himself to a moral imperative like peace in Vietnam.

LOWENSTEIN and Gans were fighting a two-front war. On the far left, radicals "took the position that [the 'Dump Johnson' movement] was a trick to destroy the peace movement," according to Lowenstein. They thought the effort would "show how weak we were," thus giving "strength to the notion that the war was popular so that it would be extended." Slightly to the left of center, "the liberal establishment, although for different reasons, generally took the same view: that you couldn't oppose Johnson effectively unless you had a major candidate, by which was normally meant Robert Kennedy. And you wouldn't get a candidate, so it was irresponsible and demagogic to oppose him at all. . . . Some [liberals] were for Johnson because they didn't really disagree very much with the war or they thought the war was a minor item compared to the good things he was doing at home. Some of them were against Johnson, but felt that it was quixotic to break with him."

Without a national figure willing to challenge the president, Gans and Lowenstein were sustained by tiny encouragements: Don Peterson, chairman of the Democratic party in the Tenth Congressional District of Wisconsin, was the highest party official supporting their effort. Alpha Smaby, a member of the Minnesota legislature, was the first elected official to give public support to the movement. "The whole Humphrey apparatus just descended on her," said Lowenstein, "but she stuck it out." For a very long time, "the nearest thing we had to a celebrity was Robert Vaughn"—quite prominent then for his starring role in *The Man from U.N.C.L.E.*[39]

Although Rauh continued to assume no one would run as a peace candidate in the primaries, he did tell Lowenstein he thought Gene McCarthy would be a stronger candidate than George McGovern. Being a Catholic, Rauh felt the Minnesotan would be "invulnerable to the soft-on-communism charge," since the Vatican had always been so fiercely anti-Communist. Once again, the power of Joe McCarthy's ghost was on display.[40]

Gene McCarthy's first serious discussions about challenging Lyndon Johnson were held in March 1967 in Manhattan with Thomas K. Finletter, Thomas Shea, and Russell Hemenway—Stevensonians who wanted an alternative to Bobby Kennedy in case Lyndon Johnson decided not to run. McCarthy said the only move that might persuade Lyndon Johnson to alter his position on the war was a direct challenge in the primaries, and he suggested he might be willing to accept a summons if no one else would. But two days later he changed his mind; he was not yet ready to confront the president.[41]

In August, Gans quit the ADA because only the organization's staff supported the "Dump Johnson" movement; so far, its board would not. Most of the telephoning around the country was done out of his apartment; at night, California congressman Don Edwards made his office telephone available. In this period, Edwards was the only elected official in Washington giving the movement any concrete support. "We were collecting lists of names of anybody who had ever signed an ad, written a letter, or said anything against the war and putting them on cards by precincts," Gans recalled.

By September the "Dump Johnson" movement was still without a candidate.* Under the pseudonym Daley Unruh, former White House aide Richard Goodwin wrote in *The New Yorker* that an unknown opponent of the war could become a national figure in a month. Practically the only direct support for the movement in the Washington press was an encouraging editorial written by *New Republic* editor Gil Harrison.[42]

Lowenstein suggested that Gans should visit Gene McCarthy's daughter Mary, a Radcliffe undergraduate. Gans had an ambiguous conversation with Mary McCarthy, but others say she had begun to press her father to make a run for the presidency. "Don't you want to be remembered in history for some nobler act than support of LBJ's reelection?" she asked. When Gans visited Minnesota in September, he got his first inkling that McCarthy might be willing to follow his daughter's advice. According to Gans, Sandy Keith, a candidate for governor, had heard McCarthy "make some private remarks about the intolerable use of power." McCarthy had said, "Something must be done."

Gans thinks Lowenstein was reluctant to approach McCarthy because he still hoped Bobby Kennedy would change his mind and challenge the president. "Finally, after I heard more and more about McCarthy, I told Allard if he wasn't going to see McCarthy, I was." When Lowenstein

---

* In the fall of 1967 Lowenstein traveled to Saigon to observe the Vietnamese presidential election. Lee Lescaze, a *Washington Post* correspondent in Vietnam, got a call from Lowenstein, whom he had never met. " I remember very well, over dinner one night he was talking about how he was going to get somebody to run in New Hampshire," said Lescaze, "and he was going to beat Johnson in the primaries. I thought he was very engaging—but I thought he was wacko." [Author's interview with Lescaze, 2/23/86.]

learned that Gans had actually made an appointment to meet with the Minnesotan, he was galvanized into action. According to Gans, Lowenstein didn't want there to be any question in McCarthy's mind about who was really running the "Dump Johnson" movement—so he made sure he got to see the senator one day before Gans did. The meeting in late October produced an agreement that McCarthy would explore the possibility of running.[43]

McCarthy's doubts about the Johnson administration's intelligence from inside South Vietnam had become specific thirty-one months earlier, after a White House briefing for two dozen senators on February 18, 1965. Rusk "advised us that the government in power in Vietnam—at that time under General Nguyen Khanh—was strongly supported, was stable, and gave every evidence it would be effective for a long time to come," McCarthy remembered. "The secretary gave us that assurance at nine or ten o'clock at night. The morning papers gave us the news the Khanh government had been overthrown. If one took into account the difference in time zones, the overthrow was being carried out at about the time that the secretary of state was speaking to the Senate group in the White House."[44] A year later he made his first formal statement in the Senate opposing the administration's policy. "The burden is on the Defense Department to prove, if it can, that the bombings have had some kind of beneficial political or diplomatic effect . . . it is my judgment that this has not been demonstrated. . . . The serious problem today is that we are called upon to make a kind of moral commitment to an objective . . . which we do not clearly understand."[45]

When the Senate voted 92 to 5 in March 1966 against a motion to repeal the Gulf of Tonkin Resolution, McCarthy was one of the five, together with Wayne Morse, Ernest Gruening, William Fulbright, and Stephen Young. The resolution gave the president the power to "take all necessary measures" to repel attacks on American forces, to "prevent further aggression," and to determine when "peace and security" had been restored. Johnson interpreted it as giving him the authority to send whatever forces he wanted to Southeast Asia. It was like "Grandma's nightshirt," he later quipped; "it covered everything."[46] Originally approved on August 7, 1964, by 82 to 2 in the Senate and 416 to 0 in the House, the resolution was in response to what a Pentagon spokesman described as a "second deliberate attack" by the North Vietnamese on an American warship. But the first shots in the initial "attack" were actually fired by Americans—and the second North Vietnamese attack almost certainly never occurred. According to Stanley Karnow, "It had not been deliberately faked, but Johnson and his staff, desperately seeking a pretext to act vigorously, had seized upon a fuzzy set of circumstances to fulfill a contingency plan."[47]

If there was a turning point in McCarthy's outrage, it probably came on August 17, 1967, when Undersecretary of State Nicholas Katzenbach told the Senate Foreign Relations Committee that Congress was "compelled" to support the president's foreign policy. Katzenbach also described the Gulf of Tonkin Resolution as "the functional equivalent" of a declaration of war. Enraged, McCarthy left the hearing room. "This is the wildest testimony I have ever heard," he told Ned Kenworthy of the *New York Times.* "There is no limit to what he says the president can do. There is only one thing to do: take it to the country."[48]

In the fall of 1967, more and more moderate officeholders were expressing doubts about the war. Massachusetts congressman Thomas P. ("Tip") O'Neill (who held John Kennedy's former Boston seat) was bombarded by questions from his twenty-two-year-old son and his twenty-year-old daughter; in September, he announced that he favored a bombing halt. "After listening to their side of the story for a year and a half, I've decided that Rusk and McNamara and the rest of them are wrong," said O' Neill. In October, a *New York Times* survey of 203 congressmen, senators, and governors revealed that thirty of them now favored a stronger peace posture; only ten wanted a wider war. Thruston Morton, a Kentucky senator and former chairman of the Republican National Committee, said he had been "all for the bombing . . . I was wrong. . . . There's going to have to be a change." Paul Findley of Illinois, Claude Pepper of Florida, Al Ullman of Oregon, and Morris Udall of Arizona (whose brother was Lyndon Johnson's secretary of the interior) were also among the new dissenters. But none of these men was even close to making the leap from challenging the war to challenging the president.[49]

McGovern, who, like most of the other antiwar senators, faced his own reelection campaign in 1968, was one of the reluctant pols who had suggested that the "Dump Johnson" people should approach McCarthy, since the Minnesotan's Senate term didn't expire until 1970. When he saw McCarthy on the Senate floor a few hours later, McGovern mentioned that he had sent some people over to talk to him about challenging the president. McCarthy said, "Yeah, I talked to them. I think I may do it." McGovern was astounded: "I just couldn't believe it. I really thought [it was just] a way of getting these people off my back."[50]

The presumed futility of challenging an incumbent president had dissuaded all other antiwar senators from confronting Johnson in the primaries. What McGovern and his colleagues had overlooked was the appeal a reputedly hopeless quest could hold for a man like McCarthy. For this enigmatic iconoclast, impossible odds were practically a prerequisite for a run for the presidency. As he suggested in his nominating speech for Stevenson in 1960, McCarthy recoiled at the spectacle of *any* politician grasping for power. When he competed with Humphrey to become Johnson's vice-president in 1964, he was shocked by Humphrey's sycophantic attitude toward the president during their joint appearance on *Meet the Press*. "I thought he was overly flattering," said McCarthy. "He mentioned Lyndon, what, fifty times? When you get to that level, you've got to keep something to yourself. . . . The explanation, and I think it's valid in some ways, is that Humphrey wanted to be president very badly."[51]

After his first election to Congress in 1948, McCarthy said, "I guess I agree with Plato that it's the philosopher who should rule."[52] In 1968 he said, "I've kind of got me hitched to Thomas More. . . . I think he was a rather interesting man because he was kind of a breakthrough. He had to accept responsibility more or less outside the pattern of a tradition of family obligation."[53]

These attitudes made McCarthy the ideal candidate for the challenge. The same calculation that held Bobby Kennedy back actually protected McCarthy, shielding him from the accusation that he might be running for president out of crass ambition. It also made him especially appealing to those appalled by the obvious pleasure Lyndon Johnson took from manipulating the power of the presidency.

MOST politicians, regardless of their position on the war, were unaware of another movement that was born in 1967 on the airwaves of a non-profit FM radio station in New York City called WBAI. This more-or-less listener-sponsored outlet, subsidized by the Pacifica Foundation (KPFA in San Francisco and KPFK in Los Angeles were the West Coast affiliates), was an East Coast locus for the counterculture. As early as 1963, Pacifica had been harassed by the Senate Internal Security Subcommittee, which investigated the backgrounds of people appearing on its stations.

Always straining the Federal Communications Commission's capacity for tolerance, WBAI broadcast everything from conspiracy theories blaming Lyndon Johnson for John Kennedy's assassination to the latest underground rock and roll. Rounding out its unpredictable format was a distinguished nightly news feature called *The War Report*. Delivered solemnly, this was the most thorough daily diary of war news available to the public. The cool recitation of grim events without television's gory pictures made the war sound particularly macabre. (A similar effect was achieved by Simon and Garfunkel's "Seven O'Clock News/Silent Night.")

WBAI's earliest morning hours belonged to disc jockeys Steve Post and Bob Fass. Very late one night in February 1967, Fass's all-night "radio unnameable" featured a tape by a young male singer whose father was the most venerated figure in folk music.

"Alice's Restaurant," by Arlo Guthrie, was a beguilingly simple tale that combined a rural arrest for littering with an inspirational visit to the Army's Whitehall Street induction center in Manhattan—and bound them together with a refrain about a restaurant run by a woman named Alice who lived in a church. In twenty hilarious minutes Arlo made the absurdity of youth logical and the logic of adults absurd; in the process he won a permanent place as one of our indispensable bards. Simultaneously he reclaimed from Bob Dylan that part of his father's mantle that he knew belonged to Arlo.

"You can get anything you want at Alice's Restaurant" became one of those code phrases that defied translation across the generation gap— likewise the "Group W bench," that hallowed place in our minds where Arlo was detained while military authorities wrestled with the question of whether he was "moral enough to join the Army, burn women, kids, houses, and villages—after being a litterbug."

As soon as Fass finished playing the tape, the station was inundated by listeners calling for more. He complied as only a noncommercial disc jockey could, replaying "Alice" over and over again all night.[54] Within weeks, other radio stations were also broadcasting the bootleg antiwar hymn. But by the time Arlo got to the Newport Folk Festival in July—despite the proliferation of cryptic "Alice's Restaurant" buttons—his song remained an almost entirely underground phenomenon. He played it first at a modest Saturday-afternoon workshop for "topical songs." The following afternoon he repeated it for thirty-five hundred; the response persuaded festival producer George Wein to add it to the evening performance. That night, before ninety-five hundred instant enthusiasts, it became the festival's climax. Thirty famous folk singers joined Arlo onstage for a refrain that doubled as the music for his coronation.* Just ten weeks later, his father, Woody, was dead at fifty-five.[55]

---

* Exactly four years earlier, Dylan had been crowned in the same place in the same fashion, when Peter, Paul and Mary spontaneously backed him on "Blowin' in the Wind." Pete Seeger, Joan Baez, Theodore Bikel, and the Freedom Singers then joined in for an extraordinary encore of "We Shall Overcome." It was probably the closest the folk world ever came to a formal passing of the torch. [Jim Miller, editor, *The Rolling Stone Illustrated History of Rock & Roll* (New York: Random House/Rolling Stone Press, 1980), 222.]

The *New York Times*—which, improbably enough, had launched Bob
Dylan's recording career with a similarly enthusiastic notice—gave Arlo a
spectacular send-off. The headline read:

NEWPORT IS HIS
JUST FOR A SONG

Arlo Guthrie Festival Hero
With "Alice's Restaurant"

Times music critic John S. Wilson called it "the most unlikely song hit
since 'Yes, We Have No Bananas.' "[56] "Alice" was finally released on an
album two months later.[57] By the end of 1968, there would still be thousands in the movement who had never heard the names of Curtis Gans or
Sam Brown or even Allard Lowenstein; but everyone loved Alice and her
restaurant.

IN OCTOBER of 1967, antiwar sentiment was becoming more pronounced
all across the country. Stop-the-Draft Week began in Boston on Monday,
October 16, 1967, when a hundred clergymen and two hundred members
of the New England Resistance marched into the Arlington Street Church,
where a century earlier, abolitionists had pleaded for the end of slavery. A
waiting crowd greeted the marchers with a chorus of "We Shall Overcome."
Dana McLean Greeley, president of the Unitarian-Universalist Association,
addressed the makeshift congregation: "I don't know what justifies a nation
in forcing young men to fight and die for a cause in which they do not
believe. That is not democracy but totalitarianism, and it is not freedom but
tyranny, if the nation is wrong." Yale chaplain William Sloane Coffin spoke
of "hundreds of history's most revered heroes—Socrates, St. Peter, Milton,
Gandhi—men who were not disrespectful of the law but who broke it as a
last resort." Then the doors opened on the center aisle, and 280 young men
approached the altar. Sixty-seven draft cards were burned over an abolition-
ist's candlestick; another 213 were turned in for presentation to the Justice
Department later in the week.[58]

That same Monday, McCarthy took the floor of the Senate to attack Dean
Rusk's newest justification for the Vietnam War—the fact that "within the
next decade or two, there will be a billion Chinese on the mainland, armed
with nuclear weapons, with no certainty about what their attitude toward
the rest of Asia will be." McCarthy accused the secretary of resurrecting

the "ancient fear of the yellow peril," and wondered out loud what effect a victory in South Vietnam could possibly have on the alleged threat of the Chinese.[59]

In the next four weeks, there were four crucial antiwar Vietnam protests—two in California, one in Washington, and one in New York—that would unravel into violence. These events would help convince liberals like McCarthy that the only alternative to challenging Johnson within the system would be unending disorder in the streets. The first protest occurred on the West Coast, just one day after McCarthy's speech attacking Rusk in the Senate. By six o'clock on the morning of October 17, three thousand protesters had surrounded the military induction center in Oakland, California. When they ignored a police order to move, twenty-five were arrested and at least twenty were injured—assaulted by the police.

Three days later, antiwar radicals learned a lot about the inspirational value of a little blood. Reacting to Tuesday's events, ten thousand people—a huge number for such a demonstration at this time—appeared at the induction center. For three hours that Friday, they behaved like seasoned urban guerrillas, blocking streets (and buses filled with inductees) with makeshift barricades of benches, garbage cans, trucks, and cars. "Whenever police attacked, demonstrators melted away and reappeared elsewhere," journalist Thomas Powers wrote. "For one brief morning opponents of the war felt they had the upper hand, that the government was powerless and could be resisted, that the war could be *stopped.* The effect on the movement throughout the country was electric."[60]

The week culminated with a memorable Washington protest organized by antiwar activist Jerry Rubin at the request of David Dellinger, a longtime pacifist.[61] It was Rubin's theatrical thought to lay siege to the Pentagon instead of the Capitol, to focus the demonstration on the heart of the American war machine. The protest began in a traditional way, with speeches in front of the Lincoln Memorial, then moved across the Arlington Memorial Bridge to Virginia. At the Pentagon itself, twenty-five radicals managed to push past a handful of MPs guarding a side entrance; inside, they were quickly arrested.

Outside, protesters gave an impeccable demonstration of the dichotomy that would simultaneously define us, divide us, and bind us together in a perpetual debate. Some of the marchers put flowers in the gun barrels of the young troops in front of them; others taunted them with ugly epithets, while a third group alternated between the two tactics. Here was a perfect fragment of our permanent competition, played out in front of the Pentagon by countercultural "flower children," by hard-core practitioners of a new radical politics, and by everyone else in between.

After the press had departed from the Pentagon on Saturday at midnight, soldiers and federal marshals began a brutal evacuation of the plaza in front of the building. The worst victims of their clubbings were women (to taunt their male friends into protecting them?). "The scene at times was one of pure horror," Powers wrote, "women beaten senseless and then dragged off into the dark with bloody, broken faces. No one moved or got up to leave despite the violence, and the marshals and soldiers slowly worked their way through the crowd."[62] The clearing action was a flagrant violation of the parade permit obtained by the organizers, which gave them the right to remain on the plaza through Sunday.[63] When Sidney Peck of the Mobilization Committee used a bullhorn to ask for a halt to the attacks until someone in authority could be located, the more radical demonstrators considered this yet another liberal cop-out. But Peck's appeal did stop the violence: Reminded of the law, the official aggressors eventually desisted.

Noam Chomsky thought the demonstration symbolized the transition from "dissent to resistance."[64] Writing in *Ramparts,* Allen Woode said, "Objectively speaking, perhaps the best thing that could have happened on October 21 would have been for somebody to have been killed. For American soldiers to have shot unarmed American civilians exercising their right of free speech would have been a blow from which the administration could never recover."

Norman Mailer memorialized his experiences at the Pentagon in *The Armies of the Night,* a pungent if somewhat self-conscious account subtitled *History as a Novel/The Novel as History.* Of all the fiction writers who dabbled in journalism in the sixties, Mailer was among the most effective, even when he insisted on referring to himself entirely in the third person: "Still, Mailer had a complex mind of sorts. Like a later generation which was to burn holes in their brain on Speed, he had given his own head the texture of a fine Swiss cheese. Years ago he had made all sorts of erosions in his intellectual firmament by consuming modestly promiscuous amounts of whiskey, marijuana, seconal and benzedrine. It had given him the illusion he was a genius, as indeed an entire generation of children would so come to see themselves a decade later out on celestial journeys of LSD."[65]

The fourth protest occurred outside the New York Hilton, where Dean Rusk was speaking on November 14. Throughout the late sixties and early seventies, the streets surrounding the Hilton were a semipermanent center of antiwar activity, attracting mobs of protesters and counterprotesters every time an important officeholder came to speak to some part of the establishment inside its ballroom.* On this particular evening the demonstrators included a large contingent from the Columbia chapter of Students for a Democratic Society, who had become increasingly militant during the previous year and a half. Some of the demonstrators got trapped against a wall; suddenly the protesters began to be clubbed from above, forcing them toward a menacing line of mounted policemen. "For a few minutes there was something close to hysteria," according to one account. Ten blocks away in Bryant Park, some of the protesters regrouped. "We're not demonstrating against Rusk," one man shouted through a bullhorn. "We're demonstrating against the American establishment, against the liberal fascists."[66] In October, Rusk had said there was "no significant body of American opinion that would have us withdraw from Vietnam."[67]

A fifth protest in Baltimore that fall was bloody but nonviolent. Five days after his brother, the Reverend Daniel Berrigan, had been arrested during the Pentagon demonstration, the Reverend Philip Berrigan and three accomplices invaded the Selective Service office in the Baltimore Customs House. Inside, James Mengel, a Unitarian minister, distributed copies of the New Testament while Berrigan, Thomas Lewis, and David Eberhardt each asked to see their draft records.[68] Once in front of the file cabinets, they removed bottles of duck's blood from their briefcases and methodically splattered the draft records of the young men registered with seventeen of the city's twenty-six draft boards. Then they waited until the FBI arrived to arrest them. The Baltimore archdiocese was not amused. Its official statement declared, "Such actions may be interpreted as disorderly, aggressive, and extreme." It added that Berrigan had acted without consulting any of his superiors.

FINALLY, Eugene McCarthy would act for several reasons. He believed that the Senate had not done enough to challenge the war, and therefore, "any senator had that responsibility." He saw "desperate need" on the part of young people to be led in a moral direction: "Their effort was rather diffused, and so far as it was manifested it was pretty radical; it was undirected, but I knew it was there." He also knew that "the

---

* In 1971 the Hilton was also the site of the makeshift bureau used by *New York Times* editors and reporters to prepare the "Pentagon Papers" for publication.

religious people were moving, and I thought they had a right to some kind of leadership."[69]

Lowenstein had at first found McCarthy "rather Hamlet-like—he said Bobby should do it. But he became progressively more encouraging."[70] Throughout the summer of 1967, McCarthy had insisted that the junior senator from New York* should be the antiwar candidate because he had the necessary money and organization. But Richard Goodwin, a former speechwriter in the Kennedy and Johnson White Houses, assured McCarthy that Bobby had made "a final decision not to run in the primaries,"[71] and Kennedy told McCarthy the same thing in private. "I think he was afraid he couldn't beat Lyndon," McCarthy said almost twenty years later, drawing a pointed contrast with himself. "'I have to think of my future,' he said. It wasn't a question of principle. It was a question of his future."[72]

Despite his disappointment that Kennedy wasn't going to be his candidate, Lowenstein was thrilled when McCarthy finally made it clear he would accept the challenge. "He had a kind of notion that he was going to lead a sort of last charge to prove his own heroism," Lowenstein recalled a year later. "It was a great moment. I remember the first question he asked me that made me just roll with joy. He said something like, 'Well, how would we do in Wisconsin? Should we go in there?' I mean it was not an announcement he would run, it was a sort of backhanded thing of asking a different kind of question. I remember saying after that, for weeks after that, that we all had our heroes—Jack Kennedy, Mrs. Roosevelt—but that none of them had ever been so heroic or had so many people owing him so much as Gene McCarthy. That's the way I felt. A lot of people felt that way, but particularly me, I think, because he had agreed to do it—when no one would."[73]

---

* Robert Kennedy had adopted the state for his Senate run in 1964.

3

Like a Rolling Stone

DAVID FROST: *"How would you like the first line of your obituary to read?"*
EUGENE MCCARTHY: *" 'He died,' I suppose. That would be most reassuring."*[1]

J UST after ten o'clock on the morning of November 30, 1967, Gene McCarthy walked into the marble-arched caucus room on the third floor of the Old Senate Office Building, the same room John Kennedy had used for the same purpose almost eight years earlier. Other politicians spend their entire lives preparing for such a moment: plotting, pleading, wheedling, and waiting, hoping somehow to make their campaigns fulfill the promise of the words "I will be a candidate for the presidency of the United States." But at the age of fifty-one, McCarthy spoke as if this act were almost an afterthought. He offered no drama, no hoopla. His gray suit, gray eyes, and gray complexion[2] were a perfect match for his very gray statement, remarkable mostly because he may have been the first man ever to announce his candidacy for president without ever saying, "I am a candidate for president." He "intended" to enter "the Democratic primaries" (not even "*presidential* primaries") in Wisconsin, Oregon, California, and Nebraska. He would decide shortly whether he would run in Massachusetts and New Hampshire as well. He never even said he was challenging the president, only "the president's position."

Like a doctor delivering a serious but survivable diagnosis, he recited the war's effects:

"The physical destruction of much of a small and weak nation by military operations of the most powerful nation in the world.

"One hundred thousand to 150,000 civilian casualties in South Vietnam alone, to say nothing of the destruction of life and property in North Vietnam. . . .

"For the United States, as of yesterday, over fifteen thousand combat dead and nearly ninety-five thousand wounded through November.

"A monthly expenditure in pursuit of the war amounting [to] somewhere between $2 billion and $3 billion."

He saw "growing evidence of a deepening moral crisis in America—discontent and frustration and a disposition to take extralegal if not illegal" actions—and he hoped to alleviate "this sense of political helplessness." He was also careful to try to preempt the knee-jerk reaction of the *Joe* McCarthyites: "As I'm sure I shall be charged—I am not for peace at any price, but for an honorable, rational, and political solution to this war, a solution which I believe will enhance our world position . . . and leave us with the resources and moral energy to deal effectively with the pressing domestic problems of the United States itself."[3]

McCarthy had stepped out of the static line of Johnson's critics, but there wasn't anything in his announcement to suggest that he shared the conviction of Gans and Lowenstein that the president could actually be beaten. "It wasn't really political, unless you wanted sort of suicide," he said.[4] Four weeks before his announcement he had told John Herbers of the *New York Times,* "I don't want to 'Dump Johnson.'" Nineteen years later, he said his highest hope at the end of 1967 had been to see Johnson renominated on a peace platform.[5]

And yet nothing about this man's style was ever so simple as it appeared. Indirection was always his method: Beyond diffidence, there was a philosophical, perhaps even a strategic reason for his subdued approach. He was following a rule he originally articulated in 1954: "The Christian in politics should shun the devices of the demagogue at all times, but especially in a time when anxiety is great, when tension is high, when uncertainty prevails, and when emotion tends to be in the ascendancy."[6]

McCarthy was born March 29, 1916, the son of an Irish-American father and a Bavarian mother. The qualities and contradictions of his character almost perfectly matched his parentage. From his father, Michael, he inherited his political savvy and a scathing sense of humor. The elder McCarthy, however, was an enthusiastic Republican, rewarded for his party labors with the postmastership in Watkins, Minnesota, a job he held for thirteen years until he was displaced by a Democrat in 1913. After that he turned to livestock.[7]

The son's lifelong preoccupation with religion began with his mother. Anna Baden attended mass every morning and was considered by many to be a "saintly person." It may also have been his mother's example that gave Gene his striking ability to project a sense of inner calm into the midst of chaos. "We respected her for the fact that she didn't become excited or angry with us," said her younger son, Austin. "This had the effect . . . of teaching us not to react in anger and with words that we would regret later. I think this was a real factor in the way Gene has reacted to things."[8]

An altar boy, Gene was educated in Catholic schools: first under German nuns in St. Anthony's redbrick school in Watkins,[9] then a final year of high school in nearby Collegeville before enrolling at St. John's University there in the fall of 1931. In college, there were early signs of what would become a famous arrogance. "He enjoyed it when someone made a fool of himself in class," commented one of his teachers.[10] He also had considerable physical grace.

His performance as a baseball player was quite a good metaphor for his future career in politics. An excellent fielder at first base, he could hit the long ball—but not very often. In hockey there was a certain caginess, at least in the eyes of his brother: "Melees would get started in our hockey games, and he would come out unscathed while the fists were flying and the blood was flowing. I think he usually had something to do with starting them, like a little trip here and a little nudge there."[11]

As an undergraduate he was extremely hardworking, earning the nickname "the Watkins Wonder" and acquiring the best academic record in the school's history. The year after his graduation, when he was only nineteen, McCarthy interrupted his studies for a master's degree at the University of Minnesota to become principal of the Tintah, Minnesota, high school. A couple of years later he took another teaching job in Mandan, North Dakota, where Abigail Quigley was teaching English and German. Until she met McCarthy, she was distressed that *he* was becoming head of the English department instead of herself; but after their first encounter, she decided he was "too handsome to be true."[12] Within a few months, they were engaged. "He was the only one I knew who went to Mass every morning. . . . I thought he must be some kind of a saint."[13] It was a very long courtship. In 1941 the relationship seemed to have ended for good when McCarthy announced he was returning to St. John's Abbey to become a Benedictine novice.

Although McCarthy lasted less than a year at the abbey and a second monastery, the experience seemed to deepen his sense of himself, giving him a peculiar, permanent aura of detachment from the rest of the world. The fact that he had even attempted the monastic life reinforced the perception (especially among rival politicians) that he was something of a mystic. Father Walter Reger, who spent more than half a century at St. John's, believed Benedictine principles were "the key to Gene, perhaps without his realizing it. He has absorbed them. He talks about moral issues and is conscious of moral and spiritual values."[14] In the words of McCarthy's biographer, Albert Eisele, he "left the monastery, but in many ways, the monastery never left him. . . . McCarthy henceforth would reflect the Benedictine approach of combining utopian ideals with the realization that utopia will never come."[15]

A severe case of bursitis in his feet earned McCarthy a 4-F deferment from the draft. He went to work for the War Department in Washington, where he helped decipher Japanese codes in the fall of 1944. The following June, five years after they had first become engaged, Gene finally married Abigail in Minneapolis.[16]

After an abortive attempt at farming in his hometown of Watkins, the McCarthys moved to St. Paul, where Gene taught economics and sociology at the College of St. Thomas. Almost immediately he became embroiled in the internal politics of Minnesota's own version of the Democratic party, the Democratic Farmer-Labor party. He met Hubert Humphrey in 1947 and quickly allied himself with the young Minneapolis mayor in his efforts to end far-left influence over the DF-L.

In 1948 McCarthy ran for Congress with a campaign that bore many of the trademarks of his presidential run twenty years later—lots of campus support, very little organization, and plenty of ad hoc committees.[17] He was also a terrible speaker. When his supporters heard a radio report that he had lost the primary election in the Fourth Congressional District, one of them insisted they say a rosary. As twelve of them began to recite it, the telephone rang with the news that the opponent's votes had been counted twice in one ward—which meant that McCarthy was the real winner.

In Congress he was known as a loner, someone who seemed to feel slightly superior to most of his colleagues. "To be blunt about it, Gene was a little on the lazy side," according to his House colleague Fred Marshall, "but he could get away with [it] because of his intelligence and his sense of humor. He didn't have to work as hard as the rest of us to accomplish what he wanted." With New Jersey congressman Frank Thompson, he helped organize a group of liberal congressmen in 1957; they quickly became known as "McCarthy's Mavericks." When he announced for the Senate the following year, the *Washington Evening Star* wrote that he had "gained the reputation for serenely cleaving to his principles, no matter what the prevailing political winds."[18]

His legislative record was neither particularly distinguished nor predictably liberal, but he was one of the very first congressmen to question the role of the CIA, calling for a congressional oversight committee of the agency in 1955. And compared with most of his colleagues, he remained unusually serene before the ghost of his namesake. In 1960, in his book *Frontiers in American Democracy*, he wrote that the United States "often tries to direct the international policies of other nations—whether they be Communist or neutrals or allies of ours—as though their foreign policies were wholly unrelated to the internal politics and economies of those nations."[19]

Two weeks before McCarthy announced for the presidency, Mary McGrory wrote that Bobby Kennedy's situation was best described by lines he quoted from Tennyson's "Ulysses" during his 1966 campaign for the Senate:

"How dull it is to pause, to make an end.

To rust unburnish'd, not shine in use."

McCarthy had explicitly offered to step aside in Bobby Kennedy's favor before taking the crucial step. Nevertheless, no one seemed more shaken by his announcement—at least in private—than the junior senator from New York. "I've never seen him so disturbed as he was when he got this information," said McGovern. "He could see the trouble this was going to present to him." Out of prescience or paranoia, Kennedy made a surprisingly accurate prediction. "He's going to get a lot of support," he said. "I can tell you right now, he'll run very strong in New Hampshire." Kennedy asked McGovern to withhold his support for McCarthy because "it would make it hard for a lot of us later on if we wanted to make some other move." McGovern knew this meant he should avoid committing himself to McCarthy because Kennedy might come in. "I think," said McGovern, that Kennedy felt, " 'My God, I should have done this. Why didn't I move earlier?' "[20]

Two days after his declaration in Washington, McCarthy flew to Chicago to speak to a meeting of dissident Democrats organized by Lowenstein and Gans. It was here that Lowenstein had originally wanted him to announce his candidacy. Rauh had convinced McCarthy that that would be a mistake, since such a radical forum might antagonize more moderate opponents of the war.

When the candidate arrived, Lowenstein was making an angry speech before twenty-five hundred committed people who were eager to vent their hatred for Lyndon Johnson. At least three thousand more listened at nearby loudspeakers. McCarthy was disgusted with Lowenstein's tone: He stood in the back of the auditorium, furiously kicking a Dixie cup against the wall, waiting for his own chance to speak. One month earlier, he had made it clear he was uncomfortable with Lowenstein's rhetoric. "The word 'Dump Johnson' has never been one of my words," he told the *New York Times*. "I think it is a bad word. I think it is inexcusable. I think it is one of the things that the press does that tends to interfere with a proper discussion of problems."[21] Lowenstein said later he hadn't even wanted to introduce McCarthy—he thought that job should go to a Midwestern Protestant like Don Peterson to make things look right for television, but then someone had suggested that Lowenstein should introduce Peterson. When, after twenty minutes, he finally got the word that McCarthy was waiting to speak, Lowenstein—as he remembered it—immediately stepped aside. Others there that day recall considerably more hesitation.

As he began, McCarthy looked grim-faced, and his delivery was just as undistinguished as it had been in Washington. This candidate would not meet the youthful passion in front of him even halfway. "He was flat," a delegate told Warren Weaver of the *New York Times*. "This is the fourth time I've heard him, and he's been flat every time. When is he going to take off?"[22] Worse still, when he was done, he didn't even bother to visit the overflow crowd outside the auditorium. Gans insisted this was *his* fault—that McCarthy didn't make the visit because Gans didn't tell him the crowd was there—but Lowenstein and practically everyone else in Chicago attributed this gaffe to laziness rather than ignorance.[23]

A schoolteacher and former speechwriter named Gerry Studds and a university official named David Hoeh were two of the seven members of the New Hampshire delegation to the Conference of Concerned Democrats that McCarthy addressed that day in Chicago. (Gene Daniel, head of the Kennedy organization in New Hampshire, came with a McCarthy button in one lapel and a Kennedy button in the other.) McCarthy wasn't ready to commit himself to running in New Hampshire, but Studds and Hoeh were "very encouraged by what he had to say." Studds had spent the Thanksgiving recess at home doing some basic statistical research on New Hampshire presidential primaries, and he came to Chicago armed with an analysis of the vote, its percentage in each town and each congressional district. "We had statistical information in our heads which we knew the administration forces never had," said Studds.[24] He presented McCarthy with a twelve-day schedule of campaigning with which the candidate could hit 75 percent of the voters. Hoeh had already run several New Hampshire campaigns, and the insurgents had studied the trends of recent elections, particularly the growth in voting strength in the southern tier of the state. This would be the hallmark of the New Hampshire campaign: so-called amateurs who turned out to be much better informed about the local electorate than their entrenched opponents.[25]

Another man in Chicago that day with two years of New Hampshire in his background was Blair Clark, a journalist with plenty of unlikely connections who had written to McCarthy from London to offer his support. At the end of November he flew to New York to see political writer Theodore White, an old friend he had known well in Paris in the early fifties. Clark was sure that White would know exactly what was going on, and together they flew out to Chicago. There White loaned Clark his press badge so that he could hear McCarthy's speech.

Clark balanced a warm manner with a biting wit, a substantial bank account with surprisingly radical politics. His mixture of old-fashioned American charm and iconoclastic intelligence attracted a startling collection of friends, ranging from reformed bank robbers to the widows of presidents. He had also helped launch the careers of a number of exceptionally powerful journalists.

A fellow member of Clark's class of '35 at St. Marks School in South borough, Massachusetts, was the poet Robert Lowell, who would become his closest friend. Lillian Hellman was another intimate. His passions encompassed everything from poetry to motorcycles. At Harvard he became president of the *Crimson* and met Jack Kennedy, another classmate. "I got Jack on the *Crimson*," Clark recalled. "He'd already written for the Hearst papers, he wanted to do something, and I thought, What the hell? He did a half-dozen pieces. He never really worked at it. He always remembered that about me: that I was a serious fellow in college and he wasn't—he was a jock trying to get on the swimming team." Ironically, Clark's father had been Joseph Kennedy's classmate in the Harvard class of '12. "Did you know Joe?" Blair once asked his father. "Yes, I knew the son of a bitch," came the quick reply.

In 1946 Clark took $60,000 he had inherited from his grandmother and used it to found the *New Hampshire Sunday News*. His star reporter was a young Harvard graduate named Ben Bradlee,* who had been four years behind him at St. Marks. "We won all the prizes," Clark remembered. "We sent the state comptroller to jail and we got the girl *out of jail* who became the basis for *Peyton Place.* Ben was a wonderful reporter." Within two years, the *Sunday News* had a circulation of thirty-five thousand, making it the biggest paper in the state. When the daily *Union-Leader* threatened to start a competing Sunday paper in 1948, Clark sold out at a substantial profit to the Union-Leader Corporation, which was co-owned by William Loeb.†

In 1961 Kennedy offered to make Clark his ambassador to Morocco, but instead Clark became vice-president and general manager of CBS News. He hired a young Texan named Dan Rather, who had distinguished himself at hurricane coverage—as well as Mike Wallace, Morley Safer, Roger Mudd, and Bill Plante. In 1962 he helped his boss, Richard Salant, persuade the network brass to replace Douglas Edwards with Walter Cronkite on the CBS *Evening News.* In the same period, Clark took a weekend cottage near West Point; there he developed one more unlikely friendship, with the school's superintendent, a general named William Westmoreland.[26]

CLARK first met McCarthy in 1965 at a party in Walter Lippmann's house in Washington. McCarthy, himself a poet, had recently met Robert Lowell, and he noticed that one of Lowell's books, *Near the Ocean,* was dedicated to Clark. "I didn't really know McCarthy," said Clark. "My contact with that world was Mary McGrory," yet another "old, good friend," who was a behind-the-scenes advisor to McCarthy in 1968. In Chicago in December 1967, Clark met with McCarthy and agreed to go to Massachusetts to research his primary prospects there. A week later the two men met in Clark's Turtle Bay town house in Manhattan. To Clark's surprise, McCarthy asked him to be his campaign chairman.

"When he asked me to be chairman, I thought he wasn't very serious about the campaign," said Clark, whose only previous association with a

---

* Bradlee was named managing editor of the *Washington Post* in 1968.

† Ironically, the very liberal Clark helped to solidify the influence of the relentlessly reactionary Loeb. For the next three decades no other small-state newspaper publisher appeared to have so much influence over national politics as Loeb, simply because the *Union-Leader* was the principal paper in the first presidential-primary state. Naturally, Loeb was particularly antagonistic toward McCarthy.

presidential candidate had been a very brief stint as Averell Harriman's press secretary during the pre-convention period in 1952. "You know—a chairman isn't me," said Clark. "I'm a journalist, a free-lancer at the time, with no political clout. I've been objective all my life. He had to have a name, a political name. So then I began wondering whether he was serious or whether that was just flattery."

McCarthy *was* serious—at least about making Clark his campaign manager—and Clark moved to Washington in December to begin the job. One of the first things he learned about was the intense dislike between McCarthy and one of the men who had played a key role in getting him into the race, Allard Lowenstein. Clark went to see Lowenstein and asked him to take a big part in the campaign, but Lowenstein thought McCarthy was uncomfortable with him. Lowenstein was right. "Al was a sort of zealot," said Clark, "and McCarthy didn't like zealots."[27]

One of Clark's greatest virtues as campaign manager was his openness, as Sam Brown discovered when he arrived unannounced in Washington to visit him. Brown camped out in the alcove outside Clark's office until Clark agreed to see him. The new campaign manager was remarkably receptive to Brown's approach. After a few minutes he reached into his pocket and wrote out a personal check for $200 so that Brown could travel to Cleveland to attend the University Christian Movement Conference.

Living at Joe Rauh's house in Washington, Clark was immediately depressed by his candidate's unwillingness to behave like a candidate. He proposed a ten-city cross-country tour, including Philadelphia, Cleveland, Chicago, Minneapolis, New Orleans, and San Francisco, because he was sure people would come out to hear McCarthy—and McCarthy rejected it. Meanwhile, Rauh was maneuvering to get McCarthy the endorsement of Americans for Democratic Action, but only after making sure the unpredictable senator would accept it. "Ironical as this will be for some future historian," Rauh told an interviewer in 1969, "McCarthy had left the ADA in the fifties because of our anti-Johnson position. He had written and said that he could no longer be in an organization so one-sided against Johnson." By 1968 McCarthy was quite ready to bury this little-known piece of history. He told Rauh he would welcome the ADA's endorsement.[28]

Clark's principal achievement in this period was to persuade McCarthy that he had to go into the New Hampshire primary. "He didn't want to go into New Hampshire," said Clark, "and I was convinced from the very beginning that he should go into New Hampshire. He wanted to start in Wisconsin, and I thought that was too late." McCarthy was invited up to Manchester to test the waters on December 14. It was a precise repeat of his Chicago performance. "It was a golden opportunity," said Studds, "and it was a disaster. McCarthy gave a speech which, while substantively fine, was totally nonpolitical—and he gave it in the flattest conceivable style. He got a standing ovation when he came in, and no one stood when he left. I remember I took the senator immediately from the podium after he finished, back to his room in the motel. I was trying to think of something appropriate to say under the circumstances. And he put his arm around me and said, 'I think we really got them that time. I could feel it.' And I said to myself, 'Oh, my God.'" On his way back to the airport, McCarthy told David Halberstam he still wasn't inclined to run in New Hampshire, which deepened the locals' depression.[29]

Within weeks of McCarthy's announcement, his performance was provoking contempt from much of the left, ever eager to eat its own young. *Ramparts* accused him of trying to destroy the peace movement. In the *Village Voice,* Jack Newfield called his speeches "dull, vague, and without either balls or poetry. . . . Make Bobby Kennedy run." I. F. Stone said, "[He] seems to lack guts. . . . We enlist in McCarthy's army but we intend to keep stirring up mutiny until the general stops yawning." Mary McGrory wrote that many liberals "think he is doing the right thing, but beg off because they feel 'he does not have a chance,' thereby making his chances all the less likely. . . . From the McCarthy point of view his effort continues as it began, a conspiracy between one man and his conscience." Clark was nonplussed. "It was almost as if he thought the mere announcement was enough," said the campaign manager.[30] "I think we may have a fraud on our hands," he confided to one young volunteer. The White House wanted the world to believe it had dismissed him as a serious threat. On December 15, the *Washington Post* quoted an anonymous official who said everyone in the administration would campaign against McCarthy, and, if he ran in New Hampshire, "his only allies would be two or three guys who hadn't made it with the party."[31] Democratic National Committee chairman John Bailey refused McCarthy's request to attend a convention planning session on January 7 to explain why "many loyal Democrats believe as I do that the administration's course in Vietnam is dangerous and wrong." Bailey said Vietnam would not be discussed at the session and added, "The Democratic National Convention is as good as over. It will be Lyndon Johnson again, and that's that."[32]

David Hoeh and Gerry Studds decided to summarize their arguments in a thousand words for the senator. *"There is nothing to be lost—and a great deal to be gained*—by coming into New Hampshire. Given the general impression that it is a 'hawkish' state and a 'conservative' state—*plus*

[New Hampshire Democratic senator Thomas] *McIntyre's extraordinary prediction* that McCarthy would get 3,000–5,000 votes (i.e., less than 10 percent) anything better than that can be hailed as a stunning performance (and we can do considerably better than that). . . . *A victory here*, which we think we ought to shoot for and which seems to us far more within the realm of possibility than it did a month ago, *would have major national repercussions*. . . . There has been *a clear panic reaction to the threat of McCarthy's candidacy among the party hierarchy in the state*—and with real reason. Many prominent Democrats have quietly refused to serve on the LBJ Committee. If we are to move on the Senator's behalf, *we must get going yesterday*."[33]

Late in December Clark bolstered these arguments on a four-hour train ride with McCarthy. "Some of the history books will say that I persuaded McCarthy to go into New Hampshire on a train journey from Washington to New York, just before Christmas," Clark later specified, "and they'll be wrong. I made the journey and put the case, but you don't persuade McCarthy to do things like that: He decides himself."[34] Then Clark went back to New Hampshire on January 2 to dine with Studds and Hoeh. While they were eating, a call came through from the senator to Hoeh, announcing he was finally ready to jump into the snows of New Hampshire. Studds and Hoeh have exactly the same memory: Clark's face "practically fell into his soup" at the news. As he would so frequently during the next eight months, Clark felt that his candidate was undercutting his authority.

The next day Studds and Hoeh called a press conference, sparsely attended because most reporters expected an announcement that McCarthy was avoiding the state. "Their expressions were rather fun to watch as we read the telegram from McCarthy, which we ourselves had written the night before," said Studds.

The difficulty of their struggle was perfectly illustrated by one aspect of their triumph: According to Studds, "this was the only time that Senator McCarthy, at least in the first two or three months, and certainly in the New Hampshire primary, said, 'I am running for the presidency of the United States.' I wrote that sentence the night before, and I was damn sure he was going to say that when he declared his entry to New Hampshire. . . . I [was] sick and tired of people telling me that's not what he is running for. So he said it that time."[35]

In January, Clark recruited Seymour Hersh, a brilliant if wildly unpredictable reporter, to be the senator's press secretary. Hersh was another friend of Mary McGrory's, and he also knew Clark's son, Tim. Like most of his fellow campaign workers, Hersh was appalled by the attitude of McCarthy's Senate staff toward their boss's campaign for the presidency. When Hersh got his first request for an interview with McCarthy, he called the senator's longtime administrative assistant, Jerry Eller, for guidance. The response: "Well, I'll tell you what you do. Wait until you get two hundred requests, and then throw them over the wall, and we'll handle them." Hersh remembered "looking at him and thinking, 'My God!'" Then Hersh approached McCarthy directly, and he agreed to the interview right away. "Actually," said Hersh, "I thought his whole staff was an unmitigated disaster."[36]

McCarthy's announcement that he would run in New Hampshire did little to dispel the skepticism about him in the rest of the country. On January 15, McGrory reported from California, "The trouble with Eugene McCarthy is that he is trying to spark an uprising without raising his voice. . . . For those who burn to man the barricades against Lyndon Johnson, this excessive restraint is dampening. Within the McCarthy camp the problem has been identified as the 'passion gap.' 'He's a Milquetoast,' sniffed a county chairwoman. 'Even if I agreed with him, he wouldn't turn me on.' A Los Angeles lady with bangs, who knows all the statistics on the war and wore a McCarthy button, sighed, 'I loved the content, but oh, the presentation. I respect his intelligence, but couldn't he pound the table a little?' "[37]

In New Hampshire, Studds was quickly discovering there was no national organization or advance staff: "We became used to the fact that there [would] be nothing but chaos on the Washington end of the telephone," he said. McCarthy's first campaign swing through the state after announcing he would run in the primary was another dud. "We made the famous mistake there," said Studds—they got the candidate to a factory gate five minutes late, and he missed most of the arriving workers. "All the national press picked up on it." On his first day in Manchester, McCarthy refused to enter a room containing two hundred potential voters. "Oh, no, that won't be nice," said the candidate. "They're eating, and I don't want to disturb their lunch." Studds was devastated.[38]

In January and February, according to Lowenstein, "McCarthy's behavior was so odd that a very serious 'Dump McCarthy' movement began among the people who were for McCarthy." There were a series of meetings about "whether he should be supported or not" and whether "another effort should be made to get Kennedy in."[39]

There were so many complaints about the candidate's pallid speaking style that Blair Clark eventually dug up a tape of McCarthy's famous speech at the 1960 convention to hear whether it was really as good as everyone's memory of it. "He had to yell to make himself heard over the noise on the floor of the convention," said Clark. "*That's* why he sounded so effective."[40]

McCarthy "drove us absolutely wild by his refusal to do the standard political things, putting a little bit of pizzazz into his speeches," said Studds. "He just plain wouldn't do it. . . . [Whenever] we got a situation when we would have a conventional political response [we would] say, 'Senator, for heaven's sake, do what everybody else does.'

"And he would say, 'No. That is not me. If this campaign means anything, it means that I am going to be myself. I am not going to be a demagogue. I am going to do it the way my judgment tells me, and you just have to trust me. I've been in the business a long time.'

"We fought with him the first two or three times when we were convinced that we knew better than he on the basis of what worked in New Hampshire. But he stuck to his guns."

Six weeks later Studds made a remarkable discovery: "Every single time—at least in New Hampshire—McCarthy seems to have been right."[41]

4

Tet: The Turning Point

"You can kill ten of my men for every one I kill of yours, but even at those odds, you will lose and I will win."
—Ho Chi Minh to the French occupying Indochina[1]

"I'm absolutely certain that whereas in 1965 the enemy was winning, today he is certainly losing."
—General William Westmoreland,
November 21, 1967[2]

"If taking over a section of the American embassy, a good part of Hué, Dalat, and major cities of the Fourth Corps area constitutes complete failure [for the Communists], I suppose by this logic that if the Vietcong captured the entire country, the administration would be claiming their total collapse."
—Eugene McCarthy, February 1968[3]

IN 1789 the general who drove the British out of the thirteen original colonies was inaugurated as America's first president. It was an equally momentous year in Vietnam, though even Americans who fought there often don't know why. In 1789 the Vietnamese used the celebration of Tet, the lunar new year, as the cover for a surprise attack on a foreign military power occupying *their* country. Vietnamese Emperor Quang Trung led one hundred thousand troops and several hundred elephants in a brilliant assault on the unsuspecting Chinese celebrating Tet in Hanoi, routing them from the city. Almost two centuries later a statue of Quang Trung occupied a prominent place in the Saigon villa of William Childs Westmoreland, the four-star general heading the American Military Assistance Command in Vietnam. The statue was the gift of a Vietnamese acquaintance.[4]

As recently as 1960, Vietcong troops had attacked the government's military headquarters in Tay Ninh (near Saigon) on the eve of Tet. Western holidays had provided similar cover: In 1944 General Vo Nguyen Giap sent his tiny Vietnam People's Army against colonial outposts on Christmas Eve and slaughtered the unsuspecting French soldiers. Yet no one in the American command seemed particularly aware of this history.[5]

In 1968 Tet's fame would be renewed as the moment when the illusions of American omniscience and omnipotence, so carefully nurtured by Lyndon Johnson and all the other post–atom bomb presidents, vanished inside the smoke that simultaneously enveloped Saigon, Da Nang, Ben Tre, Quang Tri, Huê, and almost every other major population center and military base in South Vietnam. Once again, a modern version of a Vietnamese emperor had used the sacred holiday as a cover for the bloodiest and most carefully choreographed surprise of the Vietnam War. This time it wouldn't matter that we killed so many more of them than they killed of us, because sixty-seven thousand of our "desperate" enemy had attacked everywhere at once—and not even the American embassy compound was secure. This time the shock was so great that astute men and women inside and outside the government suddenly suspended their belief in the promise of light at the end of the insidious Indochinese tunnel.

When Tet began, the unsettling images available nightly on all the network news shows had lost most of their power to shock. Newspaper stories about individual engagements had even less impact. After seven years of steadily increasing warfare, all the battles seemed to blur together into a single jumbled image: very young, helmeted GIs, bolstered by B-52 bombers, naval bombardments, napalm, Agent Orange, tanks, helicopters, and mortars, locked in perpetual conflict with a seemingly endless supply of slightly built, bareheaded men and women wearing black pajamas and sandals fashioned from the Goodyear tires salvaged from American jeeps and trucks. The mystery was why our absurd technological advantage never translated into a predictable pattern of success on the battlefield. One answer was "desire," the only thing our government was unable to manufacture. To James Kunen, the author of *The Strawberry Statement,* a memoir of the uprising in 1968 at Columbia, there were "seventeen parallels" between Manhattan cockroaches and our intractable jungle opponent: Both "are ignorant, ill-clad and underfed; they both drag away the bodies of their slain, come back no matter how many are killed, move by night, avoid prolonged engagements with the enemy, are not white, are fighting against people who are, have been fighting for generations, are of uncertain numbers, move via infiltration routes, are wily, are out-armed by the enemy, are contemptuous of death, are independent of outside control, are inscrutable, and are winning."[6]

Tet broke the monotony for the American television viewer and newspaper reader. Because of satellite technology and the absence of censorship, this engagement was reported with a bluntness and immediacy unlike anything the home front had ever experienced. Vietnam was hardly the first battlefield at which reporters were regarded as a nuisance or worse by American generals. But Vietnam probably was the first war in which Washington considered American journalists and enemy troops approximately equal threats to the policy of the president.

The imbalance between the power of the policymakers and the power of the press had reached its apogee as 1968 began. Fifty-two new correspondents arrived in Vietnam during Tet, for a total of 248 American reporters—an all-time high—to cover America's humiliation on the battlefield.[7] In Washington, relations between the press and the president's government were grim. Ten days after Tet began, Secretary of State Dean Rusk exploded at reporters during an off-the-record briefing. "There gets to be a point when the question is, Whose side are you on?" Rusk roared at the startled journalists before him. "I don't know why . . . people have to be probing for the things that one can bitch about."[8]

The shock Tet produced in individual reporters and their editors changed American attitudes much more dramatically than the courage of American troops ever could. The offensive was burned into the American memory by the coverage given two battles, one photograph, and one searing, cynical epitaph. Of these four episodes, the assault on the American embassy compound would create the deepest doubt. One reason the failure to defend the embassy was so startling was the huge proportion of Americans allotted to support and defense tasks in Vietnam. Six months before Tet, 414,000 U.S. troops were assigned to support and defense—and just fifty thousand to offensive ground operations. Under these circumstances, it hardly mattered that the attack on the embassy was, as Westmoreland has always insisted, a militarily insignificant event.

A month of bloody combat in February would produce four weeks of extraordinary change in March. Tet acted like an immense magnetic field, energizing the war's opponents and transforming the political landscape.

In Washington it actually transposed the polarities, reversing the direction of policy within the government's corridors.

The four-week-long Tet offensive would ignite seven interlocking dramas. They unfolded in Vietnam, in the press, in New Hampshire, in the White House, in the Pentagon, and in the minds of Bobby Kennedy and Lyndon Johnson. On the evening of March 31 all of them fused to form 1968's only genuine catharsis.

BUILT to be as indestructible as $2.6 million could make it, the new American embassy was ready for occupancy two and a half years after the Vietcong had destroyed the previous structure—killing twenty-two people and injuring seventy-five—with a 250-pound bomb in March 1965. The new building stood inside a four-acre compound. It had Plexiglas windows, reinforced concrete walls, and a massive terra-cotta sun screen that doubled as a blast shield, all topped off with a convenient helicopter landing pad to permit the American ambassador to avoid hostile crowds in Saigon's streets whenever that might be necessary. "We'll be able to withstand just about any type of minor attack," the building's architect boasted.[9]

In the weeks and months before Tet, the Communists imported almost a hundred tons of weapons and infiltrated a thousand Vietcong into Saigon. The new arrivals worked with scores of locals like Nguyen Van De. Hired in 1950, De (nicknamed "Satchmo") was one of the original employees of the American delegation. He joined the payroll the same year the United States first sent troops to Vietnam to teach French soldiers how to use their new American weapons. De was the most popular, and the most pro-American, of all the local workers. He had even been the ambassador's personal driver, the most coveted position in every embassy garage. Unbeknownst to his American bosses, Satchmo was also an entrepreneur, raising race horses and maintaining two households: one with a "minor" wife for the siesta hour in the city, and another with a "major" wife and six children in the suburbs. "He must be a Vietcong," American secretaries would jest, "because he's so much smarter than the other drivers." On January 31, 1968, the secretaries discovered that their surmise wasn't a joke.[10]

At 2:45 that morning, a nineteen-man Vietcong assault team left the automobile repair shop at 59 Phan Thanh Gian Street, carrying arms that had reached the city during the preholiday bustle inside baskets topped with tomatoes. The team traveled in a taxicab and a Peugeot truck. As they approached the embassy, the men in the taxi opened fire on two American

MPs guarding the gate while the truck continued around the corner to unload rockets and explosives. The MPs fired back, retreated inside, bolted the gate, and radioed at 2:47 that they were under attack. Then there was a huge explosion when a fifteen-pound charge blew a three-foot hole in the wall of the compound.

"They're coming in! They're coming in! Help me! Help me!" Those were the last words twenty-three-year-old Specialist Fourth Class Charles Daniel shouted over his radio. Daniel and his partner, twenty-year-old Private First Class William Sebast, were both facing the enemy when they died, judging from the position of their bodies. The dead Marines probably killed the two leaders of the enemy assault, who were the first invaders through the wall. An MP patrol jeep a few blocks away heard their distress call and responded immediately. As they approached the embassy, the men in the jeep were cut down by a fusillade of bullets. Sergeant Jonnie Thomas and Specialist Fourth Class Owen Mebust were the third and fourth Americans killed in the embassy engagement.

On the streets bordering the compound, four South Vietnamese policemen were the embassy's first line of defense. Three of them fled as soon as they heard the first explosions; the fourth one hid behind a concrete kiosk and stayed there until the battle was over.[11]

Saigon was twelve hours ahead of the American East Coast, so it was midafternoon when the first reports of the attack began to trickle into New York and Washington. The Associated Press was first with the news: "A suicide squad of guerrilla commandos infiltrated the capital and at least three are reported to have entered the grounds of the new U.S. Embassy near the heart of the city," the wire service reported. "U.S. Marine Guards . . . engaged the infiltrators in an exchange of fire."

In New York City, Walter Cronkite was getting ready for the CBS *Evening News* when he saw the first bulletin. "What the hell is going on?" he demanded. "I thought we were winning the war!" At the White House, National Security Advisor Walt Rostow was giving a familiar performance for four visitors from the *Washington Post*, promising them copies of captured documents revealing how well the war was going. The tension in the adjoining communications room proved more riveting than the Communist memoranda. Finally a White House aide explained the visible strain: "It appears the Vietcong are attacking the embassy in Saigon." Over at the CIA, Undersecretary of State Nicholas Katzenbach and Deputy Assistant Secretary Philip Habib were visiting the agency's new Vietnam Operations Center at its Langley, Virginia, headquarters. A CIA officer was warning the men from State of the likelihood of "massive attacks, probably at the end of the Tet holiday," when a communications officer handed him a piece a paper describing the action at the embassy. One of the visitors thought at first that he was the victim of an elaborate CIA joke.

Meanwhile, on the fourth floor of the American chancellery in Saigon, night-duty officer E. Allen Wendt had been sleeping in a small chamber when he heard an explosion "so loud that it literally shook everything" in the room. He grabbed his toothbrush and a .38 revolver and retreated into the relatively secure code room next door. Soon he was fielding phone calls from ten thousand miles away. Habib called from the State Department.

"What the hell is going on?" asked Habib.

Wendt held up the phone. "Listen to it," he said.

At that moment another rocket thudded into the embassy wall, giving Habib a very up-to-the-minute report on the battle's progress.[12]

One American helicopter tried to set down on the embassy's rooftop pad around 5 A.M., but it was driven away by hostile fire. A second helicopter did manage to land seventy-five minutes later. It evacuated casualties and deposited some M-16 ammunition—useless to the embassy's defenders because they didn't happen to have any M-16s. In the darkness, no one outside the embassy walls had discovered the hole created by the Vietcong's first explosion. The gates were locked, and for the moment, no American reinforcements were getting inside.

The real sense of urgency to reclaim the complex began after Chet Huntley's first report on NBC's news at 6:30. "Snipers are in the buildings and on the rooftops near the embassy and are firing on American personnel inside the compound," Huntley reported. After that, horrified American officials in Washington made it perfectly clear to their counterparts in Vietnam that reclaiming control of the embassy was America's number-one priority. Never mind that the three American officers' barracks, the Tan Son Nhut and Bien Hoa air bases, the compound of the South Vietnamese general staff, the South Vietnamese navy headquarters, and the studios of the Saigon radio station were also under attack;* it

---

* The attack on the radio station was one of the Vietcong's notable failures, even though a Communist sympathizer had provided the assault team with diagrams and keys for all the studios. The South Vietnamese—familiar with the importance of the broadcast outlet because of their own frequent coups d'état—had anticipated this particular danger, and the line between the station and the transmitter fourteen miles away was cut as soon as the battle began. At the transmitter, they played what they had on hand, which turned out to be a strange mix of the Beatles, the Stones, and an occasional Viennese waltz. The station was badly damaged by the Communists. Whatever equipment survived was then looted by the South Vietnamese who "liberated" it.

was the embassy—the most visible symbol of American might—that Washington wanted back.

At dawn the hole in the perimeter wall was belatedly discovered by an embassy security officer. Moments later MPs finally managed to ram a jeep through the front gate, and troops from the 101st Airborne Division started landing on the embassy roof. The siege was almost over. Now reporters were surging onto the grounds to witness the denouement. Colonel George Jacobson was the key actor in the climax. An advisor to the ambassador with the title of mission coordinator, Jacobson was also, among other things, a former magician. He first came to Saigon to be an assistant to the chief of the first U.S. Military Assistance Advisory Group in 1954—just four years after Satchmo joined the embassy staff as a chauffeur. In 1968 Jacobson lived in a villa on the embassy grounds. One of the first explosions during the attack shattered his second-floor bedroom window, covering him with glass; then he discovered that his only weapon was a single M-26 grenade. Throughout the battle he hid upstairs. Jacobson was impressed with the bravery of his attackers, who never seemed to consider the possibility of surrender. At 6:45 he noticed fresh blood on the ground floor of his villa. Very quietly, he telephoned the Marine guard across town, asking it to notify the nearby security men that the Vietcong had penetrated his house. Marines threw a grenade and then tear gas into the first floor, stunning but not killing the intruder. The next scene was captured by NBC cameraman Philip Ross for the *Huntley-Brinkley Report.* Within hours after the fact, the network's twenty million viewers sat riveted as twenty-year-old Private Paul Healey dashed across the embassy lawn to throw Jacobson a .45 pistol and a gas mask.

The last Vietcong attacker was stumbling up the stairs of Jacobson's villa to escape the tear gas. Spotting the American colonel above him, the wounded Communist rifleman fired three shots. "I was very lucky," Jacobson told a reporter a few minutes later. "He got in the first shots." But the rifleman missed, and the colonel killed him with his .45.[13]

The embassy was back in American hands by 9:15 A.M. Six Americans were dead; the bodies of nineteen Vietnamese lay on the lawn. Three of them were embassy drivers. Two of them were apparently innocent victims of the cross fire. The third one was Satchmo, the embassy's senior employee. Marines said they had seen him firing at them during the battle. In his belt was a 9-mm Browning pistol; in his pocket, a large roll of money.

William Westmoreland inspected the battle scene five minutes after the firing had stopped. Surrounded by reporters staggered by this panorama of blood and rubble in the heart of the capital, Westmoreland provided a shocking commentary: "The enemy's well-laid plans went afoul," he declared. "Some superficial damage was done to the building. All of the enemy that entered the compound so far as I can determine were killed." Actually, two of the Vietcong were wounded, captured, and later interrogated about their roles in the attack. "It was astonishing," said Lee Lescaze, a *Washington Post* man stationed in Saigon.[14]

"They looked at me as if I didn't have all my faculties," Westmoreland conceded nineteen years later.[15] But unlike the Americans who experienced it at home on the evening news, the commanding general of American forces in Vietnam was unaffected by this single battle. In delivering his upbeat assessment, Westmoreland was merely carrying out the orders he and everyone else in the administration had been getting from the president for more than a year: End this terrible talk of "stalemate" and convince your countrymen we are winning the War in Vietnam.

NEITHER the reporters who covered him nor the grunts who fought for him would ever be overwhelmed by Westmoreland's intellect. That didn't matter very much since this rather average soldier seemed to be completely compatible with Lyndon Johnson's ideas of how a commanding general should look (square build, stolid face), sound (slight South Carolina drawl), and act (very, very obedient). The two Southerners first met at West Point in 1961, when Johnson was vice-president and Westmoreland was the school's superintendent. Three years later, a month after Westmoreland's fiftieth birthday, Johnson selected him from a field of four competitors to become the new commander of American forces in Vietnam. "Westy" was already the deputy commander in Saigon; he was also the only one of the four the president knew personally. On three different visits home in 1967, Westmoreland tried to sell the war to the public, even addressing a joint session of Congress. Gene McCarthy remarked bitterly that Truman had *fired* General Douglas MacArthur for giving a political speech during the Korean War,[16] while Johnson had commanded Westmoreland to deliver one.

A staffer on the National Security Council had the job of monitoring every negative speech about Vietnam in the *Congressional Record*; by the end of the day any such speech appeared, the staffer's rebuttal had to be on the president's desk. At the White House there were both a Vietnam Information Group and a Psychological Strategy Committee to promote a favorable view of the war.[17]

In June 1967 came a new, wholly unexpected source of pressure to convince Americans they really could win the War in Vietnam. In the Middle East, Israel had responded to Egypt's decision to close the Gulf of Aqaba with an astonishingly deft military stroke, simultaneously crushing Syria, Egypt, and Jordan. In six days this tiny country had routed Egypt from the Sinai, expelled the Syrians from the Golan Heights, and conquered Old Jerusalem—as well as Jordan's West Bank. The contrast between Israeli prestidigitation in the desert and American impotence in the jungle was stunning, and stunningly depressing.

In Saigon the Joint United States Public Affairs Office was responsible for press relations *and* psychological warfare. Michael Herr "never met anyone who seemed to realize that there was a difference." Herr, who was covering the war for *Esquire,* couldn't fathom why his colleagues spent so much time interviewing senior American officials in Saigon. "What did anybody ever expect those people to *say?*" he wondered. "It could have rained frogs over Tan Son Nhut and they wouldn't have been upset; Cam Ranh Bay could have dropped into the South China Sea and they would have found some way to make it sound good for you; the Bo Doi Division (Ho's Own) could have marched by the American Embassy and they would have characterized it as 'desperate.'"*,[18]

Throughout 1967 there was growing impatience among American voters: Some wanted a much bigger war; others wanted no war at all. Practically no one wanted the conflict to continue just the way it was. "Americans do not like long, inconclusive wars," North Vietnamese premier Pham Van Dong had told author Bernard Fall in 1962, adding, "This is going to be a long, inconclusive war."[19] In these circumstances the administration's florid optimism was perceived as a political necessity. But instead of winning the hearts and minds of the American people, Johnson's cheerful words ultimately had the opposite effect. They created an atmosphere in which a seemingly suicidal Communist strategy became an extraordinary psychological defeat for the United States. To Lyndon Johnson, Tet and its aftermath were "the most disastrous Communist defeat of the War in Vietnam."[20] But to Americans who

---

* George Orwell identified this syndrome in 1945 in his celebrated essay "Politics and the English Language": "In our time, political speech and writing are largely the defense of the indefensible. . . . Thus political language has to consist largely of euphemism, question-begging and sheer cloudy vagueness. Defenseless villages are bombarded from the air, the inhabitants driven out into the countryside, the cattle machine-gunned, the huts set on fire with incendiary bullets: this is called pacification." [*The Collected Essays, Journalism and Letters of George Orwell*; volume 4, *In Front of Your Nose, 1945–1950* (New York: Harcourt Brace Jovanovich, 1968), 136.]

had heard weekly how well the war was going, the exploding offensive was like a heart attack suffered by a middle-aged man ten minutes after his doctor has told him he has the constitution of a twenty-five-year-old.

During the first three days of Tet alone, readers of the normally sober *New York Times* were bombarded with these developments:

> [Day one:] Viet Cong raiders drove into the center of seven major Vietnamese cities early today, burning Government buildings, freeing prisoners from provincial jails and blasting military installations and airfields with rockets and mortars.[21]

> [Day two:] Viet Cong commandos seized parts of the United States Embassy early today and held them for more than six hours. The Viet Cong, wearing South Vietnamese Army uniforms, held off American military policemen firing machine guns and rocket launchers. . . . For Saigon, the Embassy attack capped a night of terror . . .[22]

> [Day three:] Viet Cong forces stubbornly held pockets of resistance in Saigon and other areas today after their spectacular attacks on cities and American bases throughout South Vietnam. In one suburb northwest of the capital . . . families were serving meals to guerrillas who had routed police forces from the area.[23]

From Da Nang, *Times* correspondent Gene Roberts filed this memorable report: "Few [places] have suffered so much or endured so long a period of sustained terror as tiny Apba. . . . Tuc Dan Khoi, a truckdriver, told the story of his village in a few words of fractured English and French. 'Beaucoup VC,' he said. 'Beaucoup soldier. Beaucoup airplane. Beaucoup boom-boom.' That description summed it up."[24]

On the fourth day there were more sensational accounts, including a story about a twenty-six-year-old American civilian who was defending his Saigon home with a pistol and a high-powered rifle because law and order had broken down in the Vietnamese capital. In Washington, Mississippi senator John Stennis called the attacks "embarrassing" and "humiliating" to the Johnson administration.[25] However, on this fourth day of the offensive, every news *story* would be overshadowed by the play given to a single news *photograph*—and a television clip of the same event.

AP photographer Eddie Adams was walking through Saigon with NBC correspondent Howard Tuckner and his cameraman, Vo Suu, when they spotted a Vietcong prisoner in custody. The small man did not look at all threatening, especially with his hands tied behind his body; he wore a plaid shirt and blue shorts and walked with a slight limp. But the pistol he was carrying identified him to the South Vietnamese as a Vietcong officer. "I was standing there," said Adams, "just watching what they were doing, and all of a sudden [the national police chief, General Nguyen Ngoc] Loan—I didn't know who he was—as soon as he raised his pistol, I raised the camera." Loan waved the nearby troops away with his drawn gun. When Adams's shutter clicked, he had one of the most famous pictures of the Vietnam War: the official executioner in profile, his shirt sleeve rolled up, exposing his extended right arm, his pistol inches from the prisoner's face, which was in a grimace from the impact of the bullet. The prisoner crumpled in front of him. (NBC aired a film of the incident on the *Huntley-Brinkley Report*; an ABC cameraman was also present for the execution, but he stopped filming at the moment Loan pulled the trigger from fear of the police chief's retaliation.) After the shot, the general reholstered his pistol and turned to his witnesses. "Many Americans have been killed these last few days, and many of my best Vietnamese friends," said Loan. "Now do you understand? Buddha will understand."[26]

This image probably did more damage to the idea that America was bringing civilization to South Vietnam than any other event. The photograph was devastating. It appeared on front pages all around the world, it won the Pulitzer and eight other prizes, and through absolutely no fault of the photographer, the symbol it became was somewhat misleading. It was an honest portrait of the brutality of war and the ruthlessness of our Vietnamese ally. What it could not convey, because neither Adams nor any other photographer could reproduce the other side of the war that day in quite the same way, was the fact that the North Vietnamese were every bit as brutal as the South Vietnamese, and probably more so; they just happened to be cunning enough to commit most of their atrocities out of the range of foreigners' cameras. Most Americans never learned Loan's specific motivation: He executed the suspect after a subordinate had told him the prisoner had killed a police major who was one of the police chief's closest friends—and the rest of the major's family as well.[27]

If the definitive picture from the Tet offensive came out of Eddie Adams's camera, the definitive quote came from an anonymous American major. On February 7, a group of correspondents took a day trip organized by the American military command to Ben Tre, a city of thirty-five thousand that was the capital of Kien Hoa province in the Mekong Delta. To the dismay of the military, "each trip produced a new wave of stories of surprise attack, inadequate defense and death, destruction and discontent in the city visited," as Don Oberdorfer described the syndrome in his book *Tet!*[28] The Vietcong were under strict orders to limit unnecessary destruction, while the Americans and the South were indiscriminate in their use of firepower, according to Oberdorfer, "and seemed to value their own safety far beyond the political purpose (if any) for which they fought."

Peter Arnett, a war correspondent for the AP, found a major in Ben Tre who managed to provide a neat summary of the whole American approach to the war—at least as far as its opponents were concerned. "It became necessary to destroy the town to save it," the major explained. No official statement about the conflict ever got anything like the attention lavished on these ten words from a single officer. American doves seized on this sentence as the perfect description of the futility of our effort. In Vietnam the Army had the standard bureaucratic reaction: Rather than examine the tactics that had been used at Ben Tre, it launched an investigation to determine the identity of the errant major.

BACK in Saigon, the official American apparatus faced several serious obstacles as it struggled to restore a sense of normality to the capital city. Saigon didn't feel the same after Tet. During 1967 the only serious threats to personal safety inside the city limits had been an occasional 122-mm rocket and the notorious dragon lady, a crazed figure who rode on the back of a Honda motorcycle and fired a .45 at American officers in the street. "The Saigon papers described her as 'beautiful,'" wrote Michael Herr, "but I don't know how anybody knew that. The commander of one of the Saigon MP battalions said he thought it was a man dressed in an *ao dai* because a .45 was 'an awful lot of gun for a itty bitty Vietnamese woman.'"[29]

And while the pockets of Vietcong resistance within the city proper were pretty much eliminated by the end of the first week of the offensive, throughout February there was a daily curfew. Like everyone else, American reporters were forbidden to travel in the dark without an armed guard. "There was a terribly dramatic escort service," said Lee Lescaze, which reporters had to call every time they wanted to go to their offices during the curfew to file stories. It consisted of "MPs in flak jackets with .50-caliber machine guns mounted on their jeeps—and you really felt you were going off to war."[30] Herr thought that Saigon under the curfew looked like "the final reel of *On the Beach*, a desolate city whose long avenues held nothing but refuse, windblown papers, small distinct piles of human excrement, and the dead flowers and spent firecracker casings of the Lunar New Year.

"Tet was pushing correspondents closer to the wall than they'd ever wanted to go," Herr discovered. "In Saigon, I saw friends flipping out almost completely. . . . A friend on the *Times* said he didn't mind his nightmares so much as the waking impulse to file on them." It was also during these weeks that *Time* magazine put North Vietnamese general Vo Nguyen Giap, a leading strategist of the offensive, on its cover. The South Vietnamese permitted the distribution of the magazine—but only after a black X had been imprinted on every copy, "disfiguring but hardly concealing Giap's face," wrote Herr. "People were doing weird things that Tet."[31]

Sometimes the hardest task was reassuring new arrivals. Maynard Parker and Kevin Buckley of *Newsweek* got to Saigon three weeks after the offensive began. Buckley, fresh from the magazine's London bureau, sat on the flight into the capital with Parker and John Cantwell of *Time* magazine. Within a couple of days, Parker and Buckley were in Huê, where they split up so that they could go out with two different groups of Marines. Buckley befriended a Japanese photographer who was killed by a land mine when he chose a different path from the *Newsweek* man. Ten weeks later, Buckley was back in Saigon when Cantwell, his fellow passenger on the plane into Vietnam, drove out to the edge of the city with Bruce Pigott of Reuters and three other reporters. Pigott, Cantwell, and two of their three fellow journalists were all killed by a Vietcong who ignored their shouts of "*Bao Dai!*" (Vietnamese for "reporters.") "Kevin came back thinking this was a slightly dangerous business," Parker remembered. According to James Sterba of the *Wall Street Journal*, fifty journalists working for American news organizations were killed in Southeast Asia—compared with twelve American generals.[32]

The biggest problem for all of the permanent optimists in the American military command was the continuing presence of the flag of the National Liberation Front over the majestic city of Hué—three weeks after the Tet offensive had begun. Sitting on the bank of the Perfume River, adorned by temples and palaces, Hué was an unusually romantic Vietnamese metropolis. In the nineteenth century it had been rebuilt by Emperor Gia Long to resemble the seat of his Chinese patron in Peking. "No city got more press attention during Tet than Hué," according to journalist Peter Braestrup.[33]

Hué was the victim of one of the worst intelligence snafus of the war. A week before Tet, the U.S. command in Saigon warned Washington to expect a huge, multibattalion attack on the majestic city. But the command never provided that information to South Vietnamese or American officials in Hué. Another warning from an American military advisor stationed east of the city about the movements of three Communist battalions was discounted because he was considered a "worrier."[34] When Communist forces entered the city from three directions early on January 31, they encountered little resistance. Quickly their flag rose over the Citadel, a fortress at the center of the city.

Hué's 140,000 citizens suffered some of the worst atrocities ever committed by the Vietnamese Communists. The Vietcong arrived with a list of political opponents, government officials, foreigners, "and even the schedule of doctors on duty at the Central Hospital," according to Oberdorfer.[35] Their list of 196 targets came complete with the addresses of everyone they planned to eliminate. During their twenty-four-day occupation, the Communists murdered 2,800 civilians, including two American Foreign Service officers, two German doctors, a popular Vietnamese priest (who was apparently buried alive), and hundreds of ordinary Vietnamese considered too close to the Saigon regime. The impact of these executions on the outside world was diluted by the absence of witnesses and the fact that many of the graves remained undiscovered for more than a year. Nineteen months after Tet, three Vietcong defectors led American GIs to a secret jungle site ten miles from the city. There they found the bones of 428 victims—military men, students, civil servants, and ordinary citizens.[36]

Unlike some of their American counterparts, no North Vietnamese official ever expressed any regret over these horrors. After the war, the victorious commanders sounded like unrepentant Nazis dismissing "rumors" of a holocaust. General Tran Do, a senior Communist architect of the offensive, flatly denied to Stanley Karnow that the Hué atrocities ever occurred. He contended the films and photographs of the corpses had been "fabricated." In Hué itself a local official blamed most of the deaths on the Americans, "but he hinted that his comrades had participated in at least a share of the killing—resorting to familiar Communist jargon to explain that the 'angry' citizens of Hué had liquidated local 'despots.'"[37]

The last center of Vietcong resistance was wiped out and the city was completely "pacified" on February 25. After twenty-six days of battle, American officials said 142 Marines had been killed and 857 seriously wounded. The South Vietnamese lost 384 men; 1,800 were wounded. The Communist losses were 5,113 killed and eighty-nine captured.[38] At least six thousand houses were seriously damaged; another 4,400 were completely destroyed.[39]

DESPITE the massive coverage of Tet, the American media were slow to understand its political importance on the hustings. When Gene McCarthy was first asked in February whether the offensive would bring him votes in New Hampshire he replied, "Give it three weeks, time to sink in. By then it could make a difference."[40] As it happened, the college students neglecting their studies to spread the word about the enigmatic senator in New Hampshire were among the very first citizens to discern the flutter in the national heartbeat. The press, however, was not noticing.

Washington reporters knew McCarthy as a brilliant but rather lazy legislator, someone who was too much of an iconoclast to be considered a serious presidential candidate. Besides, his campaign was being run by people the reporters had never heard of—like Sam Brown and Curtis Gans—or people who had very little experience in politics—like Blair Clark and Seymour Hersh—so it was easy to dismiss their efforts.

Hersh was typical of the kind of McCarthy staffer who could bewilder a reporter accustomed to more predictable behavior in a campaign spokesman. Within a few years, Hersh would become famous as one of the great investigators of his generation. In *Harper's* and the *New York Times* he would break many of the biggest stories, from the My Lai massacre to details of the CIA's involvement in domestic surveillance. But in 1968 he was known only as a twenty-nine-year-old ex–wire service man with a huge ego and a bizarre sense of humor. "Sy is a fine, fine investigative journalist," said Curtis Gans, "and a complete maniac and the antithesis of a press secretary. He is also congenitally incapable of internalizing his feelings."[41]

Hersh's own account does not contradict this portrait. "I happen to be a damn good reporter," he said a year after the campaign ended. "And I can't stand bad reporters. Why should I have to live with them?" To make those long winter nights in New Hampshire a little more engaging, Hersh once recruited the two most attractive, miniskirted staffers he could find. After equipping them with four glasses and two bottles of whiskey, he dispatched them to the suite of two deserving (male) members of the fourth estate. Holding bottles and glasses in front of them, the young ladies knocked on the door and explained their mission: "Hi. Sy Hersh sent us up for a couple of hours." The press secretary stood at the dark end of the corridor to observe the reaction of his horrified victims. He noticed that despite reputations as rakes, the reporters "would get very worried about it. And they would wonder what sort of setup they were getting into." But Hersh was just having a little fun—"as much as you could."[42]

Partly because of such antics, partly because of what they perceived as McCarthy's lackadaisical approach, and largely because of Washington myopia, most reporters continued to believe in the inevitability of

Lyndon Johnson, even after Tet. That Bobby Kennedy was still insisting he would not be a candidate, even as he stepped up his attacks on the war, only strengthened the conviction of the herd. And with exceptionally bad timing, Kennedy had restated his unavailability the very day Tet began. At an off-the-record breakfast with reporters at the end of January, he derided the McCarthy campaign as "helpful to President Johnson." Then he deplored the growing gaps between the generations and the races. Kids "just don't have any respect for older people," he said. "I think these problems are going to intensify. There is a strong feeling among middle-class whites against the Negroes. In New York City, the Democratic leaders have a strong feeling against the Negroes. They just don't like them. If someone could appeal to the generous spirit of Americans to heal the race question, this is what the campaign should be about." But his running "would automatically elect a Republican by splitting the Democratic Party, and Democratic candidates would be beaten all over the country." What if Johnson decided not to run? "You're talking about an act of God," the senator replied.

For the record, Kennedy said there were "no foreseeable circumstances" that would push him into the race. During the breakfast, Peter Lisagor of the *Chicago Daily News* handed Kennedy a piece of UPI wire copy describing the first wave of coordinated attacks on seven South Vietnamese cities. "Yeah," said Kennedy sarcastically, "we're winning." But this was the day *before* the attacks on Saigon, and the scope of the unfolding disaster was not yet apparent. Kennedy's friends insisted afterward that if the breakfast had been held just a day or two later, he never would have placed such a large rhetorical roadblock between himself and the presidency.[43]

An Elmo Roper poll for *Time* published in the last week of February predicted McCarthy would get 11 percent of the New Hampshire vote, but the survey was based on three-week-old responses.[44] The McCarthy campaign "had been mounted entirely outside" Washington's traditional "terms of reference," British journalist Anthony Howard pointed out. "The power of McCarthy's appeal represented an attack on the assumptions of political writer David Broder just as much as it did on those of politician John Bailey."[45] By mostly ignoring McCarthy's campaign right through February, the press guaranteed the drama of its March denouement. Nineteen years later, McCarthy delivered this caustic verdict: "Reporters and political experts were so wrong about much of the campaign of 1968 that many, had they professional integrity, would have put away their typewriters and written no more of politics."[46]

*   *   *

THE sea change in American attitudes toward the war began at the end of February, and no one in the press played a larger role in this phenomenon than Walter Cronkite. By 1968 this newsman was revered. He was an American patriarch who was not a politician, a man with whom the camera had begun its legendary love affair eighteen years earlier. As steadily as the war consumed Lyndon Johnson's credibility, the stature of Walter Cronkite grew. While one sentence of Johnson's lugubrious prose could drive his audience away, the slightest alteration in Cronkite's inflection guaranteed national attention.

Born in 1916 in St. Joseph, Missouri, Cronkite grew up in Texas on the western edge of Houston. After enrolling at the University of Texas and reporting for the *Houston Post,* he became a battlefield correspondent for United Press during World War II. That assignment gave him a crucial credential: participation in the key experience of his generation. After the war, he moved to the medium that would make him the most trusted man in America. Cronkite joined CBS in 1950; the Vietnam generation grew up with him in the living room. He first penetrated its young psyches as a time traveler, interviewing everyone from Paul Revere to Thomas Edison on the entertainingly educational (and reliably patriotic) *You Are There.* His commanding voice and soothing manner made him a uniquely persuasive presence inside the American home. In 1962 he took the anchor seat of the CBS *Evening News.*[47]

Chet Huntley and David Brinkley had become the first superstars of an evening news program after the debut of the *Huntley-Brinkley Report* in 1956, but Cronkite was the first to master the format alone. In 1965 and 1966 the ratings race seesawed back and forth between CBS and NBC, but in the second half of 1967 Cronkite began to pull ahead of the competition. By then he was the consummate television newsman, the perfect blend of middlebrow intellect and superb showmanship. His producers referred to his solo moments in front of the camera as "the Magic." Beginning in 1968 he became the prime personality on television, just as Edward R. Murrow's extraordinary voice had dominated the radio during World War II. But only in 1968 would Cronkite act with the same courage and independence as Murrow, the reporter who first made CBS matter.

As 1968 began, Cronkite was keeping his viewers up-to-date on the usual mixture of human lunacy, tragedy, and triumph. At a time of almost total war between parents and children, this fifty-one-year-old newsman was one of the very few public men in America who could still bridge the credibility gap between the generations. In January his program covered all these events: Christiaan Barnard performed the world's second heart transplant on retired South African dentist Philip Blaiberg; baby doctor Benjamin Spock ("the father of us all"), Yale chaplain William Sloane Coffin, and three others were charged with conspiring to disrupt the draft; six LSD trippers went blind in Pennsylvania after staring at the sun (six days later, Cronkite revealed this story had been a hoax); AT&T announced the introduction of a new nationwide emergency number, 911; Eartha Kitt exploded at Lady Bird Johnson during lunch at the White House, deploring the president's war; the *Pueblo* was seized by North Korea;* and American officials wanted narcotics agents to fight marijuana use among GIs in Saigon (even as the U.S. Army was issuing amphetamines to combat troops).

During January slightly less than half of Cronkite's broadcasts led with news about Vietnam. But beginning January 30, the war dominated all of his programs. On the tenth day of Tet, Cronkite announced he was going to Vietnam to conduct a personal investigation of the offensive. Nineteen days later he was back with a lethal verdict.

Who, What, When, Where, Why (the first five questions every reporter is taught to answer) was the title of Cronkite's program at ten o'clock on the evening of February 27. *Report from Vietnam by Walter Cronkite* was the subtitle. Partly because its subject was less personal, this broadcast was not quite so dramatic as Murrow's *See It Now* body blow to Joe McCarthy fourteen years earlier. But it was still one of the most devastating television programs of all time.

Cronkite opened with a "stand-up" on location:

"These ruins are in Saigon, capital and largest city of South Vietnam. . . . Like everything else in this burned and blasted and weary land, they mean success or setback, victory or defeat, depending upon whom you talk to." In Tuy Phuoc province, CBS News correspondent Robert Schakne interviewed Captain Donald Jones, deputy pacification advisor. Jones said Tuy Phuoc "used to be considered the bowl of pacification."

"Is there any pacification program left in Tuy Phuoc district at this point?" Schakne asked.

"No," said the captain. "For most of the district, pacification does not exist. This is a war."

---

* A still unanswered question is whether this was done by the North Koreans as a favor to their North Vietnamese ally to throw the United States off-balance just before Tet. [Don Oberdorfer, *Tet!* (1971; reprint, New York: Da Capo Press, 1984), 163.]

"Are you discouraged?"

"Yes," the captain replied.

Back in New York, Cronkite delivered his conclusions, identifying them as "speculative, personal, and subjective":

"We have been too often disappointed by the optimism of the American leaders, both in Vietnam and Washington, to have faith any longer in the silver linings they find in the darkest clouds. . . . Any negotiations must be that—negotiations, not the dictation of peace terms . . . it seems now more certain than ever that the bloody experience of Vietnam is to end in a stalemate. . . . For every means we have to escalate, the enemy can match us, and that applies to invasion of the North, the use of nuclear weapons, or the mere commitment of one hundred or two hundred or three hundred thousand more American troops to the battle. And with each escalation, the world comes closer to the brink of cosmic disaster.

"To say that we are closer to victory today is to believe, in the face of the evidence, the optimists who have been wrong in the past. To suggest we are on the edge of defeat is to yield to unreasonable pessimism. To say that we are mired in stalemate seems the only realistic, yet unsatisfactory, conclusion. . . . It is increasingly clear to this reporter that the only rational way out will be to negotiate, not as victors, but as an honorable people who lived up to their pledge to defend democracy, and did the best they could.

"This is Walter Cronkite. Good night."

Never before had such an influential American identified the futility of our effort on prime-time television. The war's opponents reacted with a mixture of astonishment and glee to this battlefield conversion. Cronkite's words carried greater weight than those of any politician—and Lyndon Johnson knew that better than anyone. The fact that Johnson had enjoyed a very special relationship with CBS for thirty years only increased the size of the shock. It had been Frank Stanton (then a young assistant to CBS founder William Paley) who agreed in 1938 to make the Texas congressman's radio station in Austin a CBS affiliate—and it was that decision that made the outlet the foundation of the Johnson fortune.[48] By the time Stanton was president of CBS and Johnson was president of the United States, the two men were very close friends indeed. Stanton even redesigned the presidential desk in the Oval Office. He also provided endless technical advice in the futile effort to make the commander-in-chief look better on television.[49]

The president had unusual respect for the CBS anchor. "I can't compete with Walter Cronkite," he explained. " He knows television and he's a star. So when I'm with him, I'm on his level, and yet he knows what he's doing and so he does it better and so I lose."[50] Now the president's telegenic opposite had become his avowed enemy, and Johnson was devastated by the loss of Cronkite, the personification of CBS in the public mind. The president told his aides that if he had lost Walter, he had lost the common American.

Alone, Cronkite's words would have carried tremendous weight. But his broadcast was anything but an isolated event. At the beginning of February, Art Buchwald, the most widely read lampoonist in America, used the dateline of "Little Big Horn, Dakota" to puncture Westmoreland's incessant optimism: "June 27, 1876—General George Armstrong Custer said today in an exclusive interview with this correspondent that the battle of Little Big Horn had just turned the corner and he could now see the light at the end of the tunnel. 'We have the Sioux on the run,' General Custer told me. 'Of course, we still have some cleaning up to do, but the Redskins are hurting badly and it will only be a matter of time before they give in.'"[51] The next day, James Reston, the dean of *New York Times* columnists, paraphrased the American major in Ben Tre: "What is the end that justified this slaughter? How will we save Vietnam if we destroy it in the battle?"[52]

Most surprising of all were the doubts voiced by the *Wall Street Journal.* Four days before the CBS broadcast the bible of American capitalism delivered a broadside against the president's war: "We think the American people should be getting ready to accept, if they haven't already, the prospect that the whole Vietnam effort may be doomed, that it may be falling apart beneath our feet. We believe the administration is duty-bound to recognize that no battle and no war is worth any price, no matter how ruinous, and that in the case of Vietnam it may be failing for the simple reason that the whole place and cause is collapsing from within." The *Journal*'s sentiments were widely reprinted.

THERE were a million losers in the Tet offensive: tens of thousands killed, tens of thousands crippled, hundreds of thousands left homeless. What was most shocking about the outcome was the proof it provided of the ignorance of Americans and North Vietnamese alike. Both sides seemed to have pitiful intelligence about the real conditions inside the country where they had chosen to squander so many of their men and so much of their treasure. The North Vietnamese had predicted a massive uprising in the South and the end of its "puppet" regime after their onslaught. That was the carrot they used to get their troops to undertake suicidal missions like the embassy attack, missions whose survivors said they had never considered the equivalent of suicide. The Americans had been boasting throughout 1967 that *we* were winning the war and the Communists were on the run. Everyone was wrong.

Just four days after Tet began, Lyndon Johnson called the enemy's military effort "a complete failure" and compared the impact of the offensive with an American riot or "a very serious strike . . . they have disrupted services."[53] At the end of *two months*, 214 Koreans, 3,895 Americans, 4,954 South Vietnamese troops, 14,300 South Vietnamese civilians, and (by American estimates) 58,000 Communist troops were dead: a total of 81,363 men, women, and children shot, blown up, or buried alive. Once again, our generals rejoiced over the "kill ratios." But despite the best efforts of the president, most Americans still associated "victory" with the capture of enemy territory—and the wiser citizens noticed that what we had "won" was exactly what we *had* the day before the Tet offensive started. Well, not *exactly*: The homes of 821,000 South Vietnamese had been destroyed, so now there were 821,000 new refugees—doubling the total before Tet—as well as 81,363 new graves.[54]

By the end of February, Lyndon Johnson felt particularly chastened. He insisted that his government had anticipated the offensive, though he looks especially drawn in pictures taken January 31. The president's involvement in the minutiae of the war was legendary. In 1967 and 1968 he spent many early morning hours alone in the White House Situation Room, reading reports from the front or studying his own huge scale model of the Marine base at Khe Sanh. Sometimes, he would excuse himself from state dinners, explaining, "I've got to get back to Khe Sanh."[55] In early 1968 Khe Sanh was Johnson's special obsession. The siege went on for months, providing plenty of dramatic footage of airplanes dodging Communist anti-aircraft guns fired during very difficult resupply operations. The president worried that it would become the American equivalent of the French debacle at Dien Bien Phu, where eight thousand Vietminh and two thousand French soldiers died. In the end Khe Sanh cost the Communists ten thousand lives and the U.S. fewer than five hundred Marines. It never turned into the decisive battle Johnson had feared. Despite their heavy losses, North Vietnamese officers told Stanley Karnow they felt their strategy was worth it because it drew American troops away from the major population centers, which were their principal targets. Johnson insisted that the effort to overrun Khe Sanh "never materialized because of our bombardment." But, in Karnow's view, "Westmoreland fell for the enemy ruse."[56]

In his memoirs, Johnson praises Westmoreland and Ellsworth Bunker, who succeeded Henry Cabot Lodge as Johnson's ambassador in Vietnam, for warning him of the impending offensive a week before it began. But he also wrote, "This is not to imply that Tet was not a shock, in one degree or another, to all of us. We knew that a show of strength was coming; it was more massive than we had anticipated. We knew that the Communists were aiming at a number of population centers; we did not expect them to attack as many as they did. We knew that the North Vietnamese and the Viet Cong were trying to achieve better coordination of their countrywide moves; we did not believe they would be able to carry out the level of coordination they demonstrated. We expected a large force to attack; it was larger than we had estimated."[57] Finally, because of the president's ignorance of Vietnamese history, the timing was the biggest shock of all. "No one believed that you would have an act of this kind on a holiday after you had an honorable agreement" to suspend operations, Johnson told Walter Cronkite two years after Tet. "That was just too much to even believe a Communist would do."[58]

In 1982 CBS broadcast a documentary accusing Westmoreland and his command of purposely under-reporting enemy troop strength during 1967. The general responded with a $120 million libel suit, which he dropped three years later, after the case had gone to trial but before it reached a jury. Karnow argues that even if CBS's charges were true, "it is doubtful that [Westmoreland's] deception deprived Lyndon Johnson of the facts," since the president "always had alternate sources of information." The U.S. Army's own verdict on the surprise attack was a harsh one: A textbook prepared for West Point cadets called Tet "an allied intelligence failure ranking with Pearl Harbor."[59]

The North Vietnamese lost their best fighters. It would take them several years to replace them. In their own initial assessment of the offensive, the Communists found themselves "guilty of many errors and shortcomings."[60] Westmoreland saw Tet as something comparable to the Battle of the Bulge, Hitler's last gasp in World War II, but like almost everyone else in the administration, the general vastly underestimated the patience and resilience of his enemy. As early as 1965, the North Vietnamese had calculated they would be able to sustain the war even if they faced between eight hundred thousand and one million American and South Vietnamese troops.[61] The North had a standing army of four hundred fifty-thousand, and two hundred thousand North Vietnamese men reached the age of eighteen every year. In addition, it could call on three million men in regional, popular, and self-defense forces.[62] And although they had hoped for an uprising, the Communists approached Tet with many goals in mind. "For us, you know, there is no such thing as a single strategy," General Giap told Karnow after the war. "Ours is always a synthesis, simultaneously military, political, and diplomatic—which is why, quite clearly, the Tet offensive had multiple objectives."

One Communist goal was to drive a wedge between the Americans and their South Vietnamese allies. Their success was reflected in the rumor that swept Saigon shortly after Tet: The United States was secretly behind the Communist attacks, because we wanted to pressure the South into accepting a coalition government, to clear the way for the withdrawal of our troops. Eventually Ambassador Bunker had to go on Saigon television to deny "this ridiculous claim"—a declaration that some Vietnamese inevitably took as confirmation of their peculiar theory.[63]

Giap also hoped Tet would force Johnson into halting the bombing of all—or most—of the North. As part of that strategy, the North Vietnamese foreign minister announced on December 30, 1967, that the Communists "will" open discussions with the United States as soon as the bombing stopped.[64] And that part of his strategy worked.

Tet revealed two crucial differences between North Vietnam and the United States, differences that would largely determine the outcome of the war. The first was one of attitude. To the North Vietnamese this war was a noble venture, a compulsion, the very reason their nation had been founded: the expulsion of foreigners from their native land. To us it was an ugly quagmire, a cancer on our spirit, and—particularly after Tet—a war without a cause. The second difference was a matter of structure. Ours was a free society; theirs was not. The leaders of the North Vietnamese antiwar movement were all in jail. Starting in September 1967, more than two hundred government and party officials were arrested for their opposition to the country's war policies, according to a defector. Among them were such senior officials as Colonel Le Trung Nghia, director of Central Intelligence for North Vietnam, and Bui Cong Trung, a member of the Central Committee.[65] While some American dissenters were also in prison, after Tet the most influential opponents of the war would be in prime time on every television network.

IN MARCH it would not matter very much whether Americans wanted more war or less war. What mattered from a political point of view was their precipitous loss of faith in the abilities of its progenitor. During Tet, Americans initially reacted the way they usually do when their forces come under attack; they wanted to fight back. With multiple battles still raging, those favoring a reduction in the American role in the conflict *declined* to just 24 percent, twenty points lower than the figure recorded the previous November. But in the six weeks *after* Tet, the approval rating of Lyndon Johnson slipped from 48 percent to 36 percent, and the favorable verdict on his handling of the war plummeted fourteen points, to 26 percent.[66] Military bases had become practically the only places where presidential handlers could ensure at least the appearance of a warm welcome for Johnson.

In New Hampshire, David Hoeh and Gerry Studds had taken the titles of campaign director and coordinator in the McCarthy effort and selected the former Ralph Pell Electrical Appliance Store to be its Concord headquarters. "There were wires hanging out of the walls, it looked like a medieval torture chamber, and it took a whole day for David and me to sweep it," Studds recalled. "We sort of looked at each other and said, 'God, there are ten weeks to go. What are we going to do?'" But then "people began drifting into our office—just as if from heaven."[67] Two weeks after Tet began, Sam Brown arrived to direct the energies of the student army.

Ten days later, when television screens in every college dormitory were filled with the carnage of Tet, the stream of students arriving in New Hampshire turned into a river, then a flood. Gans had been chafing in Washington for an operational role in the field. Nineteen days before the election, Blair Clark finally dispatched him up North. "I was never as scared as I was the night I took the train to New Hampshire," said Gans. "All of a sudden all the things we'd been saying for a year seemed to be weighing on my shoulders." Gans was worried about McCarthy's attitude because the candidate acted as if he still didn't believe in the possibility of victory. In the middle of February, the senator had told Clark to raise "every dime he could because after New Hampshire the money would stop." But when Gans arrived in New Hampshire, he didn't feel nervous anymore.[68]

Perceived as amateurs by outsiders, the McCarthy campaign staff actually combined seasoned local operatives like Hoeh and Studds with extraordinary young people from all over the country. "The kids," which is what everyone called them, including themselves, were the campaign's hallmark. Beautiful, intense, and brilliant young men and women from a hundred colleges as far away as Michigan and Virginia descended on New Hampshire, desperate to define themselves.[69] A feeling of moral certainty about the iniquity of the war and a healthy desire for self-preservation: These were the essentials behind the collective decision to push for an end to the conflict, in New Hampshire or wherever they were. A sense of themselves as crusaders produced a seven-day-a-week, sixteen-hour-a-day commitment more intense than anything money could buy. Just as their parents had defined themselves as moral people by waging a just war, they would do the same thing by trying to end a pointless conflict. A sign in the Concord headquarters explained: GOD ISN'T DEAD, HE'S JUST LONELY, BUT HE JUST MIGHT COMMIT SUICIDE ON MARCH 12TH. IT'S UP TO YOU![70]

Devotion to McCarthy included a significant Oedipal element. At a moment when so many were in pitched battles with their real fathers—over everything from politics to drugs to hair length—this paternal-looking icon-oclast was an ideal surrogate. Being incomprehensible to the establishment only made him more appealing to them. As one of his speechwriters put it, "The students enjoyed Gene's respectability and wit as the outer signs of solidity, courage, and wisdom. They didn't miss his not directing them; he was the permissive father who is really wonderful but who has to be explained to outsiders." In New Hampshire, McCarthy was the ideal person to lead the vanguard of a generation hoping to define itself by living outside as many norms as possible.

McCarthy's cause attracted some of the youngest, smartest, most inde-pendent, best-educated, and worst-paid staff members in the history of American politics. It was probably the last presidential campaign in which most participants were driven by an issue, rather than drawn to a particular personality. The young men were the first American warriors to go into disguise by *removing* their beards; the young women sought the same effect by discarding their dungarees in favor of proper Peck & Peck skirts. (One woman volunteer remembers 1968 as the year you wore your blue jeans *under* your skirt when you went home for Thanksgiving.) Those who declined to become "Clean for Gene" were hidden away in basements, where they huddled over precinct maps and mimeograph machines, pro-pelled by a seamless sound track of the Beatles, the Stones, Country Joe and the Fish, and the Grateful Dead. Even the locals who had formed the Committee for Peace in Vietnam were kept in the background. "The general public considered them bearded 'peace types,'" Studds explained. "These were obviously magnificent people," but "for political purposes, with a sort of sticking in our throat, we asked them to stay out of sight. We did it because we figured this was . . . one last try within the traditional political system. . . . I remember many a conversation with people like Sam Brown and with many other young people who were working here, that this was their last effort within the system. They were prepared to go to Canada or go to jail or go into the streets if this failed. I felt that this was the last gasp within the process, and you couldn't live with yourself if you didn't do everything you could to make a try of it."[71]

A twenty-year-old college dropout named Ann Hart was one of the most effective out-of-state volunteers at the Manchester headquarters. As the daughter of Senator Philip Hart, she had politics and idealism in her blood and a childhood acquaintance with McCarthy. Her father was a much-admired liberal gentleman from Michigan. Like McCarthy, Phil Hart was first elected to the Senate in 1958, and they were reelected together in the Johnson landslide of 1964. McCarthy's daughter Ellen had been Ann Hart's classmate at Stone Ridge Academy of the Sacred Heart. For a few weeks each year, Hart, McCarthy, and Maine senator Edmund Muskie shared a house on Calvert Street in Washington while their wives and families retreated to their home states during summer vacations.

By the winter of 1968, Ann Hart's mother had become "very antiwar," but her father, like most Democratic senators, was still supporting Lyndon Johnson. Vietnam had first penetrated the inner life of the family in 1965, when the son of some close friends was killed in the conflict. It took the Marines a long time to ship Geoffrey Green's body back home to Michigan, leaving sort of an "open wound of grieving," and Ann Hart's parents spent many hours consoling the Greens. "We had never realized there was this thing called Vietnam," said Ann, who was seventeen at the time.

Phil Hart was a World War II veteran who had been seriously wounded at Utah Beach on D-day. After Geoffrey Green was buried, the senator went to Vietnam to make his own inspection. "He came back convinced this was a righteous war that had to be fought," his daughter remembered. "It took a long time for him to go against the war."

Ann Hart was one of those who recognized "something Oedipal" in all this. "McCarthy presented an alternative to my father who represented my views more closely. There was the whole 'children's crusade' aspect, with Gene as the father whom we would have liked to have. Instead of having this warmonger redneck [LBJ], we had an educated, gentle man. Instead of an eagle, we had a dove."

If her personal connection to the candidate made her a little unusual, the rest of Ann Hart's background made her the archetypal McCarthy volunteer. The oldest of eight children, she dropped out of college in the spring of 1966. Her parents would have been happier if she had stayed in school, but being "good liberals," they "wanted me to do whatever it was that I needed to do—which is either a cop-out or a liberal philosophy." After that, she was a bit "vagabondish." Like thousands of self-possessed women of her generation, she became a folk singer who accompanied herself on the guitar and sang "very earnest antiwar songs and lots of love songs." She was also quite familiar with sex, drugs, and rock and roll—the sixties trinity in permanent competition with politics for the attention of a generation. Just as emblematically, she felt disaffected by the political realities of America, but "unable to do anything much about it—except sing. I clearly was not exactly fully employed, or engaged in anything significant—and I felt it would be nice to be engaged in something significant."

As a volunteer in Washington, she was uncomfortable giving orders to women two and three times her age, but Blair Clark spotted her potential and asked if she wanted to go into the field. "There's nothing much we can offer you if you do this," said Clark. "Is there something you would like if he wins?" The raw recruit thought about that for a moment, then suggested secretary of the interior might be nice.

In New Hampshire she was seized with the sense that "this was a mission, and they needed me." Because of a natural talent for organization, she was put in charge of the main tasks in the Manchester office, including canvassing and leafleting. She experienced "a fabulous comraderie in the cause of righteousness. We really were on fire with the cause. There was a real exhilaration to being the underdog." Mary McGrory noticed that Hart also managed to teach the volunteers working the phones some very credible New England accents.[72]

At first there was almost no money, which meant very little media, forcing the campaign to adopt the novel approach of relying on real people instead of television. Soon Hart was running something resembling a "very complicated military operation," briefing busloads of volunteers on how to behave, equipping them with packets for canvassing, instructing them how to rate each voter on a scale of one to five ("ones" were definitely for McCarthy; "fives," definitely for LBJ), and making sure everyone had a gym floor or a church floor to sleep on. STRANGE POLITICS MAKE BEDFELLOWS, read one sign at headquarters. Another pictured General Douglas MacArthur with an unusually apt quote: ANYBODY WHO COMMITS THE LAND POWER OF THE UNITED STATES ON THE CONTINENT OF ASIA OUGHT TO HAVE HIS HEAD EXAMINED.[73] Personalized invitations to receptions featuring the candidate were sent to almost every voter in the state, and everyone who turned up got a personalized thank-you, with McCarthy's signature forged by a student from Rutgers.[74]

Ben Stavis, a doctoral candidate at Columbia, was delighted with the campaign's ability to apply old techniques on a statewide basis: "No one had ever thought of actually canvassing personally all the voters in the state and pulling all favorable voters. But no campaign had the thousands of people willing to do precinct work, and the dozens of diligent office and field workers to organize such a massive effort. We had created, on an amateur basis, a supermachine."[75]

The campaign consisted of equal parts of chaos, organization, energy, and creativity. Gans exercised as much control over the New Hampshire effort as anyone else, largely because of his extraordinary energy level. "When we complained about meeting at 9 A.M, he threatened to have them at 8 instead, which [he said] was the time the Kennedy staff met," Stavis wrote in his campaign memoir, *We Were the Campaign.* "Sometimes he called meetings to begin at midnight, and when they were over, he rushed to Manchester for a 2 A.M. meeting. Yet he was ready for the next day's 9 A.M. With the director keeping such hours, no one could complain about overwork."[76] Studds suggested to Gans "that if he ate a meal or two or slept an hour or two, the whole thing might go better, but clearly that was not the way he operated." Leaving Gans even less time was a most unlikely obligation: Right through the primary he was still commuting to Washington to attend Marine Corps reserve meetings.[77]

THE avowed purpose of the campaign was to end the war and replace a sense of impotence with a feeling of moral purposefulness by bringing the disaffected back into the system. Underneath, there were plenty of other subliminal agendas, but for many of us, the most powerful one would require the use of a time machine: We wanted to turn back the clock, to replace the gore of the Johnson presidency with the glamour of Camelot.

"We will never laugh again," Mary McGrory told Daniel Patrick Moynihan after John Kennedy's assassination. "No, Mary," said Moynihan. "We will laugh again, but we will never be young again."[78] For many romantics from two generations—the Americans who came of age during World War II, and their adolescent progeny—the spring of 1968 would be the last time they still believed they might yet be young again. For an instant it was an exhilarating chase: a pursuit of lapsed feelings of hope and opportunity, feelings that were gravely wounded by the bullets that killed Kennedy in Dallas, then buried alive by Johnson's war. "It was a rare moment," said Marie Ridder, a journalist who was doing research for Teddy White in 1968. "The spring of that year was a happy time in American politics. You felt you could do something."[79]

Despite McCarthy's corrosive ambivalence toward America's first political family, he understood this impulse toward a restoration, and he did not hesitate to exploit it. At David Hoeh's suggestion, McCarthy's first day on the New Hampshire campaign trail duplicated John Kennedy's itinerary of eight years earlier. Hoeh even got his candidate to pose (a little uncomfortably) in front of a bust of the late president.[80] All across New Hampshire, McCarthy invoked the Kennedy name and the spirit of the early sixties. "In 1963, America was confident," he declared on February 6. "There was an openness about America. Some of you won't recall, but in 1958 and 1959 people were saying, 'What's wrong with young America? They seem indifferent; they don't even demonstrate.' And then we offered the Peace Corps. Or John Kennedy did, and people said, 'Isn't it frightening how they respond when they're challenged?' This was the spirit of '61 and '62 and '63. . . . What is the mood of America today? What's happened to the youthful confidence, the optimism, and the openness of 1963?" And again on March 4: "In three years under President John F. Kennedy, America was on the move. Now the fabric of that great achievement is unraveling. All around us we see that the last five years have brought decay to replace progress, near despair to replace hope, and failure in war to replace success in the pursuit of peace. In 1963, when President Johnson took office, prices were stable, the economy was booming, and taxes being lowered. Today prices are rising, the Kennedy boom is slowing down, and we are being asked to raise taxes."[81] A campaign leaflet pictured McCarthy with the late president and promised to return the country to Kennedy's policies. To many McCarthy fans, the Minnesotan's self-confident demeanor was even more evocative of Jack than Bobby's was.

While McCarthy was making quiet headway on the hustings, Johnson's New Hampshire surrogates were giving the insurgent plenty of unintentional assistance. Their first mistake was the distribution of three-part numbered pledge cards, which were supposed to confirm the extent of the president's support. The first part was to be kept by the voter, the second sent to the Democratic state committee, and the third mailed to the White House. The obedient Democrat would then receive a thank-you note from New Hampshire Governor John W. King and an autographed picture of Lady Bird and Lyndon. McCarthy denounced the cards as an "invasion of the secrecy of the ballot," then wryly suggested "it's not at all inconsistent with administration policy to kind of put a brand on people."[82] "You Don't Have to Sign Anything to Vote for Gene McCarthy" was the campaign's newest slogan.[83] A decision by the president's men to permit forty-five Johnson supporters to run for just twenty-four delegate slots was another tactical error bred of overconfidence. McCarthy's people ran just one candidate for each seat, so they started with a substantial built-in advantage.

The largest miscalculation by Johnson's people was a philosophical one. Governor King, a conservative Democrat, assumed that the power of the ghosts of Munich and *Joe* McCarthy was undiminished in the Granite State. After the debacle of the pledge cards, he began an unabashed Red-baiting campaign in the worst tradition of American politics. McCarthy, said one hostile ad, is "an advocate of appeasement and surrender" and an "apostle of retreat"—the traditional formula for evoking Chamberlain's disgrace at Munich. A vote for McCarthy would "be greeted with joy in Hanoi," King declared. Another radio spot said, "Don't vote for fuzzy thinking and surrender—support our fighting men."

Like the president he was representing, King had not yet understood the multiple consequences of Tet. The destruction of Lyndon Johnson's credibility was only its first effect. What gave this campaign its lasting importance was the permanent damage it inflicted on those twin ghosts. Tet was the first event since the Democrats' "loss" of China large enough to give the party, and the country, the courage to pull back from a disastrous commitment—even though its purported purpose was the containment of communism.

"It didn't work," McCarthy said simply of the effort to paint him as soft on communism. "Lyndon did it, and Rusk did it: Hanoi and the yellow horde."* The New Hampshire vote would provide the first electoral evidence of this turnaround. Studds felt McCarthy had a large advantage over Johnson's men in style as well as substance: "Our senator and governor [were] real stemwinders and fist pounders—and lousy speakers to boot," he said. That made McCarthy "a very very appealing change of pace for the people of New Hampshire."[84]

It was a stunt rather than substance that brought the campaign some of its earliest positive press. With the state's dominant newspaper, the *Manchester Union-Leader*, owned by Neanderthal conservative William Loeb, the most important local coverage was heavily hostile. But in the middle of February, McCarthy provided the ideal photo opportunity by donning a pair of skates and joining a hockey game. Hersh said to him, "The press are

---

* There was, however, still some occasional confusion about exactly which McCarthy New Hampshire was voting for. When the senator had given a speech at a Kiwanis Club near Manchester, no one noticed the inscription on the plaque he received until after he had moved on to the next stop . Then someone picked it up and asked, "Senator, have you seen this?" It read, "From the Kiwanis, with grateful appreciation to Senator Joseph McCarthy." [Recorded interview with Gerry Studds, McCarthy Historical Archive, Georgetown University Library.] .

all there—would you please go skating?" He "wanted to go anyway," said Hersh. "He's a very good skater." It was a feat that endeared him to every news photographer, as well as New Hampshire's substantial hockey-loving French-Canadian population. Fortunately the reporters didn't see the senator in the dressing room with Hersh afterward. "He was exhausted," said the press secretary. "He said, 'Why in the hell did you let me take that third turn, huh? You should have gotten me out of there sooner.'" Hersh asked if the candidate was tired, and got "one of those long, disdainful looks."

Yet most of the national press didn't notice there was more to the McCarthy effort than an occasional display of athleticism until one week before the March 12 primary. Mary McGrory was the first reporter to "discover" the McCarthy kids, and she fell in love on the spot. McGrory is a beloved figure in Washington, admired for her warmth, her wide range of contacts, her rigorous reporting, and her distinctive writing style, qualities few columnists manage to sustain as long as she has. She had joined the *Washington Evening Star* in 1947 as a book reviewer, covered her first national campaign in 1956, and become a columnist in 1960, the year JFK was elected president. Most impressively, she had made it to the top of her profession long before men were under any pressure to accommodate the ambitions of worthy women competitors.

Partly because she knew McCarthy well, she had given his campaign thorough coverage, picking up early hints of national unhappiness with the president. On February 11, she wrote about McCarthy's endorsement by the Americans for Democratic Action. She quoted an anguished ADA member from Pennsylvania: "Look, try to understand. I started out thinking it was insane to go against the president. You know who changed my mind? The people in my district. They just cannot take what the president is doing with this war. . . . Now I can go home and face my people. I tell you, there is a feeling of protest in this country."[85]

Upon her arrival in New Hampshire, McGrory was escorted to McCarthy headquarters in Concord. "It was in the back of a building. I went in and it was total, one thousand percent activity. I hadn't seen so many people in a political headquarters since I could remember. It was just so immense you figured it had to make a difference." The first person she encountered was a French Ph.D. candidate from Yale who had a list of French-speaking voters produced by a computer run by graduate students from MIT. "The Ph.D. from Yale looked like a swan. She was absolutely exquisite, and she talked about the cake she was fed at every stop. She was worried she was going to put on weight."[86]

In Washington, Tet was already having a dramatic effect on policymakers, but its political potency was not yet understood. On the capital cocktail circuit McGrory had learned this official wisdom from her colleagues: Unkempt youths working for McCarthy were alienating "the gruff country people of New Hampshire, who hate foreigners and have a sort of professional discourtesy toward people they don't know—like the French." In New Hampshire, she went to see Bill Dunfey, a former state Democratic chairman. Dunfey had led John Kennedy's New Hampshire primary campaign eight years earlier. "He had been with Johnson, but he knew the war was wrong," said McGrory, and he was someone she always checked in with. When she repeated the official line from Washington, the pol-professor gently chided his reporter-student. "Mary," said Dunfey, "old people *like* young people—and they like having them come to their door." The next day McGrory went to a Nixon rally and saw a man named Dick Hudson "who lived quietly at home with his mother, a totally respectable Republican. He said, 'I wonder why none of the McCarthy people have come to *us*? Our neighbors on both sides have had them and we haven't had none.' And he was *so* envious."

"We were theoretically the antiwar candidate," said Gans, " but I would hold indoctrination sessions for every one of the canvassers, sorting out those who were clean. We also talked to them about what they were about: You're here because you're against the war. Well, you should know people in New Hampshire basically support the war. If you're going to talk about the war, talk about its endless nature." Tet had vastly simplified that assignment. "What you want to do," Gans continued, "is pit the image of an honest man against the image of a dishonest man." Gans even had some Vietnam literature burned to blunt the charge McCarthy was running a one-issue campaign. There was a card that looked like a tax return, to remind voters of inflation and the president's pending request for a 10 percent income tax surcharge. Gans was pushing the essence of political pragmatism, the kind the candidate so often resisted. The dimming power of the ghost of Joe McCarthy was a crucial factor in the success of this strategy. For the first time in twenty years, the fact that a presidential candidate was perceived as an honest man became more important than his opposition to a war against Communists. Polls indicated many hawks supported McCarthy in New Hampshire. David Hoeh thought people who didn't know the candidate's position on Vietnam had "transferred to McCarthy their own view of the war. The New Hampshire voter was taking both the dove and the hawk position in the same sentence. They'd say, either we ought to win the war or we ought to get out. They didn't fully understand, or they didn't listen to McCarthy's position, so they said, 'Well, look, he's an alternative. We don't like Johnson. We'll vote for him.'"

"About ten days before the campaign was over," said Gans, "McCarthy for the first time would walk into a drugstore and draw a crowd. It just became very clear this was going to be serious."

Mary McGrory's first story on the "children's crusade" was titled "Going Straight in New Hampshire: The 'Hairies' Learn How to Help McCarthy." It appeared on Tuesday, March 5, just seven days before the primary. "What is phenomenal," she wrote, "is the reception [the canvassers] have been accorded by reputedly hawkish natives who are traditionally unfriendly to strangers." One reason was that the "hairies" were no longer so hairy: "Told at the door of the Unitarian Church in Concord that his beard would keep him from engaging the voters in doorstep dialogue, [the young man] asked for a razor and on the spot shaved off a four-year-old beard." She praised the "brilliant generalship" of Sam Brown, and reported Ann Hart's biggest problem: "trying to hold back an expected invasion of 2,500 kids for the last weekend of the campaign" when she could use only a thousand. Nevertheless, the column ended noncommittally: "Sam Brown makes no great claims for the effect of his young army," it said. "'I don't know whether we're just having a good time or [whether] we could make the difference,' said Brown. 'All I know is that we're the one thing McCarthy's got that nobody else in this campaign has or could get.'"[87]

Thomas McIntyre was the conservative Democratic senator who had practically guaranteed some sort of psychological victory for McCarthy by predicting way back in December that the insurgents would get less than 10 percent of the vote. Three days before the first big influx of kids, he went on the radio to declare that their intrusion proved McCarthy had no indigenous support in New Hampshire. "That was the last we heard from anybody in the LBJ camp about the kids," said Studds, "because they made such an obvious and immediate impact and success their first weekend here." Later McGrory ran into Governor King in Washington. "These kids, these goddam kids!" the governor shouted. "They are going to beat us!" Studds had never considered King particularly insightful, "but he seemed to have caught on that time."[88]

In fact, McGrory never wrote that McCarthy would win. "I just said this was something utterly new—and that is my primitive definition of news." Her scoop was a story waiting to be discovered; by focusing on a phenomenon her colleagues had never bothered to look at, McGrory became the first person to alert the public to what would be one of the campaign's most satisfying events. "It was simply wonderful," McGrory remembered many years later. "It had emotion, it had intellectual content, it had the unexpected, and it was surprising. It was a little glimpse of Athens."[89]

This was the last fortnight in 1968 when the peace movement remained united behind a single candidate. In this final period, when the movement was not yet wasting any energy by going to war against itself, it was coming alive in many places outside New Hampshire. While chaos continued to dominate McCarthy headquarters in Washington, independent operators were mining broad veins of dissent all across the country and coming up with powerful evidence of dissatisfaction with the president. On the fifth day of March, autonomous bands of McCarthy insurgents won three significant victories thousands of miles apart. In Minnesota, McCarthy men and women humiliated the Humphrey-Johnson forces by seizing control of the precinct caucuses in three of the state's five congressional districts. In St. Paul, sixty-nine nuns turned out and stayed late for McCarthy; Humphrey's people even lost the home ward of the vice-president. "It was the voice of the doves wanting to be heard," said Minnesota state legislator Alpha Smaby—the politician Lowenstein revered because she had been the first public official anywhere to come out publicly for McCarthy. This was the most brutal infighting Minnesota had witnessed since McCarthy and Humphrey had worked together twenty years earlier to push the far left out of the Democratic Farmer-Labor party.

On the same March day in California, McCarthy's supporters held petition parties throughout the state. The revelry continued past midnight into March 6—the first day it was legal to collect signatures for the primary. They needed 13,746 names to qualify their candidate for the June contest; they got 28,000, which also gave them the top spot on the ballot. And in Massachusetts, where the president had been unable to secure the services of a surrogate to represent him, Johnson refused to put his own name on the ballot. Since McCarthy was the only candidate left in the race, the president's default handed him seventy-two first-ballot delegates to the Chicago convention—including a senator named Edward M. Kennedy.

As soon as McGrory's first column on the kids appeared, the invisible campaign blossomed into everyone's favorite political story. Now Chet Huntley and David Brinkley and Mike Wallace and Teddy White and all the other "big foots"* of the media world were trudging through

---

* "Big Foot" was originally a nickname for Hedrick Smith, a former Washington bureau chief of the *New York Times*. Its invention is generally attributed to *Times*man B. D. Ayers. It rapidly evolved into a generic term for any senior journalist with prominent elbows. Also a verb, as in "I've been big-footed."

the headquarters they had shunned, searching for new angles and creating instant stars. Ann Hart found the surge of publicity disconcerting. "I was freaked out by being put on TV a lot," she said. "They kept turning the cameras on me, and I'd have to sort of pretend I knew what I was saying. *I* was on television. People were asking me questions and listening to me and taking me seriously." She was not flattered: "I felt very appalled about that. I had always felt that people who were on that screen were somehow different and superior to me. When I realized that in fact they were just as human as I was, I was very sobered by that. I realized that this world was really in the hands of people like me—and *that* was trouble!"[90]

THE campaign that just one month earlier had appeared to have nothing now seemed to have just about everything. One weekend it had three thousand student volunteers, prompting frantic calls to prevent further arrivals—and threats of blockading the highways.[91] It had Paul Newman, whose first visit to Claremont, New Hampshire, was advanced by Tony Podesta, a student from MIT. Podesta picked Newman up at the airport, and all the way into town he prayed "that there might be a few shoppers out that he could shake hands with." In the main square, they were mobbed by two thousand people, which Podesta was certain was the entire population of the town. The neophyte advance man had never seen such a large crowd in New Hampshire. With only one other person accompanying Newman, he had no idea what to do. "Most of them were either middle-aged women or teenaged kids, and all of them had decided they wanted to walk away from that day with a piece of Paul Newman's clothing and, while they were doing it, bruising me. So we kind of rushed Paul through the crowd very quickly, hid in the barbershop for a while, and snuck out the back door." Newman told the voters, "I didn't come here to help Gene McCarthy. *I* need McCarthy's help. The country needs it." Podesta thought Newman had a big impact on the campaign. "Until that point, McCarthy was some sort of a quack not too many people knew about, but as soon as Paul Newman came to speak for him, he immediately became a national figure."[92]

The campaign also had Tony Randall and Myrna Loy and Rod Serling, whom Ann Hart admired as "a very gentle, polite man who understood that external speediness as stimulation was fairly superficial." It had a sociologist who had done motivational reseach for product sales for large corporations who gave advice on the canvassing operation.[93] And it had Carl Rogers, a Vietnam veteran with a crew cut who came up to Concord from Washington. Rogers organized other uniformed Vietnam vets and put them on Manchester street corners. Their signs read, ASK THIS VIETNAM VETERAN WHY HE SUPPORTS MCCARTHY.[94] Quite suddenly, the campaign also had a lot more money. One reason it was able to explode out of nowhere was the lack of restrictions on direct contributions from wealthy supporters to their favorite candidates. In these pre-Watergate days, there was no such thing as a Federal Elections Commission or matching federal funds for presidential candidates; a handful of generous benefactors could practically finance an entire national campaign on their own. Thus, after lean beginnings, when the money did start flowing, it came in a torrent. Blair Clark (a descendant of the family that brought Clark thread to America) wrote out a check for $25,000 in New Hampshire. Martin Peretz, a young Harvard lecturer whose second wife was an heir to the Singer sewing machine fortune, was equally generous. And Howard Stein, president of the Dreyfus Fund, opened a financial pipeline from Wall Street that provided $125,000 for New Hampshire. Stein discovered early on that being a McCarthy supporter sometimes required unusual persistence. Displaying what was initially regarded as charming diffidence—and later identified as disastrous indifference—McCarthy ignored Stein's first five offers of support. "He was the only politician my wife and I had met who didn't remember our name," said Stein. "We rather liked that."[95] One McCarthy backer bet a bookie more than $10,000 that his candidate would get over 30 percent of the vote. He got odds of twelve to one—and gave his winnings to the campaign.[96] Gans estimated the McCarthy campaign spent $250,000 in New Hampshire, although Clark believes the total was $100,000 less.[97]

"We knew for about ten days before the election that something exciting was happening," said Studds. "We didn't know what. But people began calling in from everywhere. There would be the same kind of conversation. Ronald Callahan would call up from Laconia and say, 'I don't know what it is. I don't know what it is, but something is happening.' Marc Kasky would call up from Berlin, and people would call from Keene, Portsmouth, and Nashua, and we knew something was happening."[98]

"Senator McCarthy was doing a great job," said David Hoeh. "He was coming across beautifully. He greeted people perfectly in the streets. Everything was sweet: It was calm and gentle and there wasn't this maniacal rushing around."

"I don't know what I would have done with another fifty thousand dollars," said Gans. "We had radio commercials that were on every half hour on every station in the state for the last two days of the campaign. [They said, 'Think how it would feel to wake up Wednesday morning to find out that Gene McCarthy had won the New Hampshire primary—to find out that New Hampshire had changed the course of American politics.'] We had every billboard we could grab. We had coffee at shopping centers and town dumps. We had six pieces of literature for every man, woman, and child in New Hampshire; three mailings to every Democrat; two phone canvasses; and two foot canvasses for the entire state. We had transportation to and from the polls; a modicum of TV out of Boston, Burlington, and Poland Springs, Maine, plus Manchester. We had traveling movie stars; we had Galbraith-type stars; we had Polaroids for everyone who shook hands with McCarthy. We even bought some votes. I didn't do it, but there was money transferred to the town of Berlin, where certain leaders of the town were accustomed to paying poll workers. We had an organization of nuns throughout the state. There were a couple of stupid mistakes on the Johnson side, and we only needed one. We only needed the pledge cards, which demonstrated locally what people already perceived nationally—which was arrogance."[99]

WHILE Tet was transforming McCarthy from an unknown into a media star in New Hampshire, it was creating equal turbulence in Washington. Bobby Kennedy's reluctance to run for president was dissolving even faster than Lyndon Johnson's resolve. Inside Johnson's government, Tet was driving everyone to extremes: The generals had become even more eager to escalate the conflict; the doves, more anxious to end it.

The conflict within the administration over the course of the war, which would prove so important to the outcome on the hustings, remained largely shielded from the public until two days before the New Hampshire primary. Then, on Sunday, March 10, the *New York Times* provided the first detailed report on the war about the war within the government. The story—and its timing—were a godsend to the McCarthy campaign. This was the headline that, according to Defense Secretary Clark Clifford, caused a "national disturbance:"[100]

WESTMORELAND REQUESTS
206,000 MORE MEN, STIRRING
DEBATE IN ADMINISTRATION

Nearly everyone in Washington that winter interpreted this news as part of the same trend that had brought Clifford to the head of the Defense Department ten days before the story appeared. Clifford's appointment as secretary of defense was taken as the latest evidence of the dominance of hawks over doves inside Johnson's administration. This view was based on a combination of knowledge and gossip about the gradual change in Clifford's predecessor, Robert McNamara, and the timing of his departure.

For years McNamara had been one of the war's chief architects; during most of his tenure, he was a favorite target of the war's opponents. Gene McCarthy wrote in 1967 that it was McNamara's experience as the former president of the Ford Motor Company—"an industry in which [in this bygone era] the president of one of the big three could not, by the very nature of the industry itself, ever fail"—which had given him his blind faith in the power of technology and statistics. McCarthy thought this was the reason McNamara would never understand "that all the calculators and all the computers could not in any way measure the power and the strength and the willingness to die in a cause."[101]

But McNamara's position was much more intricate than his public pronouncements suggested. For several years he had been careful to give different impressions of his views before different audiences. To the president, he had been a faithful defender of the war effort; to doves in the press, he was a man tormented over the direction of American policy. One incident in particular illuminated the complexity or, perhaps, the hypocrisy of his approach.

In February 1967, Soviet premier Aleksei Kosygin was in London during a halt in the bombing of North Vietnam. British prime minister Harold Wilson was meeting with Kosygin in the hope of igniting peace negotiations between North Vietnam and the United States. When Johnson decided this latest peace feeler was going nowhere, he wanted to resume the bombing just as soon as a previously announced truce period expired on February 11. But one veteran diplomat demurred at this prospect. David K. E. Bruce, America's ambassador to the Court of St. James's, strongly opposed the resumption of the bombing while Kosygin was still meeting with Wilson. Believing this would be a gratuitous insult to the Soviets, Bruce sent a sharp cable to Rusk outlining his objections. The ambassador wanted the bombing halt to continue at least until Kosygin had returned to Moscow. He underlined his concern by marking the cable with words reserved for the most important communications: PLEASE PASS TO THE WHITE HOUSE. On this occasion Johnson heeded his envoy's request for restraint. The following day, Bruce got a warm telephone call from

McNamara. The defense secretary thanked him effusively: Bruce had provided just the right cable, just when McNamara needed it. Bruce appreciated the call, but his deputy later learned from an eyewitness how McNamara had really reacted when the cable arrived during a meeting with the president. "What the hell does Bruce know about bombing?" McNamara demanded. "We need to resume the bombing *now*!"[102]

In his memoirs, Humphrey writes that he "never heard McNamara dissent from the President's views" on the war during their meetings with the president. "Had McNamara begun talking privately to the President against the bombing, I am certain I would have learned" of it. But the vice-president was mistaken.[103] In the spring of 1967, McNamara was closing the gap between his posture with his dovish friends and the advice he provided to the commander-in-chief. In May he argued strongly against Westmoreland's latest request for new troops. The general was asking for between eighty thousand and two hundred thousand additional men. Partly because of McNamara's effort, the president limited the increased authorization to just forty-five thousand.[104]

By the fall of 1967, McNamara had lost all faith in the bombing. Now he was even directly doubtful about the outcome of the war. On October 31, he told the president that the continuation of his present policy would be "dangerous, costly, and unsatisfactory to our people." The next day he sent Johnson another lengthy memorandum. "There is," wrote McNamara, "a very real question whether under these circumstances it will be possible to maintain our efforts in South Vietnam for the time necessary to accomplish our objectives there." He concluded with three recommendations: a public announcement that the United States would not expand its air operations or the size of its forces beyond what had already been planned, a bombing halt before the end of 1967, and a new study of military operations to reduce American casualties and increase South Vietnamese responsibility for the war.*

The supertechnocrat made it perfectly clear that he no longer shared the president's public optimism about the course of the conflict. Johnson circulated his defense secretary's proposals among his usual advisors, inside and outside the government. Former national security advisor McGeorge Bundy, retired general Maxwell Taylor, Supreme Court justice Abe Fortas, Secretary of State Rusk, and General Westmoreland all opposed an unconditional halt in the bombing, though some of these men favored one or more

---

* Unlike Humphrey, McCarthy was aware of how McNamara had changed. In an interview with the *Miami Herald* in February 1968, he said, "McNamara realized about six months ago that the war was wrong, gave up, and handed it over to the generals."

of McNamara's other suggestions. But by far the harshest reaction came from Clark Clifford, the Washington lawyer who had been a close friend of the president's for twenty-five years. He asked in his written response to the president: "Would the unconditional suspension of the bombing, without any effort to extract a quid pro quo, persuade Hanoi that we were firm and unyielding in our conviction to force them to desist from their aggressive designs? The answer is a loud and resounding 'no.'" Clifford was contemptuous of the idea that the United States should announce it was stabilizing its effort. "Can there be any doubt as to the North Vietnamese reaction? The chortles of unholy glee issuing from Hanoi would be audible in every capital of the world. Is this evidence of our zeal and courage to stay the course? Of course not! . . . The President and every man around him wants to end the war. But the future of our children and grandchildren requires that it be ended by accomplishing our purpose, i.e., the thwarting of the aggression by North Vietnam, aided by China and Russia. Free peoples everywhere, and Communists . . . [are] watching to see if the United States meant what it said when it announced its intention to help defend South Vietnam."[105]

At the end of November, Johnson accepted McNamara's resignation; six weeks later he had persuaded Clifford to replace him. Johnson's insistence that McNamara was never fired but resigned because he wanted to become president of the World Bank did nothing to diminish the impact of the change. Within the foreign policy bureaucracy the ascension of Clifford sent a single, powerful message: Lyndon Johnson was staying the course on Vietnam. "The Clifford appointment foretells no change in the war policy," Mary McGrory wrote the day the White House announced he had taken the job. "He will now be administering in public a policy he helped to formulate in private. He is a hawk."[106]

What was the president's mood in February? "He wanted to win," Clifford said many years later. The suggestion was that McNamara had "gone soft on the war." The generals felt it was time "to apply more pressure, and McNamara wanted to apply less pressure. Johnson was terribly anxious to step it up and win it. You get into a sporting contest and you want very much to win—and this is a thousand times more important than a sporting contest. Fifty-five thousand of them died,* and Johnson wanted to justify that. He wanted to justify his whole policy."[107]

---

* By March 14, 1968, 19,670 Americans had actually died. A total of 58,021 Americans were killed during the whole war. [*New York Times,* 3/15/68, and *The World Almanac and Book of Facts* (New York: World Almanac, 1988), 338.]

In this context it is possible to understand why General Earle G. Wheeler, chairman of the joint chiefs of staff, decided to use Tet as an excuse to request a large increase in American troops—not only for Vietnam, but also for depleted American outposts all around the world. The military had never got the leeway it wanted in Vietnam; now it saw the chance to widen the war there. The joint chiefs were also increasingly concerned over the depletion of American garrisons outside Southeast Asia.

Westmoreland was the first person Wheeler enlisted in his effort to get more troops. Their joint strategy to escalate the conflict at this delicate moment had two fatal flaws: It put them on a collision course with a restive American electorate, and it destroyed their credibility with their civilian superiors. In one of the least noticed ironies of the war, it made them powerful, unwitting allies of the doves.

The first thing Wheeler thought he needed to make his request plausible was a lot less optimism from Westmoreland, who had continued, right through the Tet offensive, to be just as upbeat as Washington had always ordered him to be. Wheeler felt that without some impressively bad news, it would be impossible to pry more troops out of the president. So he began to encourage his man in Saigon to describe a situation that would require reinforcements. "The United States is not prepared to accept a defeat in South Vietnam," Wheeler cabled the battlefield commander on February 8. "If you need more troops, ask for them."[108] Westmoreland was slow to understand this signal. He replied that he could probably hold Khe Sanh, but in the event he had miscalculated, he would need "reinforcements to recapture it." That wasn't the tone Wheeler was looking for.

"Please understand that I am not trying to sell you on the deployment of additional forces," Wheeler cabled back. "However . . . I do not believe that you should refrain from asking for what you believe is required." Now Westmoreland was beginning to get the message. "It seemed to me that for political reasons or otherwise, the president and the joint chiefs were anxious to send me reinforcements," he said several years later. "My first thought was not to ask for any, but the signals from Washington got stronger." By February 12, Westmoreland was fully in step with his superiors: "I am expressing a firm request for troops, not because I fear defeat if I am not reinforced, but because I do not feel that I can fully grasp the initiative from the recently reinforced enemy without them."[109] Eleven days later, Wheeler was in Saigon to finalize Westmoreland's troop requirements. Wheeler's sense of security was not enhanced by a rocket attack on the South Vietnamese capital the night he arrived.[110]

As was so often the case during the war, one of the generals' biggest problems centered on a heavily publicized body count. Westmoreland had put the Communist attack force during Tet at sixty-seven thousand. He told his visitors forty thousand enemy troops had been killed, three thousand captured, and about five thousand had been disabled or had since died of their wounds. Impressive numbers—but if they were accurate they meant two-thirds of the enemy force had been destroyed. So why would Westmoreland be asking for more troops? The solution was simple: Wheeler's staff arbitrarily added South Vietnamese guerrillas, support troops, and new recruits to the North Vietnamese regulars—and came up with a new total that was 25 percent larger than what had been previously announced. Now, an enemy force of eighty-four thousand troops had been repelled.[111]

After two days of meetings, Wheeler and Westmoreland listed three "force package requirements": 108,000 men to be deployed in Vietnam by May 1, plus two roughly equal increments to be ready by September 1 and December 31—a total of 206,000 new troops by the end of the year. Wheeler claimed there was a "clear understanding" between him and Westmoreland that only the first increment was definitely intended for Vietnam. The others were to be used to reconstitute strategic reserves elsewhere—unless the North Vietnamese made new, unexpected progress. However, nowhere in Wheeler's report to his colleagues was this "clear understanding" ever mentioned, and nearly everyone in Washington believed all of these troops were destined for the war.[112]

Back home, still unwittingly, Wheeler began to accelerate his own undoing. This was his very sober assessment of South Vietnam after Tet: "The enemy is operating with relative freedom in the countryside. . . . His recovery is likely to be rapid; his supplies are adequate; and he is trying to maintain the momentum of his winter-spring offensive. . . . The initial attack nearly succeeded in a dozen places, and defeat . . . was only averted by the timely reaction of United States forces. *In short, it was a very near thing* [emphasis added]."[113]

McNamara had just three days left as defense secretary when Wheeler's report dropped on his desk. He opposed the troop request, which he calculated would cost $10 billion in the first year alone. At a meeting of senior Pentagon civilians, Paul Ignatius, the secretary of the Navy, asked why Westmoreland needed one hundred thousand new troops so soon after the Communists had suffered a terrible defeat. Army chief of staff General Harold K. Johnson explained that the Vietcong were "actively recruiting" in the countryside. Townsend Hoopes, the undersecretary of the Air Force, thought the whole episode was appalling. He suggested that the new fighter squadrons Westmoreland wanted would jam the airfields in Vietnam and provide the Vietcong with a tempting new target.[114] Wheeler delivered his report to Johnson on February 28. Clark Clifford remembers it as "so somber, so discouraging, to the point where it was really shocking." The new defense secretary thought his president looked "as worried as I have ever seen him."[115]

The following day Undersecretary Hoopes ran into Edwin L. Dale, the *New York Times* economics writer in Washington. They met on March 1 at the home of Congressman William Moorhead, a Pennsylvania Democrat whom Dale and Hoopes had both known when all three men were students at Yale. It was a reunion of Skull & Bones, a secret society of Eli undergraduates. A couple of days earlier the *Times* had reported "indications that [Westmoreland] was seeking 100,000 to 200,000 more troops for the war effort." As an economics expert, Dale was worried about the international impact continuing escalation would have on foreign investors, who were already redeeming their dollars for gold in record amounts. "If you throw many more troops into the war, you're going to have something really grave on your hands in the gold markets," Dale told Hoopes. To the reporter's surprise, the undersecretary agreed. He said that he was one of several Pentagon officials opposed to a big troop increase.[116]

The *New York Times* has traditionally fostered internal competition rather than cooperation. Particularly in the sixties, group efforts were quite rare. One reporter working alone on each story was the preferred practice. But for seven days in March, cooperation briefly predominated inside the Washington bureau of the *Times*. As soon as Dale reported his tip to his editors, everyone understood its importance. On Monday, March 4, Hedrick Smith was detached from the State Department, Neil Sheehan was relieved of his day-to-day duties at the Pentagon, and Max Frankel pitched in from his post at the White House so that they could all work together to confirm the story as quickly as possible.

Smith was the first to hear the figure of 206,000 from a friend on Capitol Hill; by Thursday, he and Sheehan had confirmed the crucial number with three separate sources. Sheehan thought the internal dissension within the administration should be the lead of the story. Top editors in New York disagreed. They wanted the number of new troops at the top of the story, and, as it usually does, New York prevailed.

The story came off the *Times*'s Manhattan presses late in the afternoon of Saturday, March 9. Within hours nearly every leading official in Washington was familiar with its content, because almost all of them were gathered in a single ballroom for the annual dinner of the Gridiron, the establishment club of Washington journalists. As the story made its way around the room, Ben Bradlee of the *Washington Post* grabbed Chalmers Roberts, one of his best diplomatic reporters; together they got enough confirmations (or nondenials) of the *Times* scoop to permit the *Post* to run a similar piece in its final editions for Sunday.[117]

That Sunday evening NBC News aired a Vietnam special it had been planning ever since the Cronkite broadcast. NBC correspondent Frank McGee began with the report from the morning papers that a new escalation might be imminent. He ended with a conclusion that was even more pessimistic than Cronkite's: "The war, as the administration has defined it, is being lost. . . . Laying aside all other arguments, the time is at hand when we must decide whether it is futile to destroy Vietnam in the effort to save it." As McGee spoke, *Newsweek*'s presses were rushing out 2.3 million copies of a special edition that echoed the gloom of CBS, NBC, and the *Wall Street Journal.* "The war cannot be won by military means without tearing apart the whole fabric of national life and international relations," the magazine declared in an unusual editorial statement. "Unless it is prepared to indulge in the ultimate, horrifying escalation—the use of nuclear weapons—it now appears that the U.S. must accept the fact that it will never be able to achieve decisive military superiority in Vietnam."[118]

Together, these three developments created a "dream weekend" for McCarthy volunteers in their final three-day sprint in New Hampshire. In tiny Claremont, Tony Podesta received "phone calls from kids all over the United States, asking to come—this is the fifth headquarters they had tried. [We were] telling them no, we have four times as many people as we need. We had four people on permanent doughnut duty at that point."[119]

On the eve of the primary, McGrory quoted Yeats: " 'All is changed, changed utterly' . . . McCarthy has become a political star of the first magnitude. Violet-eyed damsels from Smith are pinning McCarthy buttons on tattooed mill-workers, and Ph.D.s from Cornell, shaven and shorn for world peace, are deferentially bowing to middle-aged Manchester housewives and importuning them to consider a change of commander-in-chief. . . . A kind of reconciliation process between the generations has begun. . . . McCarthy is leading the children back into the political process and thus willy-nilly into communication with their elders."

In the middle of this exhilaration, McGrory included a single dissonant note. Rumors were spreading that Robert Kennedy was reconsidering his decision to stay out of the race for the presidency—and McCarthy's kids were not amused. "He wasn't there when we needed him," a Cornell senior told the reporter. "He's a moral slob. In our crowd, we're circulating a 'Dump Kennedy in '72' letter."

"Whatever else happens on Tuesday," McGrory concluded, "Senator McCarthy has taken the place of Robert Kennedy as the symbol of hope and change among America's bright children. The question is being openly asked whether Lyndon Johnson can put the Democratic Party back into the LBJ bottle. The top is off here."[120]

McGrory revisited Bill Dunfey, her original, indispensable source. "I have driven clear across the state," said Dunfey, "and I saw something I have never seen before. I've seen groups of young people standing at intersections, with the American flag, and their literature." Thousands of student volunteers "pulled" voters who they knew were McCarthy supporters from their foot and phone canvasses. They drove them to the polls, and they watched over the polling places. At the end of a very long day, they still faced an unusual problem: They had no idea what percentage of the vote they needed to claim victory in the primary election.

Normally, a politician requires at least a plurality of the voters to be recognized as the winner. But because the press and the president's surrogates had persisted in predicting a landslide for Lyndon Johnson, the normal standards for victory did not apply here. McCarthy just needed to exceed the press's expectations—that alone would make him the "winner." Reporters decided Governor King had set the upper limit of McCarthy's appeal when King predicted he would win no more than 28 percent of the vote. (Sam Brown predicted on a piece of paper that his candidate would get 19 percent.[121])

The reluctant contender did better than that: a great deal better. When all the Democratic votes were counted, McCarthy had 23,280, or 42.4 percent of the vote—*50 percent more* than Governor King had thought possible seven days earlier. Johnson got 27,243, or 49.5 percent of the total. But when Republican write-ins were added, the president's margin shrank to just 230 votes. In the ledgers kept in the state capital, the president had "won." Everywhere else, McCarthy was magnificently victorious. The results in the separate, simultaneous election for delegates to the Democratic National Convention reinforced the idea of a McCarthy victory: In that contest, the insurgents were the *real* as well as the *perceived* winners, taking twenty of the twenty-four delegate slots. Gans was counting votes at headquarters when Mary McCarthy found him. He was the person who had told her six months earlier she had to persuade her father to run for president. "You were right, kiddo," she said.

Hawks argued the election wasn't really a verdict on the war after fewer than half the voters surveyed by NBC in an exit poll correctly identified McCarthy's position on Vietnam. But every reporter interpreted it as a devastating verdict on the president. MCCARTHY'S N.H. DREAM BECOMES LBJ NIGHTMARE, read the headline in the *Boston Globe*. "There was a terrific euphoria, no question about that," said Blair Clark. "It had the marvelous, fresh, glorious feeling of surprise," said Marie Ridder. "You hadn't had to make the hideous decision between Bobby and Gene . . . and it was just the forces of good over the forces of evil—which was wonderful."[122]

Gerry Studds was in Bedford with the senator and his family. While everyone else remained glued to their television sets, McCarthy called Robert Lowell to rejoice with him. Later, Studds explained the essentials of their victory: "We had the senator in places where normally you would never send a Democratic candidate, because nobody had taken the trouble to analyze the vote. We could also see trends over the last three primaries, where the vote was consistently increasing, and we were aware of the importance of southern towns like Salem, where we were able to project a considerably higher vote this time—and, in fact, it was.* That southern tier of the state was growing tremendously fast. McCarthy did extremely well there. We carried Rockingham County, and we carried Stratford County in the southeast. We carried Salem. We carried Portsmouth. We carried Rochester. [Johnson's people] didn't dare call the White House on election night. They didn't have an inkling that Berlin would be anything other than what it has always been, which was a reliable organization town. And we had, literally through the efforts of this Yale graduate student, Marc Kasky, carried the city of Berlin by a hundred votes. And we carried Coos County— and they just couldn't believe it. They were absolutely stunned." Despite McCarthy's hockey game, and all those French-speaking volunteers, "we never broke through the French wards in Manchester. We lost the city of Manchester by more than we lost the state of New Hampshire. We carried the state outside of Manchester."

On polling day, the senator was in what was for him a state of near euphoria—mostly, in Clark's view, "because his enemies and critics were being shown to be wrong." Informed that three dead men had been recorded as voting at an urban polling place, McCarthy quipped, "Don't release it. It was the resurrection. They came back to vote for us."[123] When it was time to claim his victory, he snubbed NBC on the ground that its set was too elaborate; instead, he traveled to an unheated garage on the other side of Manchester to give David Schoumacher a much-wanted scoop for CBS.

---

* The final vote in Salem was 53 percent for McCarthy, 40 percent for LBJ—and twelve votes for Herbert Hoover. [Arthur Herzog, *McCarthy for President* (New York: Viking, 1969), 13.]

Only afterward did he condescend to pay homage to Huntley and Brinkley, on what he called their "throne."

It was a spectacular scene at the Wayfarer Hotel, where three hundred students cheered wildly as each wave in the tide of favorable results washed over them. For once McCarthy seemed genuinely enthusiastic in front of his throng, perhaps because so many of them felt better than they ever had before or ever would again. By leaving their studies to fight for the end of an immoral war, they had proved themselves more prescient than the press, more powerful than the president, and more courageous than Robert Kennedy. As McCarthy entered the ballroom, they chanted, "Chi-ca-go! Chi-ca-go!"—the city where the Democrats would choose their nominee. "We've really bridged the generation gap," McCarthy told Ned Kenworthy of the *New York Times*. Richard Goodwin, who had joined the campaign a few weeks earlier, thought the candidate went through "an almost physical change" as he addressed his supporters: "You could see the color come into his face."[124]

"People have remarked that this campaign has brought young people back into the system," McCarthy declared. "But it's the other way around: The young people have brought the country back into the system. . . . If we come to Chicago with this strength, there will be no violence and no demonstrations but a great victory celebration. If I had failed, it would have been a great personal failure because I had the most intelligent campaign staff in the history of American politics, in the history of the world!"[125] That night, his speech stimulated unrestrained exuberance. Later, as questions about his personal performance proliferated, these words took on the darker aspect of a premonition.

5

The Truth Comes Home

"The Commander-in-Chief answers him while chasing a fly
Saying, 'Death to all those who would whimper and cry'
And dropping a bar bell he points to the sky
Saying, 'The sun's not yellow: it's chicken.'"
— Bob Dylan, "Tombstone Blues," 1965

I THINK I can get the nomination," Eugene McCarthy said the next morning in Manchester. "I'm ahead now."[1] Then he got on a plane to Washington. When it landed in the capital, he was met by Jerry Eller, his administrative assistant. "Bobby wants to see you," said Eller. "He's going to tell you he's going [to run]." Kennedy had already announced that McCarthy's performance proved that a Democrat could campaign on "issues" instead of "personality." In fact, the contrast between McCarthy's character and the president's was probably crucial to the Minnesotan's success, but that detail did not help Kennedy's case—and no one else was focusing on it the day after New Hampshire anyway. McCarthy became bitter, angry, and, for a moment, unusually determined. The night before, Kennedy had telephoned him to offer his congratulations. The reporters at National Airport drained away the winner's joy: They peppered him only with questions about Kennedy. "The happy man was put away somewhere now and the black Irishman was very much dominant," Charles Bailey wrote in the *Minneapolis Tribune*.[2] "He wouldn't even let me have my day of celebration, would he?" said the senator as his car sped off toward the Capitol.[3]

There they were again: those upstart Bostonians who always behaved as if they were endowed with a divine right to the presidency. Richard Goodwin had told McCarthy the day before the primary that Bobby now wanted to get into the race—as soon as McCarthy agreed to withdraw.* Now McCarthy knew exactly how Humphrey had felt every time *he* had tried to become president—and how Johnson felt fighting off the effort to make Bobby his vice-president in 1964. The way the Kennedy brothers coveted the presidency was one of the biggest differences between them and McCarthy. Wanting to be president—or even *saying* he wanted to be president—never came easily to the man from Minnesota. Blair Clark believed that "if he could have been anointed president, he would have been happy to exercise the powers. He wasn't afraid to exercise the powers. He'd been around Congress twenty years and he saw what schmucks most of them were and he knew how the system worked."[4] In 1986 it was still impossible to get McCarthy to be precise on this subject:

> *In the best of all possible worlds, did you* want *to be the nominee? Did you want Lyndon to be the nominee on a changed policy? Did you want Hubert to be the nominee?*
>
> "Well, I wasn't sure what would happen. I felt—it looked to me that just the fact that there could be a significant percentage of Democrats who'd say, 'We don't want this war,' could affect the policy of Johnson—moderate it—and that he could be renominated. I thought he could be renominated, but on a different platform, a modification of his war position."
>
> *Did you think that was desirable?*
>
> "I did. Yeah. I thought that was probably the ultimate that we could accomplish."
>
> *Did you want to be president in 1968?*
>
> "Well, we really didn't start out with any such hope."
>
> *I know you didn't start out . . .*
>
> "But after we got all into it, it wasn't a question of wanting it."
>
> *Do you think there was* any *time in '68 when you said to yourself, "I'd like to be president"?*
>
> "Well, ah, I—I—I suppose I could give reasons for it."
>
> *It sounds to me like you wanted to end the war, but you didn't want to be president.*

* Kennedy had asked his brother to perform this assignment, but Teddy refused to tell McCarthy on the last day of his primary campaign. [Arthur M. Schlesinger, Jr., *Robert Kennedy and His Times* (Boston: Houghton Mifflin Company, 1978), 847–848.]

"Well, you had to be president to do it. So I—I, you know I was willing. . . . I said somewhere I was willing to be president, and they said, 'Do you want to be?' and I said, 'Well, I wouldn't say I want to be, but I'm willing—willing is a much stronger commitment than wanting.'" He laughed. "We can get into a little metaphysical or philosophical distinction there. But obviously I had the feeling I knew enough about government to put together a presidency and so on."

Oh, I think you were convinced that you could *do it.*

"Yeah."

I'm just not sure you were convinced you wanted *to do it.*

"Well, it didn't have any bearing upon what we did in the campaign. We tried as hard as we could."[5]

Many people who worked for McCarthy violently disagree with that last sentence. However, practically everyone believes there was *one day* in 1968—and probably *only* one day—when McCarthy *really did want to be president.* It was Wednesday, March 13, the day after his triumph in New Hampshire. Perhaps this time he was responding to the bellowing crowd, just like an ordinary politician. He had proved himself smarter than every other "expert" on the American electorate, and he wanted to savor the rewards. His distaste for the Kennedys was another important reason for his vehemence, just as it had been in 1960, when he relished the chance to embarrass them by nominating Adlai Stevenson.

McCarthy went to see Bobby in his younger brother's Senate office in the hope of eluding the press. From McCarthy's point of view, Bobby could hardly have been in a weaker moral position. In 1967 the Minnesotan had repeatedly offered to stand aside if Kennedy wanted to make the race, and Bobby had repeatedly demurred. Kennedy "simply didn't take seriously McCarthy as a candidate," said Allard Lowenstein, who was deeply torn between the two men but remained publicly loyal to McCarthy. "That was one of the miscalculations by [Kennedy and his people]—they didn't understand that the movement was much stronger than an individual, and that given the strength of the movement, even McCarthy's odd conduct couldn't kill what was happening. They never understood the depth of feeling on the issues, and therefore the depth of gratitude to McCarthy that he made the fight when Kennedy wouldn't."

Now that McCarthy had taken the risk and proved the president was vulnerable, Bobby was rushing in to seize the spoils. "Kennedy thinks that American youth belongs to him at the bequest of his brother," wrote Mary McGrory. "Seeing the romance flower between them and McCarthy, he moved with the ruthlessness of a Victorian father whose daughter has fallen in love with a dustman."[6]

McCarthy's perception of Kennedy's moral position was irrelevant, probably invisible, to the senator from New York. Kennedy was forty-two, the same age Jack had been when he announced he was running for the presidency. In Kennedy's mind, McCarthy's success had freed Bobby from the charge that he was running for president because of personal ambition, though only the people who loved him could understand this point of view. He was determined to carry on his brother's tradition, and he had never considered McCarthy qualified for the job anyway.[7] The Minnesotan made it clear he would not welcome any competition. If Kennedy insisted on running, he should confine himself to Pennsylvania, West Virginia, and Florida, and leave the other primaries to McCarthy. He even offered to serve a single term, implying he would cede the presidency to Kennedy after that. He said he believed in one-term presidencies. Bobby was unmoved. Afterward, McCarthy complained that Kennedy had just been "fattening me up for the kill."[8]

Kennedy for several weeks had been inching toward a decision to make the race—or ever since his brother had died, depending on how you read him. Early in 1968, Teddy Kennedy spoke to George McGovern several times in the Senate gym about his brother's prospects. "Be careful what you tell him because he's thinking seriously about going in," said Teddy. "I think Bobby would go if he got a little encouragement." McGovern got the impression that "Ted didn't want him to run, and was nervous about the fact that I and others were urging him to go."[9]

In mid-February, when he was still writing speeches for McCarthy, Dick Goodwin debated Bobby's prospects with Teddy Kennedy. Both men thought Bobby had about a one-in-five chance of winning the nomination, and, as Goodwin later reported to Bobby, "Clearly all your instincts push you in this direction. If you don't do it, you won't feel good about it." Goodwin had asked Teddy what Jack's advice would have been. "I'm not so sure about that," said Teddy. "But I know what Dad would have said. . . . Don't do it." After a moment he added, "Jack would probably have cautioned him against it—but he might have done it himself."[10]

Without specifically articulating it, the two men may have identified the main reason for this very unusual uncertainty within the family: 1968 was the first year any Kennedy had faced the decision of whether he should seek the presidency without the participation of the patriarch, Joe Kennedy.

It was true that a good deal of Joe Kennedy's history had been an embarrassment to his sons. His support of isolationism in the 1930s, his friendship with Joe McCarthy, his reputation in some quarters as an anti-Semite: All these were dubious assets indeed to young men seeking high office in the 1960s under the banner of the Democratic party. Joe Kennedy's extensive womanizing wasn't written about very much during his own lifetime, so it did not become a *public* embarrassment. But combined with the spirit of competition he instilled in all of his progeny, these flagrant infidelities produced the most corrosive part of his private legacy. Kennedy brothers who had been taught to challenge each other for first place in everything also seemed to end up competing with their father (perhaps unconsciously) for the title of Greatest Possible Philanderer.

Despite these very mixed blessings, the father's twin talents for pulling strings outside the family and imposing almost absolute discipline within it were crucial to its extraordinary run of political successes during the two decades before 1968. Certainly much of the disarray within the Kennedy family during the twenty years after 1968 was caused by two terrible assassinations. But the loss of control by the patriarch after his debilitating stroke in 1962 was just as important to its public decline.

On March 1, 1968, Bobby Kennedy telephoned Theodore White. Ever since he had written *The Making of the President, 1960*, a romantic account of John Kennedy's race for the White House, Teddy White had been the Kennedys' favorite political pundit. That book also made White the unofficial head of the unincorporated fraternity of American political writers, a post he retained until his death in 1986. All the Kennedys liked to ask him for advice, and White loved to provide it. Bobby opened the phone conversation this way: "Teddy, should I run for president?"

"Exactly that, and that's all," White wrote in his notes half an hour after the conversation. Knowing the value of a dramatic pause after such a dramatic inquiry, the author did not answer for several seconds.

"Teddy, are you still there? Teddy, are you on?"

"Yes," said White. "I'm here, that's me breathing. That's a hell of a question to ask me just like that." They gossiped a bit before White gave him an answer. "I'll tell you what I say to people who ask me about you," said the author. "Bobby would run . . . but Bobby is not a martyr, and shouldn't be a martyr, and can't win. The arithmetic of the convention doesn't add up. Bobby shouldn't destroy the Democratic party just to be a martyr."

But that obviously was not the answer Kennedy was looking for. "I sit here reading my mail and it's all about the sewage system in Dunkirk, New York. Shouldn't I be doing something more? My wife and all my friends tell me 'You got to do something.' And that's not so bad, it's what I hear from myself at five o'clock in the morning. The country can't stand four more years of this."

"Constantly in this conversation," White wrote to himself, "Bobby is saying: 'That man,' 'that man is bad,' 'that man can't run this country'— meaning Johnson all the time."

Then Kennedy told White something that would have astounded almost every antiwar activist in America: Richard Daley, the mayor of Chicago, the man who ordered his police to "shoot to kill" to quell a riot, the man who was Lyndon Johnson's warmest ally at the Democratic Convention in 1968 and who would become the most famous symbol of repression in America for his treatment of antiwar protesters during that convention—Daley had admitted to Bobby Kennedy that he *hated* the War in Vietnam. The mayor said he had asked the president "two and a half years" ago to "toss in his cards" on the war.* But White elicited from Kennedy the fact that Daley had not offered his support for a race for the presidency—and Bobby had never asked for it.[11]

INSIDE the John F. Kennedy Library in Boston, there is a small screening room where a movie of Bobby Kennedy on the stump in 1968 plays over and over again on an endless loop. In it the candidate tells a young audience, "President Kennedy's favorite quote was really from Dante: that the hottest places in hell are reserved for those who, in times of moral crisis, preserve their neutrality."[12] Right through New Hampshire, every McCarthy kid was sure a space inside that circle had been reserved for Robert Kennedy. But if that quotation really was his brother's favorite, it explains Bobby's compulsion to finally act, if not the delay that preceded it.

Now, in the week before he made his fateful announcement, there was one more hesitation on Bobby's side. There was also a final, futile attempt by two McCarthy men to strike a deal that would enable the two antiwar candidates to cooperate instead of compete.

During Kennedy's meeting with Daley in February, the mayor had suggested to him a possible passageway out of his morass. If Kennedy was really only interested in running because he wanted to end the war, why not

* According to one account, there was a personal reason for Daley's position. Several years earlier, he had helped a friend's son get accepted to Harvard. The young man did very well and graduated high in his law school class. Then he was killed in Vietnam. [Lewis Chester, Godfrey Hodgson, and Bruce Page, *An American Melodrama, The Presidential Campaign of 1968* (New York: Viking, 1969), 120.]

ask the president to appoint a commission to reassess the Vietnam policy? Theodore Sorensen, who said he came up with the same idea on his own,[13] mentioned it during a meeting with the president the day before the New Hampshire primary. Three days later, Sorensen and Kennedy visited Clark Clifford together at the Pentagon. Sorensen said that if Johnson appointed a commission and made a "public statement that his policy had been in error," Kennedy would agree to stay out of the race. Clifford rejected the idea out of hand. He knew Johnson would never publicly repudiate his policy. Kennedy agreed that was unrealistic; he said a weaker statement from the president would be satisfactory. Clifford hinted that if Kennedy was planning to run to change the president's position on the war, he might be in for a few surprises.

To an outsider, Bobby once again sounded extraordinarily arrogant, although, being a Kennedy, he may have seen this as a selfless proposition: offering to let Johnson retain his office in return for a new policy on the war. Yet it seems implausible that Kennedy believed the president might agree to turn his most important foreign policy decision over to a panel of outsiders partly of Kennedy's choosing. A few hours after their meeting, Clifford telephoned the senator to say the idea was out of the question. Perhaps the main purpose of the whole odd episode was to prove to Daley that Kennedy was taking him seriously.[14]

The day after Kennedy's meeting at the Pentagon, Blair Clark telephoned Teddy White. Clark had told White a couple of weeks before the New Hampshire vote that he was planning to quit his job as campaign manager; he was disgusted with McCarthy's refusal to give him or anyone else enough power to control the whole operation. After the New Hampshire triumph, Clark forgot about his threatened departure. With Kennedy's announcement imminent, he told White, "I must avoid any confrontation. My job is to delay or postpone the confrontation between McCarthy and Kennedy." White agreed.[15]

McCarthy's wife, Abigail, assumed that Clark was a spy for the Kennedys. According to journalist Richard Stout, she ordered copies of Clark's mail sent to her home so that she could "keep track of things." But Abigail McCarthy completely misunderstood Blair Clark. There was never any question of his going to work for Bobby Kennedy; Clark's very real affection for Jack Kennedy did not extend to the younger brother. "I genuinely did not like Bobby Kennedy," said Clark. "I didn't trust him, and I didn't believe in his conversion from Joe McCarthy staffer to the ultraliberal."[16]

In a year when almost every liberal, journalist and politician alike, was suspected of some sort of divided loyalty, no one aroused more doubts than

Dick Goodwin, a friend of Bobby's who had worked in his brother's White House, then stayed on for a time under Lyndon Johnson. It was Goodwin who had predicted back in September that anyone who ran for president on an antiwar platform could become nationally known within a month. When he arrived in New Hampshire after Tet began, he told Hersh, "With these two typewriters, we're going to overthrow the government."[17] During the last days of the first primary, youthful volunteers would panic every time Goodwin disappeared, thinking his absence meant Kennedy's entrance was imminent.[18]

Clark thought Goodwin had "sort of fallen in love with McCarthy—he was deeply interested in him. If McCarthy had said, 'You become the campaign manager,' I think Goodwin would have stayed, and to hell with Bobby Kennedy. Goodwin was terribly tempted by the big role. He had seen the difficulty of getting McCarthy to do the necessary things. But I think he was tempted by the idea that *he,* unlike me, or anybody else, could make McCarthy be a serious candidate. And I don't blame Goodwin. He had this double temptation, the ambition temptation and the puppeteer temptation— making McCarthy do what was necessary. He thought McCarthy in many ways was a much more appealing character, politically, than Bobby. I knew perfectly well that he would end up with Kennedy, because I knew that [finally] he would have the sense that he couldn't make McCarthy a serious candidate, and therefore he would be frustrated."

In the days immediately after New Hampshire, Clark and Goodwin shared a common goal: They both hoped to minimize the conflict between the two antiwar political aspirants. "We talked about what we thought was the right idea," said Clark, "which was to divide up the remaining primary states." Clark believed McCarthy should avoid Indiana and Nebraska, where there was little organization and even less prospect of success. On the Kennedy side, it was too late to enter Wisconsin, and some kind of accommodation with the McCarthy campaign might lessen the bitterness of his supporters toward Bobby. Clark and Goodwin felt Kennedy and McCarthy should compete directly only in California—and may the best man win. Clark telephoned McCarthy, and he agreed to meet with Teddy Kennedy if he would fly out to Wisconsin, where McCarthy was campaigning in the next primary.[19]

ON THURSDAY, three days after New Hampshire, Bobby Kennedy telephoned Al Lowenstein, who remembered the call this way:

"Al, baby, I've decided to take your advice."

"You S.O.B. Don't come around to me with your six-month-late advice."

"Oh, don't say that," said Kennedy. "That's what everybody else is saying. You can say something original. Think of something better than that." Then Kennedy asked Lowenstein to come see him at Hickory Hill, his McLean, Virginia, home, on Friday evening—the same night his brother Teddy was flying off to Wisconsin. After a brief hesitation, Lowenstein agreed.

Earlier on Thursday, Kennedy had gone to the Senate office of his friend George McGovern. To the senator from South Dakota, "Kennedy looked absolutely fatigued and run-out. . . . I remember being shocked at the deep wrinkles. He looked so much older than I had ever seen him." McGovern was "impressed with the anguish" and "self-examination that were going on, and the struggle." Also present were New Jersey congressman Frank Thompson; Stewart Udall, whom John Kennedy had appointed as interior secretary (and Johnson kept in place); and Lee Metcalf, the senator from Montana. All four men had served together in the House with Gene McCarthy, who normally attended this semiannual gathering but never made it to this one. McGovern told Kennedy he should run, but he "didn't push it very hard" because everyone else there thought Kennedy should get behind McCarthy. "I remember being somewhat startled at how strong Thompson and Metcalf and Udall were in urging him to back McCarthy," said McGovern.[20] Udall "got the feeling that it was like a Greek tragedy . . . events themselves had been determined by fates setting the stage . . . there was really little choice left."[21]

The next day Jimmy Breslin wrote a remarkable column for the *New York Post*. It gave his quintessentially Irish perspective on two very different Irishmen: "McCarthy, the lovely poet who tells us to walk together with him in the sunlight," and "Robert Kennedy, coiled and tight Gaelic doom running through his face." Breslin had traveled to Washington with Kennedy on the shuttle.

> "Are you happy you're doing it?"
> "Yes," he said. His eyes flashed.
> "The guy did a helluva thing, didn't he?"
> "Yes." A vigorous nod.
> "Could you have done this without him?"
> "No."

In Washington, Breslin found McCarthy in a hallway outside his suite in the Old Senate Office Building. "You know," said the Minnesotan, "I was up in New York talking to a lady, this is about a week ago, and we were at this party and I guess she had a couple of drinks and she said to me, 'Bobby Kennedy is what in Ireland we call a stinker.' So I said to her, 'Oh, I wouldn't go as far as to say a thing like that.' But today, well, I'll sort of think about what she said." McCarthy laughed.[22]

Kennedy spent most of Friday politicking on Long Island. At the Westbury Manor Restaurant he was picketed by a dozen high school students. One held a sign saying, DON'T SPLIT THE PEACE MOVEMENT—MCCARTHY FOR PRESIDENT; another read, MR. KENNEDY—PLEASE DON'T BE JUST ANOTHER POLITICIAN. SUPPORT MCCARTHY. Kennedy accepted some McCarthy buttons. Then he thanked the students for their presence but declined to comment on his plans.[23]

At Hickory Hill that evening, Lowenstein said he thought he shouldn't be there since he was supporting McCarthy. Kennedy was disturbed. "That's stupid," said the senator. "We're all doing the same thing. We're trying to stop the war and beat Johnson. If you can't stay here and eat dinner and talk about it, what does that mean about the campaign?" After that, Lowenstein relented. But he said he would continue to support McCarthy publicly.[24]

As the debate around the Kennedy dinner table continued, Teddy Kennedy was on an airplane headed west with Blair Clark, Goodwin, and Curtis Gans, to find out whether any accommodation with McCarthy might be possible. They were supposed to change planes in Chicago but they missed their connection. Clark, the only prosperous man in the crowd who never behaved like a poor one, pulled out his American Express card and chartered a Learjet so they could fly on to Green Bay, Wisconsin. When they finally telephoned McCarthy's hotel from the Green Bay airport around midnight, the candidate was asleep—and he did not want to get up. "I didn't ask him to come," McCarthy told his daughter Mary, conveniently ignoring his earlier commitment to Clark.[25] When they arrived at McCarthy's hotel, Abigail said firmly that her husband had gone to bed. Clark insisted that he be roused. When McCarthy came out, he made it clear that he wasn't interested in discussing any compromise other than the one he had mentioned in Teddy Kennedy's office a couple of days earlier—the deal that left Kennedy with Pennsylvania, West Virginia, and Florida, which was not a compromise at all. He wouldn't even let Teddy Kennedy remove a proposed statement of reconciliation from his briefcase.[26] "It wasn't very verbal," said Clark. "McCarthy said something like, 'I've got to go along the way I've been going.'"*

It was dawn on Saturday when Teddy Kennedy arrived back at Hickory Hill, depressed by his pointless pilgrimage to Wisconsin. Arthur Schlesinger had spent the night in the family home. Bobby Kennedy woke him at seven o'clock to discuss this newest nonevent. "Why not come out for McCarthy?" Schlesinger asked. "Every McCarthy delegate will be a potential Kennedy delegate. He can't possibly win, so you will be the certain inheritor of his support." Like almost everyone else in the Kennedy camp, the historian had missed the campaign's most recent development: Though originally drawn to their candidate by an issue, by now many of McCarthy's supporters had fallen in love with the man. But Schlesinger's misreading didn't matter. Kennedy greeted the idea "stonily."

"I can't do that," he said. "It would be too humiliating. Kennedys don't act that way." The debate continued with others for another hour until Teddy Kennedy told everyone to shut up because his brother had made up his mind and now they would only shake his confidence. His scheduled announcement was only two hours away. "He has to be his best at this goddamned press conference," Teddy said. Schlesinger knew Teddy was right, "but all I could think of was a conversation seven years before in the same house, when Robert Kennedy asked me to stop worrying his brother about the Bay of Pigs."[27]

The *New York Times* had a bit of pointed history in its Saturday editions: The Senate caucus room where Bobby Kennedy would make his declaration was the same one in which he had sat as minority counsel during the televised Army-McCarthy hearings, the ones that were the beginning of Joe McCarthy's undoing. Bobby, of course, had not chosen this location for that reason; he was there because it was the room his brother had used to make *his* most momentous announcement eight years earlier. Robert Kennedy went before the live cameras of all three networks to disclose what was very much his own decision. His wife and his sisters were with him, but most of his advisors had been against him just an hour before he said, "I am announcing today my candidacy for the presidency of the United States."

With his wife, Ethel, and nine of their ten children in attendance—and Sorensen and Schlesinger and scores of other New Frontiersmen spread around the room—it looked quite a lot like John Kennedy's announcement. Bobby wore a blue suit and a red-and-blue tie adorned by a gold PT-109 tie

---

* Eighteen years later I said to McCarthy, "My instinct is, the last thing you wanted to be was the latest in a long line of politicians to capitulate to the Kennedy steamroller."

"Yeah, yeah," he replied.

clasp,[28] the family version of the multicolored pins worn by Secret Service men to identify themselves to one another. He used the Kennedy verb tense (present, as in "I run because I am convinced") and a venerable Kennedy slogan: "I think we can do better." But the resemblance to 1960 ended as soon as the questions began. What had been a boundless affection between the Kennedys and the press was suddenly replaced by relentless hostility.

One reporter brought up "speculations that this is opportunism on your part, that McCarthy had the courage to go into New Hampshire while you hesitated."

"I don't believe that," Kennedy snapped. "I felt, and I think it was generally accepted, that if I had gone into the primary in New Hampshire, if I had won the primary in New Hampshire or had done well in the primary in New Hampshire, it would have been felt at that time that this was a personal struggle." Of course, with another antiwar candidate as the only other declared contestant in the race, to a great many people his behavior looked even more like "personal struggle," or personal ambition, than it would have if Kennedy had run and won in New Hampshire. But even if he understood that, Bobby could never acknowledge it.

Mary McGrory wanted to know whether he would stay out of Wisconsin if McCarthy asked him to—a foregone conclusion since it was too late to get his name on the ballot.

"Certainly," Kennedy replied.

"So he could have the victory for himself," McGrory muttered, loud enough for all of her colleagues to hear her.[29]

Kennedy kept repeating that "in no state will my efforts be directed against Senator McCarthy," a meaningless statement that elicited guffaws from reporters and an angry rejoinder from his rival. In Wisconsin, the Minnesotan fired back, "An Irishman who announces the day before St. Patrick's Day that he's going to run against another Irishman shouldn't say it's going to be a peaceful relationship."[30] From then on, McCarthy abandoned his affectionate references to JFK on the campaign trail.*

James Rowe, the chairman of the Citizens for Johnson-Humphrey, was just as caustic: "I'm going to watch with fascination Bobby's efforts to

---

* In New York, a city councilman running for Congress named Edward I. Koch was scheduled to appear on McCarthy's behalf on WCBS-TV—the day after Kennedy's announcement. The councilman was debating the lawyer Louis Nizer, who was LBJ's stand-in. Koch told his law partner, Victor Kovner, that he would announce on the program he had switched his support to Kennedy. "If you do," said Kovner, "Sarah [Kovner's wife] will never speak to you again." Undaunted, Koch went ahead with his plan. He won the primary and the election in November. [Author's interview with Koch, 7/25/87.]

convince those former young supporters of his, who are now supporting Gene McCarthy, that he's neither ruthless nor a political opportunist." Lowenstein thought it was Kennedy who turned McCarthy into a folk hero, "which McCarthy would not have become to anything like the degree that happened, if Kennedy had not entered" the race when he did. His timing gave "the general sense that all of the worst images of Kennedy had been confirmed." Lowenstein thought this perception "was a very gross misreading" of his friend, but he recognized its power within the public mind.[31]

No one was more brutal about Bobby in print than Murray Kempton. Later on, no one would regret this brutality more than the great liberal columnist himself; but his subject would never know that. In the *New York Post,* Kempton called Kennedy a coward who had come "down from the hills to shoot the wounded. He has, in the naked display of his rage at Eugene McCarthy for having survived on the lonely road he dared not walk himself, done with a single great gesture something very few public men have ever been able to do: In one day, he managed to confirm the worst things his enemies have ever said about him. We can see him now working for Joe McCarthy, tapping the phones of tax dodgers, setting a spy on Adlai Stevenson at the UN, sending good loyal Arthur Schlesinger to fall upon William Manchester in the alleys of the American Historical Association. I blame myself, not him, for all the years he fooled me."[32]

And no one was more depressed than Jackie Kennedy. The rest of the family drowned their doubts in the uneven euphoria of the campaign trail. Not Jackie. Several days after Bobby's announcement, she asked Schlesinger if he knew what she thought would happen to Bobby. He did not. "The same thing that happened to Jack," she said. "There is so much hatred in this country, and more people hate Bobby than hated Jack." She had even told Bobby her view—"But he isn't fatalistic, like me," she said.[33]

By bizarre coincidence, Jackie's feeling about Bobby was identical to Martin Luther King's fatalism about himself, and King had even used similar words when he told his wife of his terrible premonition on the very day Mrs. Kennedy became a widow. Like so many millions of others, King sat in stunned silence after the televised announcement of John Kennedy's killing on November 22. Then he said to his wife, Coretta: "This is what is going to happen to me. This is such a sick society."

Two and a half years later King retained the same foreboding. "How does the movie end?" asked filmmaker Abby Mann. "It ends with me getting killed," said King.[34]

* * *

THERE were two dramas that preoccupied Lyndon Johnson during all of March: what to do about the war and what to do about his presidency. Always after his biggest surprise, Johnson insisted that the decision he announced on March 31 had been made years earlier. He told Walter Cronkite it actually went back to 1955, when Joe Kennedy approached him about running for president in 1956. He declined the patriarch's offer, and it was then that he first realized he had "serious questions in [his] own mind about being President."[35] He said this in order to prove that no one but himself had influenced the decision he made about his future in 1968. However, he also offered an uncharacteristic caveat: He admitted that he could not be "very objective" about this question.[36] The strongest evidence he offers of his decisiveness is the fact that he informed a few friends in 1967 that he wasn't planning to run for a second full term. Arthur and Mathilde Krim were especially close to the president and his wife. "He told us in November 1967 that he had made his decision not to run," said Krim. "But we never believed him." A few months later, Krim, who was chairman of United Artists, was busy raising money for the president's reelection campaign.[37]

In his memoirs, Johnson wrote that his wife's position "had remained clear and consistent" since the spring of 1964: "She did not want me to be a candidate in 1968."[38] But Lady Bird's own diary belies that statement. According to Mrs. Johnson, both halves of the presidential couple remained deeply undecided about the future as 1968 began. In the third week of January, a couple of hours before he would deliver the State of the Union Address, the president came to Lady Bird in search of advice. He carried with him the draft of a statement that would take him out of the race for the presidency.

"What shall I do?" he asked.

She looked at him with a "helpless feeling."

"Luci hopes you won't run," said Lady Bird. "She wants you for herself and for Lyn and all of us. She does not want to give you up. Lynda hopes you *will* run. She told me so this afternoon, with a sort of terrible earnestness, because her husband is going to war, and she thinks there will be a better chance of getting him back alive and the war settled if you are president. Me? *I don't know. I have said it all before. I can't tell you what to do* [emphasis added]."

Sitting in the gallery of the House chamber, not even Lady Bird knew what her husband would say as he started to speak. "As he approached the end, I tightened up in my seat. Would he end with his statement? Did I want him to? Would I be relieved if he did, or if he didn't?" The president concluded without mentioning the election, and Lady Bird never answered her own question. Johnson said afterward he had reached into his pocket to touch his withdrawal statement—and discovered it wasn't there. That saved him from confronting "the problem," but he didn't "think he would have done it then" anyway.[39]

One of the things that divided Lyndon Johnson from his critics was their perception of Vietnam as a class war. The burden borne by black soldiers was so disproportionate in the mid-sixties that it became a major scandal within the Pentagon. In 1965 blacks accounted for 24 percent of all combat deaths in Vietnam. After a concerted effort by the Defense Department to reduce minority involvement on the front lines, that number dropped to 16 percent in 1966 and 9 percent in 1968. During the whole war, low-income youths were more than twice as likely to go into combat than the children of middle- and upper-income families. A study of Chicago neighborhoods found young men with little schooling were four times more likely to be killed in Vietnam than the better-educated.[40] The inequity was reduced slightly in 1967, when graduate-student deferments were eliminated, but any knowledgeable college man could still purchase a psychological deferment for $120. "There are reputable, antiwar psychiatrists who will put one through a series of personality tests to find some tendencies they can distort," a Harvard undergraduate explained in a letter home to his parents.[41]

But Lyndon Johnson did not share this advantage of other privileged parents: Both his daughters were married to military men, and to avoid the appearance of favoritism, both of his sons-in-law did go to Vietnam. For a long time, the president enjoyed mixing with the troops. During a manic, round-the-world-in-five-days tour at the end of 1967, he insisted on a stopover in Vietnam so he could talk with American boys—in between a funeral for Australia's prime minister, a powwow with the president of Pakistan, and an audience at the Vatican with the Pope.[42]

Two weeks after Tet started, Johnson authorized emergency reinforcements of 10,500 men for the war zone. On impulse he decided to visit the Army troops departing from Fort Bragg, North Carolina, and the Marines at El Toro, California. Then he spent the night on the carrier *Constellation*, which was on its way back to duty off Vietnam. "These visits with brave men were among the most personally painful of my Presidency," Johnson wrote. He remembered one soldier in particular: "I asked him if he been in Vietnam before. He said: 'Yes, sir, three times.' I asked if he was married.

He said: 'Yes, sir.' Did he have any children? 'Yes, sir, one.' Boy or girl? 'A boy, sir.' How old is he? 'He was born yesterday, sir.'

"It tore my heart out," said the president.[43]

On board the *Constellation*, two Johnson aides, Horace Busby and Harry McPherson, asked to meet with pilots who had flown missions over North Vietnam. The president was in an adjoining stateroom, and McPherson thought his boss heard "at least part of the conversation."

It is difficult to imagine pilots in any previous American war speaking as bluntly as these men did within earshot of their commander-in-chief. A young lieutenant with an Irish name asked for permission to speak. "Granted," said a commander. McPherson re-created the scene in his memoir, *A Political Education*:

> There followed a furious assault on the bombing program. Men were being asked to fly through the heaviest antiaircraft defenses ever seen, in order to bomb meaningless targets. "I've hit the same wooden bridge three times. I'm a damned good pilot. I know I've knocked it out every time. Big deal. It takes them two or three days to put it back. And for that I've flown through SAMs [Soviet surface-to-air missiles], flak, and automatic weapons fire. I've seen the god-damned Russian freighters sitting there, and the supplies stacked along the wharves. I can't hit them. It might start a wider war. Well, the war is too wide for me right now. And it's stupid." When he was through, other young pilots took up his cause.[44]

Johnson doesn't say how these experiences affected him as he approached the two most difficult decisions of his presidency. But they could hardly have increased his appetite for another escalation of the war. In March he was under tremendous physical strain, and it was showing. On the tenth day of the month Lady Bird noticed sties were growing back on his eyes: "first one and then the other, red and swollen and painful. I thought, wryly, that his life sounded more and more like the tribulations of Job." A week later she had a "growing feeling of Prometheus Bound, just as though we were lying there on the rock, exposed to the vultures, and restrained from fighting back."[45]

MEANWHILE, Clark Clifford was busy getting reeducated about the war. Almost alone among the president's confidants, Clifford had dealt with Johnson practically as an equal, partly because he had resisted all entreaties to join the government for such a long time. He was also one of the few LBJ intimates who was older than the president. The two men had known each other since Clifford was a young counsel to President Truman, the only other full-time job he ever held in government. Tall, handsome, and always meticulously dressed, he looked more like a French count than the wealthy Washington power broker he had become. His contacts were legendary; many of his colleagues considered him the most successful lawyer in Washington.

Clifford had received his last detailed briefing about the war the previous November, when he was summoned to the State Department as one of the president's "Wise Men." Also present were Dean Acheson, who had been Truman's secretary of state when American military involvement began in Vietnam; Supreme Court justice Abe Fortas, who, like Clifford, was one of the president's closest friends; McGeorge Bundy, who was Kennedy's national security advisor; General Maxwell Taylor, a former American ambassador to Vietnam; Arthur Dean, John Foster Dulles's law partner and an armistice negotiator in Korea; Douglas Dillon, secretary of the treasury in the Kennedy administration; George Ball, Johnson's former undersecretary of state; and permanent Democratic diplomat (and former New York governor) Averell Harriman.[46]

General Wheeler gave his usual luminescent assessment of American progress on the battlefield. Dean Rusk explained that the only problem was the public's ignorance of the American Army's remarkable success. "I don't believe one single Wise Man raised any serious question," said Clifford.[47] The next day at the White House the president was delighted with his counselors. "We certainly should not get out of Vietnam," said Acheson. Getting out is "as impossible as it is undesirable," Bundy agreed. Only as they were leaving the room did one participant finally erupt. "I've been watching you across the table," said George Ball. "You're like a flock of buzzards sitting on a fence, sending the young men off to be killed. You ought to be ashamed of yourselves." No one answered back.[48]

Now, four months later, for the first time Clifford was sitting inside Johnson's government. Like nearly everyone else, he had been shocked by Tet. "I had personal daily and hourly access to civilians and all the top military. That's when I really went to work. I was finding out, in constant contacts with the joint chiefs, that we had no real plan to win the war. All we were going to do was just keep pouring men in there and hopefully attrition would finally wear down the enemy to the point where they would come forward and say, 'Let's negotiate.'"

"Do you see signs of their doing that?" Clifford asked his generals.

"No," was the reply.

"Any signs of their pulling back, cutting down on their war efforts?"

"None," he was told.[49]

The cost of two hundred thousand new troops was put at $2 billion for the remaining four months of that fiscal year, $10 billion to $12 billion for the year after that. Clifford was told that the impact on the economy might include credit restrictions and a tax increase—even wage and price controls. "Will three hundred thousand more men do the job?" He was given no assurance that they would. Then he asked for the best estimate of how long this course would take. Six months? A year? Two years? No one could agree. Worse still, Clifford couldn't even find one man who was "willing to express any confidence" in his own guesses.[50]

Lyndon Johnson's most reliable hawk was undergoing a very rapid metamorphosis. "It all began to add up to the realization on my part that we'd been through a period of the never-never land in thinking that we were going to win this," Clifford admitted many years later.[51]

He began to look for allies inside the bureaucracy. They were remarkably easy to find. Deputy Defense Secretary Paul Nitze told his boss he was ready to resign rather than testify in support of a troop increase before Congress.[52] Paul Warnke and Phil Goulding, both assistant defense secretaries, and Nicholas Katzenbach, an undersecretary of state, were also skeptical. Inside the White House, Harry McPherson, the presidential speechwriter who had listened to the pilots' harrowing accounts on the *Constellation*, was becoming doubtful about the war as well. Johnson's well-known capacity for brutal retaliation made discretion a necessity. "We had to operate very carefully, and to some extent conspiratorially," said Clifford. "The expression was, 'Is he one of us?' I can picture that was the kind of word that went around in the French Revolution."[53]

In the Senate there were several surprising defectors from the president's policy. Richard Russell, the deeply conservative chairman of the Senate Armed Services Committee, told Clifford that America never should have got involved in Vietnam. Henry Jackson of Washington, another reliable supporter of the defense establishment, was also an incipient dove. "I would suspect the reaction [Clifford] got from us was decisive in his decision making," said Jackson. "If we wouldn't support [a troop increase], who would?"[54]

OUTSIDE Washington the political news was just as sobering for the president. Wisconsin had been a center of antiwar activity for years; McCarthy's campaign was beautifully organized there, and despite Kennedy's entry, the Minnesotan was high from New Hampshire. Yet the president still didn't seem to understand. On March 17 and 18, he made two more very hawkish speeches defending his war. "We must meet our commitments in the world and in Vietnam. We shall and we are going to win! . . . We ought not let them win something in Washington that they can't win in Hué, in the I-Corps, or in Khe Sanh. And we are not going to."[55]

James Rowe was becoming alarmed. On March 19, the head of the president's reelection effort told his colleagues what McCarthy's people had known for weeks: There was a distinct possibility that the president would lose the Wisconsin primary. "Somebody ought to be blunt to the President," said Rowe. He followed up with a memo that day to his unannounced candidate. *"The President* must do something dramatic (not gimmicky) *before* the Wisconsin primary. McCarthy and Kennedy are the candidates of peace, and the President is the war candidate. He must do something exciting and dramatic to recapture the peace issue. . . . A number of 'doves' called me to say they were against the President because of his Vietnam policy but were not resentful and bitter until the Minneapolis speech called them traitors. They said he should . . . realize the country is divided over Vietnam, and impugning their patriotism, as they say the speech did, merely infuriates them."

It was another turning point. The politicians inhabited by Joe McCarthy's ghost, instead of the people they were attacking, had become national pariahs. "Some people who support your Vietnam policy telephoned to say they thought the speech 'hurt our side,'" Rowe wrote. Johnson was still talking about winning the war. "The fact is," said Rowe, "hardly anyone today is interested in winning the war. Everyone wants to get out, and the only question is how."[56]

ON March 22, the president made an announcement that some of his associates thought might be a signal of a deeper change in his thinking. William Westmoreland would leave Vietnam in the middle of the summer to become the Army chief of staff. The president named no successor, but most people assumed (correctly) that it would be Westmoreland's deputy, General Creighton Abrams.

Only Rusk and Rostow remained unwavering in their support of the president's war. And while Clifford called Rusk "my most direct and confrontational figure on the other side," even the secretary of state was ready to accept some kind of bombing halt in March, though it wasn't clear what his motive was. The president "was very disappointed in me," said Clifford. "He thought that I was going to support his policy. It made him uneasy that I had changed. He had no doubt about my loyalty to him. We'd been close friends for twenty-five years. I was older than he. What bothered him was, when I changed, he knew that I had really, basically, in my innermost being, turned dead against him. That was unsettling to him, and I can understand how it would be. I upset him, just generally, all through that period. It put a terrible strain on our relationship."[57]

Johnson wanted the Wise Men to come back one more time to give their assessment. Harriman had been silent at their last meeting in the White House. He hoped to cap his career by opening direct talks with the North Vietnamese, and he wanted very much to be the chief negotiator. He was careful to mute his criticism in front of the president, but since December he had been working hard to turn Dean Acheson around, the man who had been his rival in almost everything, ever since college. Harriman was making serious headway. When LBJ summoned Acheson to the White House on February 27, he listened to the president's tirades for forty-five minutes. Then he excused himself abruptly. Walt Rostow called to ask what was the matter, and Acheson was incredibly blunt: "You tell the President—and you tell him in precisely these words—that he can take Vietnam and stick it up his ass." Despite his undiplomatic language (which Rostow does not remember), Acheson returned to the Oval Office. "The joint chiefs of staff don't know what they're talking about," he told the president. Johnson thought that was a "shocking" statement. "Then maybe you ought to be shocked," the former secretary of state replied.[58]

The Wise Men returned to the State Department on Monday, March 25, eight days before the Wisconsin primary. They spent the afternoon reading documents. At dinner they were briefed by the State Department's Philip Habib, George Carver of the CIA, and General William DuPuy, a former Army chief of operations in Saigon. The tone had changed dramatically since November. Like everyone else, these elder statesmen had been deeply affected by Tet. Habib described the corruption that permeated the South Vietnamese government, and said it might take five or ten years to achieve any real progress. With the glowing reports of the previous November still glaring in their memories, his listeners were stunned.[59] Clifford was greatly encouraged.

The next day at the White House, Lyndon Johnson lost his war. Sitting in the honored place on the president's right in the family dining room was Dean Acheson, the man who had persuaded Harry Truman to finance France's war in Indochina. Though he probably did not realize it, he was announcing the end of an era: the era of unceasing American support for the containment of communism everywhere in the world. He said Saigon and Washington both faced the same basic problem: a lack of public support for the conflict. Someone objected to Acheson's suggestion the United States was trying to impose a military solution on Vietnam. "What in the name of God have we got five hundred thousand troops out there for?" Acheson demanded. "Chasing girls? You know damned well this is what we're trying to do—to force the enemy to sue for peace. It won't happen—at least not in any time the American people will permit." Johnson was furious. "Somebody poisoned the well," he said.[60]

THE president had scheduled a major address on the war for the evening of Sunday, March 31, two days before the Wisconsin primary. As usual, no one was sure exactly what he was going to say. Clifford was worried by the absence of any mention of a bombing halt in the early drafts. The secretary of defense didn't know the president had already agreed to one, because he had confided that fact only to his still-hawkish secretary of state.[61] Clifford was working feverishly with McPherson to turn the president around: "The way he put it was . . . 'We're going to have to get our friend out of this,'" McPherson remembered.[62] But everyone knew the idea of sending 206,000 new troops was dead—even the president had abandoned it.

Three days before Johnson was going to speak, Clifford was shocked by the draft he was shown in Rusk's office. "I said this was the wrong speech, a speech about war." The first sentence read, "I want to talk to you about the War in Vietnam." Clifford wanted that changed to "I want to talk to you about peace in Vietnam." He prevailed.[63]

On Thursday, March 28, Hubert Humphrey addressed four thousand delegates at an AFL-CIO convention in Washington. The vice-president told the cheering throng that Lyndon Johnson would be renominated in August and reelected over Richard Nixon in November. Of the president's candidacy, Humphrey declared, "Only Mrs. Lyndon B. Johnson knows more about this than Hubert Humphrey."[64]

Clifford and McPherson sat down with Johnson and the reworked speech on Saturday. The session lasted for hours. McPherson said it was unique in his experience. There were "lots of arguments about almost every section of the speech," said the speechwriter. "We literally went over it word by word and changed many parts of it." Clifford questioned "any word that gave the slightest suggestion that we would reinstitute the bombing." It would be halted north of the twentieth parallel. Johnson told McPherson not to bother with a "peroration" because he had written one of his own.

MARCH 31 started early at the White House. Johnson's daughter Lynda returned from California at 7 A.M. The night before, she had kissed her husband, Chuck, good-bye at Camp Pendleton. Chuck Robb was on his way to Vietnam; within a few days, the other presidential son-in-law would follow. When Lynda got back to Washington, her father thought "the divisions in the country had left their mark" on her: She seemed "lonely and bewildered." To her mother, she looked like "a ghost." Upstairs in the family quarters, Lynda began to unravel. Through a flood of tears she interrogated her father. Why did her husband have to fight for people who did not even want to be protected?

The president "wanted to comfort her, and I could not." Lady Bird followed her husband back into his room. His face was "sagging." She saw "such pain in his eyes as I had not seen since his mother died. But he didn't have time for grief. Today was a crescendo of a day."[65]

By the time Lyndon Johnson started speaking on national television, at nine o'clock Eastern standard time, Gene McCarthy was already delivering a speech of his own: another dull speech, a speech that never mentioned the president. The Minnesotan was appearing at tiny Carroll College in Waukesha, near Milwaukee. There was a one-hour time difference between Waukesha and Washington.[66]

At 8:44, there was shouting in the back of the Carroll College auditorium. McCarthy had no idea what was going on. Reporters started charging down the aisle, "screaming like a pack of Eumenides," according to one witness. McCarthy's aides became alarmed; they surrounded the candidate to protect him from the mob. "What is it?" McCarthy kept shouting. *"What is it?"* Now he was invisible to the audience, inaudible to the reporters. Finally, someone got through to him.

"Johnson's not running!"

That's what the reporters had been yelling.

"The crowd was saying, 'You've deposed the President,'" McCarthy remembered. "You can go over and take over the White House now."

It was one of the most thrilling moments in American politics in twenty years, the biggest shock since Harry Truman defeated Thomas Dewey. James Reston was giving a speech in the field house at Rockhurst College in Kansas City. When he read out the news, he was astonished by the "tumultuous and prolonged demonstration." Teddy White rushed into the Milwaukee hotel room of McCarthy speechwriter Jeremy Larner. "Johnson snapped!" he said. "His nerve snapped!" Goodwin was way out of control. "We've won!" he shouted. "We've won! I thought he wouldn't fold for two months more." In college towns all across the country there were spontaneous marches by candlelight. Outside the White House gates, a few dozen activists gathered under a slight drizzle and sang, "We *have* overcome."[67] This was much more than winning a primary: This was the end of a president, and no group had played a bigger role in his demise than American youth.

Only McCarthy appeared unmoved. Placed before him was the greatest opportunity for impromptu oratory of his career, one of the greatest in the history of American politics. The reporters were there, and their cameras were ready. The candidate, however, chose not to seize this moment. He wasn't a Caesar, or even a Truman. Eugene McCarthy was the only David we had ever seen slay a virtual Goliath; but he behaved like a five-year-old who recoils in shock when he discovers he can inflict pain on his twelve-year-old brother by flinging an alarm clock at his head.

"As I remember," the candidate said later, "I didn't have much to say about it at the time."[68] In fact, McCarthy spoke only two audible sentence after he understood what had occurred. "It's a surprise to me," he said. "Things have gotten rather complicated." Then he left the stage.[69]

WITH twenty words Lyndon Johnson transformed American politics and—until the following Thursday—revolutionized the way millions of Americans felt about their country and themselves. Moments after announcing a halt in the bombing of most of North Vietnam, he declared, "I shall not seek, and I will not accept, the nomination of my party for another term as your President." The White House switchboard lit up like a Univac. According to the president's log, the first call he took came from Mayor Daley, who said, "We're going to draft you."[70] Happy calls poured in from the improbable to the sublime—everyone from Abigail McCarthy to Tallulah Bankhead wanted to praise him. Standing before reporters seventy-five minutes later, Johnson confronted a flabbergasted fourth estate. Their skepticism was understandable: None of them had predicted this event, and many of them realized that the news would hit front pages everywhere on April Fools' Day.

"How irrevocable is your decision?" a reporter demanded.

"Completely irrevocable," the president replied.[71]

On Monday the stock market jumped twenty points on the largest volume since Black Tuesday in 1929. Teddy White took Johnson at his word: "This is a time too tragic and dramatic for just a gimmick. He means it."[72] On Wednesday the North Vietnamese announced they were finally ready to start peace talks. Although the United States was sending an additional 13,500 men to Vietnam, the Communists were still satisfied because they had finally got the almost unconditional bombing halt they had been angling for.

For four days in April, joy took the place of anger in America as hope replaced despair. Perhaps peace was finally at hand, and the possibility of a restoration that could put John Kennedy's younger brother in the White House had never been more real.

"I felt that I was being chased on all sides by a giant stampede," Johnson told Doris Kearns. "I was being forced over the edge by rioting blacks, demonstrating students, marching welfare mothers, squawking professors, and hysterical reporters. And then the final straw. The thing I feared from the first day of my presidency was actually coming true. Robert Kennedy had openly announced his intention to reclaim the throne in the memory of his brother. And the American people, swayed by the magic of the name, were dancing in the streets."[73]

For American youth it was a stunning event. Until now, the vanguard of the Vietnam generation had worked hard to distance itself from the previous generation, with its own culture of music, drugs, dashikis, and long hair. Now they had come together with people of all ages who hated the war as much as they did to achieve what looked (at first) like a remarkably rapid coup d'état. For the first time since the height of the civil rights movement in 1965, activist, nonradical Americans committed to change had regained their confidence in the political process. For an instant it seemed that idealists from every generation might actually join forces to stop the war, preserve the peace, discard the god of materialism, and change the world.

But this surge of euphoria was pathetically brief. It would be extinguished by all the bloody scenes yet to come in 1968, the riots and assassinations that would blot out this amazing moment: catastrophic images that would outlast and then overwhelm the nascent idealism of youth.

6

The Chimes of Freedom

"After all, what does it matter to be laughed at? The big public, in any case, usually doesn't see the joke, and if you state your principles clearly and stick to them, it's wonderful how people come round to you in the end."

—George Orwell, 1948[1]

"One has to conquer the fear of death if he is going to do anything constructive in life and take a stand against evil."

—Martin Luther King, Jr., 1965[2]

I N 1968 no other public figure lived with greater strain than Martin Luther King, Jr. By the beginning of April, the civil rights leader was at the fulcrum of all the tensions that had been building in America for a decade. Clinging to the nonviolence that so many of his former allies had abandoned, he was denounced from both ends of the political spectrum. As he had been for many years, he was sustained by a powerful and explicit faith in God. It was this faith that nourished his belief that a life's content was more important than its length, and it was this conviction that permitted him to function in terrifying circumstances almost completely without fear.

He was twenty-seven in 1956 when his house in Montgomery, Alabama, was bombed for the first time. Eleven months later, a shotgun was fired at his front door. Five weeks after that, twelve sticks of dynamite were placed on his front porch (a defective fuse prevented an explosion). During a Harlem visit in 1958, a deranged woman stabbed him in the chest with a seven-inch letter opener. The blade brushed his aorta; if he had sneezed before it was removed, he would have died. (The wound left a scar in the shape of a cross.) Four years later he was punched in the face by a twenty-four-year-old member of the American Nazi party. Instead of returning the blows, King spoke quietly to his attacker until others pulled him away. In 1964 he became, at the age of thirty-five, the youngest man ever to win the Nobel Peace Prize.[3]

When he was six, he lost his first white friend after his playmate's father insisted they not see each other. For the balance of his childhood, he hated all white people. Eight years later King and his high school teacher were forced to give up their seats to white riders during a bus ride home after a speaking contest in rural Georgia. "It was the angriest I have ever been in my life," King remembered. As an undergraduate at Morehouse College in Atlanta he got to know white students through several interracial, inter-campus organizations. Only then was he able to conquer his "antiwhite feeling" and heed his parents' injunction to "love everyone."[4] After that, his conviction that the liberation of black Americans would be equally liberating for whites became a cornerstone of his philosophy.

King's combination of energy, intelligence, courage, and oratory made him the premier activist of his generation. For twelve years he managed to keep the plight of the underprivileged near the top of the national agenda, an achievement no subsequent black or white leader has been able to replicate. He was known as a student of Gandhi, but he stressed that "passive resistance and nonviolence is the gospel of Jesus. I went to Gandhi through Jesus."[5] In 1957 King helped found what would become the Southern Christian Leadership Conference, and from then on it was the base for everything he did.[6] Apart from an occasional vacation, he was on the road almost contin-uously for the next eleven years, fighting for equal rights for black people and poor people all across the country.

Just as black performers were bringing black and white people together in boisterous celebration on the dance floor, King was uniting more blacks and whites in the common cause of moral righteousness than any other American since Lincoln. To many young people coming of age in the six-ties, this combination of integrated audiences worshiping black music and integrated crowds cheering King's rhetoric made it look as if cultural and political gaps between the races might disappear within their lifetimes. Jeremy Larner, a novelist and screenwriter who wrote speeches for Gene McCarthy in 1968, remembered the mood this way: "When people sang and danced, picketed, protested and defied authority, it really seemed we might find a way to live happily."[7] The fact that the expectations of a generation were raised so high—then dashed so quickly—made the impact of the chain of disasters that began just four days after Lyndon Johnson's electrifying withdrawal unusually intense and long-lasting.

King's deep baritone was equally effective one on one, calming poor Chicago teenagers who wanted to riot, or addressing the hundreds of thousands who gathered around the reflecting pool in Washington to hear his dream recited in careful cadences. His speech to participants in the March on Washington, in the summer of 1963, was his first nationally televised triumph.

As he stood before the Lincoln Memorial, his voice echoed up and down along the Mall. "I have a dream," he said, "that one day on the red hills of Georgia, the sons of former slaves and the sons of former slave-owners will be able to sit down together at the table of brotherhood"—and everyone listened. "I have a dream," he shouted, "that one day, even the state of Mississippi, a state sweltering with the heat of injustice, sweltering with the heat of oppression, will be transformed into an oasis of freedom and peace," and his audience shouted back, "Amen!" "This is our hope," he declared. "This is the faith that I go back to the South with. With this faith, we will be able to hew out of the mountain of despair a stone of hope. With this faith, we will be able to transform the jangling discords of our nation into a beautiful symphony of brotherhood. With this faith, we will be able to work together, to pray together, to struggle together, to go to jail together, to stand up for freedom together, knowing that we will be free one day."[8]

Even those who expected to be put off were often quickly charmed. "I thought he would be pompous," said the novelist Jose Yglesias, who wrote a profile of King for the *New York Times Magazine* in the spring of 1968. "But he was a wonderful man; he had such a witty manner about him." Yglesias discovered that "interviewers seldom have to rephrase questions; he responds to the tone and level of the question but also, as if fulfilling a personal need, to implications that at first do not seem implicit in the question: an intellectual curiosity that gives the effect of total sincerity." The novelist noticed that "King laughed with his whole body, like a man who trusts his feelings."[9]

His friends said he was different from most other public men: They considered him authentically humble. He also had a boundless enthusiasm for life, and, like several other charismatic men of the sixties, he made little effort to control his private appetites. He was not a saint, and he knew it. One of his mentors, J. Pius Barbour, remembered that "he always said that Martin Luther King the famous man was a kind of stranger to him." King said, "I am a wonder to myself . . . I am mystified at my own career. . . . There's a kind of dualism in my life."[10]

His treatment by the Federal Bureau of Investigation was perhaps the single worst domestic scandal of both the Kennedy and the Johnson administrations. Many years later, William Sullivan, the bureau's former chief of domestic intelligence, told Congress that "no holds were barred" in the FBI's effort to "neutralize" King as an effective civil rights leader. The bureau used the same techniques against King it applied to "Soviet agents."[11]

King's nemesis was Sullivan's boss, J. Edgar Hoover, the FBI director who served—and often cowed—eight successive presidents. *New York Times* columnist Tom Wicker once dubbed him "Calvin Coolidge's revenge." Appointed in 1924, Hoover died in office forty-eight years later. He rose to power after directing mass arrests of radicals during the first "Red scare" after World War I, and anticommunism was the obsession he never abandoned. Long after Joe McCarthy's death, Hoover did more than anyone else to keep the dreadful McCarthy tradition alive and well in America. He used the bureau to accumulate scurrilous information about alleged subversives, then leaked what he learned to friendly congressmen and reporters. For half a century, he was the preeminent practitioner of what historian Richard Hofstadter identified as the "paranoid style in American politics." He was an unelected government within the government, a status confirmed when President-elect Kennedy and President Johnson each made the director's reappointment one of his first official acts. Before 1965 the director was not even required to consult with the attorney general (or anyone else) before installing bugs and initiating telephone wiretaps.[12] In 1968 Gene McCarthy promised to fire Hoover if he became president. To many of his supporters, that pledge was more radical than anything he ever said about the war.

Hoover insisted that King was a menace because two of his key advisors were or had been Communists, even though there was never any evidence that they used King to promote the aims of the party.[13] It was inconceivable to Hoover that anyone who spoke regularly to a Communist was not also his pawn. To placate the Kennedys, King said he would cut off contact with these two advisors, but he failed to keep this promise. King did not share the standard Joe McCarthy–fed phobia of Communists, and he seemed less intimidated by the FBI than the Kennedys were, even though John and Robert were Hoover's theoretical superiors. The civil rights leader "sort of laughs about a lot of these things, makes fun of it," Bobby Kennedy told *New York Times* reporter Anthony Lewis.[14] An aide to Bobby Kennedy testified before a Senate committee that the attorney general tolerated the bugging of King partly because he thought Hoover would torpedo civil rights legislation pending before Congress in 1963 if Kennedy tried to halt the surveillance.[15] Another reason for keeping the director happy was his intimate knowledge of all of John Kennedy's extracurricular activities —including his affair with Judith Campbell, who was also the mistress of mafiosi Sam Giancana and John Roselli. After Hoover confronted the president with his knowledge of this four-way liaison, Campbell's visits to the White House ended abruptly.[16]

A lifelong bachelor, Hoover spent most of his time, in and out of his office, with his chief assistant, Clyde Tolson. The director's biographer, Richard Gid Powers, concluded this was a "spousal," though probably not a sexual, relationship.[17] But Hoover's own idiosyncratic lifestyle never diminished his anger at any sign of "deviance" in everyone else. The evidence his agents accumulated of King's extramarital affairs infuriated Hoover: To him this behavior was a good and sufficient reason for his ruthless persecution of the civil rights leader. The bureau made multiple attempts to leak details of King's private life to the *New York Times,* the *Los Angeles Times, Newsweek,* the *Chicago Daily News,* and the *Atlanta Constitution,* among other publications, but none of them would print what the FBI offered. In the mid-sixties, the establishment press remained appropriately reluctant to report the private details of the lives of public men. Lyndon Johnson knew of at least some of these attempts to discredit King, but he did nothing to stop them.[18]

In 1964 the bureau contacted Francis Cardinal Spellman to try to scotch a meeting between King and the Pope. Hoover was astounded when the Vatican ignored his warning. "I am amazed that the Pope gave an audience to such a degenerate," he scrawled on one news clipping. Two months later he told reporters that King was "the most notorious liar in America."[19]

A few days after that, the bureau's campaign of character assassination reached its nadir: It sent King an anonymous letter threatening him with dire consequences—unless he committed suicide. His wife, Coretta, was the first to open the letter; enclosed with it was a tape of highlights gleaned from the bureau's frequent bugging of the activist's hotel rooms. The FBI's message said, "Look into your heart. You know you are a complete fraud and a great liability to all of us Negroes" and "a dissolute, abnormal moral imbecile. There is only one thing left for you to do. You know what it is. You have just 34 days in which to do this. . . . There is but one way out for you. You better take it before your filthy, abnormal fraudulent self is bared to the nation."[20] The letter was dated thirty-four days before Christmas. King immediately suspected that it came from the FBI, and he was deeply depressed by it. He was also disgusted: "What I do is only between me and my God," he told a friend.[21] The bureau was never able to rupture King's marriage or to get the seamier side of his private life into print during his lifetime. But the knowledge that almost nothing he did was *truly* private gnawed away at King. Like John Kennedy, he had a sexual appetite that could not be satisfied within the confines of his marriage, and like the late president, the risk of disclosure never led him to adjust his conduct.

King's very unusual refusal to alter his behavior after the bureau's threats was one reason Hoover hated him so much. Another was King's criticism of the bureau's failure to protect civil rights workers in the South. But there was also a more basic problem. "I think behind it all was the racial bias," said Sullivan, "the dislike of Negroes, the dislike of the civil rights movement. . . . I do not think [Hoover] could rise above that."[22] When Bobby Kennedy had asked the director how many black agents worked for the FBI, Hoover told him truthfully that there were five—without mentioning that all of them were his personal servants.[23]

The CIA and Army Intelligence also spied on the civil rights movement.[24] And King was only the most prominent target of the extensive campaign of intelligence, provocation, and disruption directed at civil rights activists by the FBI. In 1968 the bureau boasted of "3,248 ghetto-type racial informants" who provided it with a steady stream of information.[25]

THE civil rights crusade peaked in America in 1965, when a series of bloody confrontations between civil rights protesters and local authorities in Selma, Alabama, resulted in the deaths of a black demonstrator and a white Unitarian minister. Pictures of black and white activists being attacked by local lawmen—many of them mounted on horseback—galvanized the federal government into action. On March 15, Lyndon Johnson addressed a joint session of Congress, and for the last time in his presidency, he delighted all of his liberal constituents. Calling it "deadly wrong to deny any of your fellow Americans the right to vote," he urged the rapid passage of the Voting Rights Act, which remains one of the proudest achievements of his administration. Comparing Selma with Lexington, Concord, and Appomattox, Johnson called it another "turning point in man's unending search for freedom."

"What happened in Selma is part of a far larger movement which reaches into every section and state of America," Johnson said. "It is the effort of American Negroes to secure for themselves the full blessings of American life. Their cause must be our cause too. Because it is not just Negroes, but really it is all of us who must overcome the crippling legacy of bigotry and injustice." Then, pausing dramatically between each word, the president declared, "And . . . we . . . shall . . . overcome!"[26]

In this instance, the president's penchant for the histrionic served him well. Congress rose in what Johnson remembered as a "shouting ovation," and tears came to the eyes of Martin Luther King, Jr., who was watching the president on television. His biographer, David J. Garrow, called it "an emotional peak" for King, unmatched by anything that happened before or afterward.[27] He had earned those tears. More than anyone else, it was King who created the climate that inspired a president to recite the refrain from the protest song that became the anthem for the black civil rights movement and then for all the other liberation movements that followed it.

Only four months later, Johnson signed the voting rights bill into law. "Change, real change was on the horizon," Johnson wrote, "close enough to ignite hope but far enough away to increase frustration. For all the successes of the 1960's, Negroes were excluded from real equality." Despite real progress in the South, Johnson noted, "in many ways the Northern style of discrimination—subtle, unpublicized, and deep-rooted—was even tougher to break."[28] That was precisely the lesson King (and the rest of black America) was about to learn with a vengeance.

NINETEEN sixty-five also marked the beginning of the end of the liberal consensus in America. On the left, the impatience of radical blacks was drawing them away from the nonviolence King continued to preach; on the right, cold war liberals of all colors were appalled because King's conscience compelled him to speak out against the War in Vietnam.

By 1966 the antiwhite rhetoric from some leaders of the Student Nonviolent Coordinating Committee was rupturing the civil rights movement. Stokely Carmichael said he had never known a white organization he could trust. In June, during a march through Mississippi, Carmichael crystallized the split in the movement with a two-word slogan. "We're asking Negroes not to go to Vietnam and fight but to stay in Greenwood and fight here," Carmichael told a rally in Greenwood. "We need Black Power!"

These were just the right words to make the movement's white allies edgy and its enemies furious. King immediately recognized the dangers. Nothing came of King's effort to convince Carmichael to substitute the slogan "Black Equality" for "Black Power." Carmichael wasn't interested in Christian concepts of forgiveness—or compromise. To radical young blacks, a leader's willingness to endorse Black Power quickly became a litmus test of ideological purity, but King never accepted it.[29]

The division grew wider just as the movement's focus was shifting to the North. There, in the ghettos of New York, Chicago, Newark, and Los Angeles, the deprivations suffered by blacks were primarily economic, and therefore much less susceptible to rapid change than the segregation of the South. And the willingness of the federal government to spend more money on the poor was painfully fleeting. In his first State of the Union Address in 1964, Lyndon Johnson had declared "an unconditional war on poverty," but within a year, his attention, and the resources of the nation, were rapidly being diverted to the War in Vietnam. By 1967 the disparity between the American effort to fight communism abroad and poverty at home was enormous.

King's hostility to the war grew out of his opposition to all violence, but he was also deeply disturbed by its practical consequences. "Despite feeble protestations to the contrary, the promises of the Great Society have been shot down on the battlefield of Vietnam," he told a Los Angeles audience in February 1967. "We spend $322,000 for each enemy we kill, while we spend in the so-called war on poverty in America only about $53 for each person classified as 'poor.' . . . We must combine the fervor of the civil rights movement with the peace movement. We must demonstrate, teach, and preach until the very foundations of our nation are shaken."[30]

The decision to renew his public attacks on the war in 1967 was among King's most courageous acts. He was one of the very first leaders to make the rather obvious connection between the violence in Vietnam and the growing unrest in the ghetto, and cold war liberals bitterly resented him for it. The sermon he delivered at Manhattan's Riverside Church in April 1967 marked a turning point in the national dialogue on the war. "As I have walked among the desperate, rejected, and angry young men, I have told them that Molotov cocktails and rifles would not solve their problems," King declared. "They asked me if our own nation wasn't using massive doses of violence to solve its problems, to bring about the changes it wanted. . . . I knew that I could never again raise my voice against the violence of the oppressed in the ghettos without having first spoken clearly to the greatest purveyor of violence in the world today—my own government. . . . Somehow, this madness must cease." He urged everyone who considered the war dishonorable to seek conscientious-objector status.

At the same time he proposed a special kind of revolution, the idea at the heart of the unkept promise of sixties: "If we are to get on the right side of the world revolution, we as a nation must undergo a radical revolution of values. We must rapidly begin the shift from a 'thing-oriented' society to a 'person-oriented' society."

King's courage was rewarded with some of the most vitriolic attacks of his career. The *Washington Post* said he had done "a grave injury to those who are his natural allies," and "many who have listened to him with respect will never again accord him the same confidence." *Life* magazine called his speech a "demagogic slander," adding that King "goes beyond his personal right to dissent when he connects progress in civil rights here with a proposal that amounts to abject surrender in Vietnam."[31] Even a normally sympathetic reporter like *New York Times* Southern correspondent Gene Roberts was skeptical. He wrote that King's "outspoken stand . . . has dampened his prospects for becoming the Negro leader who might be able to get the nation 'moving again' on civil rights."[32]

In private, White House sycophants like John Roche gave the president a violent assessment. Roche called King "inordinately ambitious and quite stupid." The presidential advisor said the civil rights leader had "thrown in with the Commies" because he was "in desperate search of a constituency. Communist-oriented 'peace' types have played him (and his driving wife) like trout."[33]

To those who knew of the FBI's continuing interest in King's contacts with onetime Communists, his antiwar speeches seemed to make him unnecessarily vulnerable. Roger Wilkins was a Justice Department official in the Johnson administration and a nephew of NAACP head Roy Wilkins; he hated the war, and he privately defended King's statements. "I had developed by then a standard answer: To say that a black person can only talk about civil rights is just as ghettoizing as saying you can only live in a certain neighborhood. It's even worse, because it means it's only legitimate for you to have certain thoughts on certain issues." But others strongly disagreed. "To oppose American behavior in a war and to knowingly draw charges that you were soft on communism seemed to civil rights people to be total folly," Wilkins remembered. "My uncle thought it was total folly."[34]

Only a small number of spiritual leaders connected King's antiwar position to his status as a Nobel laureate. In New York City, Rabbi David

Margolies made the point forcefully: "To suggest that the recipient of that coveted award has no right to oppose our deepening involvement in a bloody and brutal war against people of color is to deny Dr. King that which is not only his right as an American citizen, but his duty as a man of God." If King were white, the rabbi said, "no one would question the logical compulsion of his simultaneous dedication both to the civil rights movement and the cause of peace in Vietnam."[35]

IN JUNE 1967 King restated another axiom of the sixties—"There is a masculinity and strength in nonviolence"—but fewer and fewer people were listening.[36] One month earlier Stokely Carmichael had been succeeded by H. Rap Brown as chairman of the Student Nonviolent Coordinating Committee. Through the summer these two men seemed locked in a competition over who could make the most inflammatory public statement. Massive riots leveled large sections of Detroit and Newark. The president announced the appointment of a national commission to investigate the disorders. Headed by two moderates, Governor Otto Kerner of Illinois and Mayor John Lindsay of New York City, the study group was immediately denounced by the left as insufficiently radical to tell the truth about the real causes of urban unrest. Carmichael said American blacks were organizing urban guerrillas for "a fight to the death."[37] Two days later, Brown told a Washington news conference that it was "morally wrong" for King and other moderate leaders to support the president's appeal for an end to violence. "Black people have been looting," Brown said. "I say there should be more shooting than looting. . . . The white man is your enemy. You got to destroy your enemy . . . I say you better get a gun. Violence is necessary—it is as American as cherry pie."[38]

In August the federal government reported that sixty-seven hundred rioters had been arrested during disorders in twenty-eight different cities over the summer.[39] The *New York Review of Books* outraged the establishment by decorating its cover with an explicit diagram of a Molotov cocktail, a wine bottle captioned this way: "Dirt + small amount of soap powder, Gasoline (from pump), Gas-soaked rag, Fuse (clothesline)." Inside the *Review,* Andrew Kopkind wrote that King "has been outstripped by his times, overtaken by the events which he may have obliquely helped to produce but could not predict. . . . Poor blacks have stolen the center stage from the liberal elites, which is to say the old order has been shattered."[40]

At the annual convention of the SCLC in August, King was visibly struggling with all these different strains. Meeting rooms were festooned with large placards declaring, BLACK IS BEAUTIFUL AND IT'S SO BEAUTIFUL TO BE BLACK, and a resolution that was passed unanimously called for a series of "Afro-American unity conferences" to include all segments of the black community—the revolutionary, the militant, and the churchgoer. At the same time, to pacify moderates, organizers made a special effort to attract white speakers, including Atlanta mayor Ivan Allen, and one-fifth of those attending the opening banquet were white.[41]

The rising tide of black militancy was having an equally dramatic effect at the opposite end of the political spectrum. Quietly, George Corley Wallace's campaign for president was beginning to take off. The diehard segregationist had become nationally famous for literally "standing in the schoolhouse door" to block federal efforts to enforce desegregation in Alabama. His tactics earned him so much admiration at home that he was able to convince the voters in 1966 to make his wife, Lurleen, the state's new chief executive. This made it possible for him to remain in the governor's mansion, despite a state law that prohibited him from succeeding himself. By the middle of 1967, Wallace had raised $1 million for his race for the presidency, and he had taken his campaign up North. Black riots were making working-class whites on both sides of the Mason-Dixon Line uneasy—and increasingly receptive to the governor's racist appeal (although by now he was always careful to insist that he was *not* a racist).

To make his candidacy credible, he had to get on the ballot in California, a daunting task because it meant convincing 66,059 Californians to reregister as members of his new American Independent party. At the beginning of 1968, the extent of the white backlash to black militancy was on the record: 107,000 California residents had formally joined the governor's cause.[42]

IN FEBRUARY 1968 King stood at the confluence of all these violent currents. Many of his former disciples were floating away on diverging streams of dissent; even to his friends, he looked more and more like a prophet without a constituency. Inside the government, the FBI had redoubled its effort to discredit him as soon as he renewed his attacks on the war. He was physically and emotionally exhausted, and it was becoming difficult for him to disguise his despair. "I can't lose hope," he told a Washington rally. "I can't lose hope because when you lose hope, you die."[43]

On February 8, there was another spasm of violence in the South, when black students at South Carolina State College marched to protest segregation at a local bowling alley. Highway patrolmen opened fire on the demonstrators, killing three and wounding twenty-seven others. Partly because of an erroneous news story—an Associated Press dispatch describing an "exchange of gunfire" that initially went unchallenged—the incident at first attracted very little attention in the rest of the country. Seven weeks later, King sent Attorney General Ramsey Clark a telegram demanding that the government "act now to bring to justice the perpetrators of the largest armed assault undertaken under cover of law in recent Southern history." Federal charges of imposing summary punishment without due process of law were eventually lodged against nine of the patrolmen, but all were acquitted.[44]

The civil rights leader's language was becoming more extreme, and he was aware of his own role in creating a crisis of expectations. "A kind of genocide has been perpetrated against the black people," he told a Miami audience, "psychological and spiritual genocide. . . . Bitterness is often greater toward that person who built up the hope, who could say, 'I have a dream,' but couldn't produce the dream because of the failure and the sickness of the nation to respond to the dream."[45]

On February 29, his analysis received corroboration from a most unlikely source. The moderate commission the president had appointed to investigate the previous year's disorders issued a brutal indictment of white America. The final report of the Kerner Commission was very much a document of its time: It used harsh language to describe the present and made predictions for the future that bordered on the apocalyptic. The product of a fierce debate between liberals and conservatives (led by John Lindsay, the liberals prevailed), the report received tremendous attention from the press. Then, most of its recommendations, like those of every other significant study of urban unrest in America in this century, were quickly forgotten.[46] In his testimony before the commission, Kenneth B. Clark identified the problem in advance: "I read that report . . . of the 1919 riot in Chicago, and it is as if I were reading the report of the investigating committee on the Harlem riot of '35, the report of the investigating committee on the Harlem riot of '43, the report of the McCone commission on the Watts riot. . . . It is a kind of Alice in Wonderland—with the same moving picture reshown over and over again, the same analysis, the same recommendations, and the same inaction."[47]

The day after this newest study appeared, almost every newspaper account began with this quotation: "Our nation is moving toward two societies, one black, one white—separate and unequal." The report also said: "Segregation and poverty have created in the racial ghetto a destructive environment totally unknown to most white Americans. What white Americans have never fully understood—but what the Negro can never forget—is that white society is deeply implicated in the ghetto. White institutions created it, white institutions maintain it, and white society condones it. . . . Discrimination and segregation have long permeated much of American life; they now threaten the future of every American." To white Americans drawn to George Wallace (and Richard Nixon's pleas for law and order), this was the height of white liberal guilt; these voters instantly rejected the notion that they were somehow responsible for the disorder inside black slums. Lyndon Johnson, offended by his commission's tone, ignored its recommendations. Gene McCarthy, disparaged by blacks for his inability to appear emotionally committed to their cause, became the first presidential candidate in 1968 to endorse all of the commission's suggestions.

The report attacked the press for failing to communicate "a sense of the degradation, misery and hopelessness of life in the ghetto" to its mostly white audience, and it called for the recruitment of more black reporters to improve ghetto coverage.* Without drastic action, there would be "continuing polarization of the American community and, ultimately, the destruction of basic democratic values." To prevent such a catastrophe, it recommended massive federal intervention: assumption by the national government of 90 percent of the cost of welfare, and changes in regulations that would help keep families together; the immediate creation of two million new jobs; and six hundred thousand new low- and moderate-income housing units by the end of 1969. The commission asked every American to adopt "new attitudes, new understanding, and above all, new will."

The civil rights leader was delighted by the report, and he announced that he would use its recommendations as the basis for his own new agenda. King was planning a massive demonstration in Washington for the spring, a Poor People's Campaign, which would attract, among others, three thousand blacks in mule- and horse-drawn wagons from the Deep South to a campsite in the capital. Because he was seeking nothing less than a redistribution of the nation's wealth, this campaign would be radically different from his previous efforts merely to desegregate the United

---

* Nineteen years later, *New York Times* executive editor Max Frankel ordered, until further notice, the news department to hire one new black reporter for every new white reporter.

States. As Jose Yglesias explained in the *New York Times Magazine,* "The substance of the demands is revolutionary for America: class demands dramatically expressed through other than the orderly democratic process."[48] But during the third week of March, King was distracted from the planning for the Washington protest by a confrontation between black workers and the white power structure in Memphis, Tennessee.

MEMPHIS was a proud but backward city in 1968, still faithful to the traditions of the Old South. Local boosters loved to brag that it had four times been named America's cleanest metropolis, but in March it could not qualify for such a contest. A strike by its mostly black sanitation force had left garbage piled high, especially in the black neighborhoods, which did not benefit from any of the pickups performed by a handful of nonstriking workers. The sanitation men were earning $1.70 an hour and wanted a raise, which the city was willing to give; but they also wanted recognition for their union and a dues checkoff on their paychecks, which the city was refusing to discuss (even though the white transit union had already won these concessions).[49]

King first came to Memphis to support the strike on March 20. A boycott of downtown stores in solidarity with the strike had reduced their business by 35 percent, and King was impressed by the unity he found among the protesters. "I've never seen a community as together as Memphis," he remarked.[50] Eight days later King was back for what was supposed to be a nonviolent show of force. He told Norman Pearlstine, a young reporter for the *Wall Street Journal,* "Discontent among Negroes and disappointment with the white community is deeper than ever before." He described Memphis as a "prelude" to the Poor People's Campaign he would take to Washington in April.[51] But five minutes after King joined the more than twelve thousand protesters in their march down Beale Street, someone shattered a window in Pape's Men's Shop, and the sound of breaking glass set off a chain reaction. King fled with his aides as the police waded into the crowd with tear gas and billy clubs. A sixteen-year-old, whom the police identified as a looter, was shot and killed. Sixty others were injured, and at least fifty store windows were broken; there were also more than two hundred arrests.[52]

King was distraught because a march he had participated in had dissolved into violence: This had never happened to him before. "Maybe we just have to admit that the day of violence is here . . . maybe we have to just give up and let violence take its course," he told his chief aide, Ralph Abernathy. To Abernathy, King seemed dangerously depressed.[53]

Two days later, he was jolted out of his doldrums by Lyndon Johnson's stunning withdrawal. Buoyed up by the surrender of the commander-in-chief, he headed back to Memphis to demonstrate that nonviolence was not dead. King would lead another march to prove that the last one had been an aberration.

On Wednesday evening, April 3, he spoke at the Mason Temple in Memphis. To his aides, the speech was both eerie and familiar. To the audience of two thousand, it was unusually moving, even for a man they had come to revere for his oratory. King recounted the stabbing incident in Harlem a decade earlier, and the surgeon's statement that he would have died had he sneezed before the blade had been removed. He recalled a letter from a schoolgirl who had been *so glad* he hadn't sneezed. "I too am happy that I didn't sneeze," said King, for if he had, he would have missed the sit-ins of 1960, the freedom rides of 1961, the demonstrations in Albany and Selma and Birmingham, his own speech in front of the reflecting pool, and this "great community rally" in Memphis. He talked about hearing "threats" and what might "happen to me, from some of our sick white brothers." His aide, Andrew Young, recognized the litany: It was the one his leader always fell into whenever he was preoccupied with death. Then the great man ended with the words so many would remember him by, words spoken in those soaring Baptist cadences that were his heritage and his trademark:

"Well, I don't know what will happen now. We've got some difficult days ahead. But it really doesn't matter with me now, because I've been to the mountaintop. And I don't mind. Like anybody, I would like to live a long life. Longevity has its place. But I'm not concerned about that now. I just want to do God's will. And He's allowed me to go up to the mountain, and I've looked over, and I've seen the promised land. I may not get there with you. But I want you to know tonight that we, as a people, will get to the promised land. And so I'm happy tonight. I'm not worried about anything. I'm not fearing any man. Mine eyes have seen the glory of the coming of the Lord."

Few men have managed such a mystical exit.

After a late dinner he went back to his room at the Lorraine Motel, room 306, a second-floor room that opened out onto a small balcony. When he entered he discovered that his brother, A. D. King, and some other friends had arrived from Louisville. Despite his somber speech earlier, King seemed cheerful now; he talked and laughed with his visitors until dawn.

Thursday he slept almost until noon. When he got up, he was in a volatile mood. He discussed the next march through Memphis, scheduled for Monday. Despite his fears that it might be marred by violence, he was determined to go through with it: "I'd rather be dead than afraid. You've got to get over being afraid of death." Then Andrew Young came back from federal court, where he had been trying to convince a judge all day to permit Monday's march to proceed. At first King seemed angry with his assistant for failing to telephone earlier with a report; but in a moment, his manic mood turned gleeful, and their argument dissolved into a raucous pillow fight.

That evening, just before leaving for dinner, he stepped out onto the balcony. He bantered with friends, who were waiting for him below in the courtyard. As he turned to walk inside to get a topcoat, a single shot rang out from a powerful rifle, pointed at him from the boardinghouse at 422½ South Main. "Oh, Lord!" someone shouted; then the ambulance seemed to take forever. King may have lived until he reached the operating room at St. Joseph's Hospital, but he never spoke again.[54]

IN MEMPHIS, the police chief was on television a few hours later. "Looting is rampant," he said. "The National Guard is coming back." In New York, John Lindsay went to Harlem, where he was astonished by the size of the crowds. He walked the streets for a while, until the scene became unruly and his bodyguards pushed him into a limousine that belonged to Percy Sutton, the black Manhattan borough president. A would-be looter shattered a plate-glass window in a Times Square shoe store; as the police took him away, a nearby crowd chanted, "Brothers, unite!" All night long there were scattered reports of violence from Boston, Winston-Salem, Durham, Charlotte, Jackson, Mississippi, and Hartford, Connecticut. The stories coming out of Washington sounded especially ominous.[55]

There, in the black section near 14th and U streets, N. W., Stokely Carmichael addressed four hundred people in the street. "Go home and get a gun!" he shouted. "When the white man comes he is coming to kill you. I don't want any black blood in the street. Go home and get you a gun and then come back because I got me a gun." There were murmurs in the crowd: "I got my gun—you got your gun?" Carmichael was brandishing what looked like a small pistol.[56]

A King disciple whose appetite for self-aggrandizement had disturbed his leader when he was alive moved swiftly to exaggerate their intimacy after his death. On Thursday night and again on three television shows Friday morning, Jesse Jackson wore a bloodstained shirt and told reporters he was the last person to speak to King. "I saw the blood on Jesse's shirt, and I know Jesse had not been near Dr. King," said Hosea Williams, another aide. Other witnesses agreed that Jackson was standing one floor below, on the ground, when the fatal bullet struck King on the balcony; Ralph Abernathy was actually the first to cradle him.[57]

By Friday afternoon, the fires and looting had spread to within two blocks of the White House, and riot troops had taken up positions on the president's lawn.[58] On Saturday, a few college students gathered outside the gates; their single sign said, LET US LIVE TOGETHER AS BROTHERS.[59] Elsewhere, ninety-five hundred federal troops patrolled the federal city. They enforced a strict curfew from four in the afternoon until 6:30 in the morning. Machine-gun nests sprouted on the steps of the Capitol and in front of the White House. Technicians installed new buttons on the phones of senators; pushing them produced up-to-the-minute reports about which parts of the city were still safe for travel. Four people were already dead in Washington. In Minneapolis, a black man vowed to kill the first white man he saw, then pumped six bullets into his neighbor.[60] There were two killed in Detroit, and there were others dead in Tallahassee and Memphis. The fires in Washington were the worst since the British burned the White House in 1814. On the drive in from the airport, the plumes of smoke made the capital look more ominous than Saigon during Tet.[61] On Sunday, Bobby Kennedy strolled through the rubble on U Street. When a squad of Army troops mistook the senator's entourage for a new crowd of demonstrators, they raised their rifles and put on their gas masks; then the crowd got closer and the GIs smiled in embarrassment. Kennedy connected King's death to his own brother's assassination: He told an aide that Lee Harvey Oswald had "set something loose in this country."[62]

THEY buried King on Tuesday in the city of his birth. Jackie Robinson, Hubert Humphrey, Aretha Franklin, Richard Nixon, Stevie Wonder, Gene McCarthy, Marlon Brando, Nelson Rockefeller—all came to Atlanta, and tens of thousands joined them there. Rockefeller subsidized the cost of the funeral and never publicized this contribution.[63] McCarthy didn't want to go at all—he relented only when his campaign manager insisted that he attend. "I told him he had to do it as a matter of public perception," Blair Clark said. It wasn't that McCarthy didn't care; he just felt

John Kennedy in 1960;
Robert Kennedy in 1968.
Each man was forty-two
when he announced for the
presidency.

January 31: the Tet offensive. An American soldier on the balcony of the American embassy after the Vietcong had penetrated its perimeter.

A wounded Marine being evacuated from Hué and a ten-year-old "Little Tiger," who was praised for killing two Vietcong—his mother and his teacher.

Joy in New Hampshire: Eugene McCarthy savors a brief moment of euphoria after his moral victory in the first Democratic primary of the year. When Republican write-ins were counted, McCarthy had just 230 fewer votes than Lyndon Johnson.

Two and a half weeks later, on March 31, a happy Bobby Kennedy arrives home at his New York apartment—a few hours after Johnson stunned the nation by abandoning the race for the presidency.

Martin Luther King, Jr., on April 3, the day before his assassination, and J. Edgar Hoover with the Kennedys and Lyndon Johnson. The harassment of King by the FBI was perhaps the single worst domestic scandal of the Kennedy and Johnson administrations.

Bobby and Ethel Kennedy offer their condolences to Coretta Scott King.

King had briefly admired Richard Nixon when he was vice-president, but in 1968 the Republican candidate for the presidency was jeered with cries of "politicking" when he attended the slain civil rights leader's funeral.

McCarthy arriving at King's funeral: The Minnesotan came only because his campaign manager insisted on it.

One of the only photographs of McCarthy and Kennedy together in 1968, inside the Ebenezer Baptist Church during King's funeral.

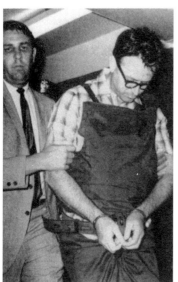

King's assassin, James Earl Ray, arriving in Memphis six weeks after he was captured at Heathrow Airport in London. Shelby County sheriff William Morris accompanies him.

April 5: Arson hits the nation's capital. After King's death, 65,000 troops were needed to put down disturbances in 130 cities. The fires in Washington were the worst since the War of 1812.

April at Columbia Universty was marked by student riots and sit-ins. The sometimes playful mood of the first days degenerated into violence as police were sent in to end the demonstrations.

April 25: Two days after students began the occupation of Columbia buildings, SDS leader Mark Rudd meets the press outside Low Library.

Kennedy in Indiana: McCarthy's campaign had Paul Newman (and his chicken bones), but Kennedy beat the Minnesotan in the primary.

May 31: Kennedy campaigns in Oakland on the eve of his only debate with McCarthy. Adoring fans stole his cuff links and squeezed his hands until they bled.

(Top) When Kennedy won the California primary, he told Kenny O'Donnell, "I feel now for the first time that I've shaken off the shadow of my brother. I feel I made it on my own."

(Middle) Claiming victory at the Ambassador Hotel: CBS had already gone off the air, but many people thought it was one of the best speeches Kennedy had ever given.

(Right) His last words were to an ambulance attendant. "Please don't," he said. "Don't lift me."

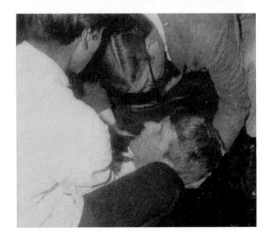

June 5: McCarthy arriving at Good Samaritan Hospital, where Kennedy would die a few hours later.

Teddy delivered a magnificent eulogy; he sounded more like Jack than Bobby had ever been able to.

Andy Warhol being taken to the hospital. The day before Kennedy was shot, Warhal had been gravely wounded by Valerie Solanas, the founder of the Society for Cutting Up Men (SCUM). Solanas fired two .32-caliber bullets into Warhol's stomach, but the artist recovered.

June 6: a Kennedy campaign office in Manhattan.

January 19: Bob Dylan makes his first concert appearance since his motorcycle accident in 1966. The Carnegie Hall tribute to Woody Guthrie ended rumors that Dylan had died—or suffered permanent brain damage. Rick Danko has his back to the camera; Robbie Robertson is at the right.

The Beatles in 1968. Six years earlier they had come "out of the sticks" to "take over the world."

July 29: Janis Joplin performing with Big Brother and the Holding Company at Newport. She was the hit of the folk festival.

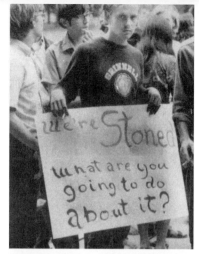

(Top left) Hippies indulging in a tribal rite in Manhattan.

(Top right) A student protest at Grinnell College (Grinnell, Iowa).

(Above) *Hair* gave Broadway audiences their first experience with full-frontal nudity.

(Right) July 28: The vice-president tries to be hip on ABC's *It's Happening*.

(Top) August 26: McCarthy comes to Chicago. His campaign was dead on arrival.

(Left) Paul Newman and Arthur Miller were both McCarthy delegates in the Connecticut delegation to the Democratic National Convention.

(Right) Student protesters in Chicago. Mayor Richard Daley hated the War in Vietnam, but almost no one knew that.

September 23: Antiwar demonstrators trying to drown out the vice-president in Cleveland. A week later, after his Salt Lake City speech, the heckling suddenly ended.

October 20: the final shock. Barbara Walters knew Jackie Kennedy was about to marry Aristotle Onassis, but NBC would not believe it—and refused to broadcast her scoop.

that most people would be there for all the wrong reasons. Many were outraged when the president failed to appear. Johnson blamed the decision on the Secret Service, which he said had warned him the trip would be too dangerous to make.[64]

The Kennedys—Bobby and Teddy—did go, and though she wasn't wearing a veil, Jackie added by her presence a terrible feeling of déjà vu. The crowd surged toward her, and she had to be pulled through the narrow door of the Ebenezer Baptist Church, the church where King had shared the pulpit with his father, the church founded by his grandfather. Nixon was jeered outside with cries of "politicking." Coretta King was dressed just like Jackie: Both wore black silk suits. Inside the church, McCarthy sat just behind Bobby Kennedy. In one of the few wire-service photos taken of the two of them together, McCarthy looked about seventy; Bobby, closer to twenty-five.[65]

King "spoke" at his own funeral; his widow insisted on it. His words flowed out of loudspeakers, the words from one of his final sermons in this same church, a sermon he had delivered two months earlier. The impact was brutal, overwhelming. "If any of you are around when I have to meet my day," the disembodied voice declared, "I don't want a long funeral. And if you get somebody to deliver the eulogy, tell him not to talk too long."

Reporters said many wept as King's words continued. "I want you to be able to say that day that I did try to feed the hungry. I want you to be able to say that day that I did try in my life to clothe the naked. I want you to say on that day that I did try in my life to visit those who were in prison. And I want you to say that I tried to love and serve humanity." He was thirty-nine when he died.

The rites took all day. The church service began at 10:43, and it was past noon before the casket was carried outside. There the mourners gathered in what Homer Bigart of the *New York Times* called "one of the strangest corteges ever seen in the land." The next day there was a huge picture of the procession on the paper's front page, nine and a half inches tall and almost seven inches wide. It showed a crowd surrounding a crude farm wagon pulled by two Georgia mules. On top of the wagon, his body was sheltered inside a gleaming African mahogany casket.

From his church they took him across town to his alma mater, Morehouse College. On the way, they sang "We Shall Overcome," the anthem King had learned from white folk singer Pete Seeger.[66] American and Georgia flags flew at half-staff outside the state capitol. Governor Lester Maddox had objected, but the secretary of state, Ben Fortson, had insisted on it. Outdoors at Morehouse, they held another service, and many fainted in the eighty-degree heat. Finally, at 5:30, he was buried at South View Cemetery, a modest hillside graveyard founded in 1866 by six blacks fed up with carrying their dead through the rear gates of the municipal cemetery.[67]

THE riots continued after his body was in the ground; Pittsburgh, Newark, Hartford, Trenton, and Baltimore all suffered serious damage. Maryland governor Spiro T. Agnew summoned middle-class blacks to his office and accused them of being part of a conspiracy behind the Baltimore riots. Richard Nixon was impressed with Agnew's toughness. Troops and National Guardsmen were everywhere—fifteen thousand in Washington, two thousand in Wilmington, four thousand in Pittsburgh, six hundred in Columbia, South Carolina. As the disorders spread from city to city, the White House worried it might actually run out of troops.[68] Even in New York, where Lindsay was praised for keeping the streets calm, there was more than $4 million in damages, and merchants complained that City Hall had covered up the extent of their losses.[69] In all, sixty-five thousand troops saw riot duty and 130 cities were struck by disturbances.

After Washington—where troop commanders were relieved that fashionable Georgetown emerged unscathed—Chicago was hit hardest.[70] Mayor Richard Daley was furious. Eleven days after the riots began, Daley stunned the nation by ordering the police to shoot to kill arsonists and "shoot to maim or cripple looters." The crime of arson, said the mayor, "is to me the most hideous and worst crime of any and should be dealt with in this fashion. I was disappointed to learn that every policeman out on the beat was to use his own discretion."[71] Less than two weeks after King's death, the polarization between ghetto blacks and middle-class whites already seemed almost complete. "A fascist's response," Jesse Jackson said of Daley's dictum. "The mayor may have a killing program for the dreamers, but he has no program that can kill the dreams."[72] The day before Daley's press conference, the city of Memphis had caved in: At last the sanitation men had won their strike.

When the riots finally ended everywhere, thirty-nine people were dead and almost twenty thousand had been arrested. All but five of the dead were black; fifteen were twenty-one or younger, including eleven-month-old Everett Austin, burned to death in his crib in a third-floor apartment on

Chicago's West Side. King's dream of a black and white coalition to push the poor out of their tenements and into the mainstream of American life had perished in the flames that scorched so many black ghettos; and the joy Lyndon Johnson had produced with his startling speech was quickly disappearing. But the drive to change America was still alive.[73]

7

Tears of Rage

"Our young people, in disturbing numbers, appear to reject all forms of authority, from whatever source derived, and they have taken refuge in a turbulent and inchoate nihilism whose sole objectives are destruction. I know of no time in our history when the gap between the generations has been wider or more potentially dangerous."
—Columbia University president Grayson Kirk,
April 12, 1968

"Grayson, I doubt if you will understand any of this . . . you call for order and respect for authority; we call for justice, freedom, and social- ism. There is only one thing left to say. It may sound nihilistic to you, since it is the opening shot in a war of liberation. I'll use the words of LeRoi Jones, whom I'm sure you don't like a whole lot: 'Up against the wall, motherfucker, this is a stick-up.'"
—Open letter to Grayson Kirk from Mark Rudd,
chairman of the Columbia chapter
of Students for a Democratic Society,
April 22, 1968[1]

AROUND the world in 1968, a loud, angry, and minutely scrutinized minority of middle-class kids emulated American blacks by taking their grievances into the streets. In the spring, young people on the left were laying siege to the established order, from Paris to Beijing. Italian students closed a dozen universities after demanding a greater voice in their administration and more assistance for needy students. In France, Daniel Cohn-Bendit, better known as "Dany the Red," spearheaded Sorbonne protests against overcrowding and the segregation of the sexes, while West Berlin's "Red" Rudi Dutschke led waves of protest against Axel Springer, a prosperous publisher accused of fostering right-wing "reaction" through his magazine empire. The German protests ballooned after Dutschke survived three bullets pumped into him by a twenty-one-year-old house painter whose hero was Adolf Hitler.

Cross-cultural inspirations traveled just as quickly among radicals as they did among musicians. Students at the Sorbonne cited China's Red Guards as their prototypes, German activist Thomas Schmitz-Bender cultivated the look of Argentinian revolutionary Che Guevara (whose diaries would be published by *Ramparts* in July), and radicals everywhere studied the sayings of Chairman Mao in his *Little Red Book*.[2]

Revolutionary activity was more widespread in Europe than at any other time since 1848, when French republicans ousted King Louis Philippe, Prince Metternich fled Vienna, and revolution swept through Italy and Germany. But in 1968, the only genuine political revolution in Europe occurred in Czechoslovakia.

There, a student demonstration in the fall of 1967 was one catalyst for remarkably rapid change. In October, two thousand students from the Prague Polytechnical University marched on the Presidential Palace to protest the lack of light and heat in their dormitories. In a pattern that would be repeated on several continents in the coming year, it was not the demonstration itself that aroused the country: It was the savage assault of the police, their clubs, and their tear gas that commanded the attention of fellow Czechs. Encouraged by the national reaction to this official violence, the students continued their protests throughout the winter. In January, political reformers did what had been unthinkable in Eastern Europe since the Soviet repression of the Hungarian uprising of 1956. At the instigation of Alexander Dubček, a gentle-looking forty-six-year-old party official with a pixyish smile, they threw out the party's conservative first secretary, Antonin Novotny, and chose Dubček as his successor. The new regime quickly transformed the country. Within three months, there was freedom of expression and a campaign to rehabilitate the victims of a previous Stalinist purge. The intoxicating scent of democracy was in the air.

A nineteen-year-old sophomore from Radcliffe was transfixed on her first visit to Prague. Martha Ritter traveled there because both of her parents had briefly lived in Czechoslovakia in 1948, and they recognized that the spring of 1968 had yielded a unique political moment: "They said, 'This is an amazing, once-in-a-lifetime opportunity. You have to go; we don't know how long this is going to last.'" When Ritter arrived, she found a city in continuous celebration: People behaved "as if they'd been let out of a closet after thirty years." Crowds would gather outside Dubček's house, just to wave at their shy hero. All over Prague, "people were debating: in restaurants, on soapboxes like [in] Hyde Park—just telling the world their views."[3]

Outside Czechoslovakia, the Prague Spring became a symbol with special power. What the Czechs achieved had more romance and more substance than any other political development in Europe in the spring of 1968. In its way, the loosening of Czech society was even more surprising than Lyndon Johnson's abdication; together they had tremendous influence. These events implied that with the right leader, sufficient determination, or (preferably) both, people anywhere—even inside a Soviet satellite—could change their country's leadership practically overnight. Even after Martin Luther King, Jr., was killed, the pictures out of Prague suggested we were still living in a revolutionary era that might yet have a happy ending.

The influence of events abroad on developments at home was undeniable, though difficult to dissect. In April the excitement in Prague helped keep many young Americans hopeful. These were the kids who were most likely to use their energies within the system, to oppose the war by working for Gene McCarthy or Bobby Kennedy—or for Nelson Rockefeller after he finally got into the presidential race. Further to the left were those who were stirred by the violent confrontations taking place in Western Europe. France came much closer to anarchy than America did that spring; if French students could practically bring their country to its knees by going into the streets, why couldn't students in the United States do the same? Among Americans inspired by this example, any lingering faith in peaceful action was overwhelmed by anger over King's assassination—and the war. These were the students who would prefer to destroy the system rather than change it. They never made up more than a tiny proportion of the American population; but the attention lavished on them by the national press in 1968—especially when they occupied college classrooms, then later on when they descended on Chicago—ensured that they were never far from the top of the nation's consciousness.

One little-noticed fact made it almost surprising that a nihilistic despair never became even more widespread among college seniors. In 1968 King's murder had given a disturbing symmetry to the scholastic lives of these students: They had been *high school* seniors when John Kennedy was killed.

Besides assassinations and an ever-present fear of the draft, there was something else at work among the young: a poorly understood malaise that nourished the usual adolescent angst. Students all over the world were unhappy with huge classes and neglectful professors; they were also beginning to feel that the materialistic life of their parents wasn't worth aspiring to. A nineteen-year-old Columbia student named James Kunen put it this way in *The Strawberry Statement*: "My friends and I became preoccupied with the common nostalgic assertion that 'these are the best years of your lives.' We could accept the fact that the college years are exhausting, confusing, boring, troubled, frustrating, and meaningless. . . . But that everything subsequent would be worse was a concept difficult to grasp and, once grasped, impossible to accept."[4]

Four years earlier, the first American students to focus national attention on this kind of alienation had been Mario Savio and his compatriots in the Free Speech Movement at the University of California, Berkeley. In the fall of 1964, the university provoked a student uprising by banning on-campus solicitation for all off-campus political activities. This action simultaneously enraged civil rights activists, Goldwater supporters, the Young People's Socialist League, and Campus Women for Peace. Berkeley was the first place where students confronted the university (and local police) on a purely political issue with the techniques of the civil rights movement. At one point even Joan Baez turned up to lead the dissenters in the singing of "We Shall Overcome." In December, the protests peaked with the arrest of 814 demonstrators who were occupying a college administration building. Less than a week later, the university capitulated to the Free Speech Movement's demands and agreed to the resumption of on-campus solicitations.[5]

Mario Savio turned twenty-two the same day the administration gave in. He was a native New Yorker who had graduated first in his class at Martin Van Buren High School. In Berkeley, a baffled *New York Times* reporter asked him why he had thrown away a semester of schoolwork to risk expulsion for campus agitation. "I spent the summer in Mississippi," Savio explained. "I witnessed tyranny. I saw groups of men in the minority working their wills over the majority. Then I come back here and found the university preventing us from collecting money for use there, and even stopping us from getting people to go to Mississippi to help."[6]

Much like Martin Luther King, Jr., Savio and his supporters believed that only "commitment" could strip life of its emptiness and its "absence of meaning in a great 'knowledge factory' like Berkeley."[7] These sentiments echoed the ideas of the Port Huron Statement, the manifesto Tom Hayden wrote for Students for a Democratic Society in 1962.

The Port Huron Statement offered a blueprint for a new "participatory democracy," and it was the closest thing the New Left in America ever had to a formal statement of intent. It began with an "agenda for a generation" and covered scores of subjects, including "students," "the military-industrial complex," and "the industrialization of the world." The section on "values" was probably most mysterious to people reading it when the statement first appeared, for it described the spirit of a counterculture that would not flower until several years later. Being ahead of its time, this section spoke with special clarity to SDS members in the vanguard of radical politics in 1968.

"We regard *men* as infinitely possessed of unfulfilled capacities for reason, freedom, and love," the manifesto declared, its sexist usage (within a radical document) clearly dating it. "Men have unrealized potential for self-cultivation, self-direction, self-understanding, and creativity. It is this potential that we regard as crucial and to which we appeal. . . . The goal of man and society should be human independence: a concern not with image or popularity but with finding a meaning in life that is personally authentic. . . . We would replace power rooted in possession, privilege, or circumstance by power and uniqueness rooted in love, reflectiveness, reason, and creativity."[8]

As early as 1965, SDS was leading the radical opposition to the War in Vietnam. At a spring march on Washington, one SDS speaker equated the killing of Vietnamese peasants by American soldiers with the murder of civil rights workers by Southern segregationists.[9] But SDS did not attract broad national attention until its Columbia chapter joined forces with black student activists to close down that university in the spring of 1968. Like their counterparts on other campuses, these students were too impatient for change to work within the system; their dream was to overthrow it.

Across the United States between January and June, there were 221 major demonstrations at 101 colleges, involving nearly forty thousand students. A survey by the National Student Association listed fifty-nine cases in which students took over a school building. "Black Power!" was the most frequent rallying cry, followed by demands for student power and opposition to the war. At Columbia these three issues fused to produce the year's most explosive campus uprising.[10]

* * *

COLUMBIA has always had to compete with Manhattan for the loyalty of its students. Its full name is Columbia University in the City of New York, and the experience of living in America's most cosmopolitan city frequently affects its students more deeply than anything that happens inside the classroom. The intensity of New York makes it easy for an undergraduate to decide that the concerns of the larger world are more important than the preoccupations of his professors—especially in a year like 1968.

Though unable to overshadow the surrounding metropolis, Columbia often behaved arrogantly toward the adjacent community. In the years before 1968, it had bought more than a hundred nearby buildings, infuriating its poorer neighbors by evicting thousands of black and Puerto Rican tenants to accommodate the needs of a steadily expanding institution.[11] (The unofficial fight song of Columbia students is "Who Owns New York?" to which the chorused answer is "*We* own New York!") In a stark geographical representation of the way it is perceived by its enemies, Columbia's Morningside Heights campus peers down at the Harlem community that borders the university on two sides.

Morningside Park acted as the local equivalent of a demilitarized zone between the venerable college (founded in 1754) and the poor black neighborhood beneath it. This neglected thirty-acre plot in the shape of a boot stretches from 110th to 123rd streets, just east of the campus. In the fifties Columbia decided that Morningside Park would be the ideal location for a new gymnasium. If the city and state approved, it would mean a new building could be erected without displacing any more local residents.

Lengthy negotiations began in 1959. Using public parkland for a private purpose required a new state law. In a gesture to the community, Columbia agreed to include some neighborhood facilities, but it planned to spend $8.4 million on its own gym, five times as much as the cost of the building designed for Harlem's needs. Worst of all was the symbolism of the architecture: In the final plan, the entrance for Columbia students would be at the top of the steeply sloping site, the one for Harlem at the bottom.[12]

Despite these inequalities, in the early sixties Columbia's plan was widely portrayed as a magnanimous gesture. But anything perceived by the community as paternalism rapidly fell out of fashion in the era of Black Power. In 1967 the university rejected a suggestion that it share the facility equally with the community; instead, to try to silence the opposition, it added a swimming pool for local residents. It wasn't enough. When ground was broken without announcement in February 1968, the gym gave years of accumulated anger a concrete focus. Harlem activists dubbed it "Gym Crow" and demanded that construction be halted. Columbia administrators tried to ignore this new wave of criticism.[13]

On the campus itself, the gym had been slow to emerge as a major issue. As late as March 6, the undergraduate newspaper, the *Columbia Spectator,* endorsed its construction. During the months before the April uprising, Columbia SDS had concentrated its energies on protests against on-campus recruitment efforts by the CIA and Dow Chemical, which manufactured napalm for use in Vietnam. Its other concerns included opposition to a university ban on indoor demonstrations and a demand that Columbia end its affiliation with the Institute for Defense Analyses. IDA conducted weapons research and studied "technical problems of counter-insurgency warfare." Further, Columbia president Grayson Kirk was one of IDA's trustees. This connection made it possible for many antiwar activists to transfer their hostility toward the war to their university.[14]

Before April, the Students' Afro-American Society had been, like SDS, uninvolved with the issue of the gym. George Scurlock, who was president of SAS until March 1968, did not remember anyone discussing it with him while he led the organization. Actually, before 1968, there hadn't been anything radical about SAS at all. Since its founding in 1964, it had functioned primarily as a book study group. "We would read things like *Invisible Man* and discuss its implications for black students on an Ivy League campus," Scurlock remembered.[15] SAS also published a scholarly journal, but until 1968 it emphasized thought over action.

It was the selection of Cicero Wilson as the new SAS president in the spring of 1968 that changed its focus, quickly bringing it into step with the more radical stance of community activists. Wilson was a native of the Brooklyn ghetto of Bedford-Stuyvesant, "the first true guy out of the community," as Scurlock described him. "He felt the need to do something demonstrably different from the middle-class 'bougie' guys who ran it before him—which was one reason he was willing to play with SDS." An SDS leader remembered Wilson as a "tough, city black kid. He really was crucial, for while he was not flamboyant, he exerted a kind of moral force on the other guys. He wasn't a 'Negro'; he was the equivalent of Malcolm X."[16]

The other vital student actor in the events of April was Mark Rudd, the twenty-year-old chairman of the Columbia chapter of SDS. The grandson of immigrants, Rudd had grown up in Maplewood, New Jersey. He had been a Boy Scout and a ham-radio enthusiast, and his father recalled that

young Mark "could be very impressed by different people he met, particularly those with some position of authority." Rudd defined the difference
between himself and "liberals" this way: "They can rationalize anything.
There will always be slums, they say, there will always be wars. . . . A
radical doesn't accept that."[17]

He was good with a crowd, excellent on camera, and, like many of the
students whom he led, he was attracted to other radicals because "there
was a sense of motion and excitement about them." Earlier that spring, he
had cut classes to take a three-week tour of Cuba. Columbia vice-president
David Truman called him "totally unscrupulous and morally very dangerous.
No one has ever made him or his friends look over the abyss. It makes me
uncomfortable to sit in the same room with him."[18]

When the New York City director of the Selective Service System came
on campus to answer questions about new draft regulations, some SDS
members wanted to interrogate the bureaucrat about the "illegitimacy"
of the draft; but Rudd was quick to see the virtue of a more flamboyant
tactic: While a group of students created a diversion in the back of the
room, another demonstrator pushed a lemon-meringue pie in the federal
official's face.[19]

One week later Rudd was at the head of what rapidly became known as
the "action faction" of SDS. Hoping to provoke a confrontation with university administrators, this group decided to violate a recently enacted ban on
indoor demonstrations. Rudd led a crowd into the university's administrative
offices in Low Library and sought a meeting with Columbia's president to
protest Columbia's membership in IDA.[20] The student radical explained,
"Confrontation politics puts the enemy up against the wall and forces him
to define himself. He has to make a choice. Radicalization of the individual
means that he must commit himself to the struggle to change society as well
as share the radical view of what is wrong with society."[21]

President Grayson Kirk was the perfect opponent for students bent on
provoking a confrontation. He was sixty-four in 1968, and, as he himself
observed, the gap between the generations had never been wider. Much
more comfortable in the company of corporate executives than he was with
undergraduates, Kirk was completely out of touch with the rapidly changing concerns of his students. "He hasn't spoken to anyone under thirty
since he was under thirty," said playwright Eric Bentley. Kirk's anointed
successor, Vice-President David Truman, was already waiting in the wings.
At a memorial service for Martin Luther King, Jr., Kirk wouldn't even link
arms during the singing of "We Shall Overcome." Students and faculty
alike were routinely told by administrators that issues like the gym and IDA

were none of their business. Government professor Herbert Deane echoed
the view that prevailed among most administrators (and inadvertently
provided the title for James Kunen's memoirs) when he stated, "Whether
students vote 'yes' or 'no' on a given issue means as much to me as if they
were to tell me they like strawberries."[22] The radicals believed they had a
moral obligation to alter these attitudes. If the university wasn't ready to
change, they would change the university.

THE Columbia sundial sits at the center of the southern portion of its elegant McKim, Mead & White campus. Anyone standing here commands a
panoramic view, reaching north to the central administration's offices in
Low Library and south to Butler Library at the bottom of the quadrangle.
Less than a hundred yards to the east sits Hamilton Hall, the main building
of Columbia College. Five undergraduate dormitories lie within earshot of
anyone using a bullhorn.

On Tuesday, April 23, four hundred students had gathered to hear an
assortment of SDS and SAS speakers talk about the war, the gymnasium,
and university discipline. Another three hundred counterdemonstrators
held signs reading ORDER IS PEACE and SEND RUDD BACK TO CUBA, while
a few hundred others with no certain political affiliation mingled among
them. SAS president Cicero Wilson was one of the first to climb on top of
the sundial.

"This is Harlem Heights, not Morningside Heights," he declared. "What
would you do if somebody came and took your property? Would you sit
still? No. You'd use every means possible to get your property back—and
this is exactly what the black people are engaged in right now."

Then Wilson gave voice to the worst fears of the administration: the
possibility that black radicals from Harlem would join forces with black
students at Columbia and burn the university to the ground. "You people had
better realize that you condone Grayson Kirk with his roughriding over the
black community. But do you realize that when you come back, there may
not *be* a Columbia University? Do you think this white citadel of hypocrisy
will be bypassed if an insurrection occurs this summer?"

While the rally continued, David Truman, Kirk's second-in-command,
tried to head off the protesters' announced plan to carry the demonstration
inside Low. He offered to speak with them instead in McMillin Auditorium, one of the largest indoor meeting places on campus. "But if we go to
McMillin," Rudd told the crowd, "we will just talk and go through a lot of

bullshit." Before Rudd could finish, a young radical in front of him shouted out, "Did we come here to talk or did we come here to go to Low?" and much of the crowd took off after him.

After an abortive effort to break through the locked doors of Low, Cicero Wilson led several hundred students away to the site of the gymnasium. There they tore down part of the fence surrounding the construction site. Several scuffles broke out with policemen, and one white student was arrested. As the demonstration broke up and stragglers marched back toward the campus, at the edge of the park they encountered another group of supporters coming toward them from the opposite direction. Then they regrouped at the sundial. Rudd shouted, "Hamilton Hall is right over there. Let's go!" And they did. By 2 P.M., the occupation of Columbia University had begun.[23]

Administrators saw themselves as victims of a carefully planned strategy to disrupt the university. A written proposal that circulated within SDS earlier that spring did recommend the occupation of campus buildings, and the radical group was unquestionably eager to provoke some kind of confrontation.[24] But participants insisted that the seizure of a building on this particular day was quite accidental. "The serendipity of it all has always been phenomenal to me," said George Scurlock. "Because the whole damn thing was such happenstance: someone said, 'Let's go over to the park'; then someone said, 'Let's go to Hamilton.' There was just this mass of people on Morningside Drive literally milling around in the street with nowhere to go, and someone said, 'Wow, a group—we need to do something!'" An official fact-finding commission agreed with this conclusion.[25]

Henry Coleman, the acting dean of Columbia College, returned to his office shortly after the demonstrators had entered Hamilton Hall; then he became their hostage. The protesters drew up a list of demands, including Columbia's disaffiliation from IDA, the end of construction of the gymnasium, and amnesty for themselves.

White radicals said later that they had stayed in Hamilton until the black students asked them to leave. According to Rudd, the blacks decided they wanted to hold the building alone.[26] Black community activists had joined the students during the night, and there were rumors that they had brought guns. Some black students have a different recollection: They say they were eager to keep the whites inside as a buffer against a possible police action. George Scurlock said the whites left only because they would not endorse the blacks' decision to lock the doors to prevent students from attending classes in the morning.[27] In any event, the very brief experiment

in black and white unity ended by dawn. All of the whites were gone by
6 A.M. Some of them broke into Low Library; there they occupied the
president's office. The police were summoned immediately, and many of
the whites fled Low when a bust seemed imminent. But the administration was thwarted when the police refused to evict the remaining whites
unless they could simultaneously arrest the blacks inside Hamilton Hall.
The university was eager to go after the whites, but scared of any confrontation with the blacks. The police explained that if the university filed
a complaint for trespass, the City of New York could hardly discriminate
on the basis of race.

Dean Coleman was released after twenty-six hours when his captors were
warned by city mediators that they might be charged with kidnapping. After
that, the positions of students and administrators steadily hardened. The
administration rejected any suggestion of amnesty, insisting that Columbia
had to set an example of firmness for other universities around the country.
Radicals derided this as Kirk's "Allen Dulles" position; then they widened
their protest. Within four days, five Columbia buildings were occupied
by protesters. Inside the president's office, the temporary tenants placed
a marker reading, OURS, on Kirk's scale model of the campus each time
a new building was taken. As moderate students threatened to evict the
protesters if the university took no action, the faculty lobbied against the
idea of police intervention, fearing a bloody denouement. Only the radicals
were exhilarated.

"It was thrilling," said Lewis Cole, twenty-one at the time of the strike,
who was an SDS leader and advisor to Rudd. He remembered the first
night of the protest this way: "It was a night on which you really felt like
you were growing up. Everything was so intensely concentrated and so
extremely focused. It was like a love affair and a great intellectual insight
happening at the same time. You've got to be some kind of Puritan to insist
that this springtime of one's exercise of power was not absolutely thrilling
for a bunch of twenty-year-olds."[28]

Within the occupied buildings, many students were getting their first
taste of communal life. The lobby of Hamilton Hall was decorated with
posters of Lenin, Che Guevara, and Malcolm X.[29] Inside Mathematics
Hall, commune leaders complained that as much money was being spent
on cigarettes as food (marijuana and liquor were banned by majority vote).
The student radio station, WKCR, announced a clergyman was needed to
perform a marriage in Fayerweather, another "liberated" building. William
Starr, a Protestant chaplain affiliated with the university, responded to the
call. The groom was dressed in love beads and a Nehru jacket; the bride

wore a white turtleneck sweater and carried a bouquet of daisies. The Reverend Starr conducted what he dubbed a "wed-in" and pronounced the bridal couple "children of the new age." The newlyweds called themselves "Mr. and Mrs. Fayerweather."[30]

Those in the buildings communicated with one another by telephone and walkie-talkie. Everywhere, stashes of green soap were preserved, to slick the stairways when the protesters decided an invasion by the police might be imminent. A demonstrator in Low suggested it might hamper the police if they undressed as the cops arrived; when a majority approved his proposal, he urged that rehearsals begin immediately.[31]

The image reproduced almost everywhere was the picture of a protester sitting at Kirk's desk, scowling through his sunglasses and puffing on one of the president's White Owl cigars. To liberals and conservatives alike, this was the enduring symbol of radical youth run amok in America in 1968. On campus, three groups were disgusted by this violation of private property in general and their beloved university in particular. These were conservative students who styled themselves the "Majority Coalition," the administration, and a large part of the faculty. They were particularly appalled by the coercive nature of the protest, which prevented so many from getting the expensive education that their parents had worked so hard to pay for.

The playfulness of the communes tended to obscure the substance of the protest. It was easy for the establishment press to dismiss the student strike as the result of a combination of spring-induced self-indulgence, the dread of exams, and a selfish opposition to the war. But black and white radicals alike had a serious message: In times of crisis, there might be some things more important than the right to go to class.

To black demonstrators, the interruption of classes was less serious than Columbia's continuing encroachment on the public property of its poorer neighbors, and peaceful protests had failed to influence President Kirk. Only after the occupation of Hamilton Hall did the administration finally suspend construction inside Morningside Park. White students argued that "speech alone" was no longer enough to end the university's coerciveness. While the protesters were certainly interfering with the rights of students to go to class, SDS argued that the real "interference" began with coercive actions by the university—actions that interfered with the lives of people in Harlem and Vietnam.[32]

The other radical argument was the idea that the majority view was irrelevant to one's opposition to the war—"Because whether it was a majority or minority who wanted the war to go on, the war was wrong," said Lewis Cole. "And even if most Americans thought it was right, it was still wrong. You did not have the right to destroy other people because you were all in agreement that they should be destroyed. That was German thinking. You didn't have that right, and it behooved us to say this war is wrong."[33]

These views, coupled with a demand for absolute amnesty for the protesters, precluded a compromise with the administration. "Amnesty," the strikers said, "must be a precondition for negotiations. Our demand for amnesty implies a specific political point. Our actions are legitimate; it is the laws and the administration's policies [that] are illegitimate."[34] Compromise was not in the interest of the radicals anyway. Only by forcing the administration to respond with violence were they likely to radicalize the liberals who had consistently rejected their tactics.

The complete polarization of the campus was finally guaranteed six and a half days after the protest began. Shortly after 2:30, on the morning of Tuesday, April 30, one thousand New York City policemen marched onto the campus in military formation to empty all five buildings of their occupants. The administration had had enough.

To the astonishment of SDS, the only completely peaceful action of the evening was the arrest of the black students inside Hamilton. Despite their radical pose, the blacks decided there was nothing to be gained from a confrontation with the police, and they had agreed in advance to refrain from violence. In one sense, it was this negotiation that made the evacuation of the rest of the campus possible—because it eliminated the single greatest fear of the administration, the ever-present possibility that Harlem would rise up in solidarity with the black students if they tried to fight off the police. Under the steady gaze of dozens of neutral observers, the blacks were led off into paddy wagons without incident.

After Hamilton, however, there was nothing but chaos: angry, bloody chaos.

Policemen who might have dreamed of sending their sons to such a prestigious place waded into crowds of privileged Ivy League students to create the closest thing to class warfare ever witnessed on the Columbia campus. The same scene repeated itself over and over again for nearly three hours. Long-haired students taunted helmeted policemen with verbal abuse and sometimes threw rocks, bottles, and chairs; they themselves were subdued with kicks, punches, and billy clubs. Many students were clearly eager for a fight, but the police were far more experienced with violence than they were, and it showed. A Spanish instructor named Frederick

Courtney was one of the innocents; as he walked off the steps of Low Library, he was set upon by plainclothesmen, knocked to the ground, and pummeled by the police.[35] Inside Avery Hall, a *New York Times* reporter named Robert McG. Thomas, Jr., was asked by a deputy inspector to leave the premises. Thomas turned to comply with the request. "I wasn't making any First Amendment effort," he remembered. Then, despite a prominently displayed press card, he was attacked by the police as he tried to leave; his head wounds required twelve stitches. "It was just one of those crazy things in the mood of the moment," the reporter said. "I was the first person they had encountered who they had to eject."[36] Some of the students inside Avery and Mathematics halls were dragged facedown over marble steps leading to police vans waiting on Amsterdam Avenue. In other parts of the campus, away from the occupied buildings, platoons of police assaulted students wherever they found them. Outside the college gates on Broadway, mounted policemen re-created scenes out of Selma as they charged anyone who looked as if he might be a demonstrator.[37] The public got a new image of the Columbia protester: Instead of a surly-looking cigar-smoking radical, they saw a cherubic face, contorted in sorrow and covered with blood.

"There was great violence"; that was the understated conclusion of the fact-finding commission chaired by Archibald Cox. Too few policemen were used because the administration had "grossly underestimated" the number of protesters inside the buildings. The Cox Commission said the administration had refused to acknowledge the fact that by the end of a week of protests, the sit-ins involved "a significant portion of the student body who had become disenchanted with the operation of their university." In all, there were 722 arrests, including 524 students taken from the buildings.[38] One hundred forty-eight people were injured; among them were twenty policemen. A spokesman for the New York City police department explained the behavior of his men: For the first time ever, they were faced "with the rejection of society by people who were brought up to inherit that society; nothing in any policeman's experience had prepared him for that."[39]

The following day the *New York Times* gave the establishment view of the event on its front page. Its tone was predictable. The paper's publisher, Arthur O. Sulzberger, was a Columbia graduate, and, like his father before him, he was a member of its board of trustees. The board had backed Kirk in his insistence that there could be no amnesty. The main story did mention allegations of police brutality. Yet, despite the experience of its own reporter, whose beating in Avery Hall was described in a separate story inside the paper, the lead article added, "The charges were challenged by some eyewitnesses."

The piece that caused the most controversy was the feature story about the riots at the bottom of the front page. It was written by A. M. Rosenthal, an assistant managing editor who while an undergraduate had begun his career at the newspaper as its part-time correspondent at the City College of New York. Rosenthal liked to boast that his first official act as metropolitan editor in 1963 had been to raise the monthly retainer of the City College correspondent to the amount received by the Columbia man.[40]

His story about the Columbia riot was very unusual for the *Times*. The managing editor was away when he wrote it, and Rosenthal had been left in charge of the newsroom. It was nearly two thousand words long, and its tone was just as emotional as the events it recounted. This was the lead: "It was 4:30 in the morning and the president of the university leaned against the wall of the room that had been his office. He passed a hand over his face. 'My God,' he said, 'how could human beings do a thing like this.'" Kirk was referring to the debris inside Low Library. The article left no doubt that Rosenthal shared the view of the Columbia president—that the property damage committed by students was the worst crime that had occurred on the campus. Later on, affidavits from several professors indicated that much of the damage in buildings other than Low Library was probably vandalism committed by policemen, not students.[41]

The next day eighty young demonstrators picketed the Fifth Avenue home of the publisher. *"New York Times,"* they shouted, *"print the truth!"* The demonstration inspired something even more unusual: a statement from Sulzberger defending the *Times*. He insisted the paper had provided "full, accurate, and dispassionate coverage."[42] The following year, Sulzberger chose Rosenthal to be the top editor on the *Times*.

Undergraduate academic activity at Columbia came to a halt under the pressure of a general strike, but three weeks later the university's ability to inspire a confrontation was undiminished. Mark Rudd and four other students were ordered to appear at the college dean's office on May 21 to enter a plea to the disciplinary charges pending against them. The students said they would refuse the summons and instead called a rally for that day. In a bizarre repetition of the earlier events, 350 students occupied Hamilton Hall. The police were called, but it was 2:30 the following morning before they arrested the protesters inside the hall. Once again, the initial arrests were peaceful, but afterward, it was a repetition of the events of April 30, only much worse. "Hell broke loose," the Cox Commission reported.[43] Fires were started in Fayerweather and Hamilton, including one that destroyed the research papers of a professor who had opposed the strike. At 4:05 A.M., Kirk panicked and ordered the police to clear the campus completely. The fighting was even fiercer than it had been on the previous occasion: In one dormitory, the police chased and clubbed students up to the fourth floor.[44] There were 177 arrests and sixty-eight injured, including seventeen policemen.

THE university community would be traumatized for years by these events. "We have suffered a disaster whose precise dimensions it is impossible to state," Richard Hofstadter told the graduating classes in his commencement address in June.[45] The split in the faculty was particularly severe. Many of the younger professors hated the administration just as much as the students did, and they sympathized with at least some of the demands of the strike. There was a common lament within the teaching staff: "Imagine how different everything would have been if Grayson Kirk had been alive." Even those who deplored the students' tactics sometimes acknowledged the importance of their message. "These kids are deeply discontent with their civilization," said Fritz Stern, a prominent member of the Columbia history department. "They don't want to be passive, affluent citizens of Westchester owning two cars. A lot of what they say deserves the most searching attention. But the means they use could discredit their goals in the eyes of others. Sometimes they are their own worst enemies."[46]

The remarkable fact was that, after the riots ended, nearly all of the strikers' demands were met. Construction of the gymnasium never resumed in Morningside Park; the university built a different one inside the main campus several years later. Columbia's connection to IDA was severed. The ban on indoor demonstrations was lifted. In August, Kirk resigned, and his chosen successor, David Truman, never got his job. Andrew Cordier, a former diplomat and dean of the School of International Affairs, was selected instead. Most of the charges of trespassing were dropped by the university. A university senate was established, forcing the administration to share power with the faculty and the student body, and Columbia College tried hard to improve the living conditions of its students. In the fall it took a dramatic step in that direction by ending all restrictions on the hours when women could visit Columbia undergraduates in their dormitories. On the football field, the Columbia marching band invented an obscene formation to celebrate this "expanding parietal."

Outside the campus, the massive coverage of the uprising had a very different effect. Together with the recent riots in black ghettos, the Columbia disturbances gave the presidential campaign a deeply unsettling background. Once again the traditional rules of society were unraveling, and no one seemed able to reverse the pattern. To the white middle class, the Columbia uprising was even more disturbing than inner-city riots. Here there was no economic explanation for the uprising; at Columbia, the rioters were their children.

8

It Takes a Lot to Laugh,
It Takes a Train to Cry

"He's a mystery man. And that makes his appeal very interesting."
—Seymour Hersh on Eugene McCarthy[1]

"If he wants to pick on us over our size, I'm willing to use that as a determinant. Or age. I don't think those should be standards, however. He plays touch football; I play football. He plays softball; I play baseball. He skates in Rockefeller Center; I play hockey. . . . If these are the bases on which you are going to make a decision . . . it'll become abrasive, I suppose."
—Eugene McCarthy on Bobby Kennedy[2]

"Those who write don't shoot and those who shoot, don't write."
—Bobby Kennedy on potential assassins[3]

UNTIL the end of March, Gene McCarthy had been battling a widely hated president and a deeply hated war. But when Lyndon Johnson disappeared from the campaign, he took with him the joy that comes with moral clarity. "I feel as if I've been tracking a tiger through long jungle grass," McCarthy said, "and all of a sudden he rolls over and he's stuffed."[4]

In place of the tiger there was the Young Turk, the Kennedy that McCarthy particularly loathed. By the end of April, there were also two new presidential candidates, although during May, the war of the Democratic primaries was confined to Kennedy and McCarthy.

The announcements of the new contestants bracketed the first bloody confrontation between Columbia students and New York City policemen. Each candidate entered the race believing he could fill a vacuum. Hubert Horatio Humphrey began his second campaign for the presidency three days before the climax of the first Columbia uprising. In 1960 Humphrey had run as the crusading liberal, the civil rights champion who always bubbled with enthusiasm. Eight years later, the enthusiasm was still there, but he had long ago exchanged his status as the First Liberal for the castrating role of Lyndon Johnson's Second Lieutenant. He had entered the race too late to participate in any of the remaining primaries—his efforts would be focused instead on the party leaders, who still controlled the selection of 60 percent of the Democratic delegates in 1968. To everyone supporting Kennedy or McCarthy, Humphrey's strategy was depressing evidence of the continuing power of the old politics. And his rhetoric had never sounded more inappropriate. When he declared for the presidency, Humphrey promised "the politics of happiness" and "the politics of joy"—less than a month after Martin Luther King's assassination.

Three days after Humphrey's announcement—and just a few hours after the first battle of Morningside Heights at Columbia—Nelson Rockefeller startled the Republicans by reversing a decision he had made just forty days earlier to ignore the presidential sweepstakes. Now the New York governor was in the race "with all my heart, my mind, and my will." While Humphrey's message made him sound almost oblivious to the upheavals all around him, Rockefeller said he had belatedly decided to challenge Richard Nixon for the Republican nomination because of the widening turmoil; he cited as reasons "the gravity of the crisis we face as a people . . . the growing unrest and anxiety at home, and the signs of disintegration abroad."[5] Michigan governor George Romney had been forced out of the race by the Nixon steamroller even before the voters went to the polls in New Hampshire. Ronald Reagan, California's chief executive, posed a faint challenge to the front-runner from the right, but without Rockefeller, Nixon would have no competition from the left. Rockefeller craved the presidency, but he had always been considered too liberal by most Republicans—in 1964 he was booed by Barry Goldwater's supporters at the national convention—and this time his late entry made him even more of a long shot.

BOBBY Kennedy brought money, brains, talent, a family tradition of invincibility, and a very different kind of hatred into the campaign. In the middle of April, a tiny newspaper in Welch, West Virginia, had greeted his appearance there with typical intensity. The paper called Kennedy "uninvited, unwanted, undesirable, unethical, un-American, unfit, unprepared, unshorn, unpopular, unloved and overrated." Welch's mayor welcomed the candidate with a piece of red carpet to contradict the newspaper.[6]

Lyndon Johnson had been despised for being old, looking ugly, talking funny, and refusing to abandon a costly war long after it seemed to have passed the point of diminishing returns. But partly because they had such clear policy differences, McCarthy had "never attacked the President's integrity, character or motives."[7] Now that McCarthy's principal opponent in the primaries was another antiwar candidate, all the energy that had been focused against the war was redirected into a bitter, personal feud.

McCarthy was a poet, always quick with a mysterious turn of phrase; with Kennedy's entry into the race, the Minnesotan became more cryptic than ever. "It's narrowed down to Bobby and me," McCarthy told two of his speechwriters, Jeremy Larner and Jonathan Schell. "So far he's run with the ghost of his brother. Now we're going to make him run against it. It's purely Greek: He either has to kill him or be killed by him. We'll make him run against Jack. . . . And I'm Jack."

"Did you understand that?" Schell asked Larner afterward.

"Half," Larner replied.

"Well, I didn't," said Schell, who then quit the campaign because he would not work against Bobby.[8]

Many years later, McCarthy said he meant that Bobby would have to run against his brother's policies, including the war. "We were saying in effect he was going to kill Jack's reputation—and he was prepared to do it. I had to do the Jack defense in a way: set Jack up and make him run against Jack."[9] McCarthy put it this way to Shana Alexander, who was covering the campaign for *Life* in 1968: "The rules of Greek drama call for stating the problem in act I, presenting the complications in act II and resolving everything in act III. I'm an act II man. That's where I live—involution and complexity. In politics, I think you must stay in act II. You can't draw lines under things, or add up scores; the complications just go on in different forms. When you get into act III, you have to write a tragedy."[10] This provided one explanation for McCarthy's seeming nonchalance in the face of defeat. Larner had another one: He thought McCarthy's reluctance to act resembled an athlete's temptation to perform under par. "If one goes all out and loses, then one is without excuse; everyone has clearly seen that the other man is better. But athletes who do not go all out end up losing to anyone who is as good as they are and to some who are worse."[11]

McCarthy classified Bobby as an act I man. "He says here's a problem. Here's another problem. Here's another. He never really deals with act II but I think Bobby's beginning to write act II now. Bobby's tragedy is that to beat me, he's going to have to destroy his brother. Today I occupy most of Jack's positions on the board. That's kind of Greek, isn't it?"[12] These were among his gentler comments about his opponent.

As soon as Kennedy entered the race for the presidency, Al Lowenstein traveled across the country to try to control the infighting within the left. He gave up after a week. In a speech to antiwar activists in California, he predicted a calamity if there "were hatred between people who agreed on the issues." Then he concluded by saying, "Bobby Kennedy is not the enemy"—and McCarthy loyalists were outraged. "It was just clear that we had to live through the next period, retaining some degree of independence from the hate, so that after the primaries were over you could move and try to do something," Lowenstein recalled. For the moment, he decided to concentrate his efforts inside New York, where he was in his own race for Congress on Long Island.[13]

Lowenstein remained officially for McCarthy and, privately, very close to Kennedy. He was disgusted with McCarthy's attacks on his opponent, but one tactic of the Kennedy campaign enraged Lowenstein. Kennedy's people were telling McCarthy supporters they had to switch to Kennedy because McCarthy could not possibly win. When he heard that, Lowenstein "blew up."

"I said that I just could not believe anybody would say that. We started a movement to stop Lyndon Johnson when you people wouldn't have a damn thing to do with it. And the argument that you people made then was that we couldn't stop Johnson. Now don't come back to us and use that same horseshit now!" Another Kennedy mistake was to offer salaries for the canvassing work McCarthy had paid for with peanut butter sandwiches. "Poverty was a dearly assumed virtue for our young affluents," Larner wrote, "and it grew easier to talk of Bobby—in public—as if he really were the little rich kid pilloried on the front page of the *Indianapolis Star* for 'trying to buy Indiana.' "[14] The arrogance of Kennedy's organization made the "determination to resist Kennedy greater," Lowenstein believed.[15]

Though the McCarthy kids bitterly resented the suggestion that their candidate might be unelectable, everyone knew there was massive disarray within his campaign. The organization had grown after the upset in New Hampshire, but McCarthy never gave anyone clear authority over the whole operation. One of his greatest failings was a dread of personal confrontation. "There were five or six times he should have stepped in, learned the situation, and made a decision," said his press secretary, Seymour Hersh. "And he steadfastly refused to."[16] Rather than dress anyone down, or push anyone out, McCarthy preferred to permit a dozen different duchies to war against one another beneath him. Each one had its own separate source of funds—or sometimes no funds at all.[17]

Blair Clark retained the title of campaign manager, but he controlled only one segment of the effort. Clark's secret bank account was called "Clergymen for McCarthy," and he kept it at the Freedom National Bank in Harlem.[18] As spending increased, McCarthy became fearful that he would be left with a campaign debt, so he installed his brother-in-law, Stephen T. Quigley, as "executive director" at national headquarters in Washington. Clark and Quigley reported independently to their candidate, and they loathed each other. Quigley seemed determined to block as many expenditures as possible. "He kept saying, 'the family is liable for it,'" Clark remembered. Clark urged the campaign treasurer, Arnold Hiatt, to persuade McCarthy to take Quigley out of the loop. Hiatt duly pleaded with McCarthy, but the candidate told him he couldn't get rid of his brother-in-law; it would be more trouble than it was worth.[19] Then Quigley went to McCarthy to make the same request about Clark. McCarthy told him to "work around Mr. Clark . . . until the whole setup could be reorganized."[20] Of course, it never was.

"There must have been ten different campaigns going on," Quigley said. "Every week there was some conspiracy by a new group to take over the campaign."[21] One reason for this chaos was the ambiguous position of the candidate's wife, Abigail McCarthy. She was smart and very tough, and she had played a pivotal role in all of his previous political contests, but now, behind the scenes, their marriage was unraveling. Rumors of McCarthy's late-night visits to one woman reporter's home in Washington reached Ben Bradlee at the *Washington Post*. Bradlee was about to become managing editor, but he was also a very old friend of Blair Clark. The newspaperman called Clark to warn him that McCarthy was attracting attention to himself. Clark went to McCarthy and told him about the rumor. The candidate said, "Thank you very much."[22] There was no publicity.*

Despite the strain in their marriage, Mrs. McCarthy remained very much involved in the campaign—even though, like everyone else, she lacked any absolute authority. She feuded constantly with Hersh and Clark.[23] "I'm not *your* press secretary," Hersh explained to Mrs. McCarthy on one occasion. "I'm your husband's."[24]

Jeremy Larner was upset by his boss's fondness for sycophants. "McCarthy's personality was central to all that happened and all that failed to happen," Larner wrote. "Criticism was impermissible, no matter its source or its quality. He seemed to feel that no one had a right to ask him to explain himself." Larner found it tough "looking back into those slate-stone eyes which bore down hard and granted you nothing. Mostly he did not reply unless you played his straight man, feeding him lines. Half his remarks came weighted with a honking 'HUNH?'—like a blow on the end of his flat strong farmer's voice. Impossible to answer anything but yes."[25] Hersh thought McCarthy became unhappy if you forgot to tell him he had given a "great speech," every day. "We got into a position where the cult began outracing the reality." Sometimes McCarthy seemed to take pleasure in humiliating his aides in front of his friends. "He can be sort of a bastard," Hersh said in 1969. "It's strictly a love-hate relationship in my case."[26]

Money became scarce again in Wisconsin. A professional stripper who joined the McCarthy campaign a few months after her husband had been killed in Vietnam had a special way of responding to the financial squeeze. According to Ben Stavis, "Whenever the finance office said it was broke, the stripper would call the major fund raisers and threaten to take off her clothes to earn money for food for the students. Fund raisers usually found money quickly."[27]

It was also in Wisconsin that Hersh finally got fed up with the infighting. His access to McCarthy was diminishing, and he was tired of being second-guessed. In a meeting with Curtis Gans and thirty other campaign workers, the press secretary complained that McCarthy wasn't doing any campaigning in inner-city neighborhoods. Hersh later said this was not the main source of his unhappiness. But the civil rights issue blew up after the *New York Times* reported that Hersh and his deputy had quit their jobs because of McCarthy's absence from the ghetto.

* The following year McCarthy separated from his wife for good. In her autobiography she wrote, "the campaign brought almost unbearable emotional strain and disaster to our family." [Abigail McCarthy, *Private Faces/Public Places* (Garden City: Doubleday, 1970), 435.]

When he could ignore the bickering, McCarthy still seemed to be riding the wave from New Hampshire. At a rally for eighteen thousand in Madison, on March 21, he said he "felt the spirit of the campaign as I had never felt it before," and he quoted Walt Whitman:

> . . . *Poets to come! orators, singers, musicians to come!*
> *Not to-day is to justify me, and answer what I am for;*
> *But you, a new brood, native, athletic, continental, greater than*
>   *before known.*
> *Arouse! Arouse—for you must justify me—you must answer.*[28]

Twelve days later, he won a great victory in Wisconsin: 56 percent of the vote, compared with just 35 percent for the lame-duck president. When Dick Goodwin left McCarthy after the primary to return to Bobby Kennedy, he told the Minnesotan that he was the front-runner now. "Goodwin was hypnotized by Gene's potential as a candidate," Larner wrote. "He speculated that Gene might have been an ineffective candidate in 1960, when the country needed to be roused, but he could be a good one now, when the needs were dignity, honesty and healing." Goodwin thought Kennedy's intensity might antagonize too many voters.[29]

A McCarthy supporter discovered a loophole in the Connecticut election law and forced a primary there for delegates to the state convention; McCarthy won a surprising 44 percent of the vote on April 10. Two weeks later, he did even better in Pennsylvania, getting 71.6 percent in a nonbinding popularity contest.[30] And in Massachusetts, where it was too late for Kennedy to enter, McCarthy finished first again on April 30.[31]

INDIANA was the setting for the first direct confrontation between Kennedy and McCarthy. Humphrey was represented by Indiana governor Roger Branigin, who was originally intended as a surrogate for Johnson. The familiar faces had all assembled around Bobby: his brother Teddy; his brother-in-law Stephen Smith; his brother Jack's speechwriter, Ted Sorensen; Jack's press secretary, Pierre Salinger; and Jack's defense secretary, Robert McNamara, who even made a TV spot for the Kennedy campaign. Kennedy got a haircut (the *Times* ran "before" and "after" pictures), and he started talking about law and order to position himself to the right of McCarthy in the conservative Hoosier state. All across Indiana he kept repeating, "I was, for three-and-a-half years, chief law-enforcement officer of the United States."[32] At the same time, a Citizens for Kennedy office in New York City issued documents suggesting McCarthy wasn't really so liberal, citing a single vote by him against a reduction in the oil depletion allowance and wrongly accusing him of failing to support a $300 million Model Cities appropriation. Most reporters concluded there was little difference between the Kennedy and McCarthy voting records. Kennedy's national staff disavowed the literature, but the pamphlet attacking McCarthy's voting record remained available at many Kennedy storefronts.[33] Kennedy's refusal to debate McCarthy added to the aura of old politics surrounding his effort.

McCarthy's kids were concerned about the "passion gap" between Kennedy and their leader. The campaign's best-known emblem matched the candidate's understatement: Tiny and round, barely half an inch in diameter, it said EUGENE in white letters on a blue background. While McCarthy said all the right things about civil rights, as Hersh put it, "he didn't show soul"; as a result, he never got anywhere with the black vote. He told students at Howard University that they should examine his record if they wanted to know what he had done for them. "Record, hell!" someone shouted from the audience. "Tell us what you *feel*."[34]

"The last thing he wanted to do was to be charismatic," said his friend poet Robert Lowell. "He was a mixture of proud contempt and modest distaste. . . . Usually the cheers were greater when he came in than when he finished speaking."[35] Kennedy's public temperament was the opposite of McCarthy's. In a spooky year, the frenzy he aroused could be frightening. In Mishawaka, Indiana, he chipped a front tooth when he was pulled out of his limousine by a wild supporter the day before the Indiana primary.[36] John J. Lindsay, a *Newsweek* correspondent, remembered Bobby getting on an airplane: "They had taken his tie off, his cuff links were gone, and his shirt . . . adhered to his chest. As he went by my seat, he put his foot up . . . on the arm of the chair. . . . They had stolen his shoe. He said, 'Don't tell me people in this country don't love me.' And then in that way of deprecating himself, he said, 'On the other hand, perhaps all they wanted was a shoe.' "[37] He was famous for changing his shirt five times a day.

Larner felt "Bobby's characteristic sins were sins of commission; Gene's, sins of omission." It was very recent history that kept so many in McCarthy's fold: "When it mattered," Larner noted, "Gene had gone into New Hampshire. Bobby, hung up, had refrained." The proudest button in the McCarthy campaign read FMBNH: "For McCarthy Before New Hampshire."[38]

In Indiana the mood of the McCarthy campaign reminded many of the earliest, desperate days of his candidacy. The advance work was bad, the crowds were small, and money was once again in short supply.[39] However, Paul Newman was still working for McCarthy, and Newman's fans were just as crazed as Bobby's. Tony Podesta re-created his New Hampshire role as the actor's chaperon. "I continued to watch Paul Newman in utter disbelief, not really willing to admit those people were actually doing what they were doing," said Podesta. The Newman motorcade was followed at all times by three or four carloads of "young, married women who were screaming all the way down the highway." On a two-lane road, one enthusiast kept trying to drive alongside Newman—in the lane of opposing traffic. "One time when she was going back into her own lane, she hit our follow-up car with the five guys in it. They stopped to get out to inspect the damage, and she said, 'Oh, let's not stop. Let's go to the airport first, I want to see him take off. My husband'll understand.'" At the airport she left her screaming child in the backseat and charged to the airplane to see her idol. To prevent a stampede, Podesta offered the other women chicken bones and beer bottles that had touched Newman's lips if they would just promise to stay off the tarmac. "We started auctioning off things he had touched, and doing a little fund raising in that way," Podesta recalled. "It was somewhat unorthodox, but, given the money we had versus the money Kennedy had, we had to resort to almost anything, and so we began to auction chicken bones."[40]

Not even Paul Newman's chicken bones were a match for the Kennedy juggernaut. In spite of the students who rode into the state on buses chartered by the Kennedy campaign and then walked around the corner to work for McCarthy, Kennedy still got a big win in Indiana. The final tally on May 7 gave the New York senator 42.3 percent, Governor Branigin got 30.7 percent, and McCarthy was a distant third with 27 percent. In his concession speech, McCarthy explained that winning wasn't the most important thing. "That isn't the way *I* was brought up," Bobby barked at the TV screen.[41]

A pall settled over McCarthy's campaign workers. Bobby had sustained his family's unbroken string of victories at the polls, and one week later he added another when he crushed McCarthy in Nebraska with 51.7 percent of the vote; McCarthy got just 31.2 percent. Now the Kennedy brothers had won twenty-seven consecutive elections. Pierre Salinger said McCarthy was no longer a "credible" candidate.[42] And the Minnesotan was even more bitter than usual in his comments to *Life*'s Shana Alexander. He said Humphrey was like a dog that barks and sits up without being asked—"He wants the office so bad, you want to give it to him." He compared Bobby to a wolverine: "kind of a torn animal. It doesn't really know its identity. It fouls up traps, or destroys what's in a trap, and its frightening snarl scares trappers in lonely camps."[43]

In private, McCarthy gave himself a little more blame for his plight—or was he just being sarcastic? Blair Clark wasn't sure when he witnessed an off-the-record conversation between McCarthy and Jimmy Breslin at the New York Hilton. The candidate told the columnist he was a victim of "acedia."

"Come again?" said Breslin.

"The sin of spiritual sloth," McCarthy explained. Clark thought that "it was an amazingly revealing line: If you wanted one fancy word to describe McCarthy's attitude toward the effort of '68, acedia would be as good as any."[44]

Larner was depressed: "The campaign was doing bad things to the candidates, bad things to the people who worked for them, bad things even to the partisans who looked on from afar with contempt for one another."[45] In the next three weeks there were two more crucial contests: Oregon on May 28 and California seven days later. McCarthy had begun his campaign amid accusations that he was only a stalking-horse for Kennedy; now Kennedy's men said a vote for McCarthy was really a vote for Humphrey, since Kennedy was the only candidate with a serious chance of stopping the vice-president. McCarthy's subdued approach to his theoretical goal always made him susceptible to the charge that his campaign was intended to benefit someone other than himself. Paradoxically, this same internal calm gave him a special appeal to voters disturbed by the continuing national turmoil.

On May 21, the growing pressures on each candidate inspired separate gaffes. After a speech at the San Francisco Press Club, Kennedy made a prediction that would haunt him for the rest of his campaign. He said, "I think that if I get beaten in any primary, I am not a very viable candidate."[46] McCarthy, interviewed the same day on an airplane on his way to Coos Bay, Oregon, told a reporter it was possible he would support Humphrey: "I don't know. I think I'll wait and see what his position is on the war." In two sentences McCarthy had confirmed the worst fears of his backers: that he secretly admired Humphrey and that he no longer had any faith in his own prospects. These rumors had picked up momentum with the arrival of two new campaign aides, Thomas Finney and Thomas McCoy, known as the "CIA twins" because of their previous government affiliation. Finney had most recently been a law partner of Clark Clifford's, another credential that increased the suspicion of many (including Blair Clark) that he was really a secret agent for Humphrey.

There was an uproar over McCarthy's comments, which the candidate tried to dismiss by pretending he had been misquoted. Unless he could repair the damage, his campaign might collapse. To McCarthy speech-writers Jeremy Larner and Paul Gorman, the misstep provided a much desired opportunity: They used it to persuade their candidate to deliver the stinging speech that he had so assiduously avoided. Larner demanded to know if McCarthy would attack Humphrey as harshly as he had Kennedy. McCarthy promised that he would; the speechwriter was prepared to quit without such an assurance.[47]

McCarthy was scheduled to speak at the Cow Palace in San Francisco the following evening. Tactically it was a crucial moment, but it was also an important intellectual occasion. Everything that was radical about the McCarthy candidacy (by the standards of 1968) was articulated in this address: his rejection of a Joe McCarthy–influenced Democratic foreign policy, his distrust of the military-industrial complex, and his eagerness to end the twenty-year-old isolation of Communist China. "Involvement in Vietnam was no accident," the senator declared. "It was written in the past, if we had only seen." The foundation of American foreign policy "has remained the same as it was in the early fifties and in the sixties: containment and a continuation of the cold war." It was "essentially the same diplomacy, assuming for itself the role of the world's judge and the world's policeman."

He attacked many of the architects of John Kennedy's foreign policy by name—Dean Rusk, Walt Rostow, McGeorge and William Bundy. "Any man who played a prominent role in developing the policies of the early sixties, I think, can be called upon to explain those policies . . . [which] grow from a systematic misconception of America and of its role in the world. I am not convinced that the senator from New York has entirely renounced those misconceptions, nor is the vice-president prepared to say that the process is wrong, as well as what it produces. If they did, in the case of the senator from New York, I would find it very difficult to explain why he would use an endorsement from the former secretary of defense." McCarthy noted he had yet to hear Kennedy criticize the military, the State Department, or the CIA.[48]

Several McCarthy aides agreed that their candidate relished his criticism of Kennedy—and mumbled his attacks on the vice-president. Larner felt that McCarthy had made it clear that he hated Bobby Kennedy and preferred

Humphrey on a "personal level." But since the speech was delivered in the evening on the West Coast, most reporters had to write their stories from the prepared text, so the subtleties of McCarthy's delivery were hidden from many readers.[49]

At last McCarthy's campaign was back on the upswing. Tom Wicker wrote in the *New York Times* that by challenging the very basis of American foreign policy—including the idea that we had a "duty to impose American idealism upon foreign cultures"—McCarthy had given himself the most radical theme of any presidential candidate.[50] For the rest of the week, McCarthy attracted large crowds, frequently greater than Kennedy's. Arthur Miller, William Styron, and Jules Feiffer were campaigning for McCarthy; the Minnesotan derided Kennedy for bringing his dog and an astronaut (John Glenn) into the state to help him.[51]

On the Saturday before the Oregon vote, McCarthy bought a half-hour of television time and invited Kennedy to join him; once again, his rival declined to confront him.[52] The same day, Drew Pearson reported that Kennedy had "ordered a wiretap" on Martin Luther King's telephone in 1963. Pierre Salinger refused to comment directly on the charge.[53]

On Sunday, McCarthy and Kennedy came within a few hundred yards of each other in Portland's Rose Garden. Larner spotted Bobby and told three McCarthy kids to stand in front of the car. "Senator McCarthy is coming," Larner told Kennedy. "Isn't that too bad," said Bobby, who jumped into his vehicle as his driver floored the accelerator, forcing Gene's campaign workers to jump for their lives. Larner shouted, "Coward!" and felt exhilarated, but by the time he heard his own cry on the evening news he was disgusted with himself. "What was *I* doing then?" he asked. "I who had joined for a cause and worked to state the issues? I had acted from instinct, just like any other hack, to embarrass the opposition. I had become in my way pretty much like everyone else on either side: a gangster in a war of two mobs in the same family."[54] It was the kind of self-doubt no one ever heard from a Kennedy operative.

Bobby made one more gaffe: He dived into the Pacific, offending the cautious sensibility of Oregonians, who never enter their ocean so early in the spring. On Tuesday the spell was finally broken; for the first time in twenty-two years, the Kennedys had lost an election. McCarthy had won Oregon with 43.9 percent of the vote. Bobby trailed with 37 percent. Kennedy sent McCarthy a congratulatory telegram, a form McCarthy hadn't bothered to observe in Indiana or Nebraska. Once again, there was pandemonium at a McCarthy headquarters, this time inside an aging athletic club near the center of Portland. A roar went up each time a new result was posted on the board; Walter Cronkite called it "a hilarious victory celebration." CBS News correspondent David Schoumacher interviewed McCarthy volunteer Teeny O'Dean on the floor of the headquarters. "Oh wow!" said Teeny. "It's just like New Hampshire—and even better!"[55]

Throughout its election-night broadcast, the network kept running Kennedy's statement that he couldn't afford to lose a single primary and remain "a viable candidate." Larry O'Brien insisted to Roger Mudd that Kennedy's campaign would bounce back in California. "I am quite confident that when we meet again, a week from tonight, my smile will be even wider than this evening."

"And you won't be sweating as much?" Mudd asked.[56]

THE next morning, Kennedy seemed suddenly desperate. He promised to quit the race if McCarthy beat him in California. And, for the first time, he agreed to a debate. "I'm not the same candidate I was before Oregon, and I can't claim that I am," he said. McCarthy switched to a larger chartered jet to accommodate his swelling press corps. Ronald Reagan said he was "delighted" by Kennedy's defeat.[57] Nevertheless, on the streets of Los Angeles that day, there were tremendous crowds, the screaming, grabbing, worshiping crowds Bobby loved, the mobs that always stole his cuff links and squeezed his hands until they bled. He said that after Oregon, Los Angeles felt like "Resurrection City."[58] The next day he took a whistle-stop tour from Fresno to Sacramento. "My family eats more tomatoes than any family I know," said Bobby, "and my wife and children all wear cotton clothes. I'm doing more for the farmer than McCarthy or Humphrey." In Watts, McCarthy gave a qualified endorsement to Black Power.[59]

On Friday, Pierre Salinger explained why only one debate was necessary between Kennedy and McCarthy: "Studies of the 1960 debates between JFK and Nixon clearly showed that the only one that anybody paid any attention to was the first."[60] McCarthy compared Kennedy's newest warning, that he would quit if he lost again, to "the threats of a child holding his breath unless you do something for him."[61]

Saturday was showdown day. The only debate between Kennedy and McCarthy would be broadcast nationally that evening by ABC. Since Kennedy had resisted this encounter for so long, most people assumed he was the underdog. He closeted himself with his aides in self-conscious emulation of the "skull sessions" his brother used in 1960 to prepare for

Nixon. McCarthy was briefed by his speechwriters, Larner and Gorman—and Robert Lowell.[62] Then Lowell paid an unofficial call on Kennedy and got a lecture on why McCarthy should get out of the race. The poet did not enjoy the experience. "I felt like Rudolf Hess parachuting into Scotland," he told Blair Clark.[63]

In different ways during the debate, each candidate managed to corroborate the worst fears of their fans, and their enemies. The main controversy started after McCarthy suggested that some ghetto residents should have the opportunity to move into the suburbs, to avoid "adopting a kind of apartheid in this country." Spotting an opportunity, Kennedy quickly distorted McCarthy's statement: "You say you are going to take ten thousand black people and move them into Orange County," he said. Orange County was very conservative and very white, and McCarthy had said nothing of the kind. Kennedy had invented the number and the location to make a none-too-subtle appeal to white racism. McCarthy partisans, outraged by the fabrication, waited impatiently for their man to correct the record. They waited in vain: McCarthy never bothered to contradict his opponent. One McCarthy aide wondered if he had "merely grown bored."[64]

In an hour McCarthy had dissipated the momentum of Oregon. The Minnesotan thought "it had turned out almost a draw."[65] Larner believed "Gene had the better of it because he was cool while Bobby was undeniably cheap; yet there was a way in which Gene lost that debate—lost as a man and as a leader."[66] Tom Finney, McCarthy's newest campaign guru, was disgusted: "He flubbed it! Blew it! Threw it away! How can you get him elected?" A *Los Angeles Times* poll said viewers, by a ratio of two-and-a-half to one, felt Kennedy had won the encounter.[67]

On Sunday in the *New York Times,* Charlotte Curtis reported the newest bumper sticker in California: FIRST ETHEL, NOW US.[68] That morning McCarthy finally hit back at his opponent. He accused Kennedy of "scare tactics" and a "crude distortion" of his proposals, but it was much too late to repair the damage. Kennedy replied that if McCarthy felt he had not been precise, "he had ample opportunity to respond when we were face to face."[69]

The day before the primary Kennedy traveled in an open car through San Francisco's Chinatown. His wife, Ethel, slumped in her seat when she thought she heard shots—six loud bangs. They were only firecrackers, and Bobby never flinched, but he did ask a reporter running alongside to climb into the car to comfort his wife.[70]

Kennedy slept late on election day; the polls said he would win. He was staying at the Malibu home of John Frankenheimer, the director of *The Manchurian Candidate*, and six of his children had been flown out from Hickory Hill to be with him. Twelve-year-old David dived into the Pacific and disappeared in the undertow. Bobby dived in after him, bruising his forehead in the course of the rescue, but father and son were both fine when they emerged from the water. Then Bobby had lunch with Teddy White. He told him he hoped McCarthy's kids would finally come over to him if he won that evening. He was tense through the afternoon until White got the first projections from CBS. The network's exit poll indicated he would beat McCarthy by eight points. For the first time since Johnson's abdication, Kennedy began to relax.[71]

THE liquor flowed happily in suite 516 of the Ambassador Hotel in Los Angeles that evening. Bobby Kennedy had won the most important victory of his life, and Oregon was just a distant memory. Jimmy Breslin was there, as were George Plimpton and Teddy White; so were Sorensen and Goodwin and Steve Smith, and occasionally Kennedy would retreat into the bathroom with one of them for a moment of privacy.[72] South Dakota had also voted that day, and Bobby had won big there, too, with 50 percent of the vote, compared with 30 percent for a delegate slate allied with Humphrey and just 20 percent for McCarthy.[73] Teddy White went on television with Walter Cronkite and called the two results "the most complete repudiation of the administration. . . . This is the clearest revolt yet of a new kind of politics against an old kind of politics."

CBS kept projecting wider and wider margins of victory for Kennedy—now Cronkite was saying he would beat McCarthy by fourteen points, 52 to 38. Bobby was unusually relaxed in a long interview with Roger Mudd. When the reporter asked him if he would run with Humphrey, Kennedy parried, "In what order?" Then he criticized Humphrey for saying that he was still ready to step aside if Johnson decided to get back into the race. "You're either in it or you're not in it," Kennedy said. Blair Clark came on the air to report McCarthy was in the race to stay, regardless of the outcome that evening. But the atmosphere was somber at McCarthy headquarters at the Beverly Hilton. The comedian Carl Reiner came onstage in the Grand Ballroom. "We're going to try desperately to make a long evening seem short," he said.[74]

CBS went off the air at 11:13 P.M. in Los Angeles, when it was 2:13 in the morning on the East Coast. Kennedy still hadn't made his formal declaration of victory, but at this hour CBS figured even the most serious political junkies wouldn't mind waiting to watch that part of the celebration the next morning. A reporter in Kennedy's suite thought the young candidate finally seemed "liberated."[75] The Kennedy magic was back, and it was definitely *Bobby's* magic. He was forty-two, but he still looked barely over thirty. To Kenny O'Donnell, one of the family's oldest retainers, Kennedy said, "I feel now for the first time that I've shaken off the shadow of my brother. I feel I made it on my own."[76]

By midnight the crowd downstairs was getting rowdy. They were singing "This Land Is Your Land" and chanting, "We want Kennedy!"[77] Bobby told Ethel he was ready to go. Inside the ballroom he stood behind a lectern with a single KENNEDY sticker stuck on it, under the logo of the hotel. He began with baseball: "I want to express my high regard to Don Drysdale, who pitched his sixth straight shutout tonight, and I hope that we have as good fortune in our campaign." He said California had voted "for peace and for justice and for a government dedicated to giving the people mastery over their own affairs." He praised McCarthy for "breaking the political logjam" and making "citizen participation a new and powerful force in our political life." And he asked McCarthy's troops to join him—"not for myself, but for the cause and the ideas which moved you to begin this great popular movement." Larner thought it was Bobby's best speech of the campaign.[78]

Then he thanked everyone: the blacks, the Mexicans, his siblings, his mother, "and all those other Kennedys"; even his dog, Freckles. "What I think is quite clear is that we can work together. We are a great country, an unselfish country, and a compassionate country." There were no policemen inside the hotel.[79] The crowd went wild, and in the film clip that would be repeated endlessly on television for the rest of the week, dozens of white boaters emblazoned with Kennedy's image bobbed happily up and down in the ballroom. Finally he was done. "My thanks to all of you. And now it's on to Chicago, and let's win there!" He gave the V sign, for victory—which also meant peace in 1968—pushed his hair off his forehead in a familiar gesture, then turned to exit through the kitchen.[80]

Andrew West, a radio reporter for KRKD, trailed Kennedy as he left the podium. West had an old-fashioned radio voice: slightly theatrical. This is what his listeners heard:

"How are you going to counter Mr. Humphrey as far as the delegate vote goes?" West asked.

"We're just going to start to struggle for it," said the candidate.

It was 12:16 A.M., and Bobby paused in the kitchen to shake hands with Jesus Perez, a dishwasher. Then West started speaking again—rather hysterically: "Senator Kennedy has been shot. Is that possible? Is that possible? Is it possible ladies and gentlemen? It is possible he has—not only Senator Kennedy. Oh, my God. Senator Kennedy has been shot, and another man, a Kennedy campaign manager—and possibly shot in the head. Rafer Johnson has a hold of the man who apparently has fired the shot." Now West sounded desperate: "He still has the gun—the gun is pointed at me right at this moment I hope they can get the gun out of his hand. Be very careful, get that gun get that gun GET THAT GUN! Stay away from the gun; stay away from the gun. His hand is frozen. TAKE A HOLD OF HIS THUMB AND BREAK IT IF YOU HAVE TO; GET HIS THUMB! All right, that's it Rafer, get it, get the gun Rafer. Hold him, hold him. We don't want another Oswald."[81]

A British reporter noted, "The blood is always so much more splotched about than you would think from pictures or movies."[82] In the ballroom next door bewilderment turned into terror. A young girl screamed, "No, God, no! It's happened again." A black man pounded the wall. "Why, God, why? Why again? Why another Kennedy?"[83] Six people in the kitchen were hit by the barrage of bullets, but only one was fatally wounded.* Most people believed Bobby never regained consciousness, but two witnesses insisted that he had talked with them. When Ethel leaned down over him, she thought she heard her husband ask, "How bad is it?"[84] And Max Behrman, an ambulance attendant, swore Kennedy spoke again when he tried to pick him up. "Please don't," said the stricken man. "Please don't. Don't lift me."[85] On the kitchen wall, five feet from where Kennedy had fallen, someone had scrawled five words: "The once and future king."[86] On West 57th Street in Manhattan, CBS News scrambled to get back on the air. "If he lives, he'll be president," someone remarked inside the control room. "And if he dies," said CBS News president Richard Salant, "we don't have a camera at the hospital."[87]

The next day, he was still alive, but there was very little hope. A twenty-four-year-old Jordanian named Sirhan Sirhan had been seized at the scene. He had fired a .22-caliber Iver-Johnson eight-shot revolver, which retailed for $30.95. "It turns out over the years that the people who shoot people

---

* The other five were Paul Schrade of the United Auto Workers Union; William Weisel, an ABC producer; Ira Godstein, a Continental News Service reporter; Elizabeth Evans, a Kennedy campaign worker; and Irwin Stoll. a seventeen-year-old supporter. Schrade was seriously wounded, but all five recovered from their injuries.

don't care if it's much of a gun," Harry Reasoner observed. When he was arrested, the assassin was carrying four $100 bills and a newspaper column that identified Bobby as a strong defender of Israel.[88]

Hubert Humphrey got a White House plane to fly the Kennedys' favorite surgeon to Los Angeles.[89] For the first time in American history, President Johnson ordered Secret Service protection for all presidential candidates. New York City policemen guarded Arab ambassadors at the United Nations after they received telephoned threats. In London, a BBC announcer said, "We pray for the American people that they may come to their senses." In Manhattan, half a dozen Secret Service men had to form a wedge through the crowd outside Jackie Kennedy's Fifth Avenue apartment building so that she could reach her limousine. Then she drove to the airport to catch another special plane to California.[90]

In Los Angeles, one minute before two o'clock on Thursday morning, almost twenty-six hours after the shooting, Frank Mankiewicz announced that Kennedy was dead. Maurice Carroll of the *New York Times* dictated the news to his colleague Albin Krebs in New York. It was more than two hours past the paper's normal closing time, but the *Times* had taken the very unusual step of staying open until 5 A.M. in case there might be such an announcement. The story of his death caught the paper's very last edition.[91] The *New York Post* put out an extra. The headline simply read, NOW RFK. For two and a half hours, Channel 11 in New York City broadcast nothing but a picture of the word SHAME.

The White House sent a Boeing 707 to pick up the body, a sister plane to the one that had carried Jack Kennedy's casket back from Dallas. Fifteen hundred watched as the blue hearse carried Bobby's body away from Good Samaritan, and others waved from overpasses as it traveled down a Los Angeles freeway. At the airport, Ethel, three months pregnant, entered the front of the plane with the coffin on a hoist. Jackie Kennedy was the first person to board through the rear entrance.

Jackie had called Leonard Bernstein from California to ask him to choose the music for the funeral. Bernstein settled on the slow movement from Mahler's Fifth Symphony and a passage from the Verdi Requiem. Then Jackie telephoned again from the airplane to say Ethel also wanted the nuns from her old school to sing certain songs from her youth, like "In Paradisum." Bernstein said that might be a problem, because a monsignor had already told him that no woman had ever sung in St. Patrick's Cathedral, and no woman ever would.[92]

It was an oppressive eighty-five degrees when the plane touched down in New York at 8:57 in the evening. Among the one thousand waiting at the airport were Governor Nelson Rockefeller and Mayor John Lindsay, each of whom had to be physically restrained from approaching the widow while she was accompanying her husband's coffin.[93] Ethel and Teddy rode in the front seat of the hearse on the way into the city. In Spanish Harlem, hundreds swarmed onto the FDR Drive. They shouted, *"Viva!"*[94]

His mother was waiting for him at St. Patrick's. As the African mahogany coffin was carried into the church, Rose Kennedy stood up from her prayers to walk behind it. Campaign aide William Vanden Heuvel found it "shocking, suddenly, to see this person, whose life had known so much tragedy, walking again behind the coffin of another murdered son." More than a hundred thousand New Yorkers filed past after her. Several strangers murmured, "Forgive us, Bobby," as they touched the casket.[95]

Bernstein had gone back to the monsignor, who continued to insist that singing nuns were out of the question inside the cathedral. But the next day it was all settled: Jackie had been to see Archbishop Terence Cooke herself at eight o'clock in the morning. It turned out that Ethel had actually been there a half-hour before Jackie and had already got the archbishop to agree to her request.[96]

Teddy Kennedy delivered a magnificent eulogy; he sounded more like Jack than Bobby had ever been able to. Sitting just ahead and to his right was Lyndon Johnson; immediately behind Johnson, Rufus Youngblood.[97] Youngblood was the Secret Service agent who had jumped on top of Johnson at the moment John Kennedy was killed in Dallas.[98] The new president had promoted Youngblood to the head of his White House detail.

The last brother began by quoting words Bobby had spoken to the young people of South Africa on their Day of Affirmation in 1966. "There is discrimination in this world, and slavery and slaughter and starvation. Governments repress their people; millions are trapped in poverty while the nations grow rich; and wealth is lavished on armaments everywhere. . . . The answer is to rely on youth—not a time of life but a state of mind, a temper of the will, a quality of imagination, a predominance of courage over timidity. . . . A young monk began the Protestant Reformation, a young general extended an empire from Macedonia to the borders of the earth, and a young woman reclaimed the territory of France. It was a young Italian explorer who discovered the New World, and the thirty-two-year-old Thomas Jefferson who proclaimed that 'all men are created equal.'"

Then Teddy spoke for himself: "My brother need not be idealized, or enlarged in death beyond what he was in life—to be remembered simply as a good and decent man, who saw wrong and tried to right it, saw suffering and tried to heal it, saw war and tried to stop it. Those of us who loved him and who take him to his rest today, pray that what he was to us and what he wished for others will some day come to pass for all the world." Here his voice was breaking: "As he said many times, in many parts of this nation, to those he touched and who sought to touch him: 'Some men see things as they are and say why. I dream things that never were, and say why not?'"[99]

AS THE body left the cathedral, television commentators broke in to announce that Martin Luther King's assassin had finally been apprehended. James Earl Ray, carrying a loaded pistol, was passing through immigration at London's Heathrow Airport on his way to Brussels when he was caught. The Royal Canadian Mounted Police had searched through two hundred thousand passport applications to find one with a picture that resembled the photograph the FBI had distributed of the wanted man. Scotland Yard had been alerted to look for a passport bearing the alias of Ramon George Sneyd. Detective Chief Superintendent Thomas Butler and Detective Chief Inspector Noel Thompson, known as the "Terrible Twins" for their tenacity, took Ray into custody. Kennedy's friends wondered whether J. Edgar Hoover had timed the announcement to upstage his enemy one last time in the middle of his funeral.[100] Earlier, FBI officials had hinted to reporters that they believed Ray was already dead.[101]

ANDY WARHOL could hear Bobby Kennedy's funeral on a distant television, but he wasn't sure exactly what it was that he heard. The day before Kennedy was shot, Warhol had been gravely wounded by Valerie Solanas, who fired two .32-caliber bullets into his stomach. Solanas was a Warhol acquaintance and the founder of SCUM—the Society for Cutting Up Men. He remembered that she had talked "constantly about the complete elimination of the male sex," saying that the result would be an "out-of-sight, groovy, all-female world." This is Warhol's account of what happened to him after the shooting:

"They took me to Columbus Hospital, on 19th Street between Second and Third Avenues, five or six blocks away. Suddenly there were lots of doctors around me, and I heard things like 'Forget it' and '. . . no chance . . .' and then I heard someone saying my name—it was Mario Amaya—telling them that I was famous and that I had money.

"I was in surgery for about five hours, with Dr. Giuseppe Rossi and four other great doctors working on me. They brought me back from the dead—literally, because I'm told that at one point I was gone. For days and days afterward, I wasn't sure if I *was* back. I felt dead. I kept thinking, 'I'm really dead. This is what it's like to be dead—you think you're alive but you're dead. I just *think* I'm lying here in a hospital.'

"As I was coming down from my operation, I heard a television going somewhere and the words 'Kennedy' and 'assassin' and 'shot' over and over again. Robert Kennedy had been shot, but what was so weird was that I had no understanding that this was a *second* Kennedy assassination—I just thought that maybe after you die, they rerun things for you, like President Kennedy's assassination."[102]

THERE were two engines at the front of the special train that carried Bobby Kennedy's body to Washington. An electrician named Vincent Emanuel rode in the second engine, which was there in case the first one had a breakdown. With him was a Secret Service man who did not want to be there at all. His name was Roy Kellerman, and he had been riding in the front seat of John Kennedy's midnight-blue Lincoln limousine when the president was killed in Dallas.[103]

Outside the train, Russell Baker remembered, "the reaction was kind of varied, as you'd expect. A lot of solemn people and a few carrying flowers and signs and whatnot. But it really impressed me to see America with its hair down on Saturday afternoon." Charles Quinn, a television man, saw someone standing way off in the distance, saluting. "You'd see another man standing with his hand over his heart; or a fire truck on top of a knoll with four or five firemen with their hands over their hearts, and the little light going around and around. And the girls on horseback; and the boats . . . all those bridges we passed over and those dozens of boats bobbing up and down in the water."[104]

In many of those who shared Bobby Kennedy's convictions but had refused to support his candidacy, guilt combined with shock to produce excruciating pain. Apart from the hideous image of a bloody puddle forming under Bobby's head on that hotel kitchen floor, nothing was more difficult to watch that week than the film of McCarthy volunteers in Los Angeles, gasping before they buried their horrified faces in their hands at the first news of the shooting.[105] Murray Kempton, who had been so brutal in print a few months earlier, spoke for many of Kennedy's former enemies in a famous column a few days after the killing: "The language of dismissal becomes horrible once you recognize the shadow of death over every public man. For I had forgotten, from being bitter about a temporary course of his, how much I liked Senator Kennedy and how much he needed to know he was liked. Now that there is in life no road at whose turning we could meet again, the memory of having forgotten that will always make me sad and indefinitely make me ashamed."[106]

David Hollander was eighteen in 1968, a Harvard freshman who loved Bobby Kennedy but campaigned for Eugene McCarthy because he thought Bobby "had been slow and played politics." When he learned that Kennedy had been shot, "I was devastated by this, because I instantly thought that I was wrong, that I should have been working for Kennedy all along. It was an irrational sort of reaction. Part of it was simply that in my heart of hearts, I had always liked him more. I was punishing him for being slow and being political. But he always appealed to me more—he was sexy, and his brother's legacy. I saw him give a speech in Albany, Indiana, in my senior year in high school, and it was just delightful. He was *really* charismatic."

Bobby had won a varsity letter in football at Harvard, and someone thought to ask the Harvard band to play at his funeral.[107] Hollander was a trumpet player in the Harvard band. "The morning of the funeral, the band is bused to Logan Airport and put on a plane to Washington," he remembered. "We go to Georgetown University, where I believe we find out that his train has killed two people on the way to Washington.* And by this time it's all just totally surreal . . . totally surreal. We go to the cemetery and we stand there, we're positioned, we play 'America the Beautiful,' and it is really like a hallucination. At this point I'd never taken any acid, but it prepared me for what came afterward. Because here comes Jacqueline Kennedy and Lyndon Johnson, the archenemy, the embodiment of evil, and the Kennedy family and the Congress and every important person in Washington are over there, like thirty feet away from us. It's really not very far, they're right there; and we're playing 'America the Beautiful' and it's—the strangeness of it is something I can't begin to express. My emotions were such a—you know, this was somebody I had worked against, and somebody who I wanted more than anything in the world to bring back to life. And these people I'm playing for I would like to kill. It was great; I was very glad I got to do that.

---

* Two people waiting in Elizabeth, New Jersey, to see the funeral train pass by had been killed by a locomotive traveling in the opposite direction. After that, all northbound trains were halted until Kennedy's had reached Washington.

"Then I went home for the summer to Indiana. About a month later all my high school classmates had a party, and we rented a cabin outside of town and we all drank a lot and there were all these Simon and Garfunkel records playing—incredibly sentimental stuff. And I see a newspaper headline about Bobby Kennedy's death, and I break down sobbing; in front of all of my friends, in front of all the jocks, and my old girlfriend and everyone I've ever known in high school. And of course I'd never done anything like this. I was quite drunk—everybody was quite drunk—and I spent the whole evening just sobbing, sobbing uncontrollably.

"And they asked what was wrong, and I said it was about Bobby Kennedy, and I don't know if they thought that was credible or not. But that is what it was about. I never discussed it with any of them ever afterward. It really was like the last straw—that there was no longer any reason to hope for anything; that the world was now just totally off its rocker, and that evil was ascendant, and was going to be."[108]

9

Rock of Ages

"Excitement wasn't in the air; it was the air."
— Greil Marcus on Beatlemania[1]

"The words are just as important as the music: there would be no music without the words."
— Bob Dylan[2]

"It was an unassailable outlet for some pure and natural expressions of rebellion. It was one channel you could take without havin' to kiss ass, you know?"
— Keith Richards[3]

"I came out of the fuckin' sticks to take over the world, it seemed to me."
— John Lennon[4]

"Nothing else can survive a holocaust but poetry and songs."
— Jim Morrison[5]

WHAT would unite the Vietnam generation after its April reverie had dissolved into a summer of despair?

There would remain a lasting legacy, a culture of sound as well as words. Of all the elements that made up the sixties, this one had the deepest impact on the whole generation, all around the world. It helped shape a common political agenda, but its influence went far beyond politics. It was by turns steel-edged, sentimental, raucous, melodious, sophisticated, and infantile, sometimes tinged with nihilism but most often blazingly upbeat.

This was the music of rock and roll. It was the transcendent achievement of the counterculture of the sixties, embodying all the virtues, shortcomings, and contradictions of that amorphous engine of change. It owed its largest artistic debt to American blacks and their forebears from Africa, where a combination of religion, magic, and music had previously provided what one critic called "a composite cultural focus."[6] Rock and roll's provenance made its impact on black artists particularly appropriate: It probably gave more of them broader and deeper recognition in Europe and America than they had ever received there before.

In the mid-fifties, it was rock and roll that had helped transform the radio into the flipside of television in American culture. As TV became steadily more homogenized and predictable, there was adventure on the radio. Very few places had as many as six TV channels, but even a small city could support a dozen radio stations, and on a clear night you might pick up a broadcast from almost anywhere on your car radio. A New York station like WABC could be heard in Albuquerque, New Mexico, and Cuba's Guantánamo Bay, while Wolfman Jack's pirate outlet south of the border, in Mexico, beamed his bizarre program west all the way to California and north as far as Canada.[*7] TV was a white medium, the one you turned on in your living room to watch *Leave It to Beaver* or *Father Knows Best*, family entertainment that reinforced the middle-class ideal of the white suburban family. With the mass production of transistors in the late fifties, radio became the medium you could enjoy anywhere, alone, outdoors, or under the covers (even after you were supposed to be asleep). What you heard put you squarely inside a world of your own, a world just as subversive as the Frank Sinatra generation feared it might be—the raucous, untamed, black and white world of Little Richard, Elvis Presley, Jerry Lee Lewis, Buddy Holly, the jitterbug, and Murray the K.

A Cleveland disc jockey named Allan Freed may have been the first person to call it "rock and roll" on a white radio station; Freed even pretended that he had invented a new term for rhythm and blues. Actually, "rock and roll" was a venerable euphemism for sex, well known for decades to connoisseurs of "race records" produced for the black market. Freed was called a "nigger lover" for making his unusual selections (and

---

* The Wolfman, who was white, refused all interviews until the seventies, to preserve the illusion that he was black.

eventually was done in by a payola scandal), but the power of the music he loved was greater than the prejudice it aroused.[8]

In 1968 the creativity of rock was pushed over the top by an unprecedented diversity, a cross-cultural exchange that was simultaneously racial, sexual, musical, and multinational. By then rock and roll included everything from soft pop to heavy metal, everyone from Laura Nyro and Smokey Robinson to Bob Dylan and Iron Butterfly, mostly because the Beatles were still competing with everyone (especially themselves) to enlarge the boundaries of what it might encompass. Stevie Wonder explained: "We all really influenced each other. That's really what it's all about."[9] Embraced by the largest generation ever—which was united almost everywhere by the radio—the music became, by the sheer force of our numbers, the dominant popular culture of the world.

The sounds were subversive in several ways—explicitly, in songs like the "I Feel Like I'm Fixin' to Die Rag," in which Country Joe and the Fish encouraged each of their listeners to be "the first one on your block to have your boy come home in a box," and more obliquely, as when the music tried to replicate (and by implication, glorify) the psychedelic experience. Sometimes, small gestures had the greatest impact. When *Rolling Stone* editor Jann Wenner asked Eric Clapton in 1967 what impressed him most about the San Francisco scene, the legendary guitar player replied it was the willingness of the Grateful Dead to play for free. "That very much moved me," said Clapton. "I've never heard of anyone doing that before. . . . There is this incredible thing that the musical people seem to have toward their audience: They want to give."[10]

For many of us, the messages implicit in the success of rock's stars were just as important as the music itself. More black singers and composers were "crossing over" to attract a larger white following than ever before. At the same moment, the emergence by 1968 of women artists like Aretha Franklin, Janis Joplin, and Grace Slick as virtual equals of men like Marvin Gaye, Jerry Garcia, and Jimi Hendrix provided subliminal evidence of sexual equality for teenagers everywhere. And at least in the case of Joplin, this equality went well beyond the easy matter of equal fame. When she wailed, "Come on, take another little piece of my heart," she wasn't merely just as famous as any male rock and roll star—she was also just as tough. Or, as critic Ellen Willis put it, "Joplin's metamorphosis from the ugly duckling of Port Arthur to the peacock of Haight-Ashbury" meant that "a woman who was not conventionally pretty, who had acne and an intermittent weight problem and hair that stuck out" could "invent her own beauty out of sheer energy, soul, sweetness, arrogance, and a sense of humor," and thereby change the very "notions of attractiveness."[11] On the other side of the sexual divide, definitions of masculinity were undergoing an equally radical transformation. With the arrival of long hair, a man could once again be cool or even macho with curls instead of a crew cut or Vitalis. And as Allen Ginsberg pointed out, simply by spending time together as "a community group," the Beatles provided "an example to youth around the world—that guys could be friends."[12] At its most fundamental level, rock and roll revealed once again how authentic equal opportunity might change the world.

IN THE decades preceding the sixties one man did more than anyone else to break down the barriers that had traditionally kept American musicians apart. His name was John Hammond, and his gigantic achievement was to integrate (almost single-handedly) black and white popular music in the United States. For fifty years he was the best musical talent scout in the world, discovering performers as diverse as Billie Holliday and Bruce Springsteen. Without him, none of the great synthesizers of the fifties and the sixties—Elvis Presley, Buddy Holly, the Beatles, and Bob Dylan—would ever have heard the work of many of the most important black artists: the singers, players, and composers who provided rock with its roots. Hammond crisscrossed the country in a variety of convertibles to discover and record scores of notable American musicians, including the greatest soul singer of 1968 and the single most important folk-rock composer-performer of them all. Only thirty years before 1968, he had organized the first major concert in America performed before an integrated audience.

He was born John Henry Hammond, Jr., in 1910, and his attitudes toward race and music were decades ahead of his time. Like a child of the sixties, he felt that music was "the catalyst for all that was to happen to me. In the grooves of those primitive early discs I found in my house, I discovered a new world, one I could enter easily and as often as I pleased by winding the handle of a phonograph."[13]

He grew up in his parents' huge four-story mansion on East 92nd Street, a few steps from Central Park. The house had two basements, two elevators, a ballroom that seated two hundred, sixteen servants, a Victrola in the front of the house for opera records, and—most important—a Columbia Grafanola in the servants' quarters, where Hammond's addiction to black music began.[14] His mother was the great-granddaughter of Cornelius

Vanderbilt, the railroad tycoon; his father, the son of the youngest Union general in the Civil War, a man who was reputed to have been Sitting Bull's only white friend.

When he was twelve, Hammond started building his record collection by spending three-quarters of his allowance on one 75¢ ten-inch Columbia or Brunswick disc every week. He was entranced by the "simple honesty and convincing lyrics of the early blues singers" and the "ingenuity of the jazz players"—and very soon he discovered that every one of his favorites was black.[15]

At twenty-one he began receiving an annual income of $12,000 from a trust fund. With the rest of his life, he demonstrated how inherited wealth can occasionally be a spur to creativity instead of killing the instinct for adventure. He disappointed his father by dropping out of Yale; then he moved into his own Greenwich Village apartment. His parents both insisted on the genetic inferiority of blacks ("Their skulls harden when they are twelve," his mother explained), but the music he adored convinced him otherwise. Hammond fell in love with black culture and did everything he could to promote it. "I did not revolt against the system," he wrote later. "I simply refused to be a part of it. . . . There was no white pianist to compare with Fats Waller, no white band as good as Fletcher Henderson's, no blues singer like Bessie Smith."[16] He was an early member of the board of the NAACP, but proving blacks were the best jazz musicians in the world was the most "constructive form of social protest" he could think of.

He pursued a double career of reviewing musicians and producing their records for publications and record companies on both sides of the Atlantic.[17] In 1933 he dropped into Monette Moore's club on 113th Street and saw Billie Holliday for the first time. He knew at once that she was "the greatest jazz singer" he had ever heard, and it was "the kind of accident" he had dreamed of. "I had found a star, and I wrote about her in *Melody Maker*," a British publication that heralded the arrival of the Beatles several decades later.[18] In the same period he befriended Benny Goodman, the legendary clarinetist, who later married Hammond's sister. At first Goodman resisted Hammond's attempts to get him to make records with black artists. "If it gets around that I recorded with colored guys, I won't get another job in this town," Goodman warned Hammond when he suggested that Goodman record something with Coleman Hawkins.

"It can't be that bad," Hammond protested.

"It's that bad," Goodman replied.[19]

But after Hammond took Goodman to hear Holliday, the clarinet player relented. In 1933 Hammond recorded Goodman and Holliday together.

Three years later, Goodman had formed the Benny Goodman Trio with Teddy Wilson and Gene Krupa, and Wilson had become the first black musician ever to integrate a white American jazz band.

Hammond's biggest breakthrough before the war was the landmark Carnegie Hall concert of 1938, which he titled "From Spirituals to Swing." With this entertainment, he did something no one had ever done before: He brought together on a single stage every phase of black music in America, "from its raw beginnings to the latest jazz."[20] With Goddard Lieberson, the future president of Columbia Records, he traveled to the backwoods of the South in search of performers. On December 23, one of the most eclectic collections of American musicians ever assembled entertained the city's first fully integrated concert audience.[21]

The concert was a smash. The music ranged from Count Basie's band to Sonny Terry, a blind harmonica player "as rough as knotty pine." Big Bill Broonzy, a primitive blues singer, enthralled the audience with a dream he'd had in which he sat in Franklin Roosevelt's chair in the White House. "The audience screamed," Hammond recalled. "They had never heard anything like this."[22]

WHAT happened to rock and roll in the sixties could not have happened without Hammond. If he hadn't gone into the music business, many of the musicians who inspired the giants of rock would have remained trapped inside the urban ghettos and country backwaters where he first found them. In the early 1940s he said, "Even in the South, there is complete acceptance of Negroes as artists." When he made that statement, it was a dream, but by 1968, largely through his efforts, it had become the truth. Black artists were not only accepted by young whites all over the country; anyone coming of age in America was an outsider to his own generation without a working knowledge of Otis Redding, Jimi Hendrix, the Supremes, the Temptations, the Four Tops, Marvin Gaye and Tammi Terrell, Martha and the Vandellas, Stevie Wonder, and Mary Wells. To millions of teenagers, no one had more cool than these artists. Even a Southern boy who hated Martin Luther King might fall in love with Diana Ross.

Hammond's impact was equally great on the other side of the Atlantic. The same black pioneers who opened up the music scene in America also became the inspiration for underprivileged young men and women across the sea, struggling musicians who dreamed that music might one day propel them out of the dreary slums of postwar Britain. The influence of

American artists was especially large in Liverpool, a decaying British port whose only cultural advantage was the presence of hundreds of "Cunard Yanks." In the 1950s, these merchant seamen brought back records from the United States by Little Richard, B. B. King, and Chuck Berry, as well as other more obscure blues artists unknown in English record shops. Without knowing it, they were carrying on the wartime tradition of lend-lease—only this time the cannon fodder coming over from America was in the form of songs called "Long Tall Sally" and "Johnny B. Goode."[23]

Black American blues was the backbone of what by the early sixties would become famous as "the Mersey Beat," but the music of Liverpool was not a simple replication of this American sound. Before it had its first rock-and-roll emporium, the city sustained a remarkable circuit of folk, blues, and country-and-western clubs, and everyone playing there drew on all of these influences.[24] "The blues is a chair," a prominent member of the Liverpool scene explained many years later. "It is the first chair. . . . You sit on that music. . . . We didn't sound like anybody else. . . . We didn't sound like the black musicians because we weren't black and because we were brought up on a different kind of music and atmosphere."[25]

The name of this speaker was John Lennon, a man with a modest Liverpool background, a singer-songwriter who remembered with great bitterness how Londoners looked down on him and his friends as "animals" because they came from the gritty industrial North.[26] For a long time, neither he nor Paul McCartney nor George Harrison nor Ringo Starr had the slightest inkling that it would be their destiny to come out of the sticks "to take over the world," but in 1962 that was exactly what they did.

After being turned down by five other recording companies, the Beatles finally got a contract with Parlophone, a unit of EMI, a thriving music conglomerate. Their first British single consisted of two McCartney-Lennon compositions: "Love Me Do" backed by "P.S. I Love You."* The record appeared in October 1962, the same month as the Cuban Missile Crisis. To hype sales, their manager, Brian Epstein, ordered ten thousand copies for the chain of department stores owned by his family. By the end of the year, "Love Me Do" had been pushed up to number seventeen on the hit parade. In February 1963 the Beatles followed it with "Please Please Me," which reached the number-one spot in less than a month. Six weeks later they released "From Me to You." In just two weeks the new song shot to the top.[27]

---

* That order wasn't reversed to Lennon-McCartney on the song credits until the second British album, *With the Beatles*. "P.S." was code for "Peggy Sue"—in honor of their idol, Buddy Holly.

Their first British album, *Please Please Me*, appeared in May. It was the best-selling album in Britain for thirty weeks, until it was replaced by their second, *With the Beatles*, which kept them at the top for the next twenty-two.[28]

Despite the rising clamor in the land of its corporate parent, Capitol Records (the American arm of EMI) refused to release any Beatles singles during the first eleven months of 1963. "They said, 'Sorry, it wouldn't mean anything in this country,'" their producer, George Martin, recalled.[29] On December 26, 1963, Capitol gave in, and "I Want to Hold Your Hand" finally arrived in America. It took five weeks to become the biggest-selling record in the United States. On February 9, 1964, the Beatles made their debut on *The Ed Sullivan Show.* In April, their records filled the first, second, third, fourth, and fifth positions on *Billboard's* singles chart. *Meet the Beatles,* their first American album on Capitol, quickly became the fastest- and largest-selling LP in the history of the United States.[30]

In his landmark essay on the Beatles, Greil Marcus argues that this was the beginning of the second pop explosion of the postwar period, the first one having become a national event with Elvis's release of "Heartbreak Hotel" in 1956. Marcus describes this phenomenon as a moment when enormous energy "is focused on, organized by and released by a single, holistic cultural entity. This entity must itself be capable of easy, instantaneous and varied imitation and extension in a thousand ways at once. . . . At its heart, a pop explosion attaches the individual to a group—the fan to an audience, the solitary to a generation—in essence, *forms* a group and creates new loyalties."[31]

Youthful anxiety in the wake of John Kennedy's assassination made American youth uniquely vulnerable to Beatlemania, but the connections between the Kennedys and the Beatles went well beyond cause and effect. On an emotional level, what Beatlemania achieved for many young people was a restoration of the feelings of hope and sheer intensity that many feared had died forever with John Kennedy. Jack and Jackie Kennedy had actually sparked the second "pop explosion" in America; the Beatles were responsible for the third.

There were many similarities between the Kennedys and the Beatles, only some of which were apparent at the moment each group was in the public eye. Most important, the Kennedys were "capable of easy, instantaneous and varied imitation and extension," and they shared the same sexy charisma of the boys from Liverpool. When John Kennedy went hatless to his own inauguration, American men stopped wearing hats; hair got longer because the president's was, the two-button suits he favored enjoyed a sudden vogue, and Jackie inspired more emulation than any other American First Lady. Like their musical successors, the Kennedys had a magnetism that exerted its pull across classes and international boundaries; both groups were masterly with the press, which played a crucial role in creating the respective myths; and like those of the Beatles, John Kennedy's sexual appetites were without discernible limit. When the Beatles were using amphetamines in Hamburg to play seven hours at a stretch, John Kennedy was traveling with speed doctor Max Jacobson to his first summit meeting with Khrushchev in Vienna. Both the Beatles and the Kennedys grew up as outsiders (the Beatles as Liverpudlians, the Kennedys as arriviste Irish), and both depended on a single string puller (Joe Kennedy, Brian Epstein) to orchestrate their triumphs. Each dynasty's impresario inspired diffidence and affection: The Kennedys were grateful to their father, and the Beatles appreciated Epstein. But Kennedys and Beatles alike worried they might become too closely identified with the less savory side of the manager's reputation, and each group lost the ability to dominate an era with the demise of its Svengali. Together, the Kennedys and the Beatles carried America and much of the world through an almost seamless eight-year era of emotional excess, from 1960 to 1968.

The very original sound of the Beatles was actually the product of an uncanny ability to synthesize everything that had come before them. That was the paradox. Their first hero was Buddy Holly (they named themselves in honor of Holly's "Crickets"), and Holly and Elvis had been the preeminent synthesizers of black and white music when the British boys first started listening to the radio. What you heard in the Beatles, Greil Marcus wrote, "was a rock and roll group that combined elements of the music that you were used to hearing only in pieces. That is, the form of the Beatles contained the forms of rock and roll itself. [They] combined the harmonic range and implicit equality of the Fifties vocal group (the Dell-Vikings, say) with the flash of a rockabilly band (The Crickets), with the aggressive and unique personalities of the classic rock stars (Elvis, Little Richard) with the homey this-could-be-you manner of later rock stars (Everly Brothers, Holly, Eddie Cochran) with the endlessly inventive songwriting touch of the Brill Building, and delivered it with the grace of the Miracles, the physicality of 'Louie Louie' and the absurd enthusiasm of Gary 'U.S.' Bonds." Rock became, "in the shape of the Beatles, a way of life."[32]

John Lennon explained the group's conquest of the colonies more simply. "It was the black music we dug," he said. "We felt that we had the message, which was 'Listen to this music.' When we came here . . . nobody was listening to rock and roll or to black music in America. We felt as though we were coming to the land of its origin, but nobody wanted to know about it."[33]

Their triumph in America made them into a worldwide phenomenon; it was also an American who would become their most important rival. He, too, was a John Hammond discovery—the least likely and most influential musical figure of his time. This artist was born Robert Allen Zimmerman on May 24, 1941, in Duluth, Minnesota, the son of Abram H. Zimmerman and Beatrice Stone. When Hammond first met him, he was twenty and called himself Bob Dylan, a name he has consistently (and implausibly) denied was inspired by Dylan Thomas. Hammond pounced on the young singer after his performance at Gerde's Folk City had received an enthusiastic review in the *New York Times*.[34] Music critic Robert Shelton, who would spend much of the next twenty-five years writing a biography of his idol, reported the new talent looked like "a cross between a choir boy and a beatnik," and, "if not for every taste, his music-making has the mark of originality and inspiration." For many months after Columbia signed him, he was known inside the label as "Hammond's folly."

His first record, *Bob Dylan*, was recorded in November 1961 and released in March 1962, just seven months before Beatlemania began in England with the appearance of "Love Me Do." For the next six years, the contest between Dylan and the Beatles would be one of the most productive of all modern musical rivalries. The Beatles made it clear that they regarded Bob Dylan as *the* musical force to be reckoned with, and Dylan reciprocated these feelings. A headline in Britain's *Melody Maker* in January 1965 read, BEATLES SAY—DYLAN SHOWS THE WAY.[35] Paul McCartney remembered, "It was really a question of everyone admiring Dylan—and we felt kind of honored that he admired us."[36]

Many saw them as polar opposites—nobody could be angrier than the Bad Boy from Hibbing, no one could be happier than Liverpool's fabulous foursome—but beneath their public postures they were far more united than divided, especially by their similar beginnings as outsiders and their common worship of Elvis, Little Richard, and Buddy Holly. Dylan was also a great synthesizer. His principal hero was Woody Guthrie, but he was also the heir to the beat tradition of Jack Kerouac, William Burroughs, and Allen Ginsberg—three writers who were all students at Columbia University at the end of World War II. Ginsberg's epic poem *Howl*, published in 1956, and Kerouac's novel *On the Road*, published in 1957, were two of the strongest literary protests against the sterility of the fifties. That was the decade Dylan remembered as a period when "our parents were in a sad situation. They were probably just into 'no down payment' and aluminum cans and mortgages and Eisenhower-McCarthy, that type of thing. I don't know what kind of knowledge they could have really passed on."[37]

While Dylan's British rivals, repackaged by their manager into lovable mopheads, were emerging as the masters of charming irreverence, Dylan was busy pushing his public persona in the opposite direction: *Abrasive* irreverence was his trademark. Uncomfortable with the reality of a not very mythic middle-class upbringing in Minnesota, he pretended to have run away from home when he "was 10, 12, 13, 15, 15½, 17 an' 18."[38] A few weeks after John Kennedy was assassinated, he was so disgusted by an award dinner of the Emergency Civil Liberties Committee, he stunned the audience by telling them he "saw a lot" of himself "in Oswald" and "I saw in him a lot of the times we're all living in."[39] Instead of charming the press, he used it to produce exchanges like these, which solidified his status as chief spokesman for an inscrutable generation:

If fortune hasn't trapped you, how about fame? Do you find that your celebrity makes it difficult to keep your private life intact?

My private life has been dangerous from the beginning. All this does is add a little atmosphere.

How do you get your kicks these days then?

I hire people to look into my eyes, and then I have them kick me.

And that's the way you get your kicks?

No. Then I *forgive* them—that's where my kicks come in.

Do you have any unfulfilled ambitions?

Well I guess I've always wanted to be Anthony Quinn in *La Strada*—not always, only for about six years now, it's not one of those childhood-dream things. Oh, and come to think of it, I guess I've always wanted to be Brigitte Bardot, too. But I don't really want to think about *that* too much.[40]

Is there anything in addition to your songs that you want to say to people?

Good luck.

You don't say that in your songs.

Oh yes I do: every song tails off with "good luck, I hope you make it."[41]

WHAT Dylan did share with the Beatles was their uncanny ability to anticipate, shape, and reflect the attitudes and anxieties of the Vietnam generation. In the first half of the sixties, when things remained relatively placid—before the escalation of the war—Dylan put the decade's agenda for change to simple but powerful music. He wrote generic antiwar songs before there was an antiwar movement ("Masters of War," "Talkin' World War III Blues," "A Hard Rain's A-Gonna Fall"), and civil rights songs ("Oxford Town" and "The Lonesome Death of Hattie Carroll") in the period when the civil rights cause was still relatively uncontroversial in one half of the country—when Northern whites, at least, still seemed united in their outrage over the abuse of Southern blacks. "Blowin' in the Wind" was his earliest, explicit call to arms—and the only modern folk song with almost as much moral resonance as "We Shall Overcome." By 1965 the runaway success of "Blowin' in the Wind"—first in the Peter, Paul and Mary version, then in everyone else's—helped to make him the most important cult figure in British and American music. To his fans, his spare arsenal—hillbilly voice, unamplified guitar, and a look-Ma-no-hands harmonica—made him the perfect David against the Goliath of society's hypocrisy. In the spring of 1965 he crisscrossed Britain with Joan Baez in a tour captured in a revealing documentary, *Don't Look Back.** On the first night in London's Royal Albert Hall, he came out looking nervous and played a very fast version of "The Times They Are A-Changin'"; after that, there was nothing but reverence.

But he already sensed that he was falling behind in the larger, unspoken contest to become the dominant cultural figure of his time. "I couldn't go much farther by myself," he said. He was tired of playing the "lone ranger" and, in any case, he had always been a rocker at heart. (Before Woody Guthrie, Little Richard was his hero.[42]) Alone, he could not approach the musical inventiveness of the Beatles. The songwriting combination of Lennon and McCartney (and the fact that George Harrison was writing on his own almost as well as both of them) was producing music that was steadily more complex. And in 1964, their first movie, *A Hard Day's Night*, had planted the Beatles' charm as deeply as their music into young psyches everywhere.

Faced with this intensifying competition, Dylan was no longer willing to fight on alone. He became a rock-and-roll star, and he never looked back. "It felt right, so it must have been right," he explained.[43] Yet many of his earliest fans, especially the older ones, were outraged. When I saw him perform again at the Albert Hall in 1966, the atmosphere had changed from a church service into a battlefield. This time the veneration lasted

---

* "Is that his philosophy?" Robert Kennedy asked Jack Newfield in 1968. "I think it's mine." [Jack Newfield, *Robert Kennedy, A Memoir* (1969; reprint, New York: Bantam, 1970), 323.]

only as long as Dylan performed without accompaniment. When he came back after the intermission with what would become the Band, reverence was replaced by something just short of bloodshed. Audience members screamed, shouted, walked out—even threw things at the stage.

The subliminal message may have caused the larger subterranean turmoil. Dylan's simultaneous abandonment of the simple style and a straightforward political message added up to an eerie early warning that an already intricate decade was about to unravel into the unimagined intensity of 1968. But no one articulated such a notion at the time. This was Dylan's typically labyrinthine response to the question that plagued him wherever he went in 1966—"Mistake or not, what made you decide to go the rock-and-roll route?"

"Carelessness. I lost my one true love. I started drinking. The first thing I know, I'm in a card game. Then I'm in a crap game. I wake up in a pool hall. Then this big Mexican lady drags me off the table, takes me to Philadelphia. She leaves me alone in her house, and it burns down. I wind up in Phoenix. I get a job as a Chinaman. I start working in a dime store, and move in with a thirteen-year-old girl. Then this big Mexican lady from Philadelphia comes in and burns the house down. I go down to Dallas. I get a job as a 'before' in a Charles Atlas 'before and after' ad. I move in with a delivery boy who can cook fantastic chili and hot dogs. Then this thirteen-year-old girl from Phoenix comes and burns the house down. The delivery boy—he ain't so mild: he gives her the knife and the next thing I know I'm in Omaha. It's so cold there, by this time I'm robbing my own bicycles and frying my own fish. I stumble onto some luck and get a job as a carburetor out at the hot-rod races every Thursday night. I move in with a high school teacher who also does a little plumbing on the side, who ain't much to look at, but who's built a special kind of refrigerator that can turn newspaper into lettuce. Everything's going good until the delivery boy shows up and tries to knife me. Needless to say, he burned the house down, and I hit the road. The first guy that picked me up asked me if I wanted to be a star. What could I say?"[44]

Twenty years later, I asked if that was "still the answer."

"Well," he said, "that's part of it."[45]

The truth was much simpler: He was in a fierce struggle to make the most influential music of his era, and it was beginning to look as if the Beatles might beat him to the punch. As early as the fall of 1964, he saw the limits of writing "for people" and being a "spokesman." Specificity was narrowing his audience unnecessarily. "From now on I want to write from inside me, and to do that I'm going to have to get back to writing like I used to when I was ten," he told an interviewer for *The New Yorker.*[46] In this quest, he was remarkably successful.

The weapons Dylan and the Beatles chose for their ultimate duel ensured a particular intimacy between them and their followers. They were the coins of the realm of a new youthful idealism: self-revelatory truths about love, fear, panic—every adolescent preoccupation. Who could make themselves sound most vulnerable in public? Who would be first to invert the macho ideals of James Dean and Marlon Brando, the heroes they had grown up with? To many listeners, these were among the unspoken goals of this competition.

The ambiguity of their words was crucial to the breadth of their appeal. In some cases, any attempt to attribute a single meaning to a particular song was to miss the point entirely. Somewhat paradoxically, it was the density of the lyrics that made them accessible to so many different types of people, simultaneously binding their fans to each other and their bards. The contest began with Dylan songs like "Don't Think Twice, It's All Right," "Chimes of Freedom," and "Tomorrow Is a Long Time"* and gathered momentum the following year with Lennon-McCartney replies like "I'm a Loser" and "I Don't Want to Spoil the Party." (In August 1964, Dylan had tried to keep the competition on an even plane by introducing the Beatles to marijuana during their first meeting in a New York City hotel room.[47]) In 1965, Dylan shot back with "It's Alright, Ma (I'm Only Bleeding)"; Lennon kept the Beatles in the game with an incredibly direct plea for "Help!" but Dylan won the first round outright when he released "Like a Rolling Stone." Whenever he wailed, *"How does it feel?"* everyone listening wailed along with him. Dylan likened the song to seeing "your victim swimming in lava . . . seeing someone in the pain they were bound to meet up with."[48] Meanwhile, in California, the Byrds came closest to fusing Dylan's words with the Beatles' music, with brilliant folk-rock versions of "Mr. Tambourine Man," "All I Really Want to Do," and "Chimes of Freedom."

Then it became a battle of albums. The Beatles offered *Rubber Soul* and *Revolver,* the first to show signs of their experiments with illicit substances, and in Nashville, Dylan produced his masterpiece, *Blonde on Blonde.* This double album had a peculiar locomotive power he has rarely been able to replicate. Blasted through KLH speakers and Koss headphones, the lyrics of "Just Like a Woman," "I Want You," "Visions of Johanna," "Stuck Inside of Mobile," and "Sooner or Later" penetrated far into the collective

---

* Written in 1963 and recorded by Elvis, but unreleased on a Dylan record until 1971.

subconscious of a generation. Dylan was "going at tremendous speed," but ten weeks later he came to a terrifying halt when the rear wheel of his Triumph motorcycle locked on a country road near Woodstock, New York, and the mystic-hero broke his neck.[49]

While Dylan recovered slowly from his accident, the hippie movement—whose antecedents, like his own, could be found in the work of Ginsberg, Kerouac, and Burroughs—was flowering into a national phenomenon. It started to receive national attention on January 14, 1967, when Ginsberg, antiwar activist Jerry Rubin, and LSD advocate Timothy Leary joined twenty thousand others in a "Gathering of the Tribes" in San Francisco's Golden Gate Park. A press release issued a few days earlier promised that "political activists" would join together with "the love generation" to "powwow, celebrate, and prophesy the epoch of liberation, love, peace, compassion, and unity of mankind." Leary was at the "Human Be-In" to promote the value of LSD, while Rubin hoped to convert the culturally alienated into standard-bearers for a new political revolution.[50]

Leary had been at Harvard until the university accused him in 1963 of carrying out dangerous experiments on undergraduates; then he was fired.[51] At the be-in, his speech was received much more enthusiastically than Rubin's strident attack on the war.[52] Although explicitly denied the "prophet status" that would have permitted him to speak for a half-hour, Leary made the most of the seven minutes allotted to him. Dressed in white pajamas, he welcomed his audience "to the first manifestation of the Brave New World." Then he made his much-quoted proposal: "Turn on to the scene. Tune into what is happening and drop out—of high school, college, and grad school, junior executive, senior executive—and follow me, the hard way."[53]

The surge in drug experimentation was portrayed as unprecedented by our parents, but it was actually a throwback to a very old American obsession. Tom Wolfe's *The Electric Kool-Aid Acid Test*, which discussed the wonders of LSD, was published in 1968—almost a century and a half after Thomas De Quincey's *Confessions of an English Opium Eater*, an 1822 best-seller that had produced a surge of interest in opium among American authors and artists. In 1900 cocaine was freely available for about $2.50 an ounce, and Coca-Cola did not replace its cocaine content with caffeine until 1903. Cocaine wasn't prohibited by federal statute until 1914, and marijuana was banned only in 1937. Amphetamines, invented in Germany in 1932, were rationed to soldiers, first during World War II and again in Vietnam, to prevent battle fatigue. And the sedate fifties were made even more so through common middle-class addictions to sleeping pills and tranquilizers dispensed by the corner drugstore.[54]

Taken by large numbers of people, LSD seemed to have the potential to alter mass attitudes more rapidly than any other sixties ingredient. But the reason it never really pushed those who used it in any particular direction had already been uncovered by the Army and the CIA. Both of these government units ran extensive experiments with lysergic acid diethylamide 25 in the fifties and early sixties. The CIA was initially ecstatic over the drug's potential as a truth serum—until it discovered that LSD was equally likely to make the user catatonic or have delusions of omnipotence, which could make a subject immune to any interrogation. Unpredictability was always at the heart of the experience.*[55]

One CIA memo called the drug a "potential new agent for unconventional warfare." That was certainly what many people hoped it would be for the swarms of hippies who descended on the Haight in the summer of 1967. Vastly more powerful than marijuana or hash, LSD was the drug that took you, instead of the other way around. In 1966 Leary had founded the League of Spiritual Discovery, explaining, "Like every great religion of the past, we seek to find the divinity within and to express this revelation in a life of glorification and worship of God."[56] Others insisted the letters should really stand for "Legalize Spiritual Discovery," which at least implied an antimaterialistic agenda. Under the proper conditions, it did have the capacity to make you feel at one with the universe, or open you up to any number of new experiences; and *seeing* the music or hearing the trees breathe certainly expanded one's consciousness in ways that were difficult to communicate once the trip was over. On the other hand, under the wrong circumstances, LSD could also make you crave suicide—or make you believe that you were already dead. The only drug of the sixties whose effects were completely predictable was the Pill; it seemed to make everyone more eager (or at least willing) to have sex.

But to the disappointment of the left, there never was any direct correlation between drug use (or promiscuity) and politics. This was one aspect of the deeper dichotomy between the recreations of the sixties and their political content. Worshiping under the banner of sex, drugs, and rock and roll, millions of young Americans smoked marijuana, tripped on acid,

---

* For several years in San Francisco, the CIA went so far as to pay prostitutes to bring their unwitting customers back to a government-financed bordello. There, in an operation codenamed "Midnight Climax," the Johns were given drinks laced with LSD so the government might evaluate its impact on average citizens. [Martin Lee and Bruce Shlain, *Acid Dreams: The CIA, LSD and the Sixties Rebellion* (New York: Grove Press, 1985), 32–33.]

sped through the decade on superfluous amphetamines, dressed wildly, danced violently, and seduced one another assiduously. Then, in roughly the same proportion as their parents, they continued to vote Republican.

The absence of any quantifiable political realignment spawned a widespread misconception: The sixties contained a period of fearful pandemonium; then the decade ended, leaving no lasting legacy. This notion was bolstered by the worst consequence of Martin Luther King's assassination— the disappearance of any national will to achieve equality between blacks and whites. But the diversity that was rock's hallmark *was* absorbed into the culture. Partly because of the impact of black and female rock-and-roll stars—and largely because of the achievements of the civil rights movement—American society opened up dramatically over the next twenty years. The example of black anger was equally important to women, who demanded the right to become lawyers instead of housewives, and to gays, who began to live more openly and honestly after the Stonewall riots of 1969. This same energy contributed to the liberation of virtually every other group that had been excluded from the mainstream or denied its legitimate claim to the levers of power in America.

JUST as the Beatles had begun their musical education with American tunes, now they were continuing their spiritual experiments with American drugs. Their first experience with LSD occurred almost two years before the Golden Gate be-in, while they were filming *Help!* Without warning, John and George were given acid-laced sugar cubes in their coffee one evening in the home of their swinging London dentist. When they finally struggled back to George's house after a very wild night on the town, John thought he was in a submarine: "It seemed to float above [George's] wall, which was eighteen-foot, and I was driving it."[57]

Sgt. Pepper's Lonely Hearts Club Band was the first synthesis of all the Beatles' experiments, musical and pharmaceutical. "They were always wanting to have new sounds and new ideas coming through," said George Martin. "I found they were almost more inquisitive than I was. In fact, in the end, it kind of exhausted me. They were saying, what new sounds can we have, what new instruments can we have? What can you do to my voice to make it different?" Paul was especially inquisitive; after hearing a Brandenburg Concerto one night on the BBC, he got Martin to insert a piccolo trumpet into "Penny Lane."[58]

With the appearance of *Sgt. Pepper's* in the middle of 1967—just as thousands were putting flowers in their hair to go to San Francisco—Beatlemania and the psychedelic era reached their common peak. Everything about the album felt like a summing-up—beginning with the cover collage, which emblematically brought together every cult figure whose impact had ever been remotely comparable with that of the Beatles, from Marx and Lenin to Marilyn Monroe and John Wilkes Booth. Mae West initially withheld her consent to be included, asking, "Why would I be part of a Lonely Hearts Club?" but she relented after the Beatles sent her a personal appeal. Only Gandhi was removed at the insistence of EMI's chairman—he was sure the Indian market would be offended to see their hero in this company.[59] It was also the first rock album with the lyrics printed on the cover (with "a splendid time" guaranteed for all), and it was one of the first to play elaborate stereo stunts, making voices and instruments vanish and reappear in the most unlikely locations, sometimes after moving straight through your head. Like a good acid trip, the energy from the music came at you in steady pulses; it was also layered, unpredictable, and ultimately comforting. Almost everyone conceded it was "art," and the fact that symphony orchestra musicians could contribute the climax only after struggling to learn how to play out of tune merely increased the irony of their participation. John described the orchestra's famous crescendo as "a sound building up from nothing to the end of the world."[60] Something else made it especially satisfactory to its fans: It proved that they lived in a time that could best be captured by a record. Only the final forty-four-second chord was a little frightening, hinting so heavily at the end of an era.

Twenty years later, nearly everything the Beatles and Dylan did in this period still stands up. But it was the impact of their competition on the rest of the music makers of the world that made it most important to its era. Only after the Beatles and Dylan were rock-and-roll musicians expected to write their own material. And the fact that a beatnik type from a dying Minnesota town and four undereducated lower-class Englishmen from the provinces were now the five most influential people of their time had a remarkable effect on record executives everywhere. For a moment, there was no one a savvy talent scout could safely ignore at first sight. That circumstance opened the commercial music world to a brief period of unprecedented experimentation. As a result, in 1968, commercial radio stations broadcast an extraordinary mixture of folk, rock, jazz, and blues.

In 1968 one of the most sensational black soloists was yet another Hammond discovery. Her name was Aretha Franklin, and she was the daughter of a Baptist minister from Detroit whose choir had once included

Sam Cooke. As soon as Hammond had listened to a primitive demo of her voice, he knew she was the best he'd heard since Holliday. In 1960 he signed her up for Columbia Records, where Goddard Lieberson had hired him earlier that year. But Hammond soon lost control of Franklin to others in the company who thought his ability to produce commercial singles didn't match the quality of his ear for new talent. Unhappy at Columbia, Aretha moved to Atlantic Records in 1965. Within two years, she had a number-one hit with "Do Right Woman—Do Right Man." From 1967 to 1970 she sold nine million singles and three million albums.[61]

Her greatest achievement in 1968 was also one of the great albums of the era. *Aretha Now* was a remarkable fusion of blues, soul, and pop. Its ten songs encapsulate most of the possibilities inherent in the collaborations that produced so much of the best music of the sixties. These black and white combinations, which had begun because of John Hammond, yielded some of their greatest dividends exactly thirty years after he produced "Spirituals to Swing." *Aretha Now* melded the talents of a black vocalist, a Jewish record producer (Jerry Wexler), and black and white songwriters (Sam Cooke, Aretha Franklin, Burt Bacharach, and Hal David, among others) to produce a joyful, soulful, sad, and touching record: a perfect emblem of its time. "I Say a Little Prayer," which was one of the album's biggest hits, was a song written by two white men (David and Bacharach) for another black vocalist (Dionne Warwick). Warwick's softer version was also very sexy, but to many listeners the soulful edge Aretha added made her interpretation sound almost like a reproach. And her rendition of the Sam Cooke classic "You Send Me" provided a wonderfully succinct summary of the difference between how it felt to be young in America in 1957 (when Cooke first recorded it) and what it was like in 1968. Aretha's version re-creates all of the sweetness of the 1957 original; but in place of the dreamlike quality Cooke infused it with, the 1968 model has a raucousness and pathos as painful and exuberant as the events of the year in which it appeared. Just listening to it was enough to make this seventeen-year-old white boy feel joyful, soulful, and cool wherever he was.

Charlie Christian was the first electric-guitar player Hammond discovered (just before World War II), and there was a direct line from Christian to B. B. King, and from King to Jimi Hendrix and Eric Clapton. The bands of the British invasion popularized King's style and created a whole new blues-influenced vocabulary for modern rock.[62] By 1968 Clapton and Hendrix were good friends: Hendrix "became a soul mate for me," Clapton recalled, "and, musically, what I wanted to hear." Hendrix had to go to England to be discovered; then he stunned the 1967 Monterey Festival when he picked out "The Star-Spangled Banner" amid feedback and fire on a flaming guitar. That performance became a legend when the movie of the festival was released at the end of 1968. Clapton was playing with Cream that year, one of the first supergroups and the granddaddy of heavy metal. In 1968 Cream's percussionist, Ginger Baker, reinvented the drum solo with a thirteen-minute amphetamine-driven, double-foot-pedaled marathon on "Toad." Clapton was "riding high" on the "Clapton Is God" graffiti found all over London, but he was brought up short when he read a negative review of his recent performances in the tenth issue of *Rolling Stone*, which came out in May. Jon Landau wrote that Clapton had become boring and repetitious. "I was in a restaurant, and I fainted," Clapton recalled. "And after I woke up, I immediately decided that was the end of the band."[63] Cream gave its farewell performance from the stage of the Albert Hall in November. It was two years before Clapton joined up with Derek and the Dominos and, despite what was by then a heavy dependence on heroin, managed to produce "Layla," a seven-minute expiation of agony that remains one of rock's most spectacular feats. Like "Somebody to Love," "Satisfaction," "Piece of My Heart," "Help!" and "Like a Rolling Stone," "Layla" is a crucial song with a unique emotional resonance for nearly every member of the Vietnam generation.

THE principal factory for black music in the sixties was founded and controlled by songwriter Berry Gordy, and it was operated entirely by blacks. Motown (originally Tamla) got its first big song in 1960 with "Way Over There" by the Miracles. Soon there was a sign reading HITSVILLE on its headquarters, and Gordy had hired everyone he needed to staff Detroit's most melodious assembly line. The singers were the stars, but the label's hidden weapons were Gordy's songwriters, especially himself, Smokey Robinson, and the teams of (Brian) Holland-(Lamont) Dozier-(Eddie) Holland, and (Nickolas) Ashford and (Valerie) Simpson. Nearly as important were the unacknowledged heroes of the studio band, great rhythm-and-blues men like bass player James Jamerson, guitarist Joe Messina, and drummer Benny Benjamin.

Motown's domination of black rock and roll began when Dozier joined up with the Hollands in 1963 to produce an incandescent "Heat Wave" for Martha and the Vandellas. The following year, the songwriting trio hit their composing stride for the Supremes with "Where Did Our Love Go," the first number one for three tough, sexy ladies who had grown up in a Detroit housing project (and were originally called the Primettes). After that first hit, the Supremes set a record for a female group, with four more number-one songs in a row and a total of twelve over the next five years. In my headphones, the Holland-Dozier-Holland/Supremes formula reached its peak with "You Can't Hurry Love" in the summer of 1966. A year later, the composing trio left Motown in a dispute over royalties, and neither the label nor the songwriting team was ever quite the same again.[64] But Ashford and Simpson (in collaboration with Marvin Gaye and Tammi Terrell) quickly picked up some of the slack with the throbbing original versions of "Ain't No Mountain High Enough" and "You're All I Need to Get By."

The beat was everything on what Gordy dubbed "the Sound of Young America," and anything might become part of the beat, including drums, tambourines, handclaps, foot stomps, wood blocks—even snow chains and ballpoint pens.[65] In the sixties, Motown Records was one of the country's most regimented factories; by 1968 it was also one of the wealthiest and most influential black-owned businesses in the world. Marvin Gaye and Stevie Wonder were the first to win contracts that gave them complete artistic freedom, and Wonder in particular used his to magnificent effect through the seventies and eighties.

Otis Redding was the greatest male soul singer of the era outside the Motown machine. Tragically, his popularity did not peak until after his death in a 1967 airplane accident. In 1968 he was a posthumous superstar with "Sittin' on the Dock of the Bay," a tremendous number-one hit. Earlier, Redding had managed to reverse the usual direction of transatlantic cross-pollination with his cover of the British-born "Satisfaction."

In its original version (released in 1965), this Mick Jagger–Keith Richards classic was the song that finally established the Rolling Stones as the Beatles' principal British rivals on both sides of the Atlantic (until then, they were outsold in America by Herman's Hermits and the Dave Clark Five).[66] The Stones worked feverishly to be the "hardest" musical choice of all. Unlike Dylan's, there was often something explicitly vulgar about their lyrics. Early on, they guaranteed their notoriety (and got briefly banned by most AM stations) by pleading, "Let's Spend the Night Together"; then Mick Jagger's looks and leaps helped push androgyny into the mainstream of popular culture. But once again appearances did not entirely match reality. To Keith Richards, the Beatles "were just as filthy as we were, really. And . . . I mean, Brian Jones used to wash his hair three times a *day,* you know."[67] To others, the Stones completed a trinity: The Beatles were the ultimate romantics, Dylan was cerebral, and the Stones stood for sex; together they made up one whole (somewhat sexist) human being.

In 1968 the Stones offered explicit sacrilege ("Sympathy for the Devil"), and when Mick shouted out "Who killed the Kennedys—when after all it was you and me," he was in perfect sync with much of young America. By then a large part of the country was consumed with guilt—and a fear that a very old American impulse toward violence was now completely out of control. It was the same atmosphere that led one radio station to play Laura Nyro's anthem, "Save the Country"—with its chorus of "Save the people, save the children, save the country, *Now!*" over and over again after the year's second major assassination.

Nyro was nineteen in 1968, and *Eli and the Thirteenth Confession*, the brilliant concept album she produced that year, was to "bright gospel rock" (her description) what *Sgt. Pepper's* had been to psychedelia.[68] In its own way, it was equally iconoclastic, being one of the first albums in which a singer-songwriter seemed to express equal passion for a woman and a man in two successive songs. Like Dylan and the Beatles, Nyro was a master of accessible ambiguity. The young singer was the Bronx-born daughter of a trumpet-playing piano tuner named Louis Nigro, and *Eli* was very much an urban album. After her own experiments with LSD, she had a clear view of what the urban battle was about: "The struggle in the city is between health and sickness—God and the Devil. That's been my experience."[69] Through Peter, Paul and Mary and the Fifth Dimension, Nyro songs like "And When I Die" and "Stoned Soul Picnic" became AM hits, but these versions rarely duplicated the power of her originals.

Dylan, who had been silent since his accident in 1966, finally emerged from his long hiatus in January 1968 with *John Wesley Harding*. (Rumors that he had been killed in his motorcycle accident didn't end altogether until he appeared at a Carnegie Hall memorial for Woody Guthrie on January 19.) With *John Wesley Harding*, he managed to alienate many of the new fans he had won when he went electric by bouncing back to a softer sound, much closer to his acoustical period than to *Blonde on Blonde*. The rest of the faithful were just grateful for *something* after what had felt like an endless absence. Produced in Nashville, the instrumentation on the new album was warm and very simple—just an unamplified guitar, harmonica, piano, bass, and drums, what the *Times* called his return "to austerity."[70] Once again, Dylan was jumping ahead of his time: The mood of the album anticipates the calm America would yearn for when 1968 was over. But when the year began, no one but Dylan understood that—probably because he had experienced the same intensity of 1968 in his own life in 1966.

In the winter of 1968, the Beatles traveled to India to meditate with the Maharishi Mahesh Yogi. Ringo gave up on the experience after only ten days (he hated the food), but the others stuck it out for almost four months more. Then they became disillusioned because of what seemed to be a not very spiritual interest on the part of their mentor in several of the female members of their party, including Mia Farrow. When John told the yogi they were leaving, he asked why. "You're the cosmic one," said John. "You ought to know." The yogi responded with a look of pure hatred.[71]

Back in the West, they pursued their plans for Apple Corps, a utopian scheme that John described as "a trick to see if we can get artistic freedom within a business structure." Artists of all descriptions were invited to submit their work, and the new company's Wigmore Street office in London was quickly swamped with submissions. In America, James Taylor was Apple's first important discovery.[72]

After *Sgt. Pepper's*, the disintegration of the Beatles was predicted more frequently than ever by the press. In August the Beatles struck back at the rumors with the biggest-selling single of their career. "Hey Jude" was number one in America for six weeks and the tenth best-selling song of all time. (At seven minutes and six seconds, it was also more than a full minute longer than Dylan's format-shattering "Like a Rolling Stone," issued three years earlier.) Paul McCartney said he wrote it originally as "Hey Jules," to cheer up John's son Julian after the boy's father left his mother, Cynthia, to live with Yoko Ono.[73] But to the legions of fans hoping to pull back from the abyss opened up by two terrible assassinations, it sounded more like an attempt to resuscitate an entire generation.

"Hey Jude," Paul sang, "Don't make it bad, take a sad song, and make it better"—and everyone listening was eager to follow his advice. The structure of the song mimicked the emotional sequence of the year: Paul's rich ballad, filled with love, dissolved into a musical picture of the apocalypse America was still struggling to escape from. The Beatles version came complete with primal screams and a fearful backing from a forty-piece symphony orchestra. They even performed the song on British and American television, reaffirming for a moment "their oneness with their audience and with each other," as their biographer, Philip Norman, remembered it.[74]

At the same time, the two-sided single gave a good précis of the differences between McCartney and Lennon, circa 1968. For several years, the two great songwriters had benefited more from their internal competition than collaboration, although each continued to perform small but crucial fixes on the other's work. Increasingly, Paul's feelings sounded like the flip side of John's politics, and that was literally the case with "Hey Jude." The B side carried John Lennon's "Revolution," the song that caused an immediate uproar all across the political spectrum. It seemed to be an attack on the recent chaos in the streets ("You say you want a revolution . . . but when you talk about destruction, don't you know that you can count me out?"), but as usual it was sufficiently ambiguous to permit several different interpretations. Robert Christgau was furious in the *Village Voice*: "It is puritanical to expect musicians, or anyone else, to hew to the proper line. But it is reasonable to request that they not go out of their way to oppose it." *Ramparts* was disgusted by one line in particular: "Don't you know it's going to be all right." "It isn't," said the magazine. "You *know* it's *not* gonna be all right." Then Michael Wood took them all to task in *Commonweal*. The Beatles weren't crazy, he insisted, they knew things were out of control, and the "shoo-be-do-wahs" with which Paul and George answered the offending prediction on a subsequent version of the song proved that. "They mean that statements about whether it is or it isn't are all part of that political crap they dislike so much," said Wood. The John Birch Society informed the world that "Revolution" took "the Moscow line against Trotskyites and the Progressive Labor party."[75]

Nineteen sixty-eight was also the year Janis Joplin shouted (with Big Brother), "I need a man to love"; the Doors demanded, "Touch me!"; the Temptations wished "it would rain"; Stevie Wonder belted out "Shoo-Be-Doo-Be-Doo-Da-Day"; Marvin Gaye and Tammi Terrell harmonized, "You're all I need to get by"; the Supremes were "gonna make you love me"; Sly and the Family Stone commanded everyone to "Dance! to the music"; the Youngbloods told us to "get together" (and sang at my senior prom); Iron Butterfly created a heavy-metal cult with "In-a-Gadda-Da-Vida"; and the Band sent their first music recorded without Dylan down from "Big Pink." Simon and Garfunkel neatly bridged the gap between culture and politics by providing the year's most popular anthem ("Mrs. Robinson") for its most influential movie (*The Graduate*);* then, together with Dustin Hoffman, they campaigned for Gene McCarthy. Even Elvis staged a comeback (and praised the Beatles) on a celebrated TV special in December. Only in 1968 could the King and all his disciples be simultaneous stars.

---

* *The Graduate* was released in December 1967. Dustin Hoffman got $25,000 for his performance.

Through television, the Vietnam generation participated in a terrible tide of death and destruction as the political center repeatedly failed to hold during the balance of the year. But in their worst moments, the children of the sixties took solace from the music that kept rolling out of the radio.

The year ended with *The White Album*, another extraordinary collection of Beatles songs, as eclectic and disjointed as 1968 itself. Because some of it was parody ("Back in the U.S.S.R.," "Honey Pie") and the fourth side was marred by John's art-rock collaboration with Yoko ("Revolution 9"), many of the critics massacred it. But every careful listener could hear that these four musicians were still more perfectly in tune with their times than all of their competitors. George bemoaned "a long, long, long time" (and recruited Eric Clapton for a magnificent guitar solo on "While My Guitar Gently Weeps"). Paul was still struggling to be cheerful, singing songs like "Rocky Raccoon" and the childlike "Ob-La-Di, Ob-La-Da." But it was John who provided the year with its awful coda. "Happiness," he sang, "is a warm gun."

10

Desolation Row

"We are living in an era when the lunatics, not the leaders, are writing the history."

—Mary McGrory[1]

"I feel like the Black Knight out in the center of the field. I turn my horse round and round; but there is no one to fight. I go to their tents to strike their shields with my lance; but not even a shield hangs there now. Only flapping rags."

—Eugene McCarthy after Bobby Kennedy's assassination[2]

"It was not in his nature to ask for something that might not be granted."

—Blair Clark on Eugene McCarthy[3]

"McCarthy still sees himself as a member of the religious nobility, who will calmly ascend to Heaven along with the other righteous, if only he pays due attention to the proper processes of life."

—Jeremy Larner[4]

IT WAS just after midnight when Gene McCarthy agreed to send Bobby a telegram to congratulate him on his California triumph. A draft of the message described a "splendid" victory; McCarthy asked Blair Clark to change the adjective to "fine," because he didn't think Kennedy's actual margin would be as large as what the networks were projecting. McCarthy was right: He lost the final tally by just 4.5 percent of the vote, with 46.3 for Kennedy, 41.8 for himself, and 11.9 percent for a slate loosely aligned with Humphrey. It seemed quite possible that McCarthy's performance in Saturday's debate had robbed him of a victory. Suddenly, CBS News correspondent David Schoumacher burst into McCarthy's hotel suite at the Beverly Hilton with the news. "Senator Kennedy has been shot," he said. "You're kidding," someone answered. "I'm not," said Schoumacher. Then he ran out to learn more.[5]

Barely two months had passed since Lyndon Johnson stunned McCarthy with his abdication. But the confusion the Minnesotan felt then was mild compared with his reaction now. In public, he made an elegant statement: "The nation, I think, bears too great a burden of guilt, really, for the kind of neglect which has allowed violence to grow here in our land." He called this calamity a "reflection of violence which we have visited upon the rest of the world, or at least on a part of the world."[6]

What he said in private was altogether different.

Blair Clark was staggered by McCarthy's first response to this second major assassination. "You know," McCarthy said, "he kind of brought it on himself." Clark remembered clearly that McCarthy had used exactly the same words when he first learned of Martin Luther King's death. Eighteen years later, McCarthy denied making such a judgment about King.* But the Minnesotan readily confirmed that he felt that Kennedy had helped to bring about his own death. "I did think so," he said. "And you know Sirhan says he did."[7]

McCarthy's explanation was one of the meanest interpretations of the tragedy ever articulated. He thought there was no reason for Kennedy to emphasize his willingness to sell arms to Israel, since this was "not an issue between him and me," and, on the basis of the Arab assassin's statements after his crime, McCarthy felt Kennedy's position on the Middle East "did stir him up" or make him go "crazy" or "whatever." In McCarthy's view this made Kennedy partly responsible for his own demise.[8]

Others blamed themselves *and* the candidates for fostering an atmosphere that might have encouraged the tragedy indirectly. Kennedy and McCarthy supporters alike wondered whether Kennedy's frenzied style of campaigning

* "Everyone knew that what King was doing . . . would expose him to attack," said McCarthy. "But I didn't say, ever say, King had done anything *particular* to provoke it, no." Clark strongly disagreed. "McCarthy said King 'never should have gone back to Memphis,'" his campaign manager recalled. "Of all the things McCarthy said, these are the quotes I remember best." [Author's interviews with Blair Clark, 3/19/86, and Eugene McCarthy, 3/27/86.]

had contributed to a general feeling of hysteria—and whether McCarthy's bitter gibes (along with those of all the other Kennedy haters) might have played an incidental role in this awful drama. However, McCarthy retained the distinction of being the only person to pin the blame for the shooting directly on its victim.

How the Minnesotan's behavior after this tragedy affected the expectations of everyone in the antiwar movement remains a crucial question—perhaps *the* crucial question—about the lasting effects of the events of 1968.

By June, millions of citizens had adopted the antiwar cause as their own, and they had begun to believe that the system might actually be made to work. The idea that ordinary people working together could wield more influence than the established power brokers was at the heart of the "new politics" practiced by the Democratic insurgents. A McCarthy advertisement put it this way: "We are the volunteers, and the mercenaries are no match for us. We are the contributors of the ten and twenty dollar bills, and together we are bigger than the big money; we are the asphalt, and we are conquering the steamroller."[9]

In the face of widespread despair over the war, it was this notion that had given so many people so much hope. But two men ensured that this grassroots concept could not be fully tested or completely played out. Because of them, there would be no final victory or cathartic defeat. One man was responsible for a heinous act of commission, the other a disturbing act of omission. But the actions of both had the same effect: They confirmed the power of the bullet to change the political process irrevocably. The men who left a movement of idealists leaderless at the moment when they most desperately needed to be led were Sirhan Sirhan and Eugene McCarthy.

Among McCarthy partisans who could see beyond their immediate grief, there were many who believed at the beginning of the summer that Kennedy's death left the presidential field wide open—and presented McCarthy with an extraordinary opportunity. But if McCarthy had been tempted to abandon the fight after Johnson's withdrawal, now it was clear that he wanted to gallop off the battlefield. Sirhan's act, he recalled, was "so out of any context" that it was surreal, "like Camus—*The Stranger*."[10] So was McCarthy's demeanor afterward.

During the plane trip on the way back from California, Tom Finney asked McCarthy how they should conduct the campaign for the next two months. "It's not going to make any difference," said the candidate. "It's all over."[11] In Washington a day later, he had lunch with Geri Joseph, a Democratic National Committee–woman from Minnesota who was supporting

Humphrey. It was "the only time in my life that I've ever seen him really incoherent," Joseph said. "One sentence didn't have anything to do with the next. . . . I think that he honestly thought that Bobby had brought some of this on himself. And this troubled him terribly, the whole violence of it. I think that he was upset that he had set himself against the Kennedys, and now this Kennedy had been killed. It wasn't really clear at all. He was just violently upset."[12]

On the eve of Bobby Kennedy's funeral, McCarthy had a private meeting with Humphrey. A vice-presidential aide recalled the discussion this way: "It was clear that what Gene was doing was trying to find a reason to drop out. He just had no more heart for it." Clark said the same aide had told him that McCarthy had given up during this encounter. But no deal was struck because Humphrey thought McCarthy was making unacceptable demands for changes in his position on the war.[13]

June was the strangest month. John Updike wondered whether God might have withdrawn his blessing from America.[14] After the Kennedy assassination, the Democratic party was in a state of nervous disarray. McCarthy's privately held conviction that the race was over was reinforced by the establishment press, which had reverted to routine disparagement of the prospects of the antiwar insurgents. A *New York Times* survey published two days after Kennedy's funeral predicted that McCarthy would get just seventy-five of the delegates pledged to Kennedy, while Humphrey would get more than four hundred. If those numbers were correct, it meant that Humphrey would get 1,600 votes, far more than the 1,312 needed for nomination.[15] But these estimates were meaningless to McCarthy lieutenants who remembered that Lyndon Johnson's renomination had been predicted just as flatly less than three months earlier. In 1968 nothing had become more debased than the conventional wisdom.

Maurice Rosenblatt had founded the liberal National Committee for an Effective Congress in 1948, and he had known McCarthy since the mid-fifties. Like so many others close to the standard-bearer, Rosenblatt thought McCarthy only "went as far towards the presidency as he wanted to go. He could have gone all the way had he wanted to. . . . After the assassination of Kennedy, he was the only voice in the land. And there were certainly no external factors standing between him and the nomination. . . . There [was] a complete vacuum at the leadership of the United States. And only one foot fit the slipper. And he was Cinderella. Now, why he didn't put his foot in that slipper . . . is a question that I can't quite decipher. . . . If ever God wanted a man to be nominated and be president, I think it was Gene McCarthy."[16]

Jeremy Larner saw the situation in almost identical terms: "Surely no politician had better credentials in restraint and dignity than Gene held at that moment—or an evener tone with which to address the nation. . . . But McCarthy could not, or would not, command his full power. The issues were not enough to maintain him, and the values which prevailed in him were not those which pertained to the state of America or the possibilities for leadership. He withdrew. . . . Gene did not resign his candidacy; he left a lottery ticket in the big barrel to await the hand of God. . . . While millions hoped for him and waited, Gene regressed to his balanced presentation of self, to the sacred ceremony of his personality."[17]

For eight days after the California primary, McCarthy made no public statements. Larner found himself preoccupied with a lyric from "Mrs. Robinson," the year's biggest hit for Simon and Garfunkel: "Where have you gone, Joe DiMaggio? A nation turns its lonely eyes to you."[18] Larner was one of many who wanted McCarthy to break his silence in the Senate caucus room, where Gene and Bobby—and Jack—had all announced their presidential candidacies. Unaccountably, McCarthy insisted that they use a tiny hearing room, which left a hundred reporters stranded outside in the hallway.

To Larner, McCarthy looked "ravaged and grim," as if he hadn't slept for a week. The *Times* said that "his face was almost as strained as the morning after" Bobby had been shot.[19] The dead senator's supporters were desperate for a gesture that would make it possible for them to forgive McCarthy for his previous behavior. Instead of trying to assuage them, McCarthy ignored them; all references to the dead senator were excised from his prepared statement.[20] In fact, he made no direct appeals to *anyone*. He wouldn't even ask undecided delegates to vote for him instead of Humphrey. "I simply will ask them to be responsible delegates and make the judgment that has to be made in August, which is a question of what issues the Democratic party is going to support at that time. . . ."

In private, his friend Gil Harrison, the editor of *The New Republic*, asked him if he felt guilty about the assassination. "No," said McCarthy, "everything I said about him was completely fair."

"If I were you, Gene," said Harrison, "I'd feel just a little guilty—it's irrational, but all the same—how could you help it?"

Of course he feels guilty, Larner thought to himself. But McCarthy would have none of it. "Kennedy said he didn't enter New Hampshire because his personality would get in the way," the candidate said of his murdered opponent. "Then he came to Oregon with his dog and his astronaut. So it was perfectly fair." Then Harrison tried to make a joke about the way some columnists were always suggesting that something was wrong with the candidate. McCarthy seemed not to hear him, but after a moment he said, "There's something wrong with McCarthy all right. But they don't know what it is."[21]

For the Minnesotan, it wasn't enough to ignore Kennedy's supporters: Now he also had to insult them. In the days and weeks immediately following Bobby's death, a tough national gun-control law became a top priority for former Kennedy supporters. Four days after McCarthy's disastrous news conference, he was asked about the new drive for country-wide gun control. "It's been my experience in twenty years in the Congress that you really ought not to put through legislation under panic conditions," he said. Larner was appalled. "The statement was more than just a political mistake," he wrote. "Twist and turn it as you would, there was a kind of meanness beyond excuse or explanation."[22]

What made it all so much worse, somehow, was McCarthy's continuing ability to say things, whenever a baffling spirit moved him, that electrified his true believers. In a meeting with *New York Times* editors two days before his gun-control statement, he talked about the importance of standing up to the Pentagon, his sympathy for protesting students ("I think it's surprising that college students have been as passive for twenty years as they have been"), and the need to recognize Communist China. He also gave an unintentionally insightful answer when one of the *Times* editors asked a very important question:

"What is going to be the reaction of these young people who came into the system to work with you if the result of it all is going to be that at the end of the campaign you lose, they lose, and what comes out is what they fought against?"

"I think it depends on how they lose," McCarthy answered. But he was not referring to his own behavior; he meant that it would depend on whether "they feel that somehow it's taken away from them by the system at Chicago."[23]

Murray Kempton had added a second role to his usual one as journalist: Now he was also running as a McCarthy delegate from New York City. Kempton noted that McCarthy had identified the thirteenth century as his own, and the columnist was intrigued by the appeal of the candidate's anti-technological bent. "From back there," Kempton wrote, "he casts a cold eye on all the institutions before which every other politician bows by habit—at the Pentagon, at the FBI, at the CIA, at everything that trusts a computer. Out of St. Thomas' quarrel with unfaithful kings comes the quarrel of Eugene McCarthy with his president and his time."[24]

Sometimes it seemed like the campaign that would not die, no matter how badly McCarthy behaved. The Minnesotan infuriated his New York supporters by doing almost no campaigning in that state's primary before the crucial vote on June 18. "McCarthy didn't throw cold water on the New York primary," said Harold Ickes, Jr., one of his campaign directors. "He pissed on it."[25] As it turned out, it didn't matter. McCarthy's fans were rigorously organized, and twenty thousand volunteers fanned out from two hundred storefronts across the state during the weekend preceding the election.[26] A ruthless unit called Junior Students for McCarthy was especially effective. Headed by twelve-year-old Randall Stempler and thirteen-year-old Nelson Gess, these juniors were formidable canvassers, and young Stempler knew why: "People don't mind talking to us about the war," he said, "because we're cute." They also had an amazing opener: "We just go up to someone and say, 'Do you believe in death?' "[27]

The *Washington Post* predicted that "most of the voters would shift to Humphrey-backed" slates, but the conventional wisdom was defective once again.[28] McCarthy won sixty-two of New York's 123 elected delegates, and Kempton was one of them. Thirty went to the candidate's dead rival, and nineteen were uncommitted; Humphrey got only twelve.[29] But when the time came for the party bosses to dole out the remaining sixty-seven delegate votes ten days later, McCarthy's people were treated contemptuously. They had originally demanded thirty-four votes, to reflect their success in the primaries; they were offered 15½—with only half of that number going to delegates recognized as McCarthy supporters by his organization. The regulars laughed when Al Lowenstein shouted, "You spit in the face of the notion that this convention is democratic." Then Lowenstein and his allies stormed out, shouting, "Fascists!" "Nazis!" and "Hacks!" It was a small-scale dress rehearsal for the way the regulars would behave and the insurgents would react two months later in Chicago, but no one realized it at the time.[30] Earlier, the delegate distribution had been even more unbalanced in Pennsylvania, where McCarthy had beaten Humphrey eight to one in the nonbinding primary. There the party's bosses had given the vice-president two-thirds of the state's 130 delegate votes. McCarthy's people called it "the Pennsylvania railroad."[31]

A balding man who dyed his remaining hair an implausible shade, often sounded fatuous, and seemed unable to free himself from the yoke of a dubious president, Humphrey came across to many as a parody of all of the establishment's failures. He hardly needed any additional disadvantages in his quest for younger supporters. However, by ignoring the primaries and getting nearly all of his delegates through the party's power brokers, the vice-president was making a difficult situation impossible. His rallies in this period were pathetic affairs, sparsely attended and frequently disrupted by angry kids shouting, "Bring the troops home!" and "Dump the Hump!"[32] His campaign was "long on delegates but woefully short of enthusiasm," Warren Weaver wrote in the *New York Times.* Throughout the summer, there was tension between what Humphrey needed to do to get nominated and what was necessary to get him elected. And that was especially true of his position on the war.

By July, Humphrey was desperate to put some distance between himself and the president, but whenever he seemed ready to announce his own position on Vietnam, Johnson carefully boxed him in. McCarthy believed that the president had given up on getting reelected so that he could retain control of his war, and all of Johnson's efforts in the pre-convention period seemed to confirm that point of view.[33] Even though the newspapers kept saying Humphrey had more than enough delegates to win on the first ballot, Johnson made sure Humphrey's strength—particularly in the South—remained sufficiently soft to keep the vice-president acutely anxious about his prospects, right through the third week of August.[34]

Three elements were pulling Humphrey in separate directions: his nostalgia for his own liberal past, his loyalty to his president, and his desperate desire to succeed him. Every time he raised the question of endorsing a complete bombing halt—one that would include all of North Vietnam, instead of most of it—the president rejected the idea out of hand. Toward the end of July, when Humphrey asked Johnson for permission to make such a statement, the president warned that he would denounce him if the vice-president insisted on pursuing this course. He also told Humphrey that any public split between them might disrupt the peace talks Averell Harriman was now conducting with the North Vietnamese in Paris—and a real breakthrough there would do more for the vice-president's campaign than any other potential development. Just for good measure, Johnson added his personal perspective. "I have two sons-in-law over there," he told the vice-president, "and I consider this proposal to be a direct slap at their safety and at what they are trying to do." A dejected Humphrey abandoned the idea of advocating a bombing halt.

Even worse than the president's bullying was the nagging fear that Johnson's withdrawal statement might turn out to be less irrevocable than it had appeared. Humphrey later said that he thought the president had the "feeling that he maybe shouldn't have resigned. There are some people who think that he was looking forward to dropping in on the convention in Chicago and being renominated by acclamation." Although Humphrey himself didn't feel this was likely, there were "people who thought it was a possibility, and I think there was a move on for that with Daley and some of them."[35]

Stymied on the war, Humphrey kept searching for new ways to attract the disaffected. Often his speeches were filled with echoes of McCarthy's other positions. In mid-July he said he "favored a shift from policies of confrontation and containment to policies of reconciliation and peaceful engagement." In the same period he endorsed a lowering of the voting age from twenty-one to eighteen and hinted that he wanted Teddy Kennedy to be his running mate. Still, none of this was enough to satisfy those waiting for clear evidence of a breach between Humphrey and the president.[36] "I'm in the middle," the candidate told Jimmy Breslin. "I've inherited every one of Lyndon Johnson's enemies. Plus some of my own that I've always had." Breslin wrote that he found it "impossible to dislike" the candidate, but "he still is disliked. They dislike the hell out of Hubert Humphrey." The columnist offered blunt advice: Humphrey must "forget about Lyndon Johnson today. Or his problem in Chicago could be more real than anybody around him suspects."[37] Then, in early August, the vice-president thought he had finally got a break. The Republicans nominated his dream opponent.

FROM the outside, the Republican conclave in Miami looked like a placid affair. "Boredom," wrote Teddy White, "lay on the convention like a mistress."[38] Richard Nixon's victory seemed practically assured. Nelson Rockefeller had spent $10 million and traveled 66,200 miles through forty-five states, but his campaign had never really taken off.[39] And while Ronald Reagan was still threatening Nixon from the right, outside his home state of California he had very little firm support. The Californian was pushing a hard line on law and order, which included his usual quota of inaccuracies. Ten days after Kennedy was shot, Reagan addressed a fundraising dinner in Indianapolis, where he assailed a "philosophy of permissiveness" and a "sick society." He also offered a shocking statistic: "In this week of tragedy, six policemen in Chicago have been killed in the line of duty." (As it happened, only two policemen had been killed in Chicago during all of 1968 up to the moment Reagan was speaking. But in a pattern that would become familiar over the next twenty years, Reagan's spokesman in Sacramento said the governor was "prepared to stand by the text" anyway.[40])

Nixon's strategy was to pretend he was invincible: He didn't even bother to arrive in Miami until 6:50 P.M. on the Monday the convention began.[41] However, his nomination was quite a bit more uncertain than his handlers had tried to make it appear. Pressed from the left and the right, he managed only 692 votes on the first ballot—just 25 more than he needed to be nominated. If Nixon had faltered in the initial voting, Reagan and Rockefeller might have continued to chip away at his delegate strength on subsequent ballots.

Two gaffes—a famous one by Rockefeller, which grew out of his indecision about whether to become a candidate, and a lesser-known one by Reagan—had made it impossible for these ideological opposites to snatch victory away from Nixon, despite what had become a tacit alliance between them to weaken the front-runner.[42]

Back in March the New York governor had performed a notorious flip-flop. A carefully orchestrated "Draft Rockefeller" movement had sprung up around the country, and Maryland governor Spiro T. Agnew was one of its earliest and most enthusiastic supporters. When Rockefeller scheduled a televised speech for March 21, nearly everyone (including the *New York Times*) predicted that he would announce his candidacy. Sensing an opportunity to take some credit for Rockefeller's decision, Agnew installed a large new color television in his office; then he invited the press to watch Rockefeller's speech with him. But unbeknownst to Agnew, Rockefeller had experienced a last-minute change of heart—and no one in the New York governor's entourage had bothered to notify his chief Maryland supporter. Witnesses swore that when Rockefeller declared, "I have decided today to reiterate unequivocally that I am *not* a candidate," Agnew's jaw dropped. The Maryland governor never forgave Rockefeller for the insult. When the New Yorker changed his mind yet again and finally got into the race in May, it was too late to recapture the affections of his former friend. At the convention, Agnew delivered eighteen crucial votes from the Maryland delegation to his new friend, Richard Nixon.[43]

For Ronald Reagan, a key target was the twenty votes of the Mississippi delegation, all of them officially committed to Nixon. Together with the Maryland votes, these would have been enough to block Nixon on the first ballot. Hoping to break the Mississippi delegation wide open, Reagan telephoned its boss, Clarke Reed, who through intermediaries had encouraged the Californian to run. However, the supposedly sympathetic Reed had actually been lying in wait for Reagan. Two years before, Reed had been in a difficult race for the governorship of Mississippi, and Reagan had never responded to Reed's appeal for an appearance to help the campaign.

Now the Mississippian was paying him back; he would do unto Reagan as Reagan had done unto him. When the governor called to ask for help, Reed turned him aside with this suggestion: "Perhaps you had better try where you have a few favors owing." All of Mississippi's votes remained firmly in the Nixon column.[44]

The Democrats were delighted with the outcome: Nixon was the Republican they particularly loved to hate. No other major party candidate had more humbling history to live down than Richard Milhous Nixon—a fact tacitly acknowledged by his fans, who that year dubbed him "the new Nixon." As author Garry Wills put it, "The entire American topography is either graveyard, for him, or minefield—ground he must walk delicately, revenant amid the tombstones, whistling in histrionic unconcern."[45] In the past, whenever Nixon had been on the verge of a great triumph, he seemed unable to control his worst instincts. In 1960 he had ruined an excellent chance to become president with a disastrous performance in his first debate with John Kennedy. Two years later, after losing the race for the California governorship, he angrily announced his retirement from politics: "You won't have Richard Nixon to kick around anymore," he promised, because this was his "last press conference." Back in 1952, in his first race for vice-president, he had barely avoided getting pushed off the ticket with Eisenhower, after reports were published about a "slush fund" inside his Senate office. On that occasion, he had managed to save himself with his famous "Checkers" speech. It was a brilliant but embarrassing performance—one of the most maudlin efforts in the history of television. The heroes of the speech were the Nixons' new dog (Checkers) and the respectable "Republican cloth coat" belonging to his wife.

The early years foretold the later man. He was born January 9, 1913, in Yorba Linda, California. In the beginning, he had done all the Horatio Alger things: joined the debating club, sold newspaper subscriptions, even played the piano in church. When his family moved to Whittier, he became the janitor for the town swimming pool. By the time Nixon entered law school at Duke, his competitive instinct was becoming more pronounced. In 1936 Nixon and two friends broke into the law school dean's office to learn his class rank. The Whittier boy had been third in his class, and he worried that if he dropped below that number, he might lose his scholarship.[46] The following year, in his very first case as a lawyer, he was sued by his own client after she accused him of unethical behavior. Nixon's firm of Wingert and Bewley paid the client, Marie Schee, $4,000 to settle her claim.[47]

If anyone might save the Democrats in 1968, it was the man John Kennedy had humiliated eight years earlier. "I've read of the new Nixon," Humphrey said shortly after the Republican had won the nomination, "in 1952, in 1956, in 1958, and in 1968. I've never known one man that had so many political face-lifting jobs in my life."[48] The Democrats' joy grew with Nixon's selection of a running mate. Fearful of delegate defections before his nomination, Nixon had struggled behind the scenes to keep Southern supporters in his column. The key to his strategy was the recruitment of Strom Thurmond, the relentlessly conservative senator from South Carolina. Thurmond's support had given Nixon crucial credibility with latent segregationists, but it came at a price: Nixon promised that the integration of public schools would not be a top priority of his administration (he explained that "freedom of choice" was more important to him), and he said he would choose a vice-president who would be "acceptable to all sections of the party."[49] That was a coded guarantee that aberrant liberals like John Lindsay and Nelson Rockefeller would not be considered for the second spot on the ticket.

Until recently, Spiro Agnew had been considered part of this same outlaw breed of progressives by those Republicans who had flocked to Barry Goldwater just four years earlier. In 1966, with the help of many liberal Democrats, Agnew had triumphed over a racist Democratic opponent in his bid for the governorship. Then he brought blacks into the state government and presided over the passage of the state's first open-housing law. But like so many other Middle Americans, he became fed up with disorder in the spring of 1968—first in the ghettos, then on the campuses—and he experienced what was practically an overnight conversion. When riots racked Baltimore immediately after Martin Luther King's assassination, he was forced to call out the National Guard to restore order. Afterward, he screamed at black moderates whom he had summoned to his office, accusing them of fostering a conspiracy. Most of his audience walked out on him. Now Agnew was against the Kerner Commission (because of its references to "white racism"), and—like Richard Daley—he was in favor of shooting looters.[50]

When Nixon chose Agnew to be his running mate, the Maryland governor was almost an anonymous figure outside his native state; a common reaction to his selection, even among political reporters, was "Spiro who?"[51] The Democrats were sure they were the beneficiaries of another blunder. The Republicans had passed over the glamour of Lindsay and Rockefeller for an unknown with less than two years' experience running a state government. But Nixon knew exactly what he was doing. Though never a reliable guide for his own political career, he was a brilliant judge of the political potential of others. After his disastrous campaigns in 1960 and 1962, he had begun the long climb back to political respectability by appearing for scores of Republican congressional candidates in 1966. In October of that year, Murray Kempton asked Nixon to predict the outcome of the election in the House of Representatives. Nixon said the Republicans would gain at least forty-six new congressional seats (a forty-seventh race, he believed, was too close to call). Kempton was deeply impressed when the actual results were tabulated: The number of Republican congressmen had increased by forty-six; then, after a recount, they won a forty-seventh seat in the district where Nixon had refused to forecast the victor.[52]

Now, in the summer of 1968, Nixon sensed much sooner than most the cumulative impact of the mayhem that had dominated the American psyche since the beginning of the year: the massive casualties in Vietnam in February and March, an assassination and riots in April, another horrible murder in June. Huge numbers of Americans had grown tired of rapid change and terrified of continuing disorder. Kennedy and McCarthy had got most of the media's attention through the spring, but the voters that would belong to Nixon were disgusted with the cacophony produced by the Democrats. Nixon deduced that these Americans now wanted a subtle stoking of their prejudices, the mostly unspoken feelings that the riots of the spring had done so much to revive—and Agnew's newly adopted rhetoric made him the perfect instrument for this strategy. At the same time, those who were frightened of hippies and drugs and riots also wanted someone who looked soothing: someone stoic, like six-foot two-inch Spiro Agnew, the candidate who had made the best-groomed list of *Men's Hairstylist and Barber's Journal*—in a year when most barbers were complaining that their business had been decimated by kids who refused to get their hair cut.[53]

"Passion," wrote Teddy White, was "the very emotion [Nixonians] sought to avoid—passion had ruined the party in 1964, passion ravaged the nation in 1968."[54] Mary McGrory thought Nixon's chances depended on a national nostalgia for "a kind of Eisenhowerian calm, after the pains and shocks and tragedies of the Democratic years. . . . [Nixon] does not seek to lead public opinion but to follow it."[55]

Even as Nixon was nominated, another riot had broken out across Biscayne Bay, in the black ghetto of Liberty City in Miami. Seventy policemen were dispatched, armed with shotguns, and four people perished in the melee.[56] The writer who may have come closest to catching the flavor of the prejudices aroused by such events was an unlikely analyst: novelist turned journalist Norman Mailer, who was covering both national conventions in 1968 for *Harper's* magazine. Mailer became irritated in Miami while waiting for Ralph Abernathy to appear at a press conference. Abernathy had succeeded King as the head of the Southern Christian Leadership Conference. Though he had been King's closest friend, Abernathy had little of the fallen leader's charm, and few reporters were enchanted with him.

As Mailer became increasingly agitated because of Abernathy's tardiness, he was astonished by the racist stream of consciousness that began to flow inside his brain. Afterward, he wrote about it with an intensity that might have embarrassed even those Republicans who felt more strongly about these matters than he did. Once again, Mailer referred to Mailer exclusively in the third person:

> The reporter became aware . . . of a curious emotion in himself, for he had not ever felt it consciously before—it was a simple emotion and very unpleasant to him—he was getting tired of Negroes and their rights. It was a miserable recognition, and on many a count, for if he felt even a hint this way, then what immeasurable tides of rage must be loose in America itself? Perhaps it was the atmosphere of the Republican convention itself, this congregation of the clean, the brisk, the orderly, the efficient. A reporter who must attempt to do his job, he had perhaps committed himself too completely to the atmosphere as if better to comprehend the subterranean character of what he saw on the surface. . . . What an obsession was the Negro to the average white American by now. Every time that American turned in his thoughts to the sweetest object of contemplation . . . nothing less than America the Beautiful herself—that angel of security at the end of every alley—then *there* was the face of an accusing rioting Black right in the middle of the dream—smack in the center of the alley—and the obsession was hung on the hook of how to divide the guilt, how much to the white man, and how much to the dark? . . . Political power of the most frightening sort was obviously waiting for the first demagogue who would smash the obsession and free the white man of his guilt.
>
> [Mailer was] heartily sick of listening to the tyranny of soul music . . . so weary of being sounded in the subway by Black eyes . . . so envious finally of that liberty to abdicate from the long year-end decade-drowning yokes of work and responsibility that he must have become in some secret part of his flesh a closet Republican. . . . Yes, he was furious at Abernathy for making him wait these crucial minutes while the secret stuff of his brain was disclosed to his mind.[57]

Nixon would go after George Wallace's voters to try to fashion a majority in the electoral college. Choosing Agnew meant a Southern strategy. It also meant that Nixon was passing the torch; his time-honored role as the party's hatchet man would now devolve upon his new running mate. In 1968 Richard Nixon would take a vague high road, promising, among other things, a "secret plan" to end the war in Vietnam. It was Agnew who would call Hubert Humphrey "squishy-soft" on communism.[58]

Meanwhile, away from Miami, Yippies, radicals, liberals, and Mayor Richard J. Daley's police force were conspiring to make the Democrats' upcoming conclave as different as anyone could imagine from the Republicans' orderly procession.

11

This Wheel's on Fire

MAYOR DALEY, A FAMILY MAN, WELCOMES YOU TO A FAMILY TOWN.
—Billboard in Chicago, August 1968[1]

"Dare to struggle, dare to win."
—Tom Hayden, quoting Mao Tse-tung[2]

"In 1968 the name Chicago won a significance far beyond date and place. It became the title of an episode, like Waterloo, or Versailles, or Munich."
—Theodore H. White[3]

". . . there are circumstances in which no one wins, in which everyone loses. . . ."
—From the Walker report on the Democratic National Convention, presented to the President's Commission on the Causes and Prevention of Violence[4]

EUGENE McCarthy's behavior during the Democratic National Convention in Chicago crippled the movement for peace; Blair Clark, Jeremy Larner, and a great many others would never forgive him for what he failed to do there.[5] The last chance to get the Democrats formally to repudiate Lyndon Johnson's war disappeared as McCarthy's will to lead dwindled away. Largely because of McCarthy's personal idiosyncrasies, the people who had worked so hard and so long to get him elected were left with nothing at the end of August but a feeling of bitter, empty failure.

That Chicago tragedy may have been avoidable; the other one was inevitable. To the left of McCarthy's kids was another group of Americans whose actions were unrelated to the Minnesotan's persistent acedia. These men and women sought a violent confrontation in Chicago as a means of proving that America had become a "police state." Goaded by Mayor Richard Daley's notorious shoot-to-kill order, the Chicago police force was more than willing to play the exaggerated role the radicals had selected for them. The behavior of the police was so egregious that by the end of the convention week, a respected Democratic senator from Connecticut was comparing Daley's henchmen with Nazis—and the radicals in the streets had attracted the sympathy of most of the liberals who had struggled to make the system more responsive.[6]

There was nothing very welcoming about Chicago in August. An electrical workers' strike, a telephone installers' strike, a bus strike, and a taxicab strike had practically paralyzed the city even before the convention began. The convention hall was ringed with barbed wire that could be electrified at the flick of a switch. Outside, the city's entire police force of twelve thousand was put on twelve-hour shifts, and they were bolstered by six thousand Illinois National Guardsmen, as well as six thousand regular troops, who were equipped with rifles, flamethrowers, and bazookas.[7] Chicago became the setting for the first great battle between American counterculture and American reaction; less than two years later, the killing of four students at Kent State University would bring this war to its peak.[8]

Mayor Daley's refusal to grant permits for anyone to camp out in his city's parks was a crucial first step toward ensuring a violent confrontation. Late Sunday evening, the day before the convention began, the pattern for the week was established when the police decided to clear Lincoln Park. As they had at Columbia, the protesters taunted the police with chants of "Pigs!" and "Oink, oink, shithead," to which the cops responded with shouts of "Kill the Commies!" before wading into the crowds with their billy clubs. When a *Newsweek* reporter flashed his credentials on an adjacent street, a policeman shouted at him, "*Newsweek* fuckers!" and clubbed him on his head and then over the rest of his body. Order wasn't restored in the streets until 2 A.M. By then, ten newsmen had been beaten.[9]

Nine months earlier, Abbie Hoffman had started with a playful notion. Hoffman was one of the first hippie (and then Yippie) impresarios, a media handler who used his sense of theater and satire to attract generous coverage from the press. He had turned thirty-two in 1968, a fact that some people thought actually made him a child of the fifties. The first discussion of what to do in Chicago during the convention had begun in his apartment on the Lower East Side on New Year's Eve, the day before 1968 began. There with Hoffman were his wife, Anita, fellow future Yippie Jerry Rubin, and Paul Krassner, editor of the *Realist*.[10] Hoffman recalled the initial planning session this way, in an interview with investigators for the official commission that reported on the Chicago uprising:

> There we were, all stoned, rolling around the floor . . . yippie! . . . And so, YIPPIE was born, the Youth International Party. What about if we create a myth, program it into the media, you know . . . when that myth goes in, it's always connected to Chicago August 25th . . . come and do your thing, excitement, bullshit, everything, anything . . . commitment, engagement, Democrats, pigs, the whole thing. All you do is change the H in Hippie to a Y for Yippie, and you got it.[11]

In the spring, Mrs. Hoffman elaborated on their plans for Chicago to a reporter for the *New York Times*. She was quoted in an article about an early-morning occupation of Grand Central Station by "3,000 chanting youths" who had painted the words "Peace Now" on the four-sided clock in the center of the terminal—just before the celebration was broken up by club-swinging policemen. In August, Mrs. Hoffman explained, there would be "a demonstration of an alternative way of life, a six-day living experience in a park in Chicago, with free food, tents, theater, underground newspapers and lots of rock bands and folk singers."[12] The Monterey Pop Festival in 1967 had been one of the Yippie organizers' inspirations.[13]

In March, the Yippies presented their first request to camp out in Grant Park during the Chicago convention, displaying the sense of humor that quickly became their trademark. A white girl in Indian costume, who called herself Helen Running Water, delivered the permit application to the deputy mayor, David Stahl. It came inside a page from *Playboy* displaying the Playmate of the Month. On the Playmate's photo were scrawled the words, "To Dick, with love—the Yippies."[14]

Yippie proposals for the summer (all of which got heavy publicity) included a plan to contaminate the Chicago water supply with a massive dose of LSD, a protest to be led by ten thousand nude bodies floating in Lake Michigan, a squad of Yippie women to seduce delegates (and spike their drinks with acid), and a separate group of "hyper-potent" hippie men to

seduce delegates' wives—and daughters. The possibility of a mass hallucination induced by a contaminated water supply aroused the most curiosity,
although one researcher had told the CIA in the early fifties that such a
strategy was impractical because chlorine would neutralize the drug's usual
effects. (The agency reacted to this opinion with a federally financed effort
to develop a chlorine-resistant form of LSD.[15])

On the more serious side of the radical political divide, David Dellinger,
who had been one of the principal organizers of the 1967 demonstration
at the Pentagon, was now working with Rennie Davis and Tom Hayden to
try to bring a more substantial protest to Chicago during the convention.
Hayden and Davis were both products of SDS; Hayden was also the author
of the Port Huron Statement and a veteran of the recent protests at Columbia,
where he had been arrested after participating in the occupation of Mathematics Hall.[16] For several weeks, Al Lowenstein considered a separate effort
to attract a hundred thousand "Clean for Gene" kids to the convention site,
but he abandoned the idea in the face of relentless hostility from Daley and
opposition from McCarthy, who feared anarchy.[17]

In one respect, America in 1968 was more like the "police state" radicals had alleged than most people suspected. That year most radical
organizations—including David Dellinger's—were thoroughly penetrated
by several different government agencies. In 1968 the CIA engaged in
domestic surveillance, which is explicitly prohibited by its charter. When
CIA director Richard Helms forwarded the results of this work to the White
House, he was careful to mention (in writing) that such memorandums could
not be widely disseminated since "the Agency should not be reporting at
all on domestic affairs of this sort."[18]

Even Mayor Daley had his own national spying operation. In 1968 he
used the Chicago Department of Investigation—an agency he had established to supply him with intelligence information—to infiltrate antiwar
organizations all over America. His agents boasted of having penetrated
dissident groups in San Francisco, Oakland, and Los Angeles, as well as
the New York branch of the National Mobilization Committee to End the
War in Vietnam. Daley's agency also used double agents to plant false
information with the protesters.[19] Robert Pierson was a Chicago policeman
who infiltrated the radicals, served as one of their bodyguards, and stayed
close to their leaders. In one piece of news footage he is even heard to shout
"Pig!" in front of his own police headquarters.[20]

The FBI was also deeply involved in the preparations for the convention. Demonstrators expecting to find shelter in the homes of sympathizers
got stuck out on the street after the FBI issued a phony list of available

rooms under a peace group's letterhead.[21] At the request of Humphrey's executive assistant, William Connell, the bureau also agreed to supply the vice-president with a special squad of agents in Chicago, similar to the one Lyndon Johnson had used to keep tabs on his enemies at the convention in Atlantic City four years earlier.[22]

The Army was represented in Chicago by at least one film unit from the 113th Military Intelligence Group. (This was the operation inadvertently captured on film by the cinematographer for *Medium Cool,* the feature film shot on the streets of the city during the riots.) Each night at ten o'clock the product of the unit's work was put on an American Airlines flight to Washington, so that the joint chiefs of staff could begin their daily briefing with their own private movie of the events in Chicago. Ten years later, Army sources estimated to CBS News that an astonishing one in six demonstrators in Chicago that week was actually some kind of government agent.[23]

THE recent violence at home had already ensured a discomfiting background for the Democrats' convention; then, the week before the party gathered, a new cataclysm abroad produced another terrible depression. Eugene McCarthy's reaction to this event was perhaps his single most self-destructive statement: It did more to undermine his credibility than everything else he did in the period after Bobby Kennedy was killed.

The last dream for a revolution with a happy ending in 1968 died on August 20, when Soviet tanks rolled into Czechoslovakia. The Soviets had decided that the winds of change within one of their satellites posed too great a threat to the rest of their empire; the invasion ended the Czechs' hopes for freedom less than nine months after their birth in the Prague spring. Soviet ambassador Anatoly Dobrynin came to the White House to inform the United States of his government's decision. A few hours later President Johnson called a meeting of the National Security Council to discuss the invasion. The president concluded there was nothing the United States could do in response—other than to cancel the upcoming summit meeting with the Soviets, which the White House had been planning to announce the very next day.[24]

The invasion was a singularly depressing event. America had fallen in love with the Czechoslovak experiment. In a forlorn act of protest, the Czechoslovak ambassador in Washington read a defiant statement from his country's national assembly. The Soviets' action provoked denunciations by spokesmen for all parts of the political spectrum—all but one. Jeremy Larner met with McCarthy early on the morning of August 21, after preparing a statement for him about the crisis. It began, "This is a tragic day for freedom," and went on to point out that the invasion was "only the latest in a series of great power interventions that had gone on since the end of World War II." It also said that America's position in Vietnam had made it easier for the Soviets to crush a reform movement within one of its neighboring countries. But once again, McCarthy insisted on flaunting his immunity to passion. "After all, Jeremy," he said, "it's not as if Hitler were marching in."

"I think it is," Larner replied, "in some ways." McCarthy promised to use the proffered statement; then he changed his mind. A half-hour later, Larner and Ken Reich of the *Los Angeles Times* both received McCarthy's revised version from a secretary. No enemy could have arranged for anything more destructive to McCarthy's campaign than what the candidate had done by himself.

The new statement declared, "I do not see this as a major world crisis. It is likely to have more serious consequences for the Communist party in Russia than in Czechoslovakia. I saw no need for a midnight meeting of the United States National Security Council." When Larner pleaded with Reich not to report these words, the *Los Angeles Times* reporter agreed to give him an hour to try to get McCarthy to retract them. But neither Larner nor Dick Goodwin could get through to the candidate in time to fix it. It was a final straw for Larner, and for thousands of other McCarthy men and women: "If people expected Gene to give the standard angry reaction, they didn't understand what real style was," the campaign aide wrote. "At that moment, I did not want Gene to be president. . . . He was making absolutely clear what he had shown us in other ways from the beginning: that his style of presenting himself was more important than his campaign for President and all it stood for." Eventually, McCarthy was prevailed upon to issue a different statement— "Of course, I condemn this cruel and violent action. It should not really be necessary to say this"—but nothing could obliterate the impact of his previous remarks.[25]

McCarthy had got so little support from fellow legislators and former Kennedy supporters that South Dakota senator George McGovern entered the race for the presidency on August 10, to give these disaffected liberals someone to rally around. Also in August, Ralph Yarborough, a much-admired Texas liberal, became the only United States senator formally to endorse Eugene McCarthy for president. As usual, McCarthy had done nothing to encourage this gesture. "I had the feeling that I had to cram my support down McCarthy's throat," said Yarborough. "He wanted to be away from any senators or politicians; he thought they were [so] commonplace, they weren't worthy of him."

To Yarborough, the Minnesotan's statement on Czechoslovakia was one of three "colossal" blunders committed by McCarthy. The second one had occurred five days earlier. McCarthy had issued a list of potential appointees to his cabinet, ranging from Coretta Scott King for ambassador to the United Nations to William Clay Ford (Henry Ford's brother and a former Goldwater supporter) for secretary of commerce. The cabinet announcement was a brainstorm that came from Richard Goodwin, one of the very few Kennedy men who had rejoined the McCarthy fold after Bobby's death. Yarborough was appalled. "He named about six millionaires and about six Republicans —not a politician in the bunch. And the politicians were going to run the convention." McCarthy had slapped "nine-tenths of all the delegates in the face by telling all of them, 'You are unworthy to be in the cabinet.'" Then, on Tuesday, August 27, the day before the balloting, McCarthy conceded that Humphrey had the nomination locked up—producing banner headlines in all of Wednesday's newspapers.

Together, these three acts extinguished whatever lingering chance McCarthy might have had to become president. "I thought, 'My God, I'm poison,'" Yarborough recalled. "He was smart as a devil until I endorsed him. Now the man's gone crazy. Says I'll fill the cabinet with millionaires and Republicans, I'll condone the Russian invasion of Czechoslovakia, and I'll admit I'm beat before I start. If there's any way a politician could liquidate himself faster, that was self-immolation. He set the torch to those political hopes with those three things. I've wondered why on earth he did it."[26]

It is impossible to prove the contention of Blair Clark, Maurice Rosenblatt, and many others that McCarthy threw away a serious chance to become president. So many delegates were controlled by the party bosses that Humphrey's nomination may indeed have been inevitable. But McCarthy's failure to mount an effective campaign between June and August did have one undeniable effect: The impotence of McCarthy's effort meant that all the pressure on Humphrey was coming from the right—from the South and from his president. And that made it impossible for Humphrey to find the courage to come out against the war. "It left Humphrey at the mercy of Lyndon Johnson—who was at his most merciless in his drive to dominate on the issue of his war," Clark wrote.[27]

The main disagreement between Johnson's men and the antiwar faction centered on whether a halt in the bombing should be absolutely unilateral or depend on some type of reciprocal action from the North Vietnamese.

But by this time, the symbolism had become far more important than the details. Lyndon Johnson desperately wanted his party to validate his conduct of that war, and to that end his men left enough Southern delegates uncommitted to keep Humphrey nervous about his fate even after he had arrived in Chicago.

Adding to the vice-president's uneasiness was a new rumor flooding the convention: Teddy Kennedy might be available for a draft. Daley fueled this idea with an announcement on the Sunday before the convention began that his delegation would remain uncommitted for another forty-eight hours. The day before, Daley had telephoned Teddy Kennedy in Hyannis Port and asked him to announce his availability for a draft. Perhaps Daley really wanted Teddy to be the presidential nominee, or perhaps this was merely a ploy to bring the Massachusetts man out of his lair—so that he could be forced to accept the *vice*-presidential nomination on a Humphrey-Kennedy ticket. Whatever Daley's real motivation, Kennedy refused to say publicly that he might be available. However, Kennedy's brother-in-law Steve Smith had gone to Chicago to test the waters.[28]

According to Teddy White, "Only if an authentic, unquestionably spontaneous, self-obvious draft developed from the convention floor, calling on him, coming to him, would he accept the nomination as his duty; but he would not in any way, by indirection or by intermediary, incubate the draft himself."[29] Perhaps that was true, though many thought Smith was contributing significantly to the incubation process. By the time Aretha Franklin opened the convention on Monday evening by belting out "The Star-Spangled Banner," rumors of a Kennedy candidacy for president were proliferating. The idea had a peculiar logic to it: Only a candidate with his magic surname could unite both the regulars who had rallied to his brother John's cause after his nomination in 1960 and the new insurgents who were desperate for any major party candidate who might carry the antiwar banner into the fall election. Goodwin started asking McCarthy whether he might throw his support to Teddy. Amazingly, McCarthy seemed amenable. The Minnesotan suggested that Steve Smith come to visit him.

On Tuesday afternoon, Smith arrived at McCarthy's suite at the Conrad Hilton. Only Smith, Goodwin, and McCarthy were present. According to Goodwin (whose version McCarthy endorses), the Minnesotan said, "I can't make it. Teddy and I have the same views, and I'm willing to ask all my delegates to vote for him."[30] McCarthy wanted to have his name placed in nomination—but then he would withdraw it, clearing the way for Kennedy. Then McCarthy added, "While I'm doing this for Teddy, I never could have done it for Bobby." *Time* magazine reported there were tears of gratitude in Steve Smith's eyes. But Smith told Kennedy friend Peter Maas, "Somebody mistook it for all the spit in them."[31]

This was as close as the Kennedy draft came to getting off the ground. It collapsed after David Schoumacher of CBS went on the air at 8:30 Tuesday evening, reporting that Smith had visited McCarthy to *ask him* to support Kennedy—something Smith had never done. Suspecting a leak from the McCarthy camp, Smith was furious. The next morning Kennedy telephoned Humphrey and told him he was definitely out of the race for good.

McCarthy's true motivation may have been a great deal less magnanimous than it appeared. According to one account, he told a friend, "I wanted Teddy to take it and then be beaten. It would have broken the chain."[32] Asked about this eighteen years later, McCarthy replied, "I think I might have said, 'Well if he wins, it's fine, if he loses, why, you're going to have to run him sometime, and that this would be a test.' I think I said something like that." If that had happened, McCarthy explained, "he'd never run now," adding, "It's still going on twenty years later."[33]

THE level of violence kept escalating all across Chicago—inside and outside the amphitheater. Indoors, Dan Rather was punched and wrestled to the ground by a security agent on the convention floor. Outdoors, comedian Dick Gregory told an "antibirthday" party for Johnson (he was turning sixty that week) that he had "just heard that Premier Kosygin has sent a telegram to Mayor Daley asking for two thousand Chicago cops to report for duties in Prague immediately."[34] Playwright Arthur Miller, who, along with Paul Newman, had become a McCarthy delegate from Connecticut, was stared at "with open, almost comical ferocity" by an Illinois delegate. "Once I tried to give him a smile of greeting, a recognition of his interest," Miller wrote. "He gave nothing, like a watchdog trained to move only on signal." Miller thought the meeting in the amphitheater was the "closest thing to a session of the All-Union Soviet that ever took place outside of Russia."[35]

It got worse on Wednesday—a great deal worse. Abbie Hoffman was arrested shortly after 8 A.M. for having the word "FUCK" printed on his forehead. That kept the Yippie leader off the streets for the next thirteen hours.[36] At the convention hall, the debate on the peace plank reached the floor. McCarthy's aides pleaded with him to do something, *anything,* to show that he was still leading the battle, to prove that he still cared about the outcome of some earthly event. "We wanted him to express what we believed in and what we would have to fight for no matter who was nominated," said Larner. "It was so frustrating because he talked about it as if it were a purely literary event."[37] Steve Mitchell, who had been Adlai Stevenson's campaign manager and was one of the few real professionals working for McCarthy, implored the candidate to break with tradition and make a passionate speech to the convention. Tom Finney agreed: Something must be done! Mitchell telephoned McCarthy three times, begging him to come. But the Minnesotan could not be moved. This time there was a new excuse for his obstinacy: "I've always been running against Johnson," he said. So if Johnson—ensconced in Texas for the week—happened to appear that afternoon, so would Gene. Johnson never left his ranch, and McCarthy remained in his room, using an orange to play mock baseball with his brother, Austin. Later in the afternoon, as the violence began heating up again in the park across from the hotel, he looked out the window. "The worst thing about what's happening," he said, "is that it leaves those kids nowhere to go." The irony of this observation never seemed to occur to him.[38]

EIGHTY percent of the voters who had participated in the primaries during the spring had voted for the antiwar policies of McCarthy and Kennedy. Many men made a last-ditch effort to persuade Humphrey to endorse the peace plank to make himself electable in the fall. Walter Mondale, who occupied Humphrey's former Senate seat from Minnesota and was co-chairman of the vice-president's campaign, argued endlessly with old Humphrey hands like Bill Connell and Max Kampelman, who never understood that it was essential for their candidate to break with the president. Another man who urged the vice-president to act boldly was Newton Minow, who had been chairman of the Federal Communications Commission under Jack Kennedy (and had become famous for calling TV "a vast wasteland"). In a memo written three weeks before the convention, Minow argued that Humphrey had to join forces with the Kennedy and McCarthy people to get a peace plank passed. "The platform thus becomes the bridge on which HHH makes the transition from LBJ to the McCarthy-Kennedy supporters." But Humphrey remained trapped by the president.[39] On Monday, August 26, the vice-president called Johnson at his ranch to make a final plea. "He told me that the plank did not meet with the policies of this government," Humphrey remembered. "I said, 'Mr. President, this is what I feel we ought to be doing for the future.' He made it clear that we were not discussing these things. He said, 'I can't go for this, and I don't think that the platform committee is going to go for it either.' I said, 'But, Mr. President, this has been cleared with Rusk and Rostow.' He said, 'Well, it hasn't been cleared with me.' "[40] Humphrey never spoke up, and on Wednesday afternoon, the peace plank was defeated, 1567¾ to 1041½. Members of the New York and California delegations slipped on black armbands, and folk singer Theodore Bikel, a New York delegate, led them in the singing of "We Shall Overcome." Others stood in the aisles, yelling, "Stop the war!" A priest knelt in the middle of the New York delegation to offer a prayer for peace. When he was done, people murmured "Shalom" and "Amen."[41] The last hope to unite the party in 1968, and for many years to come, was over.

On Wednesday afternoon nearly ten thousand people had gathered for an antiwar rally in Grant Park. By now, the ranks of the radicals were swelled by the increasingly bitter supporters of Eugene McCarthy. When a young demonstrator wearing an Army helmet started shinnying up a flagpole to remove the American flag, the police charged. While this teenager was being dragged off, a group of young men—including at least one undercover police officer—surrounded the flagpole and removed the flag. They replaced it with a red T-shirt, and a general melee followed. Demonstrators threw asbestos, floor tiles, balloons filled with paint and urine, bricks, eggs, and "all types of stones," according to the Walker report, compiled for the National Commission on the Causes and Prevention of Violence. The police responded with clubs, Mace, and tear gas. A police official testified later that "profanity and spitting did not have the same effect on the police that incidents involving the flag did." He felt that "abuse or misuse of the flag deeply affected the police." One demonstrator heard an officer yell, "Hey, there's a nigger over there we can get." According to the official report, the police "are said to have veered off and grabbed a middle-aged Negro man, whom they beat." The crowd chanted, "The whole world is watching."[42]

Grant Park was across the street from the Conrad Hilton, where Hubert Humphrey and Eugene McCarthy both had their headquarters. As the nominating speeches began at the convention hall, some seven thousand demonstrators gathered in front of the Hilton. Hundreds of people—ranging from innocent bystanders to hardened militants—were clubbed and beaten.*[43] A reporter noticed a policeman smiling happily: "They're really getting

---

* Earlier estimates that one hundred thousand demonstrators or more might descend upon the city were large exaggerations. The Walker report on the disturbances estimated the largest crowd of the week at ten thousand people, with no more than five thousand from out of town. [*New York Times,* 12/2/68.]

scared now," the officer said.[44] Massive amounts of tear gas were released, and some of it even reached the nose of the vice-president in suite 2525A of the Hilton.[45]

Looking down from his room two floors below Humphrey, McCarthy thought the police formations were "reminiscent of the formations of Hannibal's last battle"; then he compared the scene to "a surrealistic dance—the ballet of purgatory."[46] George McGovern told a *New York Times* reporter he had seen "nothing like it since the films of Nazi Germany." Inside the amphitheater, Connecticut senator Abraham Ribicoff was on the podium to nominate the South Dakotan for president. "With George McGovern as President," said Ribicoff, "we would not have to have such Gestapo tactics in the streets of Chicago." The television cameras zoomed in on the Chicago mayor. Though he could not be heard, millions of lip-reading Americans were certain Richard Daley had just said, "Fuck you," to the United States senator standing only twenty feet in front of him. Ribicoff scowled back. "How hard it is to accept the truth," he said, "how hard." Twenty years later, people were still coming up to Ribicoff at airports to praise him for his courage. However, there had also been a practical consideration behind the senator's attack. Ribicoff was up for reelection in 1968, and the McCarthy forces had never been enthusiastic about him. On Wednesday evening, Anne Wexler, a leader of the McCarthy movement in Connecticut, declared, "I'm going to get everyone to work their guts out for Abe for what he said tonight." Ribicoff was reelected by a large margin in the fall.[47]

Humphrey's nomination became official when he got Pennsylvania's 103¾ votes at 11:47 P.M. At the end of the balloting, the vice-president had 1,761¾ votes, in contrast with 601 for McCarthy, 146½ for McGovern, and 100 for other candidates. When the face of his wife, Muriel, appeared on the television in his Hilton suite, Humphrey jumped up to kiss her electronic image. A film crew for a new program called *60 Minutes*, which would begin its first season in the fall, was there to capture the moment. Reporter Marie Ridder asked McCarthy if he was bitter. "No use being bitter about Hubert," he said. "He is too dumb to understand bitterness."[48] Back inside the amphitheater, CBS correspondent Mike Wallace had just been hit on the jaw—right after a New Yorker named Alex Rosenberg became a hero to his fellow delegates when he was arrested for refusing to show his credentials to a security man on the convention floor. By the end of the week a total of sixty-five newsmen had been beaten, arrested, or both.[49] Candles borrowed from a Chicago synagogue were distributed by Lowenstein and Goodwin to McCarthy delegates for a "funeral march." Five hundred participated in the candlelight vigil on Michigan Avenue.[50]

Several Humphrey advisors, including Larry O'Brien, who had come over to his campaign after Bobby Kennedy was killed, suggested that he announce his resignation as vice-president when he accepted the nomination. Then he could fly to Massachusetts to ask Teddy Kennedy to join him as his running mate. Humphrey considered the idea for a half-hour, then abandoned it. He also considered running with Nelson Rockefeller, until an intermediary told the vice-president that the New York governor did not think he could run as a Democrat.[51]

The next night, the Democrats repeated a four-year-old tradition. In 1964, on the fourth day of their convention in Atlantic City, Bobby Kennedy had received a twenty-two-minute ovation when he arrived at the podium to introduce a movie memorializing his brother Jack. Then, most of the delegates had wept. Now, on the fourth day of their meeting in 1968, Edward Kennedy's voice was relayed by telephone from Hyannis Port so that he could introduce a similar filmed tribute to Bobby. "Even dead, and on film, he was better and more moving than anything which had happened in their convention," Norman Mailer wrote. "People were crying. An ovation began. Delegates came to their feet, and applauded an empty screen—it was as if the center of American life was now passing the age where it could still look forward; now people looked back into memory, into the past of the nation—was that possible?"

Russell Baker thought the convention was "momentarily united in emotion for the first time all week." After the ovation had gone on for five minutes, convention chairman Carl Albert called for order. The delegations from New York and California responded by singing "The Battle Hymn of the Republic." The choruses went on for ten minutes, then for fifteen, then for twenty. Three-quarters of the gallery had joined in. Signs appeared around the hall, hand-scrawled efforts reading, BOBBY BE WITH US, and a large one saying, BOBBY, WE MISS YOU. By now the Texas and Illinois delegations had sat down, to indicate the demonstration should end; but the sounds of "Glory, glory, hallelujah" would not be suppressed. Finally, Daley had had enough. He passed the word to his henchmen—who occupied the other fourth of the gallery—that they should begin chanting, "We love Daley!" Then he sent Ralph Metcalfe to the podium to request a minute of silence for Martin Luther King, Jr., and Bobby's moment was over. Russell Baker remembered that Bobby had once said, "Mayor Daley is the ball game." Tonight, Baker wrote, "Mayor Daley was pitching for Hubert Humphrey."[52]

Earlier Thursday, Humphrey had announced one of the very few wise decisions he would make in 1968. He selected Edmund Muskie, a craggy-faced senator from Maine, as his running mate. Muskie projected just the sort of calm self-confidence Humphrey needed on the ticket in a period of so much upheaval; the vice-presidential nominee would be a significant asset in the months ahead. But that evening Humphrey gave a pedestrian acceptance speech. Against the advice of his aides, it included this passage: "Where there is hatred, let me sow love. Where there is injury, pardon. Where there is doubt, faith. Where there is despair, hope. Where there is darkness, light."[53]

At 12:10 A.M. on Friday, the convention was finally adjourned. Back on the fifteenth floor of the Hilton, the McCarthy kids continued to drink and talk and play bridge into the early hours of the morning. Then there was one more outbreak of violence. The police said that they were being bombarded with objects from the hotel; a McCarthy staffer in the lobby heard four policemen discussing a report that the missiles were coming from the fifteenth floor. "Okay," said one of them, "give the order to drag them all in and give them a beating. Teach them a lesson." Using passkeys provided by the management, the police started pulling campaign workers out of their beds at 5 A.M. and beating them at random. While they were being gathered together by the police in the lobby downstairs, Goodwin was able to rouse McCarthy, who came down with his detachment of Secret Service men to confront the police. "Who's in charge?" the senator demanded. No one answered. "Just as I thought," said McCarthy. "No one is in charge." Then he told his kids to go back upstairs, four or five at a time in the elevator, "and finally they were all gone."[54]

GERRY Studds was the high school teacher who had played such a large role at the beginning of the year, when he helped Blair Clark convince McCarthy that he should enter the New Hampshire primary. Nothing had ever equaled the combination of surprise and joy they had all achieved together on that blustery Tuesday in March, that faraway moment when McCarthy had strode into the Wayfarer Hotel to incredulous cheers of "Chi-ca-go! Chi-ca-go!" It was then that McCarthy had predicted, "If we come to Chicago with this strength, there will be no violence, and no demonstrations, but a great victory celebration." Five months later, the campaign that had spent between $8 million and $23 million stumbled to a halt, dead on arrival at the Windy City.* But the spirit

---

* The lower estimate is McCarthy's, the higher is Blair Clark's. [Author's interviews with Eugene McCarthy, 3/27/86, and Blair Clark, 3/19/86.]

of New Hampshire lived on in the hearts of thousands who still cherished the dream that was born there. Studds came to Chicago in August as a McCarthy delegate from the Granite State. He remembered the week this way:

"I will never forget wandering in the park across the street from the Hilton each night after the convention adjourned. I and several other delegates from New Hampshire would wander with the kids . . . and that was one of the most moving experiences that I ever had. The kids would come up, they would see delegate credentials, and they would see McCarthy buttons—and they would see 'New Hampshire' hanging on your lapel. And they would thrust out a hand, frequently a hand covered with Vaseline or grease as a protection against Mace, and apologize for begriming you but say, 'We just had to speak to you,' and say—what sounds, I guess, in retrospect, trite things—like 'Thank you' and 'Speak for us.' But at the time, an emotion-charged time, there was nothing trite about it. It was a very moving thing."[55]

12

The Long and Winding Road

"What I think the Kennedy assassination did was to sour the whole public, and particularly the Democratic party, on the election and on the political process. We'd had the Tet offensive—which was a political disaster in this country—and then you get McCarthy on the road, you get Bobby in the primaries, and you get Martin Luther King's assassination, and the party is now torn in many ways, in disarray. . . . I think this was just too much. It was like a mental breakdown for the American political community."

—Hubert Humphrey[1]

"Never interfere with the enemy when he is in the process of destroying himself."

— Napoleon[2]

"It was as if they were building not a President but an Astrodome, where the wind would never blow, the temperature never rise or fall, and the ball never bounce erratically on the artificial grass."

—Joe McGinniss on Richard Nixon in 1968[3]

AFTER Chicago, Hubert Humphrey flew home to his hideaway in Waverly, Minnesota. On Saturday, August 31, this was his first public statement: "We ought to quit pretending that Mayor Daley did something that was wrong. He didn't condone a thing that was wrong. He tried to protect lives."[4]

To everyone who hated the war and who had watched the endless violence on television for the previous seven days—all those who had seen the pictures of bleeding boys and girls and newsmen, and the clip of a middle-aged woman who lingered in the door of a paddy wagon, refusing to be pushed inside until she had finished a final chorus of "We Shall Overcome"—to these Americans, Humphrey's first words after Chicago were shocking. Certainly the police had been subjected to massive provocation, but there was also no doubt that scores of innocent people had been beaten in the course of several different police riots.* Even a Nixon aide, H. R. Haldeman, had seemed distressed: "Slowly, we got horrified; you began to wonder what the hell was going on."[5]

Three years later, Humphrey explained his feelings to his biographer, Albert Eisele:

> Frankly, I was . . . I regret to say—so isolated from the things that were happening there and so angry with some of the activities of those that were there that it was difficult, maybe, to make a valid or good judgment. I had gone through several months of this unbelievable harassment. It's not very pleasant to be invited to a place to speak, as a guest, and have people spit on your wife, and call her every filthy name in the book when you're going into a place, to have people throw urine on you, human excreta, to have them tear your wife's coat practically off her back and call her a whore. How do you think you would like that, day after day, month after month? By people who say they believe in peace and brotherly love. I just couldn't quite take that. After a while I got to looking at these people and saying: "Well, they're just not decent people." When they throw stink-bombs in the lobby of the hotel, and when they stand down under your window and utter the most foul profanity all night long—I don't consider that peace making . . . I really don't. . . . I think it was a terrible thing.[6]

The vice-president was hardly alone in his opinion of the demonstrators. A telephone poll, the results of which were published on the same day Humphrey defended Daley, showed that only 21.3 percent of those contacted agreed that "Chicago police and National Guardsmen are using excessive force in suppressing these demonstrations." Almost 59 percent disagreed. Within five weeks, CBS received 8,670 letters for its convention coverage; they ran eleven to one against the network. A typical letter read, "Your

---

* An inspector-observer from the Los Angeles Police Department put it this way to official investigators: "There is no question but that many officers acted without restraint and exerted force beyond that necessary under the circumstances. The leadership at the point of conflict did little to prevent such conduct." [*New York Times,* 12/2/68.]

coverage was slanted in favor of the hoodlums and beatniks and slurred the police trying to preserve order."[7] But the vice-president would pay dearly for his post-convention assessment.

What Humphrey had failed to realize was the futility of competing with Richard Nixon and George Wallace for the hard-core law-and-order vote in America. As had been true all summer, his only hope for victory was to build a bridge to the disaffected wing of the Democratic party; but he would waste four decisive weeks before he finally reached that crucial conclusion.

RICHARD Nixon had a lot of dubious history to overcome in 1968, but he also had the best campaign that money could buy—the most expensive presidential campaign in the history of American politics. In this era before federal matching funds or limits on individual contributions, Nixon finance chairman Maurice Stans sat in an atmosphere of serene detachment, inside a plush Park Avenue office. He had raised and spent $8 million for Nixon before the convention, and he would raise and spend another $20 million for the general election. Ten million dollars would go to media, $2 million to citizen organizations, $2 million to logistics. Six million dollars were set aside for "extras."[8]

The Nixon campaign managers took their comforts with them wherever they went. The staff plane featured two ground-to-air telephones (a novelty in 1968), seven internal telephone lines, a radio-receiving fax machine, a teletype, and fifteen walkie-talkies with an air-to-ground or (air-to-air) reach of five miles. Reporters' luggage was never late; it was the kind of detail the press really appreciated.[9]

Frank Shakespeare was one of Nixon's media men; he said flatly that his man would win because the print media "doesn't matter anymore." Television would do it all. Nixon's campaign in 1968 was the forerunner of Reagan's strategy in 1984 of keeping the candidate relatively isolated from the press. The centerpiece was a series of ten regional one-hour programs in which Nixon would answer questions live, in front of a studio audience. It was the perfect setting for this candidate: It gave the appearance of vulnerability, while ensuring that nothing really unpredictable would happen, since the panel was chosen by Nixon's people, and the audience was entirely Republican.[10]

Joe McGinniss described the impact of these carefully staged appearances in *The Selling of the President, 1968*: "It was warmly given. Genuine. For

Nixon suddenly represented a true alternative: peace, prosperity, an end to discord, a return to the stable values that had come under such rude and unwarranted attack. Nixon was fortification, reaffirmation of much that needed to be reaffirmed. They needed him now, these Republicans, much more than they had in 1960."[11]

While Nixon seemed to be perfectly organized for victory, chaos continued to stalk the Democrats. When their convention had first been planned, everyone had conceived of it as a coronation for Lyndon Johnson; that was why it took place so late in the summer, leaving very little time to get organized before the November election. "God, it was just an unbelievable nightmare," said Larry O'Brien, who was speaking of his third campaign of the year, having worked first for Johnson and then for Kennedy. "The basic problem was the extremely limited time we had to put together a campaign organization under perhaps the most difficult circumstances that the party has faced in a long, long time."[12]

Almost immediately following his praise for Mayor Daley's police force, Humphrey began a tactical retreat. Two days after his original statement, he criticized the police for "overreacting" and added that he did not "condone" the beating of demonstrators.[13] In the second week of September, bookies were giving odds of nine to five that Nixon would be elected.[14] But the worst was yet to come.

The low point for Humphrey came in Boston on September 19. Teddy Kennedy had agreed to welcome him to a rally in his hometown, and in 1968 no Kennedy had been booed in Boston for two decades. Today would be different; the crowd started booing as soon as Teddy introduced "the next president of the United States." There were perhaps ten thousand people gathered at the intersection of Washington and Summer streets in Boston's old garment district, but five hundred protesting students from Harvard, Boston University, and other colleges had arrived there early to vent their rage. They would not forget the way the candidate had defended their enemy. Their signs read, MAYOR DALEY FOR HEART DONOR, and, DON'T HUMP ON ME, and when the vice-president of the United States tried to speak, they drowned him out with shouts of "Bullshit!" and "Sellout!" When he invoked the name of John Kennedy, they yelled, "Chi-ca-go! Chi-ca-go!" Mary McGrory thought Muriel Humphrey was close to tears.

The protesters never bothered Richard Nixon, and Humphrey was particularly angered by this double standard. McGrory explained that because the students were Democrats, they considered Nixon a "howling irrelevance"; as a result, he was allowed to continue his campaign unmolested.[15] On

September 27, a Gallup poll put Humphrey fifteen points behind Nixon—
and only seven points ahead of George Wallace.[16] Humphrey's problem was
the same one he'd had since April: To become his own man, he still had to
make a break with the president on the war. Gene McCarthy returned from
the French Riviera on September 29. He looked tan—and he was ready to
start covering the World Series for *Life* magazine. But he was still not ready
to endorse Hubert Humphrey.

Now Humphrey's situation was desperate. The campaign was very
short on cash, but Larry O'Brien decided that only a direct appeal by the
vice-president—uninterrupted by protesters—might possibly reverse the
steady decline in his fortunes. O'Brien decided to spend $100,000 to buy a
half-hour of national TV time, and he wanted Humphrey to endorse a bombing halt. After another weekend of frantic internal negotiations, Humphrey
followed his campaign manager's advice—after a fashion. On September
30, in Salt Lake City, he declared, "I would stop the bombing of the North
as an acceptable risk for peace because I believe it could lead to success in
the negotiations and a shorter war." Then came the caveat: "In weighing that
risk—and before taking action—I would place key importance on evidence,
direct or indirect, by deed or word, of Communist willingness to restore
the Demilitarized Zone."

Although the language wasn't particularly radical, there was something
very important about this speech: Humphrey delivered it after the president
had warned him against it. "Hubert, you give that speech, and you'll be
screwed," the Texan had said. Finally, Humphrey had ignored him, and the
vice-president told reporters he felt "good inside, for the first time." Kennedy men like Fred Dutton, Frank Mankiewicz, and John Kenneth Galbraith
used the occasion as their excuse to come over to the Humphrey cause. At
the University of Tennessee the next day, there were no protesters waiting
to greet the vice-president. Instead, there was a new sign: IF YOU MEAN IT,
WE'RE WITH YOU.[17] Now there was a glimmer of hope for the Democrats.

The same week as the Salt Lake City speech, Humphrey picked up more
help from an unexpected quarter. George Wallace, who was attracting
huge crowds in many states crucial to the Democrats' chances, finally
announced his choice of a running mate. He had selected General Curtis
Emerson LeMay, after Texas governor John Connally and J. Edgar Hoover
had both ignored his entreaties. Within seven minutes, LeMay had derailed
Wallace's carefully crafted appeal to discreet racism by raising the most
dangerous subject in American politics—the Bomb and when to use it. At
a joint press conference where Wallace presented his new running mate to

the world, the former Air Force chief of staff declared, "We seem to have a phobia about nuclear weapons. . . . I think there are many times when it would be most efficient to use nuclear weapons. However, the public opinion in this country and throughout the world throw up their hands in horror when you mention nuclear weapons, just because of the propaganda that's been fed to them. I don't believe the world would end if we exploded a nuclear weapon." The effect was explosive, but not in the way the Wallace campaign would have liked it to be.[18]

At the same moment, Richard Nixon's vice-presidential candidate was developing into the Humphrey campaign's other secret weapon. Ethnic slurs were one of Agnew's specialties—he referred to Polish people as Polacks and called a Japanese-American reporter "the fat Jap"; he also declared, "If you've seen one city slum, you've seen them all." Meanwhile, his opponent, Edmund Muskie, was gaining sympathy (and quiet) through the novel tactic of inviting hecklers up onstage with him to share his microphone.

The Humphrey campaign produced two brilliant ads on the subject of running mates. The first one, for television, had a voice-over of just five words: "Spiro Agnew for vice-president"—followed by crazed laughter. Then this message appeared on the screen: "This would be funny if it wasn't so serious." The effort for radio began with nothing but a thumping human heart. After several beats, a sober announcer asked, "Ed Muskie—or Spiro T. Agnew: Who would you rather have a heartbeat away from the presidency?" The *New York Times* had been running some prescient articles about how Agnew might have used his position as governor to make some money on the side, but most of the press neglected this story.[19]

New York magazine (founded at the beginning of 1968) ran an interview with Pat Nixon conducted by Gloria Steinem, and feminism met traditionalism with some amusing results. Asked whom she most admired and would want to be like, Mrs. Nixon naturally answered, "Mamie Eisenhower." Pressed for her reasons, Pat replied, "Because she meant so much to young people." Steinem was skeptical about that: She had been in college during the Eisenhower years, and she told Mrs. Nixon she really didn't think that was true. There was a long pause; then Pat held her ground: "Well, I do." After that, Steinem wrote, "the dam broke; not out-of-control, but low-voiced and resentful, like a long accusation, the words flowed out: 'I never had time to think about things like that—who I wanted to be, or who I admired, or to have ideas. I never had time to dream about being anyone else. I had to work. My parents died when I was a teenager, and I had to work my way through college. . . . I worked in a bank while Dick was in the service.' "[20]

By the middle of October, Humphrey's rebound was finally evident in the polls; Lou Harris said the vice-president had closed the gap to just five points (40 percent to 35 percent). Money was flowing into the Democratic coffers more quickly, too: Humphrey hadn't raised his first million dollars for the fall campaign until October 10, but $2 million more in contributions and loans had come in within eleven days after that.[21]

Then, two weeks before the election, America's attention was ripped away from the campaign by the year's final upheaval—its greatest non-violent shock. Jacqueline Kennedy had fled to Greece to become Jacqueline Kennedy Onassis. After her awful prediction about her brother-in-law had come true, her quest for privacy and protection had accelerated. But nearly all of her fans were outraged. In many of their wedding pictures, she towered over her new husband. *Newsweek* pointed out Aristotle Onassis was "at least 23 years her senior" and had ended his lengthy affair with Maria Callas "just this spring." Abroad, this final end to innocence was treated with special harshness. THE LATEST KENNEDY TRAGEDY, said a Paris headline, while a London tabloid asked, JACKIE, HOW COULD YOU? Only Suzy, the New York gossip columnist, was pleased. "I think they were made for each other," she said. "Who else in this world could Jackie Kennedy marry?"[22]

ONE other series of events conspired to push Hubert Humphrey to the edge of success on election day. On October 7, a Soviet diplomat told an American politician his country had finally gained serious influence over Hanoi's government. If the United States stopped the bombing of North Vietnam, the Soviets could ensure a positive response. Four days later in Paris, where Averell Harriman and Cyrus Vance were conducting peace negotiations, the North Vietnamese asked whether the bombing would be stopped "unconditionally" if they agreed to participation by South Vietnam in the talks—a key American demand at this stage of the bargaining. By October 15, South Vietnamese President Nguyen Van Thieu had told the administration he would agree to the bombing halt if his participation in the negotiations was guaranteed.

Lyndon Johnson was finally ready with his last surprise, and he dropped it on the world at the very end of October: "I have now ordered that all air, naval and artillery bombardment of North Vietnam cease as of 8 A.M., Washington time. . . . I have reached this decision . . . in the belief that this action can lead to progress towards a peaceful settlement of the Vietnamese war."[23]

Emotions surged at the prospect of peace; but these hopes were crushed within forty-eight hours. Anna Chennault, the Chinese-born widow of General Claire Chennault, commander of the Flying Tigers during World War II, had urged the South Vietnamese to reject the agreement because, she said, they would get a better deal from the Nixon administration. Mrs. Chennault was an ardent Nixon supporter, but evidence was lacking that she was operating with the knowledge of the Republican candidate. On Saturday the headline in the *New York Times* read, SAIGON OPPOSES PARIS TALK PLANS, and all again was a muddle.* Mrs. Chennault's role did not become known until after the election, because Humphrey remained unconvinced that his opponent was aware of her machinations.[24] In a final slap to his vice-president, Johnson suggested in his memoirs that Humphrey's Salt Lake City speech had made the South Vietnamese especially receptive to Mrs. Chennault's entreaties.[25]

As the campaign ended, even McCarthy endorsed Humphrey—although he did so in a backhanded fashion—and in Lou Harris's poll published on the day before the voting, the vice-president had surged into the lead, 43 percent to 40 percent.[26] That Monday, November 4, Humphrey and Muskie stood on the trunk of a convertible and got mobbed by a lunchtime crowd of one hundred thousand in Los Angeles. In Michigan, the *Detroit News* poll said Humphrey had pulled ahead of Nixon; in California, he had almost drawn even in the Muchmore survey, and his crowds that day were the best of his campaign. R. W. Apple wrote in the *New York Times*, "It seems clear that he has succeeded in doing what he has promised to do all along—bring his campaign to its zenith on election eve." Humphrey told Muskie in Los Angeles: "I feel great, just great, because this is the best it can be."[27]

The AFL-CIO registered 4.6 million new voters. The union organization had distributed 115 million pieces of literature, operated eight thousand telephones, and spent $10 million to lure labor away from Wallace back to the Democrats.[28] It was almost enough—but the final Harris poll was

---

* Earlier in 1968, Henry Kissinger had acted as Nelson Rockefeller's foreign policy advisor. Then he gravitated to the Democrats—but he also kept in touch with the Nixon campaign, feeding it covert information about Johnson's secret moves on Vietnam. This earned him Richard Nixon's undying gratitude—and a prominent place in his administration. [Stanley Karnow, *Vietnam: A History* (New York: Viking, 1983), 585.]

mistaken. On November 5, Richard Nixon was elected president by a tiny margin: 499,704 votes out of 73,186,819 cast—43.4 percent of the vote, compared with 42.7 percent for the Democrat. When the crucial states of Illinois and Ohio slipped away into the Republican column early Wednesday morning, Hubert Humphrey stood up, hitched up his pants, and turned to an aide. "Well, sir," he said, "the American people will find that they have just elected a papier-mâché man."[29]

EPILOGUE TO
THE THIRTIETH
ANNIVERSARY EDITION

If Tomorrow Wasn't
Such a Long Time . . .

*"Too much and for too long, we have confused our achievements with
our wealth, and measured our greatness with the statistics of the Gross
National Product. But the Gross National Product counts air pollution
and cigarette advertising, and the ambulances to clear our highways of
carnage. It counts special locks for our doors and jails for people who
break them. It counts Whitman's rifle and Speck's knife, and television
programs that glorify violence the better to sell goods to our children."*
—Bobby Kennedy, 1968[1]

*"You know God's not in the business of dishing out material things to
make people happy. He doesn't give you a house in the country and
expect you to be content and happy. And if he does, he doesn't give it
to you for nothing, anyway."*
—Bob Dylan, 1985[2]

*"This movement will go on because it doesn't depend on structure or
organization but just on what is in people themselves. It's like striking
a hammer on the anvil, it rings forever. It's like infinity."*
—Eugene McCarthy, while watching the riots in Chicago,
August 1968[3]

A FTER Richard Nixon's election, the Vietnam generation turned inward.
At the end of a year like this, who can wonder why? But understanding that retreat provides little comfort before a panorama of so many who
turned away from politics, and toward greed.

What did we accomplish? For a quarter century after Vietnam, America avoided similar quagmires—until George W. Bush began the hideous mistake of pouring endless blood and treasure into Afghanistan and Iraq. But the 58,021 Americans and the hundreds of thousands of Vietnamese who perished in Southeast Asia did not die in vain: Their sacrifice saved the lives of millions in the generation that followed them, who were spared the catastrophe of another useless conflict. The Democratic party abolished the unit rule at its 1968 convention; since then there has been no more block voting by state. A party commission revolutionized the way the Democrats selected their nominee, severely limiting the power of the party bosses—and putting a greater portion of the decision-making process directly into the hands of the people. But the social transformation in America during the last fifty years has been more uplifting than any political shift; that has been our success, and our failure.

Anyone who believes America wasn't changed by the sixties should consider the story of Linda LeClair. In 1968 this Barnard College sophomore publicly rejected her school's notions of propriety by announcing that she was living off-campus with her boyfriend, a Columbia junior. The uproar was immediate: dozens of stories on television, in *Time* and *Newsweek*; eleven separate articles in the *New York Times* alone.* What did her action mean about morality in America? At first Barnard gave a firm answer: LeClair would be expelled for her intolerable behavior. But as the months went by—after King was killed and the streets and television screens were filled with chaos—Barnard's resolve weakened. In April a student-faculty committee recommended that LeClair be permitted to continue her studies— as long as she was denied the use of the snack bar, the cafeteria, and the recreation room!

Two trends had intersected to produce this "watershed" event: Parents gave up trying to enforce the social norms they had grown up with at the very moment their children were insisting on the right to live with an intensity and participate in a diversity that was almost unheard of in the previous decade.†
To many of us in 1968, there was a clear message in the older generation's

---

* The mother of the publisher of the *Times,* seventy-five-year-old Iphigene Sulzberger, thought the coverage was excessive. "Why not put sex in perspective?" she asked her son. "It went on in my day too." [Gay Talese, *The Kingdom and the Power* (1969; reprint, Garden City, N.Y.: Anchor Books, 1978), 541.]

† Not unheard of in the twentieth century, however: It was a British poet, neo-pagan Rupert Brooke, who told his friends at Cambridge *before World War I* that "nobody over thirty is worth talking to," and it was his circle that pioneered nude swimming and unchaperoned camping—and favored a marriage of art and life.

retreat: A society that looked as if it might be melting down no longer had the time or the inclination to intrude upon the private lives of its citizens.

The best result of that change has been the gay revolution: a worldwide revolt which produced the largest and fastest improvement in the status of any minority in the history of the modern world.

The black civil rights movement provided an explicit model for the gay movement, and black people are the real heroes of this story. Before every-thing else that happened in the sixties, it was their rejection of the submissive roles white men had selected for them that legitimized the aspirations of every other victim of oppression. The terrible irony is that so many black Americans have yet to achieve the same dramatic improvements for them-selves that their example made possible for women and LGBT people and Asians and so many others.

Most of the turmoil of the sixties had ended by the late seventies. Students were massacred by National Guardsmen at Kent State in May 1970; Richard Nixon resigned in August 1974. After that, a relative calm reasserted itself. But the will to impose the old national conformity has never reappeared. In 1968 it was destroyed on the barricades of revolt, and a veneration of diversity is still the year's proudest legacy.

When I interviewed Bob Dylan on my birthday in 1985 (the best birth-day present ever), I asked him if he had lived longer than he expected to. "Oh, yeah," he said. "Are you kidding? Every day." It's a feeling that any-one who survived 1968 can understand. Dylan moved back to Greenwich Village from Woodstock in 1969, but when he returned, he discovered that "the spirit that had been there in the sixties wasn't there anymore." He said this about the events of 1968: "All those things like that deaden you. They kill part of your hope. And enough of those blows to your hope will make you deader and deader and deader, until a person is existing without really caring anymore, at a certain time. Yevtushenko, the Russian poet, told me an interesting thing: He said what unites people is broken hope; broken hope unites people rather than hope because broken hope people have experienced, and hope they haven't really experienced."[4]

We did experience hope in 1968: hope and ambition and amazing joy. But to millions of us, Bobby Kennedy's assassination felt like the resounding chord at the end of *Sgt. Pepper's*: a note of stunning finality.

Fifty years on, some of the traumas of 1968 have faded away. Others remain but have shifted shape, mostly but not always for the better. Still others were undreamt of. With the possible exception of a few dystopian science fiction writers, no one imagined that five decades thence an important country might be headed by a profoundly ignorant, dangerously unhinged septuagenarian sex criminal whose hair hints at extraterrestrial origins and whose prominence suggests that the challenges of the next half-century will be at least as formidable as those of the last. To meet those challenges, the coming generations will need something like the courage and imagination of the best of the '68ers. It is always time, always hard, and always necessary to strive for a newer world.

Once a year, on the fourth of April, a few hundred people gather together at the corner of North 17th Street and East Broadway in Indianapolis, Indiana. They go there to commemorate the words Robert F. Kennedy spoke at that street corner on April 4, 1968—words so powerful, they kept their city peaceful while a hundred and thirty others would burst into flame.

Bobby Kennedy was on his way to Indianapolis when word reached him that Martin Luther King, Jr. had been shot. Minutes before his plane landed, Kennedy learned that King had succumbed to his wound. Despite the warnings of the city's mayor, Richard Lugar, who feared a riot, Kennedy drove straight to his scheduled campaign rally, in the heart of black Indianapolis. He was more than an hour late. Just before he arrived, the first rumor spread through the crowd, some twenty-five hundred strong: King had been shot, but he was alive.

A moment before he began, Kennedy can be heard asking his staff, "Do they know about Martin Luther King?" Most of the crowd did not yet know that King had died.

The civil rights hero and future Congressman John Lewis, who had been working for Kennedy in the Indiana primary, has said, "That evening Robert Kennedy spoke from his soul." His speech was simple and elegant and beautiful. It may have been the best speech any Kennedy ever gave; it was certainly one of the most remarkable speeches any American has ever given. It would also be his first public mention of his brother's assassination five years before. He began this way:

> Ladies and gentlemen. I'm only going to talk to you just for a minute or so this evening because I have some very sad news for all of you. Could you lower those signs please? I have some very sad news for all of you, and I think sad news for all of our fellow citizens, and people who love peace all over the world, and that is that Martin Luther King was shot and killed tonight in Memphis, Tennessee.

The crowd shrieked. Then it fell completely silent. Kennedy went on:

Martin Luther King dedicated his life to love and to justice between fellow human beings. He died in the cause of that effort. In this difficult day, in this difficult time for the United States, it is perhaps well to ask what kind of a nation we are and what direction we want to move in. For those of you who are black—considering the evidence evidently is that there were white people who were responsible, you can be filled with bitterness, and with hatred, and a desire for revenge. We can move in that direction as a country, in greater polarization—black people amongst blacks, and white amongst whites, filled with hatred toward one another.

Or we can make an effort, as Martin Luther King did, to understand and to comprehend, and replace that violence, that stain of bloodshed that has spread across our land, with an effort to understand with compassion and love.

For those of you who are black and are tempted to be filled with hatred and distrust of the injustice of such an act, against all white people, I would only say that I can also feel in my own heart the same kind of feeling. I had a member of my family killed. But he was killed by a white man. But we have to make an effort in the United States, we have to make an effort to understand, to get beyond or go beyond these rather difficult times.

My favorite poem, my favorite poet was Aeschylus. And he once wrote: "Even in our sleep, pain which cannot forget falls drop by drop upon the heart, until in our own despair, against our will, comes wisdom through the awful grace of God."

What we need in the United States is not division; what we need in the United States is not hatred; what we need in the United States is not violence and lawlessness; but is love and wisdom, and compassion toward one another, and a feeling of justice toward those who still suffer within our country, whether they be white or whether they be black. [*First applause.*]

So I ask you tonight to return home, to say a prayer for the family of Martin Luther King–yeah, it's true. But more importantly to say a prayer for our own country, which all of us love. A prayer for understanding, and that compassion of which I spoke.

We can do well in this country. We will have difficult times. We've had difficult times in the past; and we will have difficult times in the future. It is not the end of violence, it is not the end of lawlessness, and it's not the end of disorder.

But the vast majority of white people and the vast majority of black people in this country want to live together, want to improve the quality of our life, and want justice for all human beings that abide in our land. *[Cheers.]* And dedicate ourselves to what the Greeks wrote so many years ago: to tame the savageness of man and make gentle the life of this world. Let us dedicate ourselves to that, and say a prayer for our country and for our people. Thank you very much.

The speech lasted less than six minutes.

Two months and one day later, another assassin murdered Robert Kennedy. Not every American lamented his death. But scores of millions did, including thousands of Democrats who had fought him in the presidential primaries—and now mourned him with as much pain as anyone.

As his funeral train moved slowly to his burial ground, like Lincoln's a century before, the tracks were lined with silent, solemn, often weeping mourners. And for a moment, savageness was nearly tamed, and life was made gentle.

—Charles Kaiser,
New York City,
December 2017

ACKNOWLEDGMENTS

W HEN I began writing for the *New York Times* in 1971, there were old Royal manual typewriters sitting on steel desks, instead of computer terminals perched on Formica. A remarkable group of reporters and editors gave unstintingly of their knowledge and themselves to a twenty-year-old neophyte who had never written a newspaper story before in his life.

I was hired by Arthur Gelb, a brilliant metropolitan editor who taught everyone the value of enthusiasm. The demeanor of the senior men in the city room belied the paper's forbidding reputation: Dick Shepard, Emanuel Perlmutter, Pat Spiegel, Ed Ranzal, Sy Peck, George Barrett, Danny Blum, and Murray Schumach were always eager to guide the untutored, and they gave me the best education I have received away from my parents' dinner table. Younger editors and reporters were just as generous—Joe Treaster, Steve Weisman, Jim Wooten, Bob McFadden, Bill Farrell, Grace Lichtenstein, Larry Van Gelder, Mike Knight, Gene Roberts, Les Ledbetter, John Darnton, Bob Semple, Charlotte Curtis, Gerry Fraser, Ruth Adler, Mike Kaufman, Tom Wark, Marvin Siegel, Frank Prial, Paul Montgomery, Mike Leahy, Joe Vecchione, Clyde Haberman, Deirdre Carmody, Irv Horowitz, Paul Delaney, Bob Thomas, David Burnham, Fred Ferretti, Joe Lelyveld, Mickey Carroll, Frank Clines, and Marty Arnold all pushed me to make my writing as fair and accurate and interesting as I could. Pat Wallace and Shelly Binn never let anyone forget how a gentleman behaves; Joe Schoener of the Associated Press and Steve Marcus of the *New York Post* performed the same function when I worked in the press room at New York's City Hall.

Peter Kihss was the greatest reporter I have ever known. In his time, he set the standard for fairness and thoroughness in American journalism. Covering everything from the civil rights movement to the Great Blackout of 1965, and covering all of it brilliantly, he gave of himself without limit to anyone seeking the truth. All of his colleagues agreed that he deserved the Pulitzer Prize more than any other reporter; but he never won one.

At *Newsweek* and the *Wall Street Journal* I received wise counsel from many colleagues, especially Lucy Howard, Nancy Stadtman, Margaret Joskow, Elsie B. Washington, Lester Bernstein, Allan Mayer, Shew Hagerty, Ken Auchincloss, Susan Fraker, David Ansen, Cathleen McGuigan, Walter Clemons, David Gelman, Mary Murphy, Lynn Langway, Charles Michener, Pat King, Jim Baker, Ted Slate, Mark Stevens, Annalyn Swan, Jennifer Boeth, Ray Anello, Ann Graves, George Hackett, Jean Strouse, Lynn Povich, James LeMoyne, Peter Goldman, Michael Lerner, Norman Pearlstine, Lee Lescaze, Kathy Christensen, Meg Cox, Laura Landro, and Jim Stewart.

In my first jobs, I summarized speeches for Harold Lever and wrote speeches for John Brademas, splendid bosses (and legislators) who inaugurated my professional writing career. John Burke, George Scurlock, and Lionel and Diana Trilling were my guides during my undergraduate years at Columbia.

In writing this book, I have benefited enormously from the work of other students of the period. Among the best works about the major events of the sixties are *Vietnam*, by Stanley Karnow; *The War at Home*, by Tom Powers; *Teti*, by Don Oberdorfer; *Bearing the Cross*, David Garrow's indispensable biography of Martin Luther King, Jr.; and *Robert Kennedy and His Times*, by Arthur Schlesinger, Jr. Albert Eisele's *Almost to the Presidency* provides thorough portraits of Hubert Humphrey and Eugene McCarthy; *Nobody Knows*, by Jeremy Larner, is the best book about McCarthy's presidential campaign. *The Rolling Stone History of Rock & Roll*, edited by Jim Miller, is a superb guide to the music of the period; within it, Greil Marcus's stunning essay on the Beatles remains the single finest piece of writing about them and their time.

Perry Wolff and Shareen Brysac generously shared their research for the excellent CBS documentary *1968*, which they produced in 1978. Henry Gwiazda and Fred Knubel were particularly helpful at the John F. Kennedy Library and Columbia University, respectively. The staff of the Georgetown University Library led me through the extensive oral history of Eugene McCarthy's presidential campaign. Harry Oppenheimer nourished the author in more ways than one.

John Hawkins was the first person to encourage me to write this book. Luis Sanjurjo gave it a wonderful early reading and made me believe in it. Bob Dylan, Eugene McCarthy, Roger Wilkins, Ann Hart, and Mary McGrory were especially generous with their time and their memories. Maynard Parker and Lee Lescaze helped me to see Tet from the inside, and David Hollander shared the surrealistic experience of playing in the Harvard band at Bobby Kennedy's funeral. Adam Hirsh convinced me that people conceived in 1968 could be as interested in the year as those of us who lived through it. Philip Gefter, Charles Gibson, Jeff Katzoff, Lanning Melville, Irene Cornell, Gray Coleman, and John Regier made sure my enthusiasm never waned.

Constant encouragement and warm hospitality flowed from Sean and Debbie O'Neill, Jody and Andrew Heyward, Maureen Orth, Tim Russert, Janet Suzman, Harriet Fier, Steve Rattner, Maureen White, Bill Hartman, Peter Day, Nancy, Louis, and Dennis Hector, Margot and Ray Hornblower, Didier Malaquin, Ellen Fleysher, Joyce Purnick, Zarrina, Anthony and Juliet Kurtz, the Audiberts, Ellen Chesler, Mat Mallow, Molly Ivins, Richard White, Fred Bleakley, Murray Kempton, Merry McInerney, Frank Engelbert, Greg and Madeline Jaynes, Syd Schanberg, Rod Routhier, Louis Brown, Jack Foley, Arthur Lubow, Scot Haller, Ben Brafman, Linda Lake, Janet Jennings, Job Potter, Martha Ritter, Joe Kanon, David Dunlap, Lynn Darling, Kevin Goldman, Lynda Dunn, Martar Rose, Craig Unger, Sharon Delano, Sam Shapiro, Sarah Burke, Cathy and Hannah Kaiser, Chuck and Sharon Stouter, Priscilla Schwarz, and John Stouter.

Linda Amster provided extraordinary research assistance, and, more important, her friendship. Ed Koch, Nick Rostow, John Fairchild, and Arthur Sulzberger, Jr., showed steady interest in my progress. Bart Gorin found great pictures for the book and a macabre sound track of Bobby Kennedy's assassination.

Gail Gregg, Andrew Tobias, Stephanie Lane, Judy Hottensen, Hope Kostmayer, Susy Bolotin, Frank Rich, Jean Highland, Susan Solomon, Ginger Crosby, and Helen and Jose Yglesias gave different sections of the manuscript careful readings and improved it with many excellent suggestions. All of the errors and omissions, however, are my own.

Priscilla Greeley Hardiman, Marcia Chambers, Stanton Wheeler, Maralee Schwartz, John Flannery, Bettina Gregory, Heyden White, Alice McGillion, David White, Justin Feldman, Eleanor Randolph, Nancy Lunney, Mary DeBourbon, Patience O'Connor, Bruce Knecht, Christina Orth,

Paul Kaiser, Tema and Mark Silk, Sarah and Bob Hyams, Tammy Kaiser, Becca and Lee Cooprider, Herb and Joy Kaiser, Tom Stoddard, John Brecher, and Dorothy Gaiter were great listeners and devoted supporters. Eden Lipson and Neal Johnston were stern but warm critics. Sydney Korzenik offered spiritual guidance to two generations of Kaisers.

Judy Hottensen has been my publishing partner for every edition of *1968 in America*, from 1988 through 2018. Julia Berner-Tobin's meticulousness was indispensable for the new introduction and the new epilogue of the thirtieth anniversary edition.

My brother Bob pointed me toward newspapering, and my brother David introduced me (in 1968) to the letters, essays, and journalism of my hero, George Orwell. Mark Polizzotti is a good friend and a brilliant editor who refused to settle for anything less than my best. Renata Adler, Judy Knipe, and Steve and Nancy Shapiro gave me hope when I needed it most. Eric Gelman and Eloise Salholz conspired in a loving act of friendship; Paul Goldberger has shared his warmth and his intelligence ever since we began our careers together on the *Times*. Jane Berentson never let me forget how important this project was to both of us. For almost thirty years, the Husteads have been the Kaisers' most steadfast supporters. Henry Kaiser taught me the importance of iconoclasm; Paula and Ros Kaiser have been loving allies all my life. Charlotte, Emily, Daniel, and Thomas were wonderfully tolerant of their uncle's recent neglect. Judy Barnett guided me through the sixties and beyond. Rafael Yglesias wrote a book explaining all aspects of the publishing business, then personally supervised every stage of this project; he and Margaret Joskow also loaned me their house on the coast of Maine so that I could begin writing. Rich Meislin rescued the manuscript and its manufacturer on more than one occasion. For two decades, Blair Clark has given me his wisdom, boundless enthusiasm for my work, and every other type of encouragement imaginable. Michael Kaiser's affection bolsters everything I do. Ann Jensen and Sal Matera provided all types of sustenance, including food, criticism, and love, whenever my sanity seemed in doubt; Sal also gave these pages the single most meticulous reading they have received. My parents were the first people to convince me I could write. They gave me confidence, then never stopped nurturing it. My uncle Jerry Kaiser, who died on January 14, 1968, was my favorite person in the world. For me, that was the hardest day of the year, and the decade. Since then, Jerry has been the inspiration for much of what I've done.

Joe Stouter contributes more to my life than everyone else. I could not have written a single page without him.

NOTES

Preface

1. Andy Warhol and Pat Hackett, *POPism, The Warhol '60's* (New York: Harcourt Brace Jovanovich, 1980), 255.
2. Shareen Brysac, producer, and Perry Wolff, executive producer, *1968: A CBS News Special* (New York: CBS, broadcast 8/25/78).

Introduction: Bringing It All Back Home

1. *Time,* 4/8/66.
2. *New York Times,* 6/19/67.
3. Quoted in Richard T. Stout, *People* (New York: Harper & Row, 1970), 128.
4. *Americans in the 1960's: A Study of Public Attitudes* (New York: Yankelovich, Skelly and White, Inc., prepared for the John F. Kennedy Library, 1978), 18.
5. Albert Eisele, *Almost to the Presidency* (Blue Earth, Minn.: The Piper Company, 1972), 189.
6. Author's interview with David Hollander, 9/16/85.
7. Peter Collier and David Horowitz, *The Kennedys* (New York: Summit Books, 1984), 283.
8. Author's interview with Christina Orth, 7/7/86.
9. Author's interview with Jane Berentson, 7/7/86.
10. Author's interview with Sal Matera, 7/7/86.
11. Anthony Scaduto, "Bob Dylan," quoted in *Rolling Stone Illustrated History of Rock & Roll*, Jim Miller, editor (New York: A Random House/Rolling Stone Press Book, 1980), 179–180.
12. Greil Marcus, ed., *Rock and Roll Will Stand* (Boston: Beacon Press, 1969), 52.
13. *Newsweek,* 2/24/64.
14. *Rolling Stone,* 10/22/87.
15. Letter dated October 24, 1963, from George A. Eddie to the photo editor of *Newsweek* (author's private collection).
16. Ibid.
17. *Duluth Sunday News-Tribune,* 10/20/63.
18. Cameron Crowe interview with Bob Dylan, quoted on record sleeve of *Biograph* LP C5X 38830 (New York: Columbia Records, 1985); and author's interview with Dylan, 11/13/85.
19. Bob Dylan, "Like a Rolling Stone." In *Lyrics, 1962-1985* (New York: Knopf, 1985), 191.

Chapter 1: Four Democrats, Three Ghosts, One War

1. Lyndon Baines Johnson, *The Vantage Point, Perspectives of the Presidency, 1963–1969* (New York: Holt, Rinehart and Winston, 1971), xi.
2. David Frost, *The Presidential Debate, 1968* (New York: Stein and Day, 1968), 120.
3. Gay Talese, *The Kingdom and the Power* (Garden City, N.Y.: Anchor Books, 1978), 405.
4. Official Associated Press tabulation of December 17, 1960, as reproduced in Theodore H. White, *The Making of the President, 1960* (New York: Atheneum, 1961), Appendix A.
5. Albert Eisele, *Almost to the Presidency* (Blue Earth, Minn.: The Piper Company, 1972), 147. Justin Feldman, a friend of both Kennedy's and Roosevelt's, disputes this version, saying Bobby had mentioned the receipt of the tip about Hubert's draft record to FDR, Jr., but Bobby did not say whether it was true—nor did he recommend that FDR, Jr., repeat it. [Author's interview with Justin Feldman, 9/9/86.]
6. Ibid., 152.
7. Ibid.,112.
8. Author's interview with Eugene McCarthy, 3/27/86.
9. Eisele, *Almost to the Presidency*, 148
10. Ibid., 149.
11. Ibid., 152–153.
12. Author's interview with Eugene McCarthy, 3/27/86.
13. Author's interview with Mary McGrory, 4/13/87.
14. Author's interviews with Eugene McCarthy, 3/27/86, and Philip M. Kaiser, 3/20/86.
15. Johnson, *The Vantage Point*, 91.
16. Theodore H. White, *The Making of the President, 1964* (New York: Atheneum, 1965), 259–260.
17. Arthur M. Schlesinger, Jr., *Robert Kennedy and His Times* (Boston: Houghton Mifflin, 1978), 649.
18. Doris Kearns, *Lyndon Johnson and the American Dream* (New York: Harper & Row, 1976), 200.
19. Ibid., 200.
20. Eric Goldman, *The Tragedy of Lyndon Johnson* (New York: Alfred A. Knopf, 1969), 78–79.
21. Kearns, *Lyndon Johnson and the American Dream*, 340–341.
22. Author's interview with Mary McGrory, 4/13/87; and Jean Stein, *American Journey, The Times of Robert Kennedy*, George Plimpton, editor (New York: Harcourt Brace Jovanovich, 1970), 146–147.
23. Author's interview with Mary McGrory, 4/13/87; and Stein, *American Journey*, 147.
24. White, *The Making of the President, 1964*, 259.
25. Schlesinger, *Robert Kennedy and His Times*, 600.
26. *Americans in the 1960's: A Study of Public Attitudes* (New York: Yankelovich, Skelly and White, Inc., prepared for the John F. Kennedy Library, 1978), 136a.
27. Stanley Karnow, *Vietnam, A History, The First Complete Account of Vietnam at War* (New York: Viking, 1983), 249.
28. John S. Bowman, general editor, *The Vietnam War, An Almanac* (New York: World Almanac Publications, 1985), 54. The report was adopted by the Indian and Canadian members of the International Control Commission, and rejected by the Polish member.

29. Karnow, *Vietnam*, 248.
30. Bowman, *The Vietnam War*, 54–63.
31. Recorded interview with George McGovern, 7/16/70, John F. Kennedy Library, Oral History Program, Boston.
32. Ronnie Dugger, *The Politician, The Life and Times of Lyndon Johnson* (New York: W. W. Norton, 1982), 350.
33. Quoted in Schlesinger, *Robert Kennedy and His Times*, 100.
34. Quoted in James MacGregor Burns, *John Kennedy, A Political Profile* (New York: Harcourt Brace, 1959), 142.
35. Schlesinger, *Robert Kennedy and His Times*, 100.
36. Burns, *John Kennedy*, 149–150.
37. Schlesinger, *Robert Kennedy and His Times*, 599.
38. Letter to Mrs. A. L. Schwarzbach of Daly City, California, Robert F. Kennedy archives at John F. Kennedy Library, Boston.
39. Stein, *American Journey*, 50.
40. Dugger, *The Politician*, 349.
41. Eisele, *Almost to the Presidency*, 99.
42. Ibid., 98.
43. Dugger, *The Politician*, 350–355.
44. Bowman, *The Vietnam War*, 33.
45. Ibid., 34.
46. Karnow, *Vietnam*, 137.
47. Quoted in Dugger, *The Politician*, 361.
48. Eisele, *Almost to the Presidency*, 112.
49. Ibid., 113.
50. Karnow, *Vietnam*, 250.
51. Ibid., 288–311.
52. Kearns, *Lyndon Johnson and the American Dream*, 310–311.
53. Nancy Zaroulis and Gerald Sullivan, *Who Spoke Up* (Garden City, N.Y.: Doubleday, 1984), 101.
54. Author's interview with Eugene McCarthy, 3/27/86.
55. Author's interviews with Mary McGrory, 4/13/87, and Eugene McCarthy, 3/27/86.
56. David Halberstam, *The Best and the Brightest* (New York: Random House, 1972), 533.
57. Eisele, *Almost to the Presidency*, 142.
58. Ibid., 252–254.
59. *Americans in the 1960's*, 41, 43.
60. Ronald Steel, *Walter Lippmann and the American Century* (Boston: Atlantic-Little, Brown, 1980), 573–583.
61. Thomas Powers, *The War at Home* (New York: Grossman Publishers, 1973), 139; and Zaroulis and Sullivan, *Who Spoke Up*, 108–110.
62. Powers, *The War at Home*, 273; and recorded interview with Joseph Rauh, 6/10/69, McCarthy Historical Project Archive, Georgetown University Library, Washington, D.C.

Chapter 2: Blowin' in the Wind

1. Lady Bird Johnson, *A White House Diary* (New York: Holt, Rinehart and Winston, 1970), 469.
2. Jeremy Larner, *Nobody Knows* (New York: Macmillan, 1970), 17.

3. Nancy Zaroulis and Gerald Sullivan, *Who Spoke Up* (Garden City, N.Y.: Doubleday, 1984), 108–9.

4. *Americans in the 1960's: A Study of Public Attitudes* (New York: Yankelovich, Skelly and White, Inc., prepared for the John F Kennedy Library, 1978), 86, quoting Harris poll, 4/68.

5. David J. Garrow, *Bearing the Cross, Martin Luther King, Jr., and the Southern Christian Leadership Conference* (New York: William Morrow, 1986), 11–13, 82.

6. Henry Hampton, executive producer, *Eyes on the Prize, America's Civil Rights Years, 1954–1965*, Part 2 (Boston: PBS, broadcast 1/29/87).

7. Author's interview with Curtis Gans, 7/6/86; and Garrow, *Bearing the Cross*, 127.

8. Garrow, *Bearing the Cross*, 129.

9. Thomas Powers, *The War at Home* (New York: Grossman Publishers, 1973), 24.

10. Robert Shelton, *No Direction Home, The Life and Music of Bob Dylan* (New York: Beach Tree Books/William Morrow, 1986), 87; and *Rolling Stone Illustrated History of Rock & Roll*, Jim Miller, editor (New York: A Random House/Rolling Stone Press Book, 1980), 275.

11. Powers, *The War at Home*, 268–69.

12. Zaroulis and Sullivan, *Who Spoke Up*, 110–113.

13. Author's interview with Curtis Gans, 7/6/86.

14. Milton Viorst, *Fire in the Streets* (New York: Simon & Schuster, 1979), 387.

15. Author's interview with Curtis Gans, 7/6/86.

16. Richard Cummings, *The Pied Piper* (New York: Grove Press, 1985), 94. Gans can't remember but says the money-raising story is possible.

17. Viorst, *Fire in the Streets*, 389.

18. Ibid., 391.

19. Ibid., 392.

20. Author's interview with Curtis Gans, 7/6/86.

21. For "slept through": Ibid.; and recorded interview with Seymour Hersh, 9/9/69, McCarthy Historical Project Archive, Georgetown University Library, Washington, D.C.

22. Frank Cormier, *LBJ, The Way He Was* (Garden City, N.Y.: Doubleday, 1977), 231.

23. Author's interview with Curtis Gans, 7/6/86; and Powers, *The War at Home*, 274.

24. Zaroulis and Sullivan, *Who Spoke Up*, 108.

25. Author's interview with Richard Cummings, 3/1/85.

26. Eugene J. McCarthy, *The Limits of Power, America's Role in the World* (New York: Holt, Rinehart and Winston, 1967), 99.

27. Powers, *The War at Home*, 272.

28. Author's interview with Curtis Gans, 7/6/86.

29. *New York Times*, 5/21/67, quoted in Powers, *The War at Home*, 269.

30. Recorded interview with Joseph Rauh, 6/10/69, McCarthy Historical Project Archive, Georgetown University Library, Washington, D.C.

31. Author's interview with Curtis Gans, 7/6/86; and Powers, *The War at Home*, 273.

32. Author's interview with Curtis Gans, 7/6/86.

33. Recorded interview with Sam Brown, 1969, McCarthy Historical Project Archive, Georgetown University Library, Washington, D.C.

34. Ibid.

35. Author's interview with Curtis Gans, 7/6/86; and recorded interview with Sam Brown, McCarthy Historical Project Archive.

36. Author's interview with Mary McGrory, 4/13/87.
37. Jack Newfield, *Robert Kennedy: A Memoir* (1969; reprint, New York: Bantam, 1970), 206–207; and Arthur M. Schlesinger, Jr., *Robert Kennedy and His Times* (Boston: Houghton Mifflin, 1978), 825.
38. Author's interview with Justin Feldman, 9/9/86.
39. Recorded interview with Allard Lowenstein, 1969, McCarthy Historical Project Archive, Georgetown University Library, Washington, D.C.
40. Recorded interview with Joseph Rauh, McCarthy Historical Project Archive; this is Rauh's recollection of Lowenstein's recollection of Rauh's remark. Rauh did not remember saying it but trusted Lowenstein's memory. Lowenstein gives the same version in recorded interview with Allard Lowenstein, McCarthy Historical Project Archive.
41. Albert Eisele, *Almost to the Presidency* (Blue Earth, Minn.: The Piper Company, 1972), 273; and Richard T. Stout, *People* (New York: Harper & Row, 1970), 58.
42. Arthur Herzog, *McCarthy for President* (New York: Viking, 1969), 32.
43. Stout, *People,* 73; and author's interview with Curtis Gans, 7/6/86.
44. Eugene J. McCarthy, *The Year of the People* (Garden City, N.Y.: Doubleday, 1969), 17.
45. Stout, *People*, 49.
46. Stanley Karnow, *Vietnam, A History, The First Complete Account of Vietnam at War* (New York: Viking, 1983), 366–374.
47. Ibid., 373.
48. Eisele, *Almost to the Presidency*, 276.
49. Don Oberdorfer, *Tet!* (1971; reprint, New York: Da Capo Press, 1984), 84–85.
50. Recorded interview with George McGovern, 7/16/70, John F. Kennedy Library, Oral History Program, Boston.
51. Author's interview with Eugene McCarthy, 3/27/86.
52. *Minneapolis Tribune*, interview with Eugene McCarthy, quoted in Eisele, *Almost to the Presidency*, 84.
53. David Frost, *The Presidential Debate, 1968* (New York: Stein and Day, 1968), 33.
54. *Current Biography*, 2/82, s.v. "Arlo Guthrie."
55. *New York Times*, 7/18/67.
56. Ibid.
57. *Current Biography*, 2/82. s.v. "Arlo Guthrie."
58. Zaroulis and Sullivan, *Who Spoke Up*, 133–134.
59. Powers, *The War at Home*, 279.
60. Ibid., 236–237.
61. Ibid., 234.
62. Ibid., 240.
63. Ibid., 240–241.
64. *New York Review of Books*, 12/7/67.
65. Norman Mailer, *The Armies of the Night* (New York Signet/New American Library, 1968), 15.
66. Powers, *The War at Home*, 245.
67. McCarthy, *The Year of the People*, 42.
68. *Ramparts*, 9/28/68.
69. Author's interview with Eugene McCarthy, 3/27/86; and McCarthy, *The Year of the People*, 26.

70. Eisele, *Almost to the Presidency*, 277–278.
71. McCarthy, *The Year of the People*, 51.
72. Author's interview with Eugene McCarthy, 3/27/86.
73. Recorded interview with Allard Lowenstein, McCarthy Historical Project Archive.

Chapter 3: Like a Rolling Stone
  1. David Frost, *The Presidential Debate, 1968* (New York: Stein & Day, 1968), 33.
  2. Richard T. Stout, *People* (New York: Harper & Row, 1970), 81.
  3. *New York Times*, 12/1/67.
  4. Author's interview with Eugene McCarthy, 3/27/86.
  5. Ibid.
  6. *Commonweal,* quoted in Albert Eisele, *Almost to the Presidency* (Blue Earth, Minn.: The Piper Company, 1972), 114.
  7. Eisele, *Almost to the Presidency*, 29.
  8. Ibid., 28.
  9. Ibid., 29–30.
 10. Ibid., 34.
 11. Ibid., 35.
 12. Ibid., 36–37.
 13. Ibid., 38.
 14. Ibid., 40.
 15. Ibid., 39.
 16. Ibid., 40.
 17. Ibid., 80–81.
 18. Ibid., 121–123.
 19. Ibid., 161–171.
 20. Recorded interview with George McGovern, 7/16/70, John F. Kennedy Library, Oral History Program, Boston.
 21. Quoted in Eisele, *Almost to the Presidency*, 285.
 22. *New York Times*, 12/4/67.
 23. Author's interview with Curtis Gans, 7/6/86; and recorded interview with Allard Lowenstein, 1969, McCarthy Historical Project Archive, Georgetown University Library, Washington, D.C.
 24. Recorded interview with Gerry Studds, 1/30/69, McCarthy Historical Project Archive, Georgetown University Library, Washington, D.C.
 25. Ibid.
 26. Author's interview with Blair Clark, 3/19/68.
 27. Ibid.
 28. Recorded interview with Joseph Rauh, 6/10/69, McCarthy Historical Project Archive, Georgetown University Library, Washington, D.C.
 29. Recorded interview with Gerry Studds, McCarthy Historical Project Archive; and Lewis Chester, Godfrey Hodgson, and Bruce Page, *An American Melodrama, The Presidential Campaign of 1968* (New York: Viking, 1969), 85.
 30. For reactions to McCarthy: Arthur Herzog, *McCarthy for President* (New York: Viking, 1969), 78; and author's interview with Blair Clark, 3/19/86.
 31. Eugene J. McCarthy, *The Year of the People* (Garden City, N.Y.: Doubleday, 1969), 67.
 32. Eisele, *Almost to the Presidency,* 291.

33. Chester, Hodgson, and Page, *An American Melodrama*, 85–86; and recorded interview with Gerry Studds, McCarthy Historical Project Archive.
34. Eisele, *Almost to the Presidency*, 288.
35. Recorded interview with Gerry Studds, McCarthy Historical Project Archive; recorded interview with David Hoeh, 1/30/69, McCarthy Historical Project Archive, Georgetown University Library, Washington, D.C.; and author's interview with Blair Clark, 3/19/68.
36. Recorded interview with Seymour Hersh, 9/9/69, McCarthy Historical Project Archive, Georgetown University Library, Washington, D.C.
37. *Washington Evening Star*, 1/15/68.
38. Recorded interview with Gerry Studds, McCarthy Historical Project Archive.
39. Recorded interview with Allard Lowenstein, McCarthy Historical Project Archive.
40. Author's interview with Blair Clark, 3/19/86.
41. Recorded interview with Gerry Studds, McCarthy Historical Project Archive.

Chapter 4: Tet: The Turning Point
1. Stanley Karnow, *Vietnam, A History, The First Complete Account of Vietnam at War* (New York: Viking, 1983), 17.
2. Edward Hersh, producer, Av Westin, executive producer, *Our World* (New York: ABC News, broadcast 2/5/87).
3. Don Oberdorfer, *Tet!* (1971; reprint, New York: Da Capo Press, 1984), 174.
4. Ibid., 71.
5. Ibid.
6. James Simon Kunen, *The Strawberry Statement* (New York: Random House, 1969), 67.
7. Oberdorfer, *Tet!*, 183. There were also 260 correspondents from other countries besides America and Vietnam—an increase of 86 from the month before.
8. Herbert Y. Schandler, *The Unmaking of a President: Lyndon Johnson and Vietnam* (Princeton: Princeton University Press, 1977), 85.
9. *New York Times*, 1/31/68.
10. Oberdorfer, *Tet!*, 35.
11. Ibid., 7–9.
12. *Our World*, ABC, broadcast 2/5/87.
13. *New York Times*, 1/31/68.
14. Author's interview with Lee Lescaze, 2/23/87.
15. *Our World*, ABC, broadcast 2/5/87.
16. Albert Eisele, *Almost to the Presidency* (Blue Earth, Minn.: The Piper Company, 1972), 287. The remark was to John S. Knight, then publisher of the *Miami Herald*.
17. Oberdorfer, *Tet!*, 99–100.
18. Michael Herr, *Dispatches* (New York: Alfred A. Knopf, 1971), 189.
19. Oberdorfer, *Tet!*, 50.
20. Lyndon Baines Johnson, *The Vantage Point, Perspectives of the Presidency, 1963–1969* (New York: Holt, Rinehart and Winston, 1971), 393.
21. Tom Buckley, *New York Times*, 1/30/68.
22. Ibid., 1/31/68.
23. Charles Mohr, *New York Times*, 2/1/68.
24. *New York Times*, 2/1/87.
25. Ibid., 2/2/68.

26. Oberdordfer, *Tet!*, 165–166; and Stanley Karnow, *Vietnam, A History, The First Complete Account of Vietnam at War* (New York: Viking, 1983), 529. Adams interview from *Our World*, ABC, broadcast 2/5/87. Loan quote and story about the ABC cameraman from Tuckner, quoted in *Journalism Quarterly,* Summer 1972.
27. Interview with Eddie Adams in *Newsweek,* 4/15/85, 65.
28. Oberdorfer, *Tet!*, 184.
29. Herr, *Dispatches*, 44.
30. Author's interview with Lee Lescaze, 2/23/87.
31. Herr, *Dispatches*, 68–70.
32. Author's interviews with Maynard Parker, 3/23/87, Kevin Buckley, 6/14/88, and James Sterba, 6/14/88.
33. Karnow, *Vietnam*, 529; and Peter Braestrup, *Big Story*, vol. 1 (Boulder: Westview Press, 1977), 265.
34. Oberdorfer, *Tet!*, 209.
35. Ibid., 207.
36. Ibid., 214–215.
37. Karnow, *Vietnam*, 530.
38. Oberdorfer, *Tet!*, 231–232.
39. Braestrup, *Big Story*, 268.
40. Eisele, *Almost to the Presidency*, 294.
41. Author's interview with Curtis Gans, 7/6/86.
42. Recorded interview with Seymour Hersh, 9/9/69, McCarthy Historical Project Archive, Georgetown University Library, Washington, D.C.
43. Oberdorfer, *Tet!*, 114; and Lewis Chester, Godfrey Hodgson, and Bruce Page, *An American Melodrama, The Presidential Campaign of 1968* (New York: Viking, 1969), 106–109.
44. Eisele, *Almost to the Presidency*, 296; and Chester, Hodgson, and Page, *An American Melodrama*, 98.
45. Quoted in Eugene J. McCarthy, *The Year of the People* (Garden City, N.Y.: Doubleday, 1969), 82.
46. Eugene McCarthy, *Up 'Til Now* (San Diego: Harcourt Brace Jovanovich, 1987), 186.
47. Author's interview with Blair Clark, 3/19/86.
48. David Halberstam, *The Powers That Be* (New York: Alfred A. Knopf, 1979), 439–440.
49. Ibid., 431.
50. Ibid., 434.
51. *Washington Post*, 216/68.
52. *New York Times*, 2/7/68.
53. Ibid., 2/3/68.
54. Oberdorfer, *Tet!*, frontpiece, 179. Doubling the total: Cronkite says eight hundred thousand were officially listed as refugees before Tet on *Who, What, When, Where, Why* (New York: CBS News, broadcast 2/27/68).
55. Lady Bird Johnson, *A White House Diary* (New York: Holt, Rinehart and Winston, 1970), 632.
56. Johnson, *The Vantage Point*, 384; and Karnow, *Vietnam,* 540–542.
57. Johnson, *The Vantage Point*, 384.
58. *LBJ: The Decision to Halt the Bombing* (New York: CBS, broadcast 2/6/70).
59. Karnow, *Vietnam*, 543; and Lieutenant Colonel Dave R. Palmer, *Readings in Current Military History*, quoted in Schandler, *The Unmaking of a President*, 75.

60. Karnow, *Vietnam*, 544.
61. Oberdorfer, *Tet!*, 51.
62. Ibid., 53.
63. Ibid., 180–181; and Karnow, *Vietnam*, 536.
64. Karnow, *Vietnam*, 538.
65. Oberdorfer, *Tet!*, 65–66.
66. Karnow, *Vietnam*, 546.
67. Recorded interview with Gerry Studds, 1/30/69, McCarthy Historical Project Archive, Georgetown University Library, Washington, D.C.
68. Author's interview with Curtis Gans, 7/6/86.
69. Mary McGrory, *Washington Evening Star*, 3/5/68.
70. Quoted in Theodore H. White, *The Making of the President, 1968* (New York: Atheneum, 1969), 84.
71. Jeremy Larner, *Nobody Knows* (New York: Macmillan, 1970), 35–36; and recorded interview with Gerry Studds, McCarthy Historical Project Archive.
72. Author's interviews with Mary McGrory, 4/15/87, and Ann Hart, 5/4/87.
73. Arthur Herzog, *McCarthy for President* (New York: Viking, 1969), 95; and White, *The Making of the President, 1968*, 84.
74. Ben Stavis, *We Were the Campaign, New Hampshire to Chicago for McCarthy* (Boston: Beacon Press, 1969), 20.
75. Ibid., 28.
76. Ibid., 15.
77. Recorded interview with Gerry Studds, McCarthy Historical Project Archive; and author's interview with Curtis Gans, 7/6/86.
78. McGrory does not remember this conversation; this is Moynihan's recollection. [Author's interview with Mary McGrory, 4/15/87.]
79. Recorded interview with Marie Ridder, 2/9/70, McCarthy Historical Project Archive, Georgetown University Library, Washington, D.C.
80. Eisele, *Almost to the Presidency*, 293; and recorded interview with David Hoeh, 1/30/69, McCarthy Historical Project Archive, Georgetown University Library, Washington, D.C.
81. Transcripts of McCarthy's speeches, Robert F. Kennedy campaign files at John F. Kennedy Library, Boston.
82. Eisele, *Almost to the Presidency*, 296.
83. Herzog, *McCarthy for President*, 90.
84. Ibid; author's interview with Eugene McCarthy, 3/27/86; and recorded interview with Gerry Studds, McCarthy Historical Project Archive.
85. Recorded interview with Seymour Hersh, McCarthy Historical Project Archive; and *Washington Evening Star*, 2/11/68.
86. Author's interview with Mary McGrory, 4/15/87.
87. For New Hampshire campaign and "children's crusade": Ibid; author's interview with Curtis Gans, 7/6/86; recorded interviews with Gerry Studds and David Hoeh, McCarthy Historical Project Archive; and *Washington Evening Star*, 3/5/68.
88. Recorded interview with Gerry Studds, McCarthy Historical Project Archive.
89. Author's interview with Mary McGrory, 4/15/87.
90. Author's interview with Ann Hart, 5/5/87.
91. Herzog, *McCarthy for President*, 94.

92. Recorded interview with Anthony Podesta, 8/5/69, McCarthy Historical Project Archive, Georgetown University Library, Washington, D.C.

93. Author's interview with Ann Hart, 5/5/87; and recorded interview with David Hoeh, McCarthy Historical Project Archive.

94. Stavis, *We Were the Campaign*, 13–14.

95. Herzog, *McCarthy for President*, 82.

96. Ibid., 89.

97. Author's interviews with Curtis Gans, 7/6/86, and Blair Clark, 3/19/86.

98. Recorded interview with Gerry Studds, McCarthy Historical Project Archive.

99. Recorded interview with David Hoeh, McCarthy Historical Project Archive; and author's interview with Curtis Gans, 7/6/86.

100. Author's interview with Clark Clifford, 6/1/87.

101. McCarthy, *The Year of the People*, 18.

102. Author's interview with Philip M. Kaiser (3/20/86), who was Bruce's deputy in London; and Johnson, *The Vantage Point*, 253–255.

103. Hubert H. Humphrey, *The Education of a Public Man, My Life and Politics* (Garden City, N.Y.: Doubleday, 1976), 347.

104. Johnson, *The Vantage Point*, 369–370.

105. Ibid., 372–378.

106. *Washington Evening Star*, 1/20/68.

107. Author's interview with Clark Clifford, 6/1/87.

108. Schandler, *The Unmaking of a President*, 94-95.

109. Ibid., 96–99.

110. Ibid., 108.

111. Oberdorfer, *Tet!*, 261–262.

112. Schandler, *The Unmaking of a President*, 108–112.

113. Ibid., 112.

114. Oberdorfer, *Tet!*, 265.

115. Karnow, *Vietnam*, 551.

116. Oberdorfer, *Tet!*, 267.

117. Ibid., 267–271.

118. *Newsweek*, 3/19/68.

119. Recorded interview with Anthony Podesta, McCarthy Historical Project Archive.

120. *Washington Evening Star*, 3/10/68.

121. Recorded interview with David Hoeh, McCarthy Historical Project Archive.

122. Author's interview with Blair Clark, 3/19/86; and recorded interview with Marie Ridder, McCarthy Historical Project Archive.

123. Recorded interview with Gerry Studds, McCarthy Historical Project Archive; author's interview with Blair Clark, 3/19/86; and Herzog, *McCarthy for President*, 97.

124. Larner, *Nobody Knows*, 41.

125. Herzog, *McCarthy for President*, 98.

Chapter 5: The Truth Comes Home

1. Theodore H. White, *The Making of the President, 1968* (New York: Atheneum, 1969), 89.

2. Quoted in ibid., 90.

3. Albert Eisele, *Almost to the Presidency* (Blue Earth, Minn.: The Piper Company, 1972), 300.

4. Author's interview with Blair Clark, 3/19/86.

5. Author's interview with Eugene McCarthy, 3/27/86.

6. Recorded interview with Allard Lowenstein, 1969, McCarthy Historical Project Archive, Georgetown University Library, Washington, D.C.; and Arthur Herzog, *McCarthy for President* (New York: Viking, 1969), 104–105.

7. "Gene McCarthy's not competent to be president of the United States," he told George McGovern on March 14, 1968. Recorded interview with George McGovern, 7/16/70, John F. Kennedy Library, Oral History Program, Boston.

8. Herzog, *McCarthy for President*, 106.

9. Recorded interview with George McGovern, John F. Kennedy Library, Oral History Program.

10. Arthur M. Schlesinger, Jr., *Robert Kennedy and His Times* (Boston: Houghton Mifflin, 1978), 846.

11. Transcript of March 1, 1968, telephone conversation, "typed out at 6:10 this evening." From Theodore H. White Archive, Harvard University, Cambridge, Mass. White's abbreviated version of this conversation appears in pages 159–160 of *The Making of the President, 1968*. "Toss in his cards" has become "cashed in his chips" in the published account. White's advice to Kennedy, as well as Kennedy's references to Johnson, is not included.

12. Robert F. Kennedy presidential campaign film, 1968. Permanent exhibit, John F. Kennedy Library, Boston.

13. Schlesinger, *Robert Kennedy and His Times*, 851; and Lewis Chester, Godfrey Hodgson, and Bruce Page, *An American Melodrama, The Presidential Campaign of 1968* (New York: Viking, 1969), 121.

14. Chester, Hodgson, and Page, *An American Melodrama*, 120–124; and Schlesinger, *Robert Kennedy and His Times*, 851–854.

15. Memorandum of March 15, 1968, telephone conversation between eleven and twelve in the morning, Theodore H. White Archive, Harvard University, Cambridge, Mass. White's final notation on the page: "Pressure cooker stuff."

16. For sending Clark's mail home: Richard T. Stout, *People* (New York: Harper & Row, 1970), 168. For Clark's feelings about Bobby Kennedy: author's interview with Blair Clark, 3/19/86. In Chester, Hodgson, and Page, *An American Melodrama*, 90, Clark is quoted as saying to Hersh, "All we want to do is get Kennedy in," but Clark is certain he never said that.

17. Chester, Hodgson, and Page, *An American Melodrama*, 93.

18. Mary McGrory, *Washington Star*, 3/10/68.

19. Author's interview with Blair Clark, 3/19/86.

20. Recorded interview with Allard Lowenstein, McCarthy Historical Project Archive; and recorded interview with George McGovern, John F. Kennedy Library, Oral History Program.

21. Schlesinger, *Robert Kennedy and His Times*, 853.

22. *New York Post*, 3/15/68.

23. *New York Times*, 3/16/68.

24. Recorded interview with Allard Lowenstein, McCarthy Historical Project Archive.

25. Herzog, *McCarthy for President*, 108.

26. Ibid., 109.

27. Schlesinger, *Robert Kennedy and His Times*, 856–857.

28. Jules Witcover, *85 Days, The Last Campaign of Robert Kennedy* (New York: G.P. Putnam's Sons, 1969), 87.

29. *New York Times*, 3/18/68.

30. Ibid.

31. Ibid; and recorded interview with Allard Lowenstein, McCarthy Historical Project Archive.

32. "Senator Kennedy, Farewell," *New York Post*, 3/26/68, quoted in Schlesinger, *Robert Kennedy and His Times*, 861.

33. Schlesinger, *Robert Kennedy and His Times*, 857.

34. David J. Garrow, *Bearing the Cross, Martin Luther King, Jr., and the Southern Christian Leadership Conference* (New York: William Morrow, 1986), 307, 469 .

35. *LBJ: Why I Chose Not to Run* (New York: CBS, broadcast 12 /27/69).

36. Cronkite: "Mr. President, many of the reports since you left the presidency have suggested that you were run out of the presidency. Is there any aptness to that analysis?"
    Johnson: "Well, I don't think I'd be very objective about that, Walter; I don't think so. If it gives the coiners of it satisfaction, then I don't want to deprive them of it, if they enjoy it. But I don't think that it's an accurate phrase at all. And if you're asking me in an indirect way whether I had any doubt about my election as president, the answer is an absolute, positive, 'No.'" *LBJ: Why I Chose Not to Run*, CBS, broadcast 12/27/69.

37. *New York Times*, 4/14/86.

38. Lyndon Baines Johnson, *The Vantage Point, Perspectives of the Presidency, 1963–1969* (New York: Holt, Rinehart and Winston, 1971), 327.

39. Lady Bird Johnson, *A White House Diary* (New York: Holt, Rinehart and Winston, 1970), 617–619; and *LBJ: Why I Chose Not to Run*, CBS, broadcast 12/27/69.

40. Lawrence M. Baskir and William A. Strauss, *Chance and Circumstance, The Draft, the War and the Vietnam Generation* (New York: Vintage Books, 1978), 8–11.

41. Letter home from David Kaiser to his parents, April 15, 1969. My middle brother eventually joined the Army reserves to avoid the draft and probable combat. My oldest brother got a physical deferment because of a bad back. I drew number 126 in the lottery—and put myself in the pool the year they called everyone up to number 125.

42. Johnson, *The Vantage Point*, 378–380.

43. Ibid., 387–388.

44. Harry McPherson, *A Political Education* (Boston: Little, Brown, 1977), 426.

45. Johnson, *A White House Diary*, 638, 641.

46. Walter Isaacson and Evan Thomas, *The Wise Men. Six Friends and the World They Made* (New York: Simon and Schuster, 1986), 677.

47. Author's interview with Clark Clifford, 6/1/87.

48. Isaacson and Thomas, *The Wise Men*, 679–680.

49. Author's interview with Clark Clifford, 6/1/87.

50. *Foreign Affairs*, 47:4, 610–611.

51. Author's interview with Clark Clifford, 6/1/87.

52. Herbert Y. Schandler, *The Unmaking of a President: Lyndon Johnson and Vietnam* (Princeton: Princeton University Press, 1977), 214.

53. Author's interview with Clark Clifford, 6/1/87.

54. Schandler, *The Unmaking of a President*, 210–211.

55. *Public Papers of Lyndon Johnson, 1968–69*, 402–413.

56. Schandler, *The Unmaking of a President*, 225, 249.

57. Author's interview with Clark Clifford, 6/1/87; for Rusk's willingness: Schandler, *The Unmaking of a President*, 237.

58. Isaacson and Thomas, *The Wise Men*, 686–687, 806.

59. Stanley Karnow, *Vietnam, A History, The First Complete Account of Vietnam at War* (New York: Viking, 1983), 562.

60. Ibid., 561–562.

61. Ibid., 563, 564.

62. Schandler, *The Unmaking of a President*, 247; and McPherson, *A Political Education*, 431.

63. Schandler, *The Unmaking of a President*, 273.

64. UPI dispatch, *Los Angeles Times*, 3/29/68.

65. Johnson, *The Vantage Point*, 431; and Johnson, *A White House Diary*, 642.

66. Some accounts say McCarthy stopped to watch the beginning of Johnson's speech on a TV set in a press room adjoining the auditorium, but McCarthy does not recall that. Author's interview with Eugene McCarthy, 3/27/86.

67. For McCarthy speech and Johnson announcement: *Washington Post*, 4/1/68; and Herzog, *McCarthy for President*, 119–120.

68. Author's interview with Eugene McCarthy, 3/27/86.

69. Herzog, *McCarthy for President*, 119–120.

70. President Lyndon B. Johnson, Daily Diary, March 31, 1968, p. 10.

71. Johnson, *The Vantage Point*, 436.

72. *Peace, Politics and the President: CBS News Special Report* (New York: CBS, broadcast 4/1/68).

73. Doris Kearns, *Lyndon Johnson and the American Dream* (New York: Harper & Row, 1976), 343.

Chapter 6: The Chimes of Freedom

1. From the essay "In Defence of Comrade Zilliacus," in Sonia Orwell and Ian Angus, editors, *The Collected Essays, Journalism and Letters of George Orwell*, vol 4: *In Front of Your Nose, 1945–1950* (New York: Harcourt Brace Jovanovich, 1968), 399–400.

2. David J. Garrow, *Bearing the Cross, Martin Luther King, Jr., and the Southern Christian Leadership Conference* (New York: William Morrow, 1986), 393.

3. Ibid., 59, 83, 89, 109, 221.

4. Ibid., 33–38.

5. Ibid., 75.

6. Ibid., 90.

7. Letter from Jeremy Larner to the author, 4/17/86.

8. Garrow, *Bearing the Cross*, 283–284.

9. Author's interview with Jose Yglesias, 3/1/88; and *New York Times Magazine*, 3/31/68.

10. Garrow, *Bearing the Cross*, 289.

11. United States Senate, *Supplementary Detailed Staff Reports on Intelligence Activities and the Rights of Americans*, Book III, *Final Report of the Select Committee to Study Governmental Operations with Respect to Intelligence Activities* (Washington, D.C.: Government Printing Office, 4/23/76), 81.

12. *Supplementary Detailed Staff Reports*, 114.
13. *Supplementary Detailed Staff Reports*, 85.
14. Recorded interview with Robert F. Kennedy, 12/64, John F. Kennedy Library, Oral History Program, Boston.
15. *Supplementary Detailed Staff Reports*, 118.
16. Richard Gid Powers, *Secrecy and Power: The Life of J. Edgar Hoover* (New York: The Free Press, 1987), quoted in *New York Times*, 3/8/87.
17. Ibid.
18. David J. Garrow, *The FB.I. and Martin Luther King, Jr., From "Solo" to Memphis* (New York: W. W. Norton, 1981), 127–130.
19. Ibid., 121–122.
20. *Supplementary Detailed Staff Reports*, 160.
21. Garrow, *The FB.I. and Martin Luther King, Jr.*, 134.
22. *Supplementary Detailed Staff Reports*, 91.
23. Powers, *Secrecy and Power*, quoted in *New York Times*, 3/8/87.
24. Shareen Brysac, producer, and Perry Wolff, executive producer, *1968: A CBS News Special* (New York: CBS, broadcast 8/25/78).
25. Garrow, *Bearing the Cross*, 607.
26. *New York Times*, 3/16/68.
27. Garrow, *Bearing the Cross*, 409.
28. Lyndon Baines Johnson, *The Vantage Point, Perspectives of the Presidency, 1963–1969* (New York: Holt. Rinehart and Winston, 1971), 164–167; and Garrow, *Bearing the Cross*, 408–409.
29. Thomas Powers, *The War at Home* (New York: Grossman Publishers, 1973), 152–153.
30. Ibid., 160–161.
31. For King's speech and press reaction: Garrow, *Bearing the Cross*, 552–554; and Powers, *The War at Home*, 160–163.
32. *New York Times*, 4/14/67.
33. Garrow, *Bearing the Cross*, 554.
34. Author's interview with Roger Wilkins, 2/3/88.
35. *New York Times*, 4/23/67.
36. Garrow, *Bearing the Cross*, 566.
37. *New York Times*, 7/26/67.
38. Ibid., 7/28/67.
39. Ibid., 8/9/67.
40. *New York Review of Books*, 8/24/67.
41. *New York Times*, 8/19/67.
42. Lewis Chester, Godfrey Hodgson, and Bruce Page, *An American Melodrama, The Presidential Campaign of 1968* (New York: Viking, 1969), 285–287.
43. Garrow, *Bearing the Cross*, 596.
44. *New York Times*, 2/8/88.
45. Garrow, *Bearing the Cross*, 598.
46. *New York Times*, 3/3/68.
47. *Report of the National Commission on Civil Disorders* (New York: Bantam Books, 1968), 483.
48. *New York Times Magazine*, 3/31/68.

49. *Wall Street Journal*, 3/8/68, 4/8/68.
50. Garrow, *Bearing the Cross*, 605–606.
51. *Wall Street Journal*, 3/29/68.
52. *CBS News Special Report: The Death of Martin Luther King, Jr.* (New York: CBS, broadcast 4/4/68).
53. Garrow, *Bearing the Cross*, 611–612.
54. For King's speech and final hours: Garrow, *Bearing the Cross*, 620–624; *New York Times*, 4/5/68; and interview with the Reverend Samuel Kyles, *CBS News Special Report: The Death of Martin Luther King, Jr.*, CBS, broadcast 4/4/68.
55. *New York Times*, 4/5/68.
56. Ibid.
57. ". . . angered his leader": Garrow, *Bearing the Cross*, 616; Williams quote from *New York Times Magazine*, 11/29/87.
58. Theodore H. White, *The Making of the President, 1968* (New York: Atheneum, 1969), 208.
59. *New York Times*, 4/6/68.
60. Ibid., 4/13/68.
61. Author's interview with Leslie Slote, 6/6/86.
62. *New York Times*, 4/8/68; and Arthur M. Schlesinger, Jr., *Robert Kennedy and His Times* (Boston: Houghton Mifflin, 1978), 877.
63. Author's interview with Leslie Slote, 6/6/86.
64. For McCarthy's attitude: author's interview with Blair Clark, 3/19/86; and for Johnson's: Johnson, *The Vantage Point*, 176.
65. *New York Times*, 4/10/68; and Associated Press photograph, distributed 4/9/68.
66. Garrow, *Bearing the Cross*, 98.
67. *New York Times*, 4/10/68.
68. Author's interview with Matthew Nimetz, 8/8/86.
69. *New York Times*, 4/16/68, 5/16/68.
70. *Los Angeles Times*, 4/13/68.
71. *Chicago Tribune*, 4/16/68.
72. *Time*, 4/26/68.
73. For casualties, including Austin: *New York Times*, 4/13/68.

Chapter 7: Tears of Rage

1. For Kirk and Rudd: Jerry L. Avorn et al., *Up Against the Ivy Wall, A History of the Columbia Crisis*, Robert Friedman, editor (New York: Atheneum, 1969), 25–27.
2. *Newsweek*, 5/6/68.
3. Author's interview with Martha Ritter, 3/1/88.
4. James Simon Kunen, *The Strawberry Statement* (New York: Random House, 1969), 14.
5. *New York Times*, 12/12/64; and *New York Times Magazine*, 2/14/65.
6. *New York Times*, 12/9/64.
7. *New York Times Magazine*, 2/14/65.
8. James Miller, *Democracy Is in the Streets* (New York: Simon and Schuster, 1987), 332–333.
9. Ibid., 231.
10. *New York Times*, 8/27/68.
11. Ibid., 4/26/68.
12. Ibid.

13. *Crisis at Columbia, Report of the Fact-Finding Commission Appointed to Investigate the Disturbances at Columbia University in April and May 1968* (New York: Vintage Books, 1968), 81–82.
14. Avorn et al., *Up Against the Ivy Wall*, 17–18.
15. Author's interview with George Scurlock, 3/2/88.
16. Author's interview with Lewis Cole, 3/3/88.
17. *New York Times*, 5/19/68.
18. Ibid.
19. Avorn et al., *Up Against the Ivy Wall*, 32.
20. *New York Times*, 4/26/68.
21. Avorn et al., *Up Against the Ivy Wall*, 33.
22. Ibid., 119–120.
23. Ibid., 37–48; and *New York Times*, 4/24/68.
24. Avorn et al., *Up Against the Ivy Wall*, 34–35.
25. Author's interview with George Scurlock, 3/2/88; and *Crisis at Columbia*, 189.
26. Avorn et al., *Up Against the Ivy Wall*, 62–63.
27. Author's interview with George Scurlock, 3/2/88.
28. Author's interview with Lewis Cole, 3/3/88.
29. *New York Times*, 4/24/88.
30. Kunen, *The Strawberry Statement*, 33–34; and *Life*, 5/10/68.
31. Avorn et al., *Up Against the Ivy Wall*, 118.
32. Ibid., 84.
33. Author's interview with Lewis Cole, 3/3/88.
34. Avorn et al., *Up Against the Ivy Wall*, 174.
35. Ibid., 188.
36. Author's interview with Robert McG. Thomas, Jr., 3/4/88. Interim police report quoted in Avorn et al., *Up Against the Ivy Wall*, 191, and *New York Times*, 5/1/68.
37. Avorn et al., *Up Against the Ivy Wall*, 194–196.
38. *Crisis at Columbia*, 190.
39. Theodore H. White, *The Making of the President, 1968* (New York: Atheneum, 1969), 221.
40. Author's interview with A. M. Rosenthal, 7/73.
41. *New York Times*, 5/1/68; and Avorn et al., *Up Against the Ivy Wall*, 201–202.
42. Gay Talese, *The Kingdom and the Power* (1969; reprint, Garden City, N.Y.: Anchor Books, 1978), 537–540.
43. *Crisis at Columbia*, 181.
44. Ibid., 182.
45. The Columbia University Commencement Address (New York: Columbia University, delivered 6/4/68).
46. *New York Times*, 5/19/68.

Chapter 8: It Takes a Lot to Laugh, It Takes a Train to Cry

1. Recorded interview with Seymour Hersh, 9/9/69, McCarthy Historical Project Archive, Georgetown University Library, Washington, D.C.
2. Richard T. Stout, *People* (New York: Harper & Row, 1970), 197.
3. Jerry Bruno and Jeff Greenfield, *The Advance Man* (New York: William Morrow, 1971), 117.

4. Albert Eisele, *Almost to the Presidency* (Blue Earth, Minn.: The Piper Company, 1972), 307.
5. *New York Times*, 5/1/68.
6. *Welsh Daily News*, quoted in *Senator Robert F. Kennedy, A Chronology of His Activities and National and World Events, January 4, 1968–June 3, 1968.* Prepared by Gabe Bayez, Wolper productions (author's private collection).
7. Eugene McCarthy, *Up 'Til Now, A Memoir* (San Diego: Harcourt Brace Jovanovich, 1987), 196.
8. Jeremy Larner, *Nobody Knows* (New York: Macmillan, 1970), 64.
9. Author's interview with Eugene McCarthy, 3/27/86.
10. Quoted in Eisele, *Almost to the Presidency*, 310.
11. Larner, *Nobody Knows*, 31.
12. Quoted in Eisele, *Almost to the Presidency*, 310.
13. Recorded interview with Allard Lowenstein, 1969, McCarthy Historical Project Archive, Georgetown University Library, Washington, D.C.
14. Larner, *Nobody Knows*, 69.
15. Recorded interview with Allard Lowenstein, McCarthy Historical Project Archive.
16. Recorded interview with Seymour Hersh, McCarthy Historical Project Archive.
17. Larner, *Nobody Knows*, 32; recorded interview with Seymour Hersh, McCarthy Historical Project Archive; and author's interview with Blair Clark, 3/19/86.
18. Arthur Herzog, *McCarthy for President* (New York: Viking, 1969), 134.
19. Author's interview with Blair Clark, 3/19/86.
20. Recorded interview with Stephen T. Quigley, 9/26/69, McCarthy Historical Project Archive, Georgetown University Library, Washington, D.C.
21. Eisele, *Almost to the Presidency*, 316.
22. Author's interview with Blair Clark, 3/19/86.
23. Ibid.
24. Recorded interview with Seymour Hersh, McCarthy Historical Project Archive; and Stout, *People*, 168.
25. Larner, *Nobody Knows*, 7, 33, 64.
26. Recorded interview with Seymour Hersh, McCarthy Historical Project Archive.
27. Ben Stavis, *We Were the Campaign, New Hampshire to Chicago for McCarthy* (Boston: Beacon Press, 1969), 38.
28. For Hersh's attitude: recorded interview with Seymour Hersh, McCarthy Historical Project Archive; for McCarthy's: Eugene J. McCarthy, *The Year of the People* (Garden City, N.Y: Doubleday, 1969), 98–99.
29. Larner, *Nobody Knows*, 66.
30. Eisele, *Almost to the Presidency*, 310.
31. Stout, *People*, 240.
32. Lewis Chester, Godfrey Hodgson, and Bruce Page, *An American Melodrama, The Presidential Campaign of 1968* (New York: Viking, 1969), 164.
33. *New York Times*, 5/6/68.
34. Recorded interview with Seymour Hersh, McCarthy Historical Project Archive; and Eisele, *Almost to the Presidency*, 310.
35. Jean Stein, *American Journey, The Times of Robert Kennedy*, George Plimpton, editor (New York: Harcourt Brace Jovanovich, 1970), 304.
36. *New York Times,* 4/4/68.

37. Stein, *American Journey*, 299

38. Larner, *Nobody Knows*, p. 72.

39. Stout, *People*, 221.

40. Recorded interview with Anthony Podesta, 8/5/69, McCarthy Historical Project Archive, Georgetown University Library, Washington, D.C.

41. Chester, Hodgson, and Page, *An American Melodrama*, 177; and Theodore H. White, *The Making of the President, 1968* (New York: Atheneum, 1969), 175.

42. McCarthy, *Up 'Til Now*, 193.

43. Quoted in Eisele, *Almost to the Presidency*, 313.

44. Author's interview with Blair Clark, 3/19/86; and Herzog, *McCarthy for President*, 161–162.

45. Larner, *Nobody Knows*, 99.

46. Chester, Hodgson, and Page, *An American Melodrama*, 300.

47. Larner, *Nobody Knows*, 94.

48. Quoted in Chester, Hodgson, and Page, *An American Melodrama*, 302–303.

49. Larner, *Nobody Knows*, 96–97.

50. *New York Times*, 5/30/68.

51. Ibid.

52. Chester, Hodgson, and Page, *An American Melodrama*, 304–305.

53. McCarthy, *The Year of the People*, 164–165.

54. Larner, *Nobody Knows*, 101–102.

55. *CBS News Special: Campaign '68: The Oregon Primary* (New York: CBS, broadcast 5/28/68).

56. Ibid.

57. All quotes from *Los Angeles Times*, 5/30/68.

58. *Senator Robert F. Kennedy, A Chronology of His Activities and National and World Events.*

59. Chester, Hodgson, and Page, *An American Melodrama*, 337; and *New York Times*, 5/31/68.

60. *Senator Robert F. Kennedy, A Chronology of His Activities and National and World Events.*

61. *Hartford Courant*, 6/1/68.

62. Chester, Hodgson, and Page, *An American Melodrama*, 338–339.

63. Stein, *American Journey*, 309–310.

64. Chester, Hodgson, and Page, *An American Melodrama*, 344; and Herzog, *McCarthy for President*, 187–188.

65. McCarthy, *The Year of the People*, 171.

66. Larner, *Nobody Knows*, 112.

67. McCarthy, *The Year of the People*, 171; Eisele, *Almost to the Presidency*, 310; Herzog, *McCarthy for President*, 187–188; Arthur M. Schlesinger, Jr., *Robert Kennedy and His Times* (Boston: Houghton Mifflin, 1978), 912; and *Los Angeles Times*, 6/3/68.

68. *New York Times*, 6/2/68.

69. Larner, *Nobody Knows*, 118.

70. Jack Newfield, *Robert Kennedy, A Memoir* (1969; reprint, New York: Bantam, 1970), 326–327.

71. White, *The Making of the President, 1968*, 181.

72. Newfield, *Robert Kennedy, A Memoir*, 331–332.
73. *Time*, 6/14/68.
74. *CBS News Special, Campaign '68: The California Primary* (New York: CBS, broadcast 6/4/68, 11:30 P.M.–2:13 A.M. EDT).
75. Newfield, *Robert Kennedy, A Memoir*, 334.
76. Lester David and Irene David, *Bobby Kennedy: The Making of a Folk Hero* (New York: Dodd, Mead & Company, 1986), 316.
77. Newfield, *Robert Kennedy, A Memoir*, 339.
78. Larner, *Nobody Knows*, 121.
79. *Time*, 6/14/68.
80. Larner, *Nobody Knows*, 121; and *CBS News Special, Robert F. Kennedy, 1925–1968* (New York: CBS, broadcast 6/6/68).
81. For time of shooting: *New York Times*, 6/7/68; for name of dishwasher: *Time*, 6/14/68; and for tape of West: Fred W. Friendly and Walter Cronkite, *I Can Hear It Now/The Sixties* (New York: Columbia Records, M3X 30353).
82. Chester, Hodgson, and Page, *An American Melodrama*, 355.
83. Newfield, *Robert Kennedy, A Memoir*, 343.
84. Dr. James L. Poppen, quoting Ethel Kennedy in a United Press International dispatch, *New York Times*, 6/8/68.
85. *CBS News Special Report, The Shooting of Robert F. Kennedy* (New York: CBS, broadcast 6/5/68, 10–11 P.M.).
86. Chester, Hodgson, and Page, *An American Melodrama*, 355.
87. Author's interview with Warren Mitofsky, 3/21/88.
88. *Time*, 6/14/68.
89. *New York Times*, 6/6/68.
90. Ibid.
91. Author's interview with Maurice Carroll, 4/1/88.
92. Stein, *American Journey*, 25–26.
93. Ibid., 10, 25–26.
94. Ibid., 11; and *New York Times*, 6/7/68.
95. Stein, *American Journey*, 11.
96. Ibid., 27.
97. Photograph in *Washington Post*, 6/9/68.
98. Theodore H. White, *The Making of the President, 1964* (New York: Atheneum, 1965), 32.
99. *Washington Post*, 6/9/68.
100. Ibid.
101. Author's interview with Robert G. Kaiser, 3/1/88.
102. Andy Warhol and Pat Hackett, *POPism, The Warhol '60's* (New York: Harcourt Brace Jovanovich, 1980), 271, 274.
103. Stein, *American Journey*, 31.
104. Ibid., 32–34.
105. Permanent exhibit at the John F. Kennedy Library, Boston.
106. *New York Post*, 6/11/68.
107. Schlesinger, *Robert Kennedy and His Times*, 67.
108. Author's interview with David Hollander, 9/16/85.

Chapter 9: Rock of Ages

1. *Rolling Stone Illustrated History of Rock & Roll*, Jim Miller, editor (New York: A Random House/Rolling Stone Press Book, 1980), 181.
2. The Editors of Rolling Stone, *The Rolling Stone Interviews* (New York: St. Martin's Press/Rolling Stone Press, 1981), 12.
3. *Rolling Stone,* 12/10/87.
4. *The Rolling Stone Interviews*, 153.
5. Ibid., 55.
6. Robert Palmer, "Rock Begins," in *Rolling Stone Illustrated History of Rock & Roll,* 5.
7. Renata Adler, "The New Sound, Circa 1964," *The New Yorker,* 2/20/65; and *Rolling Stone Illustrated History of Rock & Roll*, 93.
8. *Rolling Stone Illustrated History of Rock & Roll*, 92.
9. *Rolling Stone*, 11/5/87.
10. *The Rolling Stone Interviews*, 28.
11. *Rolling Stone Illustrated History of Rock & Roll*, 276.
12. Simon Albury and John Sheppard, producers, Ron Caird, executive producer, *Sgt. Pepper's Lonely Hearts Club Band* (London: Grenada Television, 1987).
13. John Hammond, with Irving Townsend, *On Record* (New York: Summit Books, 1977), 29.
14. Ibid., 25–30.
15. Ibid., 30.
16. Ibid., 67–68.
17. Ibid., 158.
18. Ibid., 91–93.
19. Ibid., 110.
20. Ibid., 199.
21. "Talk of the Town," *The New Yorker*, 12/5/59.
22. Hammond, *On Record*, 199–206.
23. "Cunard Yanks," from Stephanie Bennett and Patrick Montgomery, producers, Stephanie Bennett and Jeannie Sakol, executive producers, David Silver, writer, *The Compleat Beatles* (Delilah Films, 1982); John Lennon interviewed by Jann Wenner, 12/8/70, reproduced in *The Rolling Stone Interviews*, 153.
24. *The Rolling Stone Interviews*, 153.
25. John Lennon in *The Rolling Stone Interviews*, quoted in *Rolling Stone Illustrated History of Rock & Roll*, 177.
26. John Lennon: "We were the ones that were looked down upon as animals by the southerners, the Londoners." *The Rolling Stone Interviews*, 153.
27. Peter Brown and Steven Gaines, *The Love You Make* (New York: McGraw-Hill, 1983), 88–89.
28. *Rolling Stone Illustrated History of Rock & Roll*, 178.
29. *The Compleat Beatles.*
30. *Rolling Stone Illustrated History of Rock & Roll*, 178.
31. Ibid., 29, 179–180.
32. Ibid., 185.
33. *The Rolling Stone Interviews*, 148.
34. Author's interview with Bob Dylan, 11/13/85.

35. Quoted in Robert Shelton, *No Direction Home: The Life and Music of Bob Dylan* (New York: Beech Tree Books/William Morrow, 1986), 288.
36. *The Compleat Beatles.*
37. Author's interview with Bob Dylan, 11/13/85.
38. "My Life in a Stolen Moment," in Bob Dylan, *Lyrics, 1962–1985* (New York: Alfred A. Knopf, 1985), 70.
39. *The New Yorker*, 10/24/64.
40. *Playboy*, 3/66.
41. Press conference at KQED-TV, San Francisco, 12/65, printed in *Rolling Stone*, 12/14/67.
42. Author's interview with Bob Dylan, 11/13/85.
43. Ibid.
44. *Playboy*, 3/66.
45. Author's interview with Bob Dylan, 11/13/85.
46. *The New Yorker*, 10/24/64.
47. Brown and Gaines, *The Love You Make*, 155–158.
48. Jules Siegel, *Saturday Evening Post*, 7/30/66.
49. Interview with Jann Wenner, *Rolling Stone*, 11/29/69.
50. Martin Lee and Bruce Shlain, *Acid Dreams, The CIA, LSD and the Sixties Rebellion* (New York: Grove Press, 1985), 160; and Thomas Powers, *The War at Home* (New York: Grossman Publishers, 1973), 209.
51. Powers, *The War at Home*, 204.
52. Lee and Shlain, *Acid Dreams*, 164.
53. Powers, *The War at Home*, 209.
54. *Wall Street Journal*, 12/3/84.
55. Lee and Shlain, *Acid Dreams*, 32–33.
56. *New York Times*, 9/20/66.
57. *The Rolling Stone Interviews*, 140.
58. *The Compleat Beatles.*
59. *Sgt. Pepper's Lonely Hearts Club Band*, Grenada Television, 1987; and Philip Norman, *Shout! The Beatles in Their Generation* (New York: Simon and Schuster, 1981), 291.
60. Norman, *Shout!*, 290.
61. Hammond, *On Record*, 346–348; and *Rolling Stone Illustrated History of Rock & Roll*, 249.
62. *Rolling Stone Illustrated History of Rock & Roll*, 255.
63. Interview with Eric Clapton, *Rolling Stone*, 6/20/85.
64. *Rolling Stone Illustrated History of Rock & Roll*, 235–246.
65. Ed Ward, Geoffrey Stokes, and Ken Tucker, *Rock of Ages* (New York: Summit Books, 1986), 297.
66. *Rolling Stone Illustrated History of Rock & Roll*, 194.
67. *Rolling Stone,* 11/5/87.
68. *The Music of Laura Nyro* (New York: Warner Bros. Publications, Inc., [n.d.]), 121.
69. *New York Times*, 10/6/68.
70. *New York Times*, 1/11/68.
71. Norman, *Shout!*, 324.
72. Ibid., 322–326.
73. *The Rolling Stone Interviews*, 304.

74. Norman, *Shout!*, 328.
75. Reviews of "Revolution" all quoted in Jon Wiener, "Beatles Buy-Out," *The New Republic*, 5/11/87.

Chapter 10: Desolation Row

1. *Washington Evening Star*, 6/9/68.
2. To Shana Alexander, quoted in Albert Eisele, *Almost to the Presidency* (Blue Earth, Minn.: The Piper Company, 1972), 338.
3. Unpublished article by Blair Clark, author's private collection.
4. Letter from Jeremy Larner to the author, 4/17/86.
5. Author's interview with Blair Clark, 3/19/86, and *Washington Evening Star*, 6/5/68.
6. Jeremy Larner, *Nobody Knows* (New York: Macmillan, 1970), 121.
7. Author's interviews with Blair Clark, 3/19/86 and 3/26/88, and Eugene McCarthy, 3/27/86.
8. Ibid.
9. Eugene J. McCarthy, *The Year of the People* (Garden City, N.Y.: Doubleday, 1969), 84.
10. Author's interview with Eugene McCarthy, 3/27/86.
11. Eisele, *Almost to the Presidency*, 321.
12. Ibid., 338.
13. Ibid.; and author's interview with Blair Clark, 3/19/86.
14. Norman Mailer, *Miami and the Siege of Chicago* (New York: New American Library, 1968), 15.
15. *New York Times*, 6/10/68.
16. Recorded interview with Maurice Rosenblatt, 2/4/70; McCarthy Historical Project Archive, Georgetown University Library, Washington, D.C.
17. Larner, *Nobody Knows*, 123–124.
18. Ibid., 125.
19. Larner, *Nobody Knows*, 124; and *New York Times*, 6/13/68.
20. Larner, *Nobody Knows*, 124.
21. Ibid., 127–131.
22. Ibid., 132.
23. *New York Times*, 6/14/68.
24. *New York Post*, 6/18/68.
25. Eisele, *Almost to the Presidency*, 340.
26. *Washington Post*, 6/18/68.
27. Lewis Chester, Godfrey Hodgson, and Bruce Page, *An American Melodrama, The Presidential Campaign of 1968* (New York: Viking, 1969), 407–408.
28. *Washington Post*, 6/18/68.
29. Eisele, *Almost to the Presidency*, 333.
30. Chester, Hodgson, and Page, *An American Melodrama*, 409–410.
31. Eisele, *Almost to the Presidency*, 331.
32. Chester, Hodgson, and Page, *An American Melodrama*, 416.
33. Author's interview with Eugene McCarthy, 3/27/86.
34. Eisele, *Almost to the Presidency*, 351–352.
35. For Johnson's threat and Humphrey's concern: Ibid., 337–338.
36. *New York Times*, 7/13/68 and 7/19/68; and *The New Republic*, 7/13/68.
37. *New York Post*, 7/24/68.

38. Theodore H. White, *The Making of the President, 1968* (New York: Atheneum, 1969), 243–244.
39. Ibid., 235.
40. Chester, Hodgson, and Page, *An American Melodrama*, 363.
41. Ibid., 456.
42. White, *The Making of the President, 1968*, 236.
43. Chester, Hodgson, and Page, *An American Melodrama*, 222–223; and White, *The Making of the President, 1968,* 231.
44. Chester, Hodgson, and Page, *An American Melodrama*, 466.
45. Garry Wills, *Nixon Agonistes, The Crisis of the Self-Made Man* (Boston: Houghton Mifflin, 1970), 3.
46. David Abrahamsen, *Nixon vs. Nixon, An Emotional Tragedy* (New York: Farrar, Straus & Giroux, 1977), 117–119.
47. Ibid., 122–128.
48. *New York Times*, 8/20/68.
49. Chester, Hodgson, and Page, *An American Melodrama*, 460, 481.
50. Ibid., 490–494.
51. Ibid., 490.
52. Author's interview with Murray Kempton, 4/1/88.
53. Chester, Hodgson, and Page, *An American Melodrama*, 492.
54. White, *The Making of the President, 1968*, 242.
55. *Washington Evening Star*, 8/7/68.
56. Bruce Porter and Marvin Dunn, *The Miami Riot of 1980, Crossing the Bounds* (Lexington, Mass.: Lexington Books, 1984), 13.
57. Mailer, *Miami and the Siege of Chicago*, 51–53.
58. Chester, Hodgson, and Page, *An American Melodrama*, 628.

Chapter 11: This Wheel's on Fire

1. Arthur Herzog, *McCarthy for President* (New York: Viking, 1969), 255.
2. James Miller, *Democracy Is in the Streets* (New York: Simon and Schuster, 1987), 298.
3. Theodore H. White, *The Making of the President, 1968* (New York: Atheneum, 1969), 257.
4. *New York Times*, 12/2/68.
5. Author's interviews with Blair Clark, 3/19/86, and Jeremy Larner, 3/26/86.
6. *The New Republic*, 9/7/68; and *New York Times*, 12/2/68.
7. *New York Times*, 12/2/68; and Lewis Chester, Godfrey Hodgson and Bruce Page, *An American Melodrama, The Presidential Campaign of 1968* (New York: Viking, 1969), 521, 540.
8. Miller, *Democracy Is in the Streets*, 310–311.
9. David Farber, *Chicago '68* (Chicago: University of Chicago Press, 1988), 180–183; and Chester, Hodgson, and Page, *An American Melodrama*, 522–523.
10. Farber, *Chicago '68*, 4.
11. Chester, Hodgson, and Page, *An American Melodrama*, 514.
12. *New York Times*, 3/24/68.
13. Farber, *Chicago '68*, 4.
14. Farber, *Chicago '68*, 36–37.

15. Chester, Hodgson, and Page, *An American Melodrama*, 519–520; and Martin Lee and Bruce Shlain, *Acid Dreams, The CIA, LSD and the Sixties Rebellion* (New York: Grove Press, 1985), 21.

16. Miller, *Democracy Is in the Streets*, 291–292.

17. Chester, Hodgson, and Page, *An American Melodrama*, 519.

18. Shareen Brysac, producer, and Perry Wolff, executive producer, *1968: A CBS News Special* (New York: CBS, broadcast 8/25/78); and memorandum from Helms to Walt W. Rostow, 9/1/67.

19. *Washington Post*, 8/18/78.

20. *1968: A CBS News Special*, CBS, broadcast 8/25/78.

21. Ibid.

22. Memorandum from J. Edgar Hoover, 8/15/68.

23. *1968: A CBS News Special*, CBS, broadcast 8/25/78.

24. Lyndon Baines Johnson, *The Vantage Point, Perspectives of the Presidency, 1963–1969* (New York: Holt, Rinehart and Winston, 1971), 487–488.

25. Jeremy Larner, *Nobody Knows* (New York: Macmillan, 1970), 168–172.

26. Recorded interview with Ralph Yarborough, 7/10/69, McCarthy Historical Project Archive, Georgetown University, Washington, D.C.

27. Unpublished article by Blair Clark, author's private collection.

28. White, *The Making of the President, 1968*, 281–283.

29. Ibid., 283.

30. Author's interview with Eugene McCarthy, 3/27/86.

31. Chester, Hodgson, and Page, *An American Melodrama*, 571–573.

32. Ibid., 576.

33. Author's interview with Eugene McCarthy, 3/27/86.

34. White, *The Making of the President, 1968*, 284–285; and Chester, Hodgson, and Page, *An American Melodrama*, 578.

35. *New York Times Magazine*, 9/15/68.

36. Farber, *Chicago '68*, 194.

37. Author's interview with Jeremy Larner, 3/26/86.

38. Herzog, *McCarthy for President*, 274; and Albert Eisele, *Almost to the Presidency* (Blue Earth, Minn.: The Piper Company, 1972), 356.

39. Newton Minow, memorandum to William Benton, 7/31/68.

40. Eisele, *Almost to the Presidency*, 347.

41. Chester, Hodgson, and Page, *An American Melodrama*, 581.

42. *New York Times*, 12/2/68; and Farber, *Chicago '68*, 195–196.

43. Farber, *Chicago '68*, 199–200.

44. Chester, Hodgson, and Page, *An American Melodrama*, 583.

45. *New York Times*, 8/29/68.

46. Memorandum from Marie Ridder to Theodore H. White, "Wednesday Night [8/28/68]," Theodore H. White Archive, Harvard University, Cambridge, Mass.

47. *New York Times*, 8/29/68; and Chester, Hodgson, and Page, *An American Melodrama*, 584–585.

48. Memorandum from Marie Ridder to Theodore H. White, "Wednesday Night [8/28/68]," Theodore H. White Archive.

49. *1968: A CBS News Special*, CBS, broadcast 8/25/78.

50. Chester, Hodgson, and Page, *An American Melodrama*, 583–586; and Farber, *Chicago '68*, 202.
51. Eisele, *Almost to the Presidency*, 359–360.
52. Theodore H. White, *The Making of the President, 1964* (New York: Atheneum, 1965), 292; Norman Mailer, *Miami and the Siege of Chicago* (New York: New American Library, 1968), 204–205; and *New York Times*, 8/30/68.
53. Eisele, *Almost to the Presidency*, 362–363.
54. White, *The Making of the President, 1968*, 309–310; Chester, Hodgson, and Page, *An American Melodrama*, 591; and author's interview with Eugene McCarthy, 3/27/86.
55. Recorded interview with Gerry Studds, 1/30/69, McCarthy Historical Project Archive, Georgetown University Library, Washington, D.C.

Chapter 12: The Long and Winding Road

1. Albert Eisele, *Almost to the Presidency* (Blue Earth, Minn.: The Piper Company, 1972), 332.
2. Quoted in Theodore H. White, *The Making of the President, 1968* (New York: Atheneum, 1969), 321.
3. Joe McGinniss, *The Selling of the President, 1968* (1969; reprint, New York: Pocket Books, 1970), 33.
4. *New York Times*, 9/2/68.
5. White, *The Making of the President, 1968*, 321.
6. Eisele, *Almost to the Presidency*, 364.
7. *60 Minutes* (New York: CBS, broadcast 10/8/68, 10 P.M. EDT).
8. White, *The Making of the President, 1968*, 329; and Lewis Chester, Godfrey Hodgson, and Bruce Page, *An American Melodrama, The Presidential Campaign of 1968* (New York: Viking, 1969), 607.
9. White, *The Making of the President, 1968*, 327.
10. McGinniss, *The Selling of the President, 1968*, 54, 58–69.
11. Ibid., 65.
12. Eisele, *Almost to the Presidency*, 367.
13. *New York Times*, 9/3/68.
14. *New York Post*, 9/10/68.
15. *Washington Evening Star*, 9/20/68, 9/22/68; and White, *The Making of the President, 1968*, 336.
16. Eisele, *Almost to the Presidency*, 377.
17. Eisele, *Almost to the Presidency*, 377–379; and *Newsweek*, 10/14/68.
18. Chester, Hodgson, and Page, *An American Melodrama*, 699.
19. McGinniss, *The Selling of the President, 1968*, 146.
20. Gloria Steinem, *Outrageous Acts and Everyday Rebellions* (New York: Holt, Rinehart, and Winston, 1983), 241.
21. Eisele, *Almost to the Presidency*, 382.
22. All quotes from *Newsweek*, 9/28/68
23. *New York Times*, 11/1/68.
24. White, *The Making of a President, 1968*, 376–381.
25. Lyndon Baines Johnson, *The Vantage Point, Perspectives of the Presidency, 1963–1969* (New York: Holt, Rinehart and Winston, 1971), 548.

26. White, *The Making of a President, 1968,* 382.
27. *New York Times,* 11/5/68; and Eisele, *Almost to the Presidency,* 390.
28. Eisele, *Almost to the Presidency,* 390.
29. Ibid., 392.

Epilogue: If Tomorrow Wasn't Such a Long Time . . .
1. *Washington Post,* 11/6/68.
2. Author's interview with Bob Dylan, 11/13/85.
3. *Washington Evening Star,* 8/29/68.
4. Author's interview with Bob Dylan, 11/13/85.

INDEX